THE ENDS OF THE BODY: IDENTITY AND COMMUNITY IN MEDIEVAL CULTURE

The Ends of the Body

Identity and Community in Medieval Culture

EDITED BY SUZANNE CONKLIN AKBARI
AND JILL ROSS

UNIVERSITY OF TORONTO PRESS
Toronto Buffalo London

© University of Toronto Press 2013
Toronto Buffalo London
www.utppublishing.com

ISBN 978-1-4426-4470-0

Library and Archives Canada Cataloguing in Publication

The ends of the body : identity and community in medieval culture / edited by Suzanne Conklin Akbari and Jill Ross.

Includes bibliographical references and index.
ISBN 978-1-4426-4470-0

1. Human body – Social aspects – Europe – History – To 1500. 2. Human body – Symbolic aspects – Europe – History – To 1500. 3. Identity (Psychology) – Europe – History – To 1500. 4. Individuality – Europe – History – To 1500. 5. Community life – Europe – History – To 1500. 6. Literature, Medieval – History and criticism. 7. Human body in literature. 8. Human body in art. 9. Civilization, Medieval – Sources. I. Akbari, Suzanne Conklin II. Ross, Jill, 1961–

CB353.E53 2012 940.1 C2012-904804-6

University of Toronto Press gratefully acknowledges the financial assistance of the Centre for Medieval Studies, University of Toronto in the publication of this book.

University of Toronto Press acknowledges the financial assistance to its publishing program of the Canada Council for the Arts and the Ontario Arts Council.

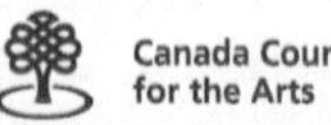

University of Toronto Press acknowledges the financial support of the Government of Canada through the Canada Book Fund for its publishing activities.

Contents

Illustrations

Preface

This volume has, appropriately, had a long gestation, and the editors would like to thank those who have provided support both material and moral. The Social Sciences and Humanities Research Council of Canada provided substantial support to the 2006 conference that initiated this volume (award number 646-2005-1003) and generated the earliest versions of some of the essays collected here. The conference was also supported generously by the University of Toronto, especially the Centre for Medieval Studies. As the volume progressed, with new essays being solicited and older versions being reconfigured in different ways, we profited from the advice of colleagues at Toronto and elsewhere, and would especially like to thank Isabelle Cochelin, Nick Everett, Brent Miles, Will Robins, and David Townsend. We are also grateful for publication subvention funds provided by Toronto's Centre for Medieval Studies, the Centre for Comparative Literature, and the Department of English. Most recently, we have been grateful for intelligent and insightful readers of the manuscript on behalf of the University of Toronto Press, and for the unfailing guidance of their superb editor Suzanne Rancourt.

Both Suzanne Akbari and Jill Ross would like to thank those students in Medieval Studies, Comparative Literature, English, and History who participated in our seminars on body and identity over the past few years, and whose thoughtful engagement in those courses have contributed indirectly – but no less meaningfully – to what is valuable and useful in this book. Suzanne Akbari would also like to thank Eddie Akbari, and Yasin, Sara, Camilla, and John Akbari, who have made her work on this project easy with their practical assistance and loving support; and Jill Ross is grateful for the enthusiastic support of Mark Meyerson and Ben and Sam Meyerson.

THE ENDS OF THE BODY

Introduction
Limits and Teleology: The Many Ends of the Body

SUZANNE CONKLIN AKBARI AND JILL ROSS

As everyone knows, the end of the body is in the grave, as bone and muscle, corpuscle and fibre, are disassembled into their constituent elements. But, as everyone also knew (at least during the Middle Ages), the end of the body was also at the end of time, as soul and restored flesh were reunited in the glorified body that the righteous individual would enjoy, bathed in the bliss of the Beatific Vision. Monumental tombs of the period – such as the one depicted on the medieval manuscript page reproduced on this book's cover – emphasize these two opposed states of corporeal being by placing a sculpted effigy of the perfect, glorified body at the top of the tomb, while engraving at its base an image of the bones and scraps of earthly flesh, devoured by worms. In this view of embodied human nature, the ends of the body are double – both abject and exalted – or even multiple, as the *telos* or end-point of the human being is most fully realized in the reunion of soul with glorified flesh after the Resurrection. Yet the ends of the body are even more various than these, for as historians such as Peter Brown, Caroline Bynum, and Miri Rubin (to name just a few) have shown, throughout the Middle Ages, the body was *the* preeminent symbol of community. Body was not only that which was most intimately personal and most proper to the individual, but also that which was most public and representative of the interlocked nature of the group. Just as each member of the body is both partaker and a part, so too the members of the community, when conceived as a body, participate in the being of the whole and contribute to its welfare. To be excluded from the communal body is to be cut off, even to be annihilated.

The essays in this volume trace out these multiple ends of the body, ranging from the personal, private space of the individual to the public, shared space of the community. They share a focus on the productive capacity of the body, whether expressed through the many aspects of the flesh's materiality – generation, reproduction, gestation, digestion, and so on – or through the body's role in performative expressions of meaning, as in gesture, dance, or other forms of motion. Some essays trace the use of physical remnants of the body in the form of relics or memorial monuments that replicate the form of the body as foundational elements in communal structures; others explore how bodies were used as models of communities themselves, whether torn into pieces in a replication of the disordered bonds of society or afflicted with degenerative illness in a reminder of the decaying nature of a postlapsarian world. Still other essays explore the rhetorical valences of body, whether in popular vernacular literature, learned Latin writings, or the oral performance of sermon delivery.

Before turning to a summary of the essays contained in this volume, the following pages seek to lay out in some detail the development of study of the body in medieval culture as it has evolved over the past two decades, and to establish the role of *The Ends of the Body* within this field. While the topic of embodiment is far from new in medieval studies, this volume is novel in its focus on the role of space and time in the deployment of the body as a symbol of both individual and collective identity. The ends of the body are markers of limitation in terms of both space and time; yet even as the body signifies limit and constraint, it simultaneously – and paradoxically – offers virtually unlimited potential for growth, development, and expansion. This dynamic aspect of embodiment is often expressed, in medieval texts, through a nuanced engagement with the various processes of the body: the physiology of conception, gestation, and birth; the humoral systems of the body, with their multiple sites of digestion and incorporation; disease, aging, and corruption of the flesh, as well as the passage into death itself. At other times, the dynamic aspect of embodiment is expressed through performance, whether literally acted out within the text or used as a metaphorical system that employs the body as a flexible symbol to denote religious, civic, national, or ethnic communities. Here, movement of the body in space – through gesture, dance, ritual, dramatic performance, or the gathering of many bodies into a single ordered grouping – produces an implicit timeline that juxtaposes the body's initial place of origin with the end-point of the body's motion.

The role of the body as the metaphorical heart of human culture has been made eminently clear by the work of anthropologists, cultural and social historians, philosophers, linguists, archaeologists, and literary scholars over the last twenty years. As medievalists have embraced Roy Porter's invitation issued in 1991 to forge a history of the body that seeks to assert the pre-eminence of the body in the discourses of the humanities and to work against the distorting philosophical and cultural orthodoxies that subordinate body to mind or soul, a new history of the body in the Middle Ages has emerged. Writing in 2001, Porter reflects on the proliferation of historical work on the body that has made it 'the historiographical dish of the day' (236) with both satisfaction and disgruntlement. While clearly relishing the surge in body history whose wave he was able to ride, he also is troubled by what he sees as an inability by historians to distinguish between theories and representations of the body in the past and actual social practices; a tendency to reduce the body to a passive object that is produced, constrained, and ruled by regimes of knowledge and power; the uncritical, anachronistic application of modern theory (he takes particular aim at Freud and Lacan) to bodies of the past; and by the reductive occlusion of popular bodies by those rendered visible in the more accessible texts of high culture (237).

In attempting to circumscribe and categorize the omnipresence of the body in history, Porter devises a scheme that posits seven different perspectives from which scholars may approach the historical body: the body as human condition that can be accessed through religious and philosophical discourse that engages with questions of birth, death, and resurrection; the visual form of the human body in its historically reconstructed physicality; the intersection of anatomy and culture; the dynamic relationship of body, mind, and soul in the production of a 'self'; the gendering and sexing of bodies; the management of the body by political authority; and the role of the body in the civilizing process. While Porter's scheme aims at a comprehensive, synthetic view of somatic history that is sensitive to current debates on the body, its heuristically driven categorization presents a somewhat fragmented view of the body parcelled off into artificially discrete sections. Collections of essays focusing on the body in the Middle Ages are faced with the similarly daunting task of defining and circumscribing the parameters of the medieval body. Sarah Kay and Miri Rubin, in *Framing Medieval Bodies*, rely on modern theoretical frames such as Marxism, feminism, race and gender theory, deconstruction, and phenomenology to organize the specific textual and historical soundings of medieval bodies (6–7). Other collections such as that by Linda Lomperis either privilege a modern discourse (in this case, feminist theory) on the body through which to reinvigorate readings of medieval corporeality, or use the coherence of a particular medieval discourse such as theological writing or religious discourse in general to organize approaches to the body.[1]

The present collection seeks to explore how medieval notions of corporeality were elaborated not only in spatial but also in temporal terms. In its focus on the role of space and place, this collection shares some common ground with the provocative set of essays published in 2003 by Jeffrey Jerome Cohen and Gail Weiss: their *Thinking the Limits of the Body* explores how theories of space have inflected representations of the body, medieval to postmodern, in literature, film, and popular culture. The extraordinary heterogeneity of subject matter in that volume is centred on a theoretical core, that is, the 'limit': for Cohen and Weiss, the limit is at once both empowering and controlling, grounded in desire that is itself limitless.[2] The present volume, by contrast, takes as its subject the specifically pre-modern body as manifested in literature, history, and art, in a collection of essays that illustrate the interplay between individual and community in medieval discourses of the body. They show how body was used to represent community, both in the ecclesiastical and in the proto-national framework, and yet was also simultaneously seen as the fundamental expression of individual identity. In the discourse of body as community as understood in spatial terms, the 'ends' of the body demarcate the boundary line of the group, the line that divides those who are included from those who are excluded; yet in the discourse of the body as community as understood in temporal terms, the 'end' of the body marks the moment of dissolution, when the spatial boundary ceases to be. A similar complexity informs the discourse of body as individual: understood in spatial terms, the 'ends' of the body mark the limit separating inside from outside, that which is whole and clean from that which is fragmentary and dirty. In temporal terms, however, the 'ends' of the individual body are even more fraught with ambivalence: understood as flesh, the body ends in age, weakness, death, and decay. Understood in terms of the eternal linkage of soul and body, however, the 'ends' of the body lie in the beatific state of the resurrected body at the end of time. Time and space are thus intimately linked in medieval discourses of the body.

Although the first thing that comes to mind when one thinks of an 'end' is the closing off of future possibility, the idea of ends can, in fact, be both productive and prolific. As Vincent Leitch points out in his reflection on the 'ends' of theory in the early twenty-first-century academy, the idea of end encompasses many concepts:

> The word has numerous connotations: withering, eclipse; fullness, closure; termination, catastrophe, death; turning or stopping points; goals and targets. It summons an array of phenomena: finitude, beginnings and middles,

> expected change, nostalgia, mourning. It suggests remains, revenants, immortality. When *ends* designates regulated or calculated passing, it evokes cyclical patterns as well as shelf life, fusing historiography and fashion ... Ends, like origins, appear multiple and complex. (124)

Medieval discourse renders a similarly polyvalent understanding of 'end.' Of the ten scriptural meanings of *finis* provided by Rabanus Maurus in his ninth-century allegorical dictionary of the Bible, *Allegoriae in universam sacram scripturam* (*PL* 112, 932B–932D), several are bound up with the idea of the body: as biological process, as boundary, and as chronological terminus. *Finis*, of course, is the death of the flesh ('mors carnis') that enables the paradoxically related meaning of 'end,' that of eternal life, which can consist either of 'gaudium eternum' ('eternal joy') or, of what Rabanus gives as another synonym of *finis*, 'fovea,' the pit of eternal punishment or damnation. The end of life, which constitutes both beginning and end, is bounded by a finite sense of time, a finitude that circumscribes the body in terms that are physical as well as chronological. Rabanus reads the 'ends of the earth' ('fines terrae') or the outer reaches of the world ('extremitas orbis') as akin to the external shell of the body that houses the interior qualities found in the new man who will be judged by God: 'By *end* is meant the outer boundary of the world, as in the song of Hannah: "The Lord will judge the ends of the earth," since the newest man will be judged according to that which will have been found in him' ['Per *finem* extremitas orbis, ut in cantico Annae: "Dominus judicabit fines terrae," quod secundum id quod in novissimo homo fuerit inventus, judicabitur' (*PL* 112, 933A)]. Moreover, Rabanus also aligns these 'ends of the earth' with the 'internal thoughts' that inhabit the body: 'By *end*, is meant internal thoughts, as in the Psalms: "In his hand are the ends of the earth," that is, it is in his power to arrange all the internal thoughts of the soul' ['Per *finem*, internae cogitationes, ut in Psalmis: "In manu ejus sunt omnes fines terrae," id est, in potestate ejus est disponere omnes internae cogitationes animae' (932D)]. In his encyclopaedic work, *De universo*, Rabanus marks the congruence between the ends of body, time, and space when he establishes both the body and time as the parameters or instruments by which to conceptualize the notion of measurement: 'Measurement is something circumscribed by its mode or time. It is either of the body or of time' ['Mensura est res aliqua modo suo vel tempore circumscripta. Haec aut corporis est aut temporis' (*De univ.* VIII.2, *PL* 111, 485C)]. Finally, the *fines* of the body are fully displaced from the spheres of time and space when the body's ends become the very biological processes internal to it and on which depend its continuing existence in time and space. Rabanus, in the *Allegoriae in universam sacram scripturam* (932B), asserts that *finis* can be substituted for 'food that has been consumed,' thereby suggesting that the biological ends of consumption, nutrition, and digestion are just as important as the body's more abstract teleological and instrumental ends.

While Rabanus's integrative treatment of bodies and ends attests to the creative force of this nexus of ideas, and the extent to which medieval readers and writers were attentive to the extraordinary dynamism and generative nature of the body, it has been only in the last twenty years that scholars in medieval studies have begun to perceive the nuanced representations of the body that inhabit virtually every level of medieval discourse. The growing interest of medievalists in the body as a serious subject of research and discussion follows upon a more general rehabilitation of the body in the humanities. The neglect of the body has deep philosophical roots in the privileging of soul over body in Plato's thought, and especially in the subordination of body to mind in the influential *cogito* of Descartes. As many feminist scholars have demonstrated, the impetus for such a refusal of the body lies in the long-standing misogynist association of the feminine with the passive, labile realm of the material whose instability and alliance with the senses threatened the primacy of the active, rational male principle. Feminist theory has veered from collusion with the rejection of the body, particularly the female body marked as maternal, because of the socially limiting consequences of such a differentiated body,[3] to the embrace of the postmodern, which enables the opening up of all rigidly constructed dichotomies such as 'male' and 'female' and 'body' and 'mind' to reveal the provisional, culturally constructed nature of all such repressive binary categories of thought. As recent work in feminist thought has evinced, the space between naive essentialism and radical constructivism has yielded to a more materialist understanding of body and gender, one where bodies are understood not solely as textual entities, but as material beings whose physical labour generates the social practices and products undergirding a larger matrix of social and economic relations of production (Weissberger xvi; McNally).

Some of the best medievalist work engages with the body both as a dematerialized, abstract, representational effect and as a fully concrete, historically embedded agent fully immersed in the particulars of its social and cultural 'situation' (Moi 59–83). Caroline Bynum's groundbreaking work on the body in medieval religious and theological discourse is exemplary in this regard. In *Jesus as Mother*, Bynum demonstrates the gender-bending potentiality of the body when it inhabits discourse. Sex is severed from gender when biologically female qualities such as the bearing and nursing of children are detached from the body and discursively applied to male bodies that now appropriate the dematerialized qualities of maternity in their pastoral relationships. In other essays such as 'The Female Body and Religious Practice in the Later Middle Ages,' Bynum's focus shifts to the signifying functions embedded in the actual bodies of spiritually powerful women. In her analysis of the strikingly somatic quality of late medieval female piety, Bynum is attentive to both the new valorization of women's bodies and the meanings with which they are charged, and to the continuity with past paradigms of body and soul and male/female dimorphism, paradigms which in the Middle Ages were never as unbridgeably dichotomous as both ancient and modern thought make them out to be. Bynum inserts the bodily practices of late medieval pious women into the currents of physiological, theological, natural philosophical, and folk discourse in order to provide a more nuanced approach to what she terms 'a turning point in the history of the body in the West' ('Female Body' 182). Her more recent work has continued her project of destabilizing any easy or pat distinctions between body and soul by an exhaustive treatment of the resurrection of the body in early Christianity until the fourteenth century that soundly demonstrates the imbrication of body and soul in medieval theological thought and ecclesiastical practice. The body, as 'the carrier or the expression ... of what we today call individuality' (*Resurrection* 11), asserted itself in all its material glory and was not automatically relegated to the back seat of the spiritual bus.

To think of the body in connection with the Last Judgment and Resurrection is to think of the body in teleological terms, as a kind of seed that comes to full fruition as glorified flesh only at the end of time. This temporal dimension of corporeality has continued to inform Bynum's more recent work, not only in her collection of essays on metamorphosis (*Metamorphosis and Identity*) but in her groundbreaking study of late medieval devotion to the wounded body of Christ, *Wonderful Blood*. Here, Bynum rethinks the nature of material body through a close examination of the veneration of Christ's blood, which was both visible evidence of the sacrificial redemption of man and a focus for empathetic identification with those who witnessed Christ's suffering and death. While Bynum outlines the medieval dichotomy of 'sweet, healthy, inside blood' (*sanguis*) and 'corrupt, separated, outside blood' (*cruor*), she emphasizes the extent to which medieval blood piety resisted this straightforward distinction: 'the complex blood rhetoric of medieval devotion, soteriology, and praxis does not seem to be a conflation, or alternately a reversal, of two structurally dichotomous "bloods"' (*Wonderful Blood* 17, 19). The fluidity of blood itself was a representation of its ability to resist the binary distinctions of inside and outside, clean and polluted, static and changeable.

The rigid categories of the encyclopedic tradition were also challenged by the nature of embodiment. In his thirteenth-century *De proprietatibus rerum*, Bartholomaeus Anglicus inserts the body into a hierarchical presentation of all creation, following his account of God and the angels with an account of the properties of the human soul, and then with an account of the properties of the body. Immediately, however, Bartholomaeus's account of the body is complicated by the different ways in which body can be divided up, in terms of its fourfold humoral composition (described in book 4 of the *De proprietatibus rerum*) or in terms of its various members (described in book 5). In terms of its humoral composition, the human body appears as a microcosm of the greater universe: the four humours correspond to the four seasons of the year, the four physical elements of creation, and so on. The humoral fluids flow through the body just as rivers flow through the landscape. Similarly, the human body appears as a microcosm not of the natural world, but of the political world, with its individual members each doing its part to maintain the health of the body politic. In both anatomical and physiological terms, body was the organizing principle for understanding both the natural and the social world. Crucially, however, this corporeal principle was rooted in a theological framework: not just any body was the template for these correspondences, but specifically the body of Christ. This can be seen, for example, in the Ebstorf world map, which depicts Christ's body as coterminus with the ecumene. The circular periphery of the known world is marked by the termini of Christ's body – feet at the bottom, hands at the side, and head, crowned with thorns, in the easternmost region at the top of the map. On the parchment skin of such a medieval map, the template of Christ's body as the model for all forms of community was made manifest not only in symbolic terms, but in material terms as well.

The self-reflexive exploitation by medieval literary texts of the corporeal nature of the very manuscripts they inhabit makes medieval literature the natural locus for the exploration of crucial questions of bodily identity and textuality. Sarah Kay's work on the relationship between 'textual content and the material state of the page' ('Original Skin' 36) considers how the skin of both manuscript parchment and characters who undergo judicial flaying use the surface of the skin to peel back layers of textual meaning, to reveal the interplay of interiority and exteriority as determinants of an essential identity, and to shape the relationship between bodily mortality and textual invulnerability (47). The insistently material, corporeal nature of medieval manuscript culture haunting medieval texts also asserts itself in the common metaphorical convergence of text and body in much medieval writing. The recognition of the integumental nature of many medieval texts, especially those classical texts whose *auctores* concealed deeper meanings inside layers of fable or myth, as akin to the dressing up of a body of truth in clothes or skin that must be removed, has led many critics to explore the corporeal implications of metaphor, allegory, and allegoresis. Suzanne Akbari's work on figuration highlights the tight nexus between bodily transformation and the integumentary nature of language (*Seeing Through the Veil* 11–18, 109–13; 'Metaphor and Metamorphosis'), while Jill Ross focuses on the hermeneutic implications of textual garments whose qualities of seamlessness or raggedness condition the reading process (Ross 16–49). The construction of a literary text as the proportionate, harmonious arrangement of parts forming a pleasing body is deeply rooted in both the classical rhetorical and poetic traditions inherited by and elaborated upon in the Middle Ages (Valenti). Both the Ciceronian view of a speech as a body possessing joints, blood, and a complexion (*De oratore* III.96, 199) and the Horatian recommendation that a poem's body be a seamless unity and not a hodgepodge of animal and human body parts (*Ars poetica* 1–5) became fundamental tenets of medieval literary theory.

The textual body swathed in layers of verbal clothing and meaning is, more often than not, gendered as feminine. Topping Horace's monstrous body is the head of a beautiful woman (*Ars poetica* 4), which functions to indicate the kind of ideal aesthetic appeal a poem should have instead of the incoherent joinings held up by Horace as a negative exemplum of poetic practice. Feminist scholars in particular have been innovative in their exploration of the implications of the conjoining of woman's body and text. Critics such as E. Jane Burns, Carolyn Dinshaw, Helen Solterer, Karma Lochrie, and Gayle Margherita explore how both the somatized space of the page and the textualized openings of the female body can become sites where the contestation of hegemonic, patriarchal discourse and structures of power are articulated and played out. Other scholars like Peggy McCracken and Barbara Weissberger explore the sexualized metaphors used in medieval literary discourse to describe the female body as wielding a power that is politically threatening and culturally compelling, and whose materiality often cannot be contained within the bounds of dominant symbolic structures. Critics like Louise Vasvári have productively assimilated Bakhtin's seminal treatment of the carnivalesque materiality of the body that disrupts and contests hegemonic discourse to analyse the eruption of the feminized *bas corporel* within the dialogically structured *Libro de buen amor*, which juxtaposes officially sanctioned clerical discourse with that stemming from lower, popular strata.

Scholarly interest in the material and gendered nature of literary bodies has also been nourished by the work of queer theorists, whose insights into the historical and ideological processes governing the construction of sexuality have revealed the fictional nature of gender and have destabilized the temporal 'always already' that substitutes the dynamic, contingent nature of gender formation with one that is a fully formed and immutable reification of gender (Burger and Kruger xi–xiii). Complementing the work of social historians (Bennett, Brundage, Boswell), cultural historians (Jordan, Murray, Dinshaw), and historians of science (Cadden, Laqueur), literary scholars have been front and centre in exploring and unsettling the sexed and gendered bodies that inhabit medieval texts. Collections of essays such as *Queer Iberia*, *Queering the Middle Ages*, and *The Tongue of the Fathers* attest to the pan-European breadth of queer readings of medieval literary texts, while recent monographs focus on the slippery nature of masculinity and the problematization of sodomy in French and English texts (Burgwinkle), the rereading of canonical texts (Klosowska, Schibanoff, Burger, Gaunt), and a queer re-evaluation of the entire generic system out of which literary texts are produced (Pugh). Some of the most stimulating developments arising from queer studies of pre-modern culture have centred on the relationship of temporality and identity, suggesting that an affective connection to the past can be not alienating, but empowering. As Carolyn Dinshaw has influentially argued, temporal distance can be not erased but, perhaps, elided through the 'touch' of present and past ('Chaucer's Queer Touches'; *Getting Medieval* 1–3, 54). In this view, the body serves as the medium through which the other is encountered and recognized, where continuities are traced even as, simultaneously, difference is acknowledged.

The focus on temporality in *The Ends of the Body* is somewhat different: here, pre-modern discourses of the body are illustrated in their historical and literary contexts, where individual and group identities are expressed through images of the body and where beginning and endings – both personal and communal – are articulated by reference to corporeal states of being. Body appears sometimes as the vehicle of transcendence, sometimes as the site of performance, sometimes as the symbolic foundation of the community. Body is not only the flesh that pulses with dynamic fluids, but also the flesh that yields to dismemberment, decay, and death. As the body moves from one state of being to another, both its formal state and its material nature undergo change, mediated through physiological processes such as gestation, digestion, corruption, and decay. Similarly, as the body moves in space, in performative actions such as gesture, dance, or ritual, the body serves as the singular point of reference throughout that sequence of movements as they are extended in time. In either of these two frames of reference, body serves as a focal point through which discourses articulate both the nature of the individual and the nature of the community, through identifying the limits or ends of the body.

The essays in the first part of this collection, 'Foundations,' centre on the ways in which bodies – whether actual fragments of bone and skin or their representation in image or phrase – are the cornerstones upon which communities are built. In 'Books, Bodies, and Bones: Hilduin of St-Denis and the Relics of St Dionysius,' Anna Taylor describes how the ninth-century relics of Dionysius were coupled with a manuscript containing writings attributed to the saint along with accounts of his life and martyrdom. Like the body, the book was thought to provide 'a connection between the devotee and the saint, between the temporal and the eternal'; for medieval worshippers, therefore, the physical proximity of the two at St-Denis provided an even more powerful link with the saint, surmounting the boundaries of space and time. The reliquary containing the saint's bones heightened this sense of sacred power, its shining jewels a 'mirror' of the 'transformed bodies of the end days.' Together, relic and word provided the sacred centre about which the monastic community was unified, in turn affirming St-Denis's role as the spiritual wellspring of a specifically national Christendom in medieval France.

Christine Kralik's 'Death Is Not the End' is an art historical essay on the image of death and its devotional function in the Berlin Hours of Mary of Burgundy and Maximilian I. In the lavishly illustrated manuscript of the Berlin Hours, the theme of the 'Three Living and the Three Dead,' extant as both visual image and narrative unit in a wide range of medieval texts, appears in the local, private setting of an individual prayer book. The patronage of Mary of Burgundy and her consort provided a highly specific context within which the pictorial convention was adapted, showing how a widespread motif could be tailored to meet the spiritual needs of an individual patron. The high status of that patron, however, ensured that her Book of Hours would be passed on to other aristocratic readers, so that individual private devotion was, inevitably, always linked to a community of readers who participated in prayer not collectively, but sequentially. Mary of Burgundy's patronage thus established a devotional pattern for the noble readers who would follow in her footsteps, meditating on the same images of the 'Three Living and the Three Dead' that Mary had meditated upon prior to her own death.

Part one concludes with Amy Appleford's 'The Good Death of Richard Whittington: Corpse and Corporation,' in which the pictorial and verbal description of Whittington's end helps to assure the continuation of 'an associated collective body, the Mercers' Company, by means of another perpetual corporate entity, the Almshouse poor-folk.' Here, the individual body serves as the symbolic foundation for two communities: the charitable organization of the Almshouse, and the politically engaged fraternity of tradesmen. Like Kralik, Appleford focuses on fifteenth-century views of embodiment; here, however, the focus is not on aristocratic courtly culture but rather on civic community formation. For Appleford, as for Kralik and Taylor, the death of the individual serves as the cornerstone for communal devotion, whether uniting the monastic community (St Dionysius), the devout women of an aristocratic lineage (Mary of Burgundy), or the rising middle-class readers of the urban centre (Richard Whittington).

The second part of this volume, 'Bodily Rhetoric,' explores the poetic linkage of body and meaning in Latin and vernacular texts. Body serves as a vehicle for meaning sometimes through an emphasis on its materiality and the physiological processes it undergoes, and sometimes through an emphasis on its role in performative action. In 'An Epic Incarnation of Salvation: The Function of the Body in the *Eupolemius*,' Sylvia Parsons explores how, in eleventh-century Latin literature, classical rhetorical strategies intersected with the Christian theology of salvation. In the *Eupolemius*, the central figure of 'Messiah' emerges as the focal point of a salvation history that chronicles the Jewish people ('Judas') and the Gentiles ('Ethnis'). Parsons shows how genre and embodiment are intricately linked in the *Eupolemius*, with the epic genre featuring 'violent combat,' 'corporeal norms that define appropriate participants,' and the equation of 'the destruction of bodies with cultural values worthy of poetic commemoration.' In keeping with the conventions of the epic genre, bodies are dismembered in service to the effort to construct poetic monuments: the ultimate sacrificial death, the crucifixion of Christ as 'Messiah,' is presented in epic terms in the *Eupolemius*, generating 'a transformative conflation, rather than an ironic distancing, of its divergent modes of imagining the body.' The epic genre, moreover, is combined with the satiric in the *Eupolemius*, with its 'ridiculous and disgusting excess of corporeality': this violation of 'generic propriety' allows the poem to enter a parodic mode, in which 'the two systems of meaning coexist' in what might be called 'a quandary of irony.' The birth of Christ, however, calls into question the rhetorical and generic excess of the poem, for the integumental quality of the incarnation – in which the Word of God is literally 'wrapped up' in Mary's flesh – evokes the allegorical mode, where body is no longer aligned with meaning, but rather with the outer shell or wrapping that contains it. As Parsons shows, in the *Eupolemius*, body proves to be the fundamental vehicle not only for ornamental language, but also for the performative speech of the divine.

The vernacular literature of Ireland is the subject of Sarah Sheehan's 'Losing Face: Heroic Discourse and Inscription in Flesh in *Scéla Mucce Meic Dathó*.' This saga – which dates back at least to the tenth or eleventh century, and perhaps earlier – recounts the violent interactions of heroic men who express their status through acts of mutilation and violence. The dominant heroes 'signify their dominance in resolutely corporeal terms, using mutilated male bodies to affirm their position at the top of the warrior hierarchy.' Through these acts, the Irish heroes accrue honour and confer shame on their enemies, performing what Sheehan identifies as 'a semiotics of the body' in which 'warrior honour is specifically grounded in the materiality of the body and is consequently as vulnerable as the body itself.'

Masculine authority continues to be the focus of attention in Jill Ross's 'The Dazzling Sword of Language: Masculinity and Persuasion in Classical and Medieval Rhetoric': here, the rhetorical prescriptions of writers such as Cicero, Quintilian, and Augustine are interpreted as opportunities for masculine display. Figurative tropes such as the 'polished, glittering sword' appear as verbal weapons that affirm the status and authority of the speaker not just in gendered terms, but in terms that explicitly ground the potency of language in the phallic power of the male body. The implicit threat of dismemberment or mutilation contained in the rhetorical 'sword' of language both subjugates the audience and elevates the manly speaker.

Part three, 'Performing the Body,' turns to the ways in which the individual body functions as the medium through which the social body is maintained, whether in punitive, sacramental, or pastoral terms. In addition, these essays also gesture towards the ways in which the body at times threatens to escape from the social controls placed upon it. In 'Amputating the Traitor: Healing the Social Body in Public Executions for Treason in Late Medieval England,' Danielle Westerhof moves beyond analyses of treason executions that interpret the dismemberment of the traitor as a symbolic amputation of a weakened limb of the body politic. Instead, Westerhof suggests, the body of the traitor both represented 'the corrupted body social' and was itself figured as 'a corruption to be expelled from it during the process of the public execution.' The traitor's body thus became the stage upon which political power and, in particular, governmental surveillance could be played out in terms readily understood by 'those for whom the executions were staged.' Public executions thus performed a ritualistic 'act of cleansing the social body from disease,' educating the audience of the dramatic spectacle about the proper, well-policed boundaries of social order.

In '"A Defect of Mind or Body": Impotence and Sexuality in Medieval Theology and Canon Law,' Catherine Rider describes the evolution of theological and legal perspectives on male sexual potency, from Augustine through the canonists of the twelfth and thirteenth centuries. The legal ramifications of impotence were discussed and adjudicated in a wide range of social settings but had particular force in the case of those who wished to enter holy orders, because the sacraments could be consecrated only by those men who were fully 'whole,' both anatomically and physiologically. Rider shows how the increasingly elaborate views of impotence presented by canonists and theologians were inflected by contemporary scientific perspectives, especially the work of Albertus Magnus. The re-emergence and elaboration of Aristotelian theories of causality made scientists and canonists alike rethink the causes of impotence, integrating medieval science with theology. Here, the body's ability to perform is itself policed by legal, theological, and medical disciplines.

This part concludes with Linda Jones's 'Bodily Performances and Body Talk in Medieval Islamic Preaching,' which, like Westerhof's opening essay, shows how the body could serve as a medium through which the audience might be educated. Jones surveys 'the representation, function, and cultural import of the body' in late medieval sermons delivered in the Iberian Peninsula and the Maghreb: by placing these sermons in the context of Islamic theological and legal texts, she shows how the relationship of body to soul served as a pattern in prescribing righteous behaviour. Jones points out that 'spiritual dispositions,' whether virtuous or deviant, were necessarily 'imagined as embodied': instead of a stark binary distinction between body and soul, medieval Muslim preachers distinguished between moral opposites, such as remembering and forgetting God, or showing and withholding gratitude. In this formulation, 'body talk' provided a 'focusing lens' through which right and wrong behaviours could be made intelligible to the community of the faithful.

Part four, 'Material Body,' comprises three essays that turn from the anatomy of the body to the processes of corporeal being, ranging from the energetic flow of humoral liquids to the decay and dissolution of the flesh after death – or, as Elma Brenner shows, even before death. In 'The Leprous Body in Twelfth- and Thirteenth-Century Rouen: Perceptions and Responses,' Brenner chronicles the social and cultural history of Mont-aux-Malades, an important leper house in Normandy that was not simply a haven for the physically afflicted, but also a focus of lay piety. The community at Mont-aux-Malades maintained strong connections with the city of Rouen, showing that those who became lepers were not simply cast out of their place in society, but maintained it in some sense, albeit at a distance. The distinctive practices of Mont-aux-Malades show that there was a great range in the actual treatment of lepers and in social attitudes towards the leprous body: while the disfigurement caused by leprosy was clearly shocking and disturbing to medieval communities, the leper's 'bodily appearance had only a limited significance.' Social ties were not dissolved entirely by the scourge of leprosy, even though the flesh itself might be in an apparent state of decay.

The dissolution of the flesh remains central in Wendy Matlock's 'The Feminine Flesh in the *Disputacione betwyx the Body and Wormes*,' which focuses on a late medieval debate poem that, uniquely, features a female corpse. As in Christine Kralik's art historical essay on the Berlin Hours of Mary of Burgundy, gender here appears as a category that inflects the status of the body, even after death. By figuring the allegorical body as female corpse, Matlock argues, the poem sheds light on 'the perceived relationship between femininity and carnality so frequently asserted in medieval texts.' Moreover, the conventional binary opposition of body and soul is here recast as an opposition of body and worms: the living, wriggling bodies of the worms thus provide the dynamic counterpart to the body that gradually surrenders to its annihilation. The work thus functions as an aid to devotion, emerging from a Carthusian monastic community but addressing an increasingly broad audience of lay readers of the vernacular.

Part four – and the volume as a whole – concludes with Suzanne Akbari's 'Death as Metamorphosis in the Devotional and Political Allegory of Christine de Pizan.' In this essay, death appears not as the site of bodily dissolution and decay, but rather as the site of bodily revivification: in the devotional allegory of Christine's biography of Charles V, the late monarch sheds his corporeal vestments for the eternal life of the soul, and the French nation maintains its body politic even as its head – the king – is replaced. In the biography of Charles V, as in the political allegory of Christine's *Corps de policie*, the body politic is figured in terms that are simultaneously Christological and physiological, with the flow of *vertu* throughout the flesh appearing simultaneously as humoral liquid and spiritual nectar. Together, the essays that make up *The Ends of the Body* illuminate the interplay of individual and community in pre-modern culture, and show the interrelation of space and time through the symbolic system of the body.

NOTES

1 See, for example, Biller and Minnis, eds., *Medieval Theology and the Natural Body*, or MacDonald, Ridderbos, and Schlusemann, eds., *The Broken Body: Passion Devotion in Late Medieval Culture.*

2 'We are interested in what limits propose ... what they make possible ... what they incorporate ... as well as how the limits are themselves constructed in and through particular cultural matrices which they cannot escape but always exceed. Limits, in other words, are grounded in desire' (Cohen and Weiss, 'Bodies at the Limit' 2–3).

3 See, for example, Susan J. Hekman's treatment of Simone de Beauvoir's understanding of the idea of otherness and the feminine in *The Future of Differences: Truth and Method in Feminist Theory* 1–17.

WORKS CITED

Akbari, Suzanne Conklin. 'Metaphor and Metamorphosis in the *Ovide moralisé* and Christine de Pizan's *Mutacion de Fortune*.' In *Metamorphosis: The Changing Face of Ovid in Medieval and Early Modern Europe*. Ed. Alison Keith and Stephen Rupp. Toronto: Centre for Reformation and Renaissance Studies, 2007. 77–90.

– *Seeing Through the Veil: Theories of Vision and the Development of Late Medieval Allegory*. Toronto: University of Toronto Press, 2004.

Bartholomaeus Anglicus. *De proprietatibus rerum*. Frankfurt, 1601. Rpt. Frankfurt: Minerva, 1964.

– *De proprietatibus rerum, Books 1–4*. Ed. Baudouin Van den Abeele. Turnhout, Belgium: Brepols, 2007.

Bennett, Judith. *History Matters: Patriarchy and the Challenge of Feminism*. Philadelphia: University of Pennsylvania Press, 2006.

– *Women in the Medieval English Countryside: Gender and Household in Brigstock Before the Plague*. New York: Oxford University Press, 1987.

Biller, Peter, and A.J. Minnis, eds. *Medieval Theology and the Natural Body*. York: York Medieval Press, 1997.

Blackmore, Josiah, and Gregory S. Hutcheson, eds. *Queer Iberia: Sexualities, Cultures, and Crossings from the Middle Ages to the Renaissance*. Durham, NC: Duke University Press, 1999.

Boswell, John. *Christianity, Social Tolerance and Homosexuality: Gay People in Western Europe from the Beginning of the Christian Era to the Fourteenth Century*. Chicago: University of Chicago Press, 1980.

– *Same-Sex Unions in Premodern Europe*. New York: Villard Books, 1994.

Brundage, James A. *Law, Sex and Society in Medieval Europe*. Chicago: University of Chicago Press, 1987.

Burger, Glenn. *Chaucer's Queer Nation*. Minneapolis: University of Minnesota Press, 2003.

Burger, Glenn, and Steven F. Kruger, eds. *Queering the Middle Ages*. Minneapolis: University of Minnesota Press, 2001.

Burgwinkle, William E. *Sodomy, Masculinity and Law in Medieval Literature: France and England, 1050–1230*. Cambridge: Cambridge University Press, 2004.

Burns, E. Jane. *Bodytalk: When Women Speak in Old French Literature*. Philadelphia: University of Pennsylvania Press, 1993.

Bynum, Caroline Walker. 'The Female Body and Religious Practice in the Later Middle Ages.' In *Fragmentation and Redemption: Essays on Gender and the Human Body in Medieval Religion*. New York: Zone Books, 1991. 181–238.

– *Jesus as Mother: Studies in the Spirituality of the High Middle Ages*. Berkeley: University of California Press, 1982.

– *Metamorphosis and Identity*. New York: Zone Books, 2005.

– *The Resurrection of the Body in Western Christianity, 200–1336*. New York: Columbia University Press, 1995.

– *Wonderful Blood: Theology and Practice in Late Medieval Northern Germany and Beyond*. Philadelphia: University of Pennsylvania Press, 2007.

Cadden, Joan. *Meanings of Sex Difference in the Middle Ages: Medicine, Science and Culture*. Cambridge: Cambridge University Press, 1993.

Cohen, Jeffrey Jerome, and Gail Weiss. 'Bodies at the Limit.' In *Thinking the Limits of the Body*. Ed. Jeffrey Jerome Cohen and Gail Weiss. Binghamton, NY: SUNY Press, 2003. 1–10.

Dinshaw, Carolyn. 'Chaucer's Queer Touches / A Queer Touches Chaucer.' *Exemplaria* 7 (1995): 75–92.

– *Chaucer's Sexual Poetics*. Madison: University of Wisconsin Press, 1989.

– *Getting Medieval: Sexualities and Communities, Pre- and Postmodern*. Durham, NC: Duke University Press, 1999.

Gaunt, Simon. *Gender and Genre in Medieval French Literature*. Cambridge: Cambridge University Press, 1995.

Hekman, Susan J. *The Future of Differences: Truth and Method in Feminist Theory*. Cambridge: Polity Press, 1999.

Jordan, Mark D. *The Invention of Sodomy in Christian Theology*. Chicago: University of Chicago Press, 1997.

Kay, Sarah. 'Original Skin: Flaying, Reading and Thinking in the Legend of Saint Bartholomew and Other Works.' *Journal of Medieval and Early Modern Studies* 36, no. 1 (2006): 35–73.

Kay, Sarah, and Miri Rubin, eds. *Framing Medieval Bodies*. Manchester: Manchester University Press, 1994.

Klosowska, Anna. *Queer Love in the Middle Ages*. New York: Palgrave Macmillan, 2005.

Laqueur, Thomas. *Making Sex: Body and Gender from the Greeks to Freud*. Cambridge, MA: Harvard University Press, 1990.

Leitch, Vincent. 'Theory Ends.' *Profession 2005*. New York: Modern Language Association, 2005. 122–8.

Lochrie, Karma. *Heterosyncracies: Female Sexuality When Normal Wasn't*. Minneapolis: University of Minnesota Press, 2005.

– *Margery Kempe and Translations of the Flesh*. Philadelphia: University of Pennsylvania Press, 1991.

Lomperis, Linda, and Sarah Stanbury, eds. *Feminist Approaches to the Body in Medieval Literature*. Philadelphia: University of Pennsylvania Press, 1993.

MacDonald, A.A., H.N.B. Ridderbos, and R.M. Schlusemann, eds. *The Broken Body: Passion Devotion in Late Medieval Culture*. Groningen: Egbert Forsten, 1998.

McCracken, Peggy. *The Romance of Adultery: Queenship and Sexual Transgression in Old French Literature*. Philadelphia: University of Pennsylvania Press, 1998.

Margherita, Gayle. *The Romance of Origins: Language and Sexual Difference in Middle English Literature*. Philadelphia: University of Pennsylvania Press, 1994.

McNally, David. *Bodies of Meaning: Studies on Language, Labor, and Liberation*. Albany: State University of New York Press, 2001.

Moi, Toril. *What Is a Woman and Other Essays*. Oxford: Oxford University Press, 1999.

Murray, Jacqueline. 'Gendered Souls in Sexed Bodies: The Male Construction of Female Sexuality in Some Medieval Confessors' Manuals.' In *Handling Sin: Confession in the Middle Ages*. Ed. Peter Biller and Alastair J. Minnis. Woodbridge, Suffolk: Boydell and Brewer, 1998. 79–93.

Murray, Jacqueline. 'Historicizing Sex, Sexualizing History.' In *Writing Medieval History*. Ed. Nancy Partner. London: Hodder Arnold, 2005. 133–52.

Porter, Roy. 'History of the Body.' In *New Perspectives on Historical Writing*. Ed. Peter Burke. University Park: Pennsylvania State University Press, 1991. 206–32.

– 'History of the Body Reconsidered.' In *New Perspectives on Historical Writing*. Second edition. Ed. Peter Burke. University Park: Pennsylvania State University Press, 2001. 233–60.

Pugh, Tison. *Queering Medieval Genres*. New York: Palgrave Macmillan, 2004.

Rabanus Maurus. *Allegoriae in universam sacram scripturae*. *Patrologia Latina* 112, cols. 849A–1088C.

– *De universo*. *Patrologia Latina* 111, cols. 9A–614B.

Ross, Jill. *Figuring the Feminine: The Rhetoric of Female Embodiment in Medieval Hispanic Literature*. Toronto: University of Toronto Press, 2008.

Schibanoff, Susan. *Chaucer's Queer Poetics: Rereading the Dream Trio*. Toronto: University of Toronto Press, 2006.

Solterer, Helen. *The Master and Minerva: Disputing Women in French Medieval Culture*. Berkeley: University of California Press, 1995.

Townsend, David, and Andrew Taylor, eds. *Tongue of the Fathers: Gender and Ideology in Twelfth-Century Latin*. Philadelphia: University of Pennsylvania Press, 1998.

Valenti, Rossana. 'Metafore del corpo nella tradizione retorica Latina: il termine "articulus."' *Bolletino di Studi Latini* 28 (1998): 391–401.

Vasvári, Louise. 'The Novelness of the *Libro de buen amor*.' In *A Companion to the 'Libro de buen amor*.' Ed. Louise M. Haywood and Louise O. Vasvári. London: Támesis, 2004. 165–81.

Weissberger, Barbara. *Isabel Rules: Constructing Queenship, Wielding Power*. Minneapolis: University of Minnesota Press, 2004.

PART ONE

Foundations

1 Books, Bodies, and Bones: Hilduin of St-Denis and the Relics of St Dionysius

ANNA TAYLOR

On the evening of 8 October 827, Emperor Louis the Pious sent the abbey of St-Denis near Paris a Greek codex containing mystical theological works and letters whose author claimed to be Dionysius the Areopagite, a convert of the apostle Paul.[1] The abbot Hilduin, the other monks, and a number of lay people were performing the Night Office for the feast of their patron saint when, as Hilduin later tells the emperor, the advent of the codex caused a number of miraculous healings. In a letter to Louis (BHL 2173), Hilduin says:

> For we received, as a great offering, a gift for our devotion, as if conveyed from heaven, those same original books ... on the very vigil of holy St Dionysius.[2] Divine grace followed to such a degree that on the same night nineteen most noteworthy healings occurred. Sick people, both well known individuals and those who live close to our neighbourhood, were cured of various illnesses. Lord Christ deigned to work for the praise and glory of his name, through the prayers and merits of his most excellent martyr.
>
> Autenticos namque eosdem libros ... in ipsa uigilia sollemnitatis sancti Dionisii, pro munere magno suscepimus, quod donum deuotioni nostrae ac si caelitus allatum, adeo diuina est gratia prosecuta, ut in eadem nocte decem et nouem nominatissimae uirtutes in aegrotorum sanatione uariarum [*MGH*: uariam] infirmitatum ex notissimis et uicinitati nostrae personis contiguis, ad laudem et nominis sui gloriam, orationibus et meritis excellentissimi sui martyris Christus dominus sit operari dignatus. (Hilduin, *Rescriptum* 330, my translation)

Just as relics brought into proximity with one another might incite each other to perform miracles, when Dionysius's book and bones were brought together in the same abbey they caused wondrous healings.[3] Like the bones that were the physical remains of the saint, the books that were the remains of his mind had miraculous properties.

This codex, now Bibliothèque nationale de France, MS grec. 437, is fairly small (216 folios, 238 x 155 mm) and utilitarian, devoid of illumination or decoration. Compared to the gold gospel book decorated with precious stones ['evangelium aureum ex lapidibus pretiosis ornatum'] that Michael sent to St Peter's in 824 (*Epistola ad Hludowicum* 479), the codex was unimpressive. The prestige and expense of a gift directly reflected the status of its recipients, and the modest-looking codex, written in Greek, and so comprehensible to only a small number of monks, presented a dilemma.[4]

By presenting the Pseudo-Dionysian codex like a relic that prompted miracles, Hilduin transformed the unassuming book into a religious artefact (cf. Jeauneau, 'L'abbaye de Saint-Denis' 365). After briefly discussing the contexts of Hilduin's correspondence with Louis and his other works on Dionysius – the unusual prose and verse passions of the saint – I propose a reading of these texts. Both the abbot and the emperor used the language of relics to discuss books. I suggest that Hilduin took the identification of the corporeal and intellectual remains of the saint even further; he described the codex like a relic and enshrined it in the *passiones*, which then functioned analogously to reliquaries.

Drawing on the early ninth-century uncertainty about what objects could be considered holy, Hilduin used ideas about saints' relics to make the Greek codex into a potent object that redounded to the greater glory of his patron saint while reaffirming the identification of St-Denis's patron Dionysius, the first bishop of Paris, with the Greek Pseudo-Dionysius. I suggest that by taking sections of the codex, translating them into Latin, and incorporating them into other texts – the prose and verse *Passiones Dionysii* – Hilduin makes the Pseudo-Dionsyian work accessible and meaningful and presents it to his readers, including his patron Louis, as a sacred object.

Hilduin, in fact, consciously transforms the book into an object whose words and material presence are akin to a reliquary that both contains and makes present the sacred body of the saint, a presence that inhabits the object as both physical icon and ephemeral words. The simultaneous insistence on the visual, imagistic beauty of the book as relic, and on the power of its words to replicate that sanctity, complicates any easy dichotomy between iconoclastic suspicion of holiness conveyed by physical, visual means, and the embrace of the material as a vehicle of divinity.

The Context: Iconoclasm

The advent of the Pseudo-Dionysian codex and Hilduin's response to it occurred during the Carolingian and Byzantine debates on iconoclasm (Irigoin 21).[5] In 824 Michael II and his son Theophilus sent legates to Louis the Pious with a letter describing both Michael's own recent ascent to power and his moderate iconoclast agenda of removing at least some pictures from the churches so that people would not worship them. Appealing to the idea of unity between east and west, he requested his Frankish counterpart's help against the iconodules who had fled to Rome and were creating trouble there (Michael, *Epistola* 479–80). In response to the legation, Louis summoned a synod of bishops to Paris to discuss the proper uses of images (*Libellus Synodalis Parisiensis* 534). The *Libellus* of the Paris synod of 825 cited scriptural, patristic, and poetic sources and advocated a middle course, arguing that images should neither be worshipped nor destroyed. During the eighth- and ninth- century iconoclasm controversies, writers embraced a range of positions between the extremes of iconoclasm and iconodulism (Noble 102). These debates in the east and west were not only about the treatment of images but engaged with a wider set of concerns about the relative value of different forms of representation in conveying the divine, the relationship between the material and the spiritual realms, and what objects could be holy or *res sacratae* (Appleby, 'Holy Relic' 333). Thus, the discussion concerned not only images, but writing, relics, and other means of describing, communicating with, or honouring God and the saints. For example, in the mid-820s, Claudius the iconoclast bishop of Turin destroyed not only images but also saints' relics, and the theologians whom Louis brought in to refute the bishop's arguments discussed not only the appropriate uses of images but also the functions of relics, pilgrimages, and the sign of the cross.[6] Not only theological treatises, but also art and poetry raised these issues (Diebold, *Word and Image*, chapter 4).[7]

Pseudo-Dionysius and Iconoclasm

Carolingian writers had at least some knowledge of Pseudo-Dionysius's theology before 827. Pope Paul I may have sent a codex of Pseudo-Dionysius to Pepin the Short around 758, although, if so, the fate of this codex is unknown (Paul I, *Epistola* 529).[8] Various writers drew on Pseudo-Dionysius's authority to support their points in the debates on images. Pope Hadrian's letter of 791 to Charlemagne and the *Libellus* of the Paris synod quote from him (Hadrian, *Epistola* 32 citing Pseudo-Dionysius, *Ep.* 10 and *Celestial Hierarchy* 1.3; *Libellus Synodalis* 512 with identical citations). Andrew Louth has pointed out that since Greek and Latin writers regularly refer to the same few passages of Pseudo-Dionysius, they probably drew on the florilegium of excerpts defending images compiled in the eighth century by John of Damascus in Palestine rather than the entire works (Louth, 'St Denys the Areopagite and the Iconoclast Controversy' 330). With his use of visual imagery and his Neoplatonic insistence that the divine be accessed through the material world, Pseudo-Dionysius could be used to support an iconophile position, and writers deployed the denatured excerpts to argue in favor of images (Louth, 'St Denys the Areopagite and the Iconoclast Controversy' 328 and '"Truly Visible Things"' 18).

The identification of the western Dionysius with his eastern namesake, the supposed author of the theological works, had already begun before 827. Raymond Loenertz shows that the Latin prose *Passio Dionysii*, known from its incipit as *Post beatam et gloriosam* (BHL 2178), was written between 817 and 834 (Loenertz, 'La légende Parisienne' 221–8). This *passio* briefly identifies the Parisian bishop with Paul's convert, although it neither uses the term Areopagite nor mentions the writings. Other evidence implies that the Byzantines recognized the conflation of their saint with the Parisian martyr. Soon after the *Post beatam et gloriosam* was composed, a Greek translation (BHG 554) was available in the east, and before 834 the iconophile Palestinian monk Michael the Synkellos used it to compose a Greek encomium for the saint's feast day (BHG 556) (Loenertz, 'Le panégyrique' 97). The exchange between Francia and Byzantium consisted not only of books and letters, but also of saints' lives and offices.

It seems likely that the Byzantines recognized the value of the gift of the Pseudo-Dionysian codex. The legates of 824 may have observed the importance of St Dionysius to both Louis and his arch-chaplain, Hilduin. At least one of these legates, Theodore, had a documented interest in hagiography (Loenertz, 'La légende Parisienne' 233–4). In an epigraph to the Greek *passio* of the iconoclast St Anastasia (BHG 81), Theodore writes that he translated the passion from a Latin original (BHL 404) when he was at Rome as 'an ambassador for the Orthodox faith' in 824 (the epilogue is printed along with the Greek passion in Halkin 131). Further the composite Dionysius, as a saint common to east and west, embodied the unity and 'caritas, quae inter nos est,' that Michael II hoped to foster between himself and Louis (Michael, *Epistola* 479, line 43). Perhaps Michael II also intended the gift to persuade Louis of the Byzantine iconoclast position; like Anastasia, and other saints martyred by pagans, the Parisian Dionysius was a destroyer of idols, and the Pseudo-Dionysian corpus, unlike the excerpts, did not lend itself to an iconophile agenda (Louth, 'Truly Visible Things' 22).[9] Modern scholars have suggested that the legates intended the gift specifically for Hilduin, with his powerful position at court, or even that he had a hand in procuring the book that was so relevant to his abbey's patron saint (Irigoin, 20; Jeauneau, 'L'abbaye de Saint-Denis' 365).

Hilduin and St-Denis

Hilduin had been appointed arch-chaplain to Louis's court in 819 or 822 (Tardif, 112; Lapidge, 58). He was also abbot of several important houses, including St-Denis just north of Paris. St-Denis was a prosperous royal abbey that received patronage from the Merovingian and Carolingian kings.[10] By the time Hilduin became abbot, in 814 or 815, St-Denis had about 150 residents (Félibien, *Pièces jutificatives*: no. lxxii; Crosby 95).

Hilduin may have been involved in the iconoclasm controversy. Some scholars assert that he directed the Synod of Paris (Louth, 'St Denys the Areopagite and the Iconoclast Controversy' 336; Lowden 250), and in the poem *De imagine Tetrici*, composed in 829, Walafrid Strabo seems to accuse Hilduin of idolatry. In this 268-line work, Strabo – the tutor of Louis's youngest son Charles (later known as Charles the Bald) – describes a golden statue of the infamous king Theoderich, which Charlemagne had set up outside his palace in Aachen (Herren, 'The *De Imagine Tetrici*' 120). After describing the statue and its parade of followers cavorting to the discordant sounds of a Byzantine organ (a gift that Louis had received from the east in 829), Walafrid praises, or appears to praise, a number of figures from Louis's court, including Hilduin. Louis is described as Moses (line 148). Hilduin is depicted as Moses's wayward priest, 'magnus Aaron.' Walafrid alludes to Aaron's garments adorned with pomegranates ['punica mala'] and bells ['tintinabula'] as described in Exodus (28.33–4) and then continues:[11]

> And he promptly celebrates the heavenly rituals with holy observance.
> You, moist Thetis, will lack water
> Before this great priest will burn the accursed idols –
> Idols, which have destroyed a holy people with axes;
> 'The greedy man has idols,' so you say, apostle of Christ.
> Go forth, ornament of the world, enjoy better fates;

Live blessedly before God, may you gain a happy end.

Et diuina sacro celebrat celer orgia cultu.
Ante tibi contingit aquis, Thetis uda, carere,
Idola quam tantus coquat exercranda sacerdos
Idola, quae plebem strauere securibus almam
Idola auarus habet, tu dicis, apostole Christi.
I decus, I mundi, melioribus utere fatis,
Vive deo felix, felici fine potire.

(Walafrid Strabo, *De imagine*, lines 184–90;
trans. Herren, 'The *De Imagine Tetrici*' 136–7, adapted)

The passage from Exodus that Hilduin draws upon introduces the episode of the Golden Calf (Ex. 32:1–6, 20–35), a story about worshipping images and the harsh punishment meted out for it. Referring to Achilles's mother, the sea goddess Thetis, Walafrid says she will lack water before Aaron (that is, Hilduin) would burn ['coquere'] the idols.[12] In other words, Hilduin, unlike Moses in Exodus, will never destroy the *idola*. The anaphora of the word *idola* in the first position in three consecutive lines, ringing like one of Aaron's bells, emphasizes the crime. The *idola* that this Aaron will not destroy should be despised ['execranda'] and, like the golden calf, are highly destructive for the people. The scriptural equation of avarice and idolatry reinforces the message (Ephesians 5.5; cf. Colossians 3.5). One strand of Carolingian exegesis of this scriptural equivalency interpreted avarice as – in Diebold's words – 'service to the wrong thing or people' (Diebold, 'The Carolingian Idol' 455). This interpretation of the line suggests a veiled accusation against Hilduin, who would shortly turn against Louis. The ominous line 189 ('melioribus utere fatis') comes from a passage in the *Aeneid* in which the shade of the Trojan Deiphobus, who was horribly mutilated in the sack of Troy, wishes Aeneas a better destiny – an ambivalent blessing indeed given the misery of Deiphobus's end (*Aen.* 6.546). Despite Hilduin's patronage of Walafrid, it seems that in *De imagine Tetrici*, the young poet accuses his mentor of idolatry, greed, and perhaps even treachery.[13]

Walafrid's poem, with its themes of discord and self interest, may look ahead to the unrest of 830 when Louis's sons Lothar and Pippin rebelled against him (Godman, *Poets and Emperors* 133). That year Louis exiled Hilduin for backing the rebellion. Hilduin's student Hincmar intervened with the emperor and in 831 Hilduin was recalled and restored to some of his abbacies, but not the arch-chaplaincy (Crosby 167). Meanwhile, Hilduin had other problems. Despite repeated attempts to reform St-Denis, Hilduin was unable to impose monastic rule on all the inhabitants (Crosby 82). He was also entangled in a costly building project – a new crypt at St-Denis – which would allow many more pilgrims access to the relics (Félibien clxviii).

In 832, the emperor instructed Hilduin to send him works on Dionysius. In his letter to Hilduin (BHL 2172), transmitted with Hilduin's prose *Passio Dionysii* in several manuscripts, Louis asked Hilduin to collect the references ['notitia'] to Dionysius from a number of sources: Greek histories, other Greek books ['ex libris ab eo patrio sermone conscriptis'], Latin books, the little book of the saint's passion ['libellum passionis ipsius'], and the volume of ancient charters stored in the church in Paris ['in tomo cartis uetustissimis armario Parisiacae ecclesiae'] (Louis the Pious, *Epistola* 327). Hilduin was asked to combine these into one text: 'render them into one body and then compose a uniform text' ['in corpus unum redigas atque uniformem textum exinde componas']. The emperor then directed Hilduin to send the volume ['corpus unum'] along with hymns and readings for the Night Office of the saint, and a second volume ['alter uolumen']:

> Thus, when these things have been collected … we wish you to unite them also with the acts, which were added to it, together with the hymns that you have about that most glorious martyr and priest, and a Night Office. But both differently and with an eye to completeness, collect whatever there is about him in a second volume, and send or hand it to us, copied out in a lucid and correct manner, as quickly as possible.

> His ita contextis uolumus ... et gesta quae eidem subnexa[14] sunt, una cum ymnis, quos de hoc gloriossimo martire atque pontifice habes, et officium nocturnale subiungas. Sed et differenter ac cum integritate sui quaeque ex eo reperta sunt in altero volumine colligas, nobisque distincte et correcte transcripta quantocius dirigas aut presentes. (Louis the Pious, *Epistola* 327; my translation)

So, Louis requested two *uolumina* on Dionysius. The first *uolumen* was to comprise both the collected works about Dionysius, rendered by Hilduin into a *uniformis textus*, along with the acts, hymns, and Night Office of Dionysius. The second *uolumen* was to be an anthology of the complete works pertaining to Dionysius, collected ['colligere'] and copied out ['transcripta']. Although Louis's language is somewhat ambiguous, and hinges on the interpretation of the verb *componere* (which here could mean to compose or compile), it seems that the emperor asked Hilduin to provide him with one *uolumen* composed of original works and one anthology collected and copied from various sources. Since we know that Hilduin wrote hymns and offices for Dionysius (Huglo 74), it is plausible that Louis intended volume one to be Hilduin's compositions and volume two to be his source materials, 'whatever information was found' ['quaeque ... reperta sunt'] in his researches. This interpretation also explains Louis's different requirements for the two *uolumina*; the first was to be rendered ['redigere'] into a uniform fabric or text ['uniformis textus'], the second to be copied out clearly and accurately ['distincte et correcte transcripta'].

Hilduin, in his reply to Louis (BHL 2173), transmitted with some manuscripts of the prose *Passio Dionysii* (BHL 2175), states that he had gathered (*colligere*) the material Louis had requested. Hilduin wrote that he had found materials in Greek and Latin books about 'dominus et patronus noster Dionysius' and had compiled them, as requested, into one book: 'in unam collecta' (Hilduin, *Rescriptum* 328). As the accompanying prose passion reveals, Hilduin chose to interpret the emperor's request as a demand for a new *Passio* of Dionysius. In his reply, Hilduin does not mention the 'alter uolumen' that Louis had requested. Nonetheless Hilduin probably did send Louis a second volume on Dionysius. This second volume certainly met Louis's requirement that it be compiled *differenter* from the first part. Rather than being an anthology, however, the second part of Hilduin's work was probably a verse passion.

The Prose and Verse *Passiones Dionysii*

Hilduin's prose passion is extant in numerous manuscripts dating from the tenth to the fifteenth centuries.[15] The lone manuscript copy of the verse passion of Dionysius (no BHL), the eleventh-century composite manuscript Oxford, Bodleian, Bodley, MS 535 (S.C. 2254), contains no author's name (Madan and Craster 280–1). Michael Lapidge identifies Hilduin as the author of the verse life. Lapidge uses the evidence of the twelfth-century historian Sigebert of Gembloux, who states that 'Hilduin, abbot of Saint-Denis of Paris, wrote to the Emperor Louis in both styles, that is in prose and meter, the life of this Dionysius' ['Hilduinus abbas de Sancti Dionysii Pariensis scripsit ad Ludowicum imperatorem utroque stilo, id est prosaico et metrico, vitam ipsius Dionisii'] (Sigebert, *Catalogus* 76, 132; Lapidge 67). Lapidge has interpreted this passage to mean that Hilduin wrote two passions in the *geminus stilus* that paired verse and prose texts (Lapidge 67).[16] In the seventeenth century, Le Mire says that a manuscript containing Abbot Hilduin's prose and verse works on Dionysius existed at Gembloux (Le Mire 71; Lapidge 68). Scholars have failed to find this manuscript among the dispersed holdings of Gembloux's library and had presumed the metric work to be lost until Lapidge's discovery (Lapidge 68). The first section of the Oxford manuscript, fols. 1–38, contains 2200 lines of Latin dactylic hexameter, divided into four books (and therefore in agreement with Le Mire's description).[17] Lapidge asserts, on stylistic grounds, that the poem was composed in the ninth or tenth century (Lapidge 73). Although the extant manuscript is from the late eleventh century, the poem it contains must have been written before 960, since Hrotsvita of Gandersheim's *Passio S. Dionysii egregii martyris* (BHL 2186) draws upon it (Lapidge 75). Further, as I argue below, a poem by Hilduin's later contemporary, Sedulius Scottus (fl. 848–59), also alludes to it (Sedulius, *Mock Epyllion* in Godman, *Poetry of the Carolingian Renaissance* 293–301). The metrical *passio* follows the structure of Hilduin's prose *passio* and borrows much of its language as well (Lapidge 72). Lapidge's argument – based on the verse *Passio Dionysii*'s profound similarities with the prose text, its ninth-century style, and its structural consistency with the book that Sigebert and Le Mire note – is persuasive.

Although no dedication accompanies the verse *passio* in the surviving manuscript, it is highly likely that, as Sigebert claims, it was sent to Louis. In the central Middle Ages, verse saints' *vitae* and *passiones* were sometimes sent to kings and emperors; Charles the Bald received both Milo's verse *Vita Amandi* (BHL 333) and Heiric's verse *Vita Germani* (BHL 3458). As monumental undertakings that demonstrated the author's erudition while flattering the recipient's culture and intellect, verse texts were gifts fit for kings. For Louis, who was famously adverse to pagan culture, the Latin epic was especially thoughtful, allowing him – in moments of leisure between quelling restive relatives – the pleasures of classicizing Latin verse in palatable Christianized form (Hilduin, *Passio Dionysii (metrica)*, fol. 36r). Verse composition is time-consuming, so it is probable that Hilduin, writing the prose *passio*, supervising the production of Louis's manuscript, and continuing his reform and building projects, would have taken several years to write the epic poem.[18] If, as Sigebert says, Hilduin dedicated the verse and prose works to Louis, then he probably sent the metric *passio* later than the prose version.

Narrative Overview of Hilduin's Verse and Prose *Passiones Dionysii*

Hilduin's prose and verse versions of the *Passio Dionysii* contain essentially the same narrative. As mentioned above, Hilduin, following a brief suggestion in an earlier passion (BHL 2178), identifies the Parisian Dionysius, traditional patron of St-Denis, with the homonymous eastern saint, the supposed author of the Greek codex. Both Hilduin's prose and verse passions fall into three thematic sections. Hilduin derives the first section, on the saint's education and conversion by Paul in Athens, from sources on the Areopagite; the second section from the Pseudo-Dionysian writings; and the third from sources on the life and death of the Parisian bishop. Both the first and third sections also depend heavily on Hilduin's imagination (Luscombe 138). The second part of the narrative is a series of summaries and quotations from the Pseudo-Dionysian letters and the mystical theology. The third section deals with Dionysius's mission to convert the Gauls and his martyrdom. In this final section the saint and his companions Eleutherius and Rusticus are decapitated on the hill of Montmartre (named 'hill of the martyrs' for this reason). After death, Dionysius becomes a cephalophore, a decapitated martyr who carries his own head.[19] Elaborating on the brief notice in BHL 2178 (*Post beatam* 794, cap. 13), Hilduin describes the striking scene of the mutilated saint, accompanied by a host of singing angels and illuminated by a celestial light, who carries his own head five miles to the future site of St-Denis.

Hilduin's passions contain a number of novel emphases and features: the thorough integration of the two Dionysii, the elaboration of the cephalophory, and, most strikingly, the inclusion of large portions of the Pseudo-Dionysian writings.[20] Thus, Hilduin embellishes Dionysius, depicting his abbey's patron as a colourful and compelling saint – a mystic, cephalophore, martyr, and scriptural figure (Spiegel 141). One of the ways that Hilduin created a more dynamic saint, enhanced the prestige of St-Denis's relics, and substantiated the identification of the two Dionysii was by drawing on the idea of books as relics. When we return to his correspondence with Louis, we will see that the emperor shared this set of ideas.

Books as Relics

As noted above, Hilduin describes the Greek codex of Pseudo-Dionysius acting like a corporeal relic. Louis also uses language reminiscent of relics. Directing Hilduin to collect works on Dionysius, he tells him to combine these into one text: 'redact into one body and thence compose a uniform text' ['in corpus unum redigas atque uniformem textum exinde componas']. The choice of metaphor – a body of works – is appropriate because Louis goes on to liken the books to relics. Louis says that he desires the collection of works on Dionysius as a pledge or symbol [*pignus*] of the saint's presence. The term *pignus* is one commonly applied to relics, for example, by Gregory of Tours (*De gloria confessorum* 309) and various early medieval hagiographers (Dado, *Vita Eligii* 673; Bobolenus, *Vita Germani* 38).

Louis uses the language of relics to describe the books and also attributes relic-like functions to them. As the saint was believed to be alive and present in his corporeal relics, so to – in Louis's estimation – Dionysius is present in his books. Thus, if Louis possesses the books, he will have access to the saint himself. Louis instructs Hilduin to assemble the works for him:

> since we believe that we have the greatest and very sweetest token of the desired presence of this our very lord and consoler, where ever we may be, if, in words, either through prayer or conversation or reading, we converse with him, or about him, or read things by him.
>
> quoniam maximum valdeque dulcissimum pignus desiderabilis presentiae ipsius domni et solatiatoris nostri, ubicumque simus, habere nos credimus, si cum eo uel de eo aut ab eo dictis oratione, conlatione siue lectione conloquimur. (Louis, *Epistola* 327)

No matter where he is, says Louis, he will be able to take comfort in the saint's presence [*presentia*], through his words. Like the saint's body, his books will provide a connection between the devotee and the saint, between the temporal and the eternal.

Hilduin's reply to Louis, quoted at the beginning of this paper, in which he describes a book behaving like a relic, is congruent with the emperor's ideas about saints' books and bodies. In creating the picture of the wonder-working Pseudo-Dionysian codex, Hilduin could have drawn on several different traditions about miraculous books, the interchangeability of books and bodies, and the overlapping functions of books and relics. Hilduin's description of the codex is part of a long line of marvellous books, going back at least as far as the Sibylline oracles. In a poem from the fifth century, Paulinus of Périgueux recounts a healing book; he writes that his nephew was healed by a scroll containing the *Miracula* of St Martin (Paulinus, *Versus* lines 29–47).[21] There is a particularly strong Irish and English tradition of miraculous books and, given the insular presence at the Carolingian court and at St-Denis (Lapidge 60, 63–4), these traditions may have informed Hilduin's ideas about how to present the codex.[22]

The equation of book and relic is also given force by the Christian idea of Christ as the Word. As the Word of God is made flesh, so the words of the saint (the Pseudo-Dionysian theology contained in the codex) are akin to the saint's incorrupt flesh and bones. Numerous classical precedents show the transformation of bodies into books.[23] Late antique and early medieval examples attest to the conflation of books and bodies, and depict writing upon the body in verse.[24] For example, in the third hymn from Prudentius's *Peristephanon* (BHL 2699), the virgin martyr Eulalia, mutilated by her torturers, says that God writes on her body (lines 136–8). In Prudentius's ninth hymn (BHL 1625), Cassian, the patron saint of teachers, is killed in the arena by his pagan students, using their writing implements as weapons. Thus, the two saints' bodies, written upon in their own blood, become in suffering and death a book for the faithful to read. Prudentius's verse passion describes the martyr's skin as a page: 'the mutilated and dampened page reddens from the puncture' ['rubet ab ictu curta et umens pagina'] (Prudentius, *Per.* 9, line 50, line 58; Jager, *Book of the Heart* 88–90).[25] The body stands in for or becomes a book for the faithful to venerate and read.

The second Byzantine iconoclast persecution provides a more literal example of the inscription of bodies. In 836, according to several hagiographical sources, the rabidly iconoclast emperor Theophilus (son of Michael II) ordered the foreheads of two Palestinian monks tattooed with lines of bad Greek verse as punishment for their iconodulism (*Life of Michael the Synkellos* 84; Barber 111–12).[26] The inscribed saints, Theodore and Theophanes, students of Michael the Synkellos mentioned above, were afterwards known as the *Graptoi*, or written ones (Mullett 156).

Around the same time in the west, Rabanus Maurus, abbot of Fulda and later archbishop of Mainz, writes on bodies in a different way when he depicts figures, such as Christ, Louis the Pious, and himself, in his collection of acrostic picture poems, *In honorem sanctae crucis* (Rabanus Maurus: A5, B1, B28). In these *carmina figurata*, each page is a grid of letters superimposed on an image or pattern. The words can be read in the usual way, from left to right, but the letters within the components of the picture (such as Christ's halo or Louis's shield) can also be read as miniature poems within the larger *carmen*.

Readable Reliquaries

Reliquaries also likened bodies (in the form of relics) to texts and rendered them readable. A bare relic, like a book written in a foreign language, was all but illegible. Relics without a narrative were simply 'bags of bones' (Geary 5). Relics were social products – they possessed individual identity and therefore significance because the communities that kept them agreed to attribute meaning to them (Gajano 259; Schmitt 151). Hagiographical stories, rituals, liturgy, architecture, paintings, and reliquaries all created the social recognition necessary for a functioning saint (Schmitt 151). Thus the reliquary functioned as a *memoria* of the saint whose otherwise nondescript bones were lodged within (Schmitt 149).[27]

Some manufacturers of reliquaries incorporated textual elements into the design to resist the threat of identity loss. By including *cedulae*, scraps of paper inscribed with the saint's name, in the reliquary with the holy remains they ensured the saint's identity would be remembered. With the labels attached, the relics themselves could literally be read inside their casing (Van Os 146, 161). Six reliquaries that Rabanus Maurus commissioned between 835 and 838 were inscribed on the outside with verse *tituli* in a variety of meters and sometimes written in gold (Appleby, 'Rudolf' 431–2).[28] Rabanus's younger contemporary at Fulda, Rudolf, records that the abbot added verses composed in metric form [*metrica lex*] and written in golden letters [*aureae litterae*] (Rudolf, *Miracula* 332). Like the Pseudo-Dionysian Greek codex, such readable reliquaries embodied both text and relic.

A reliquary could also suggest that the relics were themselves a text. In 835, Rabanus commissioned a reliquary in the form of the Ark of the Covenant, complete with cherubim and covered entirely in gold (*Catalogus abbatum Fuldensium* 273; Rudolf, *Miracula* 333). Theodulf of Orleans discussed the Ark of the Covenant as a manufactured object that could not be used to support iconodule arguments because it had been made at God's command (*Opus Caroli Regis* 1.2; Diebold, *Word and Image* 101–3). (Theodulf also employed the image of the Ark in the mosaic of his church at Germigny built around 805 [Appleby, 'Rudolf' 440].) The original Ark was constructed to hold the tablets of Mosaic law, but Rabanus's version replaced those texts with the documents of the new dispensation, the saint's bones (Appleby, 'Rudolf' 434–6).[29]

Reliquaries also communicated the meaning of their contents through decoration. Some reliquaries depicted the saint's story in images, or gold and gems (Van Os 25–7).[30] The reliquary's ornamented exterior was not an arbitrary display of wealth. Rather, it was ostentatious in the most literal meaning of the term, intended to show the power and glory of the saint it contained (Van Os 104). The exterior of a reliquary described in the ninth-century *Miracula* of Barnardus (BHL 995) lets a viewer know [*scire*] the *uirtus* of the saint. The gold and silver ornamentation and the skilled craftsmanship [*fabrile opus*] of this object are signs [*indicia*] of the *sacratis-*

simum corpus inside.[31] Precious stones had allegorical meanings that the viewer could decode (Stock 68–9), and the jewelled exterior looked forward to the heavenly Jerusalem, the golden-walled, gem-encrusted city described in the *Book of Revelation* (Revelation 21:18–21; Schmitt 52–3). Important books, especially those intended for the altar, could resemble jewelled reliquaries. Like the *evangelium* Michael II sent to St Peter's in 824, these books were highly decorated, encrusted with precious stones and metals, and could even be encased in book shrines (Diebold, *Word and Image* 28–31).

The reliquary communicated not just the presence of the remains, but also their invisible meaning. The gold, silver, and gems mirrored the incorruptible glory of the saint within, which itself prefigured the transformed bodies of the end days (Schmitt 153; Shortell 38). The relics were promises [*pignora*] of the saint's presence [*presentia*] and ultimate resurrection; they were pieces of the celestial and eternal embedded in the mundane and temporal world (Canetti 1). Bernard of Angers says in his *Miracula* that Fidis's remains are precious because she is a pearl [*margarita*] of heavenly Jerusalem (1:13). The reliquary conveyed the theological truths of resurrection and saintly efficacy and goaded the viewer to contemplate the power and glory of God as revealed in His saint.

The excerpts of Pseudo-Dionysius employed in the late eighth- and early ninth-century writings on images support the idea that a reliquary's exterior pointed to the spiritual *uirtus* within. According to this theology, 'visible things are clearly images of the invisible' ['manifeste imagines sunt uisibliles inuisibilium'] (Pseudo-Dionysius, *Ep.* 10, as cited in Hadrian, *Ep.* 32–3, and *Libellus Synodalis* 512). Further, the human mind can only attain transcendence *through* the contemplation of material things. The 'immaterial ranks are fashioned in different colors and composed in diverse manners' ['incorporea agmina diuersis coloribus effigurantur, conpositionibus uariis'] and allow us to reach the 'invisible and most beautiful … image' ['inuisibilem pulcherrimamque … effigiem'] (Pseudo-Dionysius, *Celestial Hierarchy* 1.3, cited in the same sources). In the twelfth century, Abbot Suger of St-Denis, influenced by interpretations of Pseudo-Dionysian thought, expresses a similar idea when talking about the meditative functions of gems embedded in architecture.[32] In short, a precious and richly ornamented reliquary ensured that the bones would be understood as saints' relics and even conveyed information about the particularities of that saint, while the light from the cut and polished surfaces encouraged the viewer towards a transcendent comprehension of spiritual realities.

Crypts and reliquaries served certain similar functions, albeit on different scales. Reliquaries were constructed to look like crypts (Van Os 116, 138), and the highly ornamented *crypta* that Hilduin added to the church of St-Denis was much like a reliquary. Consecrated in 832, it was built to contain the relics of Dionysius and other saints. In the eleventh century, Haimon describes the gems embedded in the crypt's walls ['criptula quaedam aureis gemmis extrinsecus decorate' (Félibien clxviii)].[33] As Hilduin's sly program of relic acquisition for St-Médard (discussed by Patrick Geary) and his construction of the new crypt at St-Denis show, the abbot of St-Denis was well able to manipulate the meaning and placement of relics to increase his communities' power and prestige and thus his own status (Geary 40–6, 118–20).

Hilduin's *Passiones* as Reliquaries

As we have seen above, Hilduin treated the saint's codex as a relic. I suggest that by excerpting, translating, and presenting the text from this codex in his *Passiones Dionysii*, he also created framing texts that were analogous to reliquaries; Hilduin took the text of Paris, BNF, MS grec. 437 and encased it in literary settings – words rather than gold and gems – that communicated its importance. By translating the Pseudo-Dionysian text from Greek to Latin and enclosing it in prose and verse, Hilduin made it accessible, explained its meaning, and enhanced its status. Hilduin describes how he encapsulated the story of the dead saint's cephalophory in verse:

> Now it is permitted to sing and *to enclose in metric verse*
> how the triumphant martyr then bore the shining banners,
> arising as a pall-bearer of these things after death.
>
> praeclara dehinc tulerit uexilla triumphans
> Martyr post obitum existens baiulus horum
> Iam cantare libet, ac stricto claudere uersu.
> (Hilduin, *Passio Dionysii (metrica)*, fol. 33v, my translation, my emphasis)[34]

In the poem, Dionysius the cephalophore is his own pall-bearer [*baiulus*], and Hilduin metaphorically makes the case or tomb (the *strictus uersus*) that encloses the saint. In a similar example from the verse *Vita Germani*, written about forty years later, Heiric of Auxerre describes the poet's words as the *monumenta* (memorial or book, but also tomb) of the saint's *gesta*: 'let me run sweetly through monuments of your deeds, and the whole web of your life' ['Gestorum michi dulce foret monumenta tuorum / Et uitae totum plectro percurrere textum' (Heiric, *Vita Germani* 444)].

Like the artisans at Conques who transformed a Roman imperial mask into a house for St Foy's remains, Hilduin took the precious materials at hand (the saint's *pignora*, as Louis called them, as well as the classical tradition of epic poetry) and reworked them into something new and more fitting for his times. Like those artisans, Hilduin employed originally unrelated fragments from diverse times and places to create something at once unusual, memorable, and strikingly innovative.[35] Verse, in particular, was understood as a jewelled, decorative, and prestigious form suited to conveying mystical and eternal themes (Roberts, passim; Appleby, 'Rudolph' 431; Cox Miller, 'Relics, Rhetoric' 49–50). Similarly, by taking fragments of the Pseudo-Dionysian codex (which had already demonstrated its power as a relic) and embedding them in verse, Hilduin incorporated and transformed the Pseudo-Dionysian corpus into an appropriate new form.

Hilduin's *Vita Dionysii* is unique among the Carolingian *vitae* and *passiones metricae* because it incorporates sections of prose, without putting them into verse. Manuscripts of other *vitae* and *passiones metricae* contain prose *capitula*, summary lists of the headings or chapter titles of each book. Hilduin's verse and prose *Passiones Dionysii*, however, contain the translated *capitula* of *other* texts – the Pseudo-Dionysian works. The prose *capitula* stand out particularly obviously in the *passio metrica*, where they break the visual flow of the lines of verse. So, on folios 10v and 11r of the verse *Passio Dionysii*, a poetic description of Pseudo-Dionysius's writing is followed by the capitula for the *Celestial Hierarchy*, with the chapter numbers written in red. Because they include the *capitula* from the Pseudo-Dionysian codex, Hilduin's verse and prose *Vita Dionysii* have a certain physical resemblance to copies of the Pseudo-Dionysian corpus, or at least to translations of it. A reader glancing through Hilduin's *passiones* for *capitula* would have found the chapter titles for Pseudo-Dionysius's *Celestial Hierarchy* or his *Ecclesiastical Hierarchy* and could have reasonably assumed that these works were among the texts included in the manuscript, although they are not (Hilduin, *Passio Dionysii (metrica)*, fols. 10v, 11v).

The passions, however, *are* in part translations and summaries of certain Pseudo-Dionysian works. Both passions contain Latin versions of letters from the Pseudo-Dionysian corpus. In the prose passion these are prose texts (as one would expect), and in the verse *passio* they are (again, as one would expect) redacted in verse, but with exceptions. In the verse *Passio Dionysii*, Hilduin has not versified Pseudo-Dionysius's letter to Apollophanius, but simply reused the exact Latin text that occurs in the prose

Passio Dionysii (fol. 15r).[36] The poet also included, in prose, Pseudo-Dionysius's letter 10, addressed to John the Evangelist on Patmos (fol. 19v). (This is the letter that is excerpted in the debates on images.)

So, by including entire letters in prose, verse redactions of other letters, and the prose *capitula* of Pseudo-Dionysius, Hilduin gave his verse *Passio* a strange and inconsistent quality. Blocks of prose interrupt the verse narrative, just as a whole section on Pseudo-Dionysius's writings interrupts the story of the saint's life. Why did Hilduin leave sections of the verse *Passio Dionysii* in prose? I suggest that, given Hilduin's interests in relics and given the interchangeability of bodies and books, Hilduin included pieces of Pseudo-Dionysian prose into his own verse narrative, because he saw his poem as a reliquary that enclosed [*claudere*] the life and works of Dionysius in metric verse [*strictu uersu*]. Like the bones in a monstrance reliquary, the Pseudo-Dionysian fragments – the *pignora* – could clearly be discerned from the precious materials surrounding them, and, like a relic within a reliquary, the literary remains were less decorative and immediately impressive than the ornamental casing that emphasized and revealed their holiness.

In the 820s and 830s, writers and statesmen contested the status of various material objects and forms of representation as channels to the divine. At the same time, artisans manufactured objects – such as Rabanus Maurus's *arca* reliquary – that equated the corporeal and the textual, alluding to a long classical and Christian tradition of conflating books and bodies. Hilduin utilized ideas about books and bodies and took advantage of the nebulous conception of the holy to fashion a new *res sacrata*, the Pseudo-Dionysian codex, and new reliquaries for it. Hilduin may have been accused of iconodulism in the past, but in this instance, he chose to represent not an image, but a book as an object imbued with sacred power. The mystical theologian Pseudo-Dionysius provided evidence that both written text (his own works) and the contemplation of material objects could offer one access to the divine. In Hilduin's scheme, the Pseudo-Dionysian codex, as a miraculous relic and as a piece of writing excerpted and enshrined in literary reliquaries, functioned as both object and text. Hilduin's letter and *passiones* allowed a reader to contemplate the divinity that endowed the codex and its mystical contents with such power.

Books and Relics as Gifts

Hilduin's compositions functioned as gifts in a network of exchange that included books and relics. Both were important gifts that established ties of patronage (Head 65–82). Hilduin understood the importance of relics as gifts; his present of part of St Sebastian to Abbot Boso of Fleury caused great popular excitement at the latter's cloister (Adrevald of Fleury 65). Books were, likewise, the object of exchange between important individuals and institutions, as Emperor Michael's gift of the Pseudo-Dionysian codex to Louis and Louis's *munus magnum* of that codex to St-Denis attest. Gifts established reciprocal ties (Lowden, passim). Such reciprocity was implied when Louis sent the Pseudo-Dionysian book to St-Denis and then requested two *uolumina* on Dionysius, thus binding his wayward abbot Hilduin into a network of favour, exchange, and obligation. By writing the two *passiones*, I have suggested, Hilduin transformed the Pseudo-Dionysian text into a new and powerful narrative and sent it to Louis, returning the favour and expressing his role in the network. By composing a verse passion – a specialized and difficult work – Hilduin provided the emperor with something as great or even greater than the gift Louis had donated to St-Denis. By giving the emperor new works in exchange for the Pseudo-Dionysian corpus, the poet of St-Denis thus reinvested himself in an economy of patronage and literary exchange, following his brief fall from favour.

Dionysius's Afterlife

If Hilduin composed the verse *Vita Dionysii* to enhance his standing with Louis, it is unclear whether the ploy worked. He was never reappointed arch-chaplain, but he and his abbey continued to receive favour under Louis and to participate in imperial ritual (Lapidge 60–1). Hilduin certainly popularized the version of Dionysius who was both the Areopagite and a cephalophore.[37] The tradition that the Pseudo-Dionysian writings were miraculous is also attested in a later *vita*.[38] The many extant manuscripts of Hilduin's prose *Passio Dionysii* show that it was widely distributed. As is usually the case with prose and verse works on the same saint, the metric version was less popular. Nonetheless, traces in other authors suggest that it was also influential. Just as Hilduin drew on a range of sources to create his text, so other writers excerpted the verse *Passio Dionysii.* As Lapidge notes, the short tenth-century *Passio S. Dionysii egregii martyris* (BHL 2186), one of several metric *passiones* composed by the nun Hrotsvita, borrows from Hilduin's verse text (Lapidge 75). Hrotsvita incorporates fragments of the original metric *Passio Dionysii* into new lines of verse. Hrotsvita's use of the poem shows that, even though we possess only one manuscript of Hilduin's metric *Passio Dionysii*, other copies circulated at least as far as Hrotsvita's abbey in Gandersheim.

A very different poem by one of Hilduin's contemporaries also alludes to the verse *Passio Dionysii.* As Lapidge notes, the scholar Sedulius Scottus probably dedicated a poem to Hilduin (Lapidge 63–4; Sedulius, *Carmen* 76). Sedulius also wrote a classicizing mini epic on a gelded ram. This humorous piece takes as its subject a humble sheep who lived a simple and holy life (printed in Godman, *Poetry of the Carolingian Renaissance* 298–9). The joke here is that a sheep's life of moderation and abstinence is like the life for which a saint is praised. The holy sheep wore a coarse wool shirt and did not ride a horse, but went about on his own feet. He ate grass and drank water and never attended banquets. He protected his flock, just as a bishop would. The protagonist of this miniature epic is a parody of the loftier subjects, the saintly bishops, who feature in grander poems, the full-scale epic *vitae* and *passiones metricae.*

Sedulius's mock saint is both implicitly a bishop (he leads the flock) and explicitly a martyr (he is killed by a pack of evil dogs). Some early medieval verse passions feature martyrs, such as St Agnes (BHL 161) and St Christopher (BHL 1776), but few of the martyrs – apart from Dionysius – are bishops, abbots, or any other kind of saint who has a flock.[39] Despite their ardent desire for martyrdom, most of the founding bishops featured in Carolingian metric *vitae*, such as Amand and Germanus, died disappointingly natural deaths. The *Passio Dionysii* is the only metric life or passion from this era that I have found of a martyr-bishop. This suggests that Sedulius is parodying not just any bishop but the martyr-bishop Dionysius, and not just any piece of verse hagiography but the *Passio Dionysii* of his probable acquaintance Hilduin. Sedulius's account of the holy sheep's utterances provides further evidence for this hypothesis. Sedulius says that the sheep was a mystic: '"Báá" seu "béé" – mystica verba dabat' ['"baa" or "bee," he was giving mystic pronouncements'] (line 116). By interpreting what is incomprehensible (the sheep's bleating) as mystical, Sedulius may be mocking the use of Greek among Louis's circle or the flawed translations of Greek texts by men, like Hilduin, whose understanding of the language was limited.[40] The depiction of the sheep as a mystic also suggests that the gelded ram stands for Dionysius. If medieval verse passions of martyr-bishops are unusual, mystical martyr-bishops seem otherwise non-existent. A mystic is a contemplative, whereas the bishops of the early saints' lives are men of action. Only in the composite figure of Dionysius, fabricated from originally disparate *personae*, do the different kinds of saint coincide. Further, the sheep's *mystica verba* appear to be an allusion to the *mystica orsa* that Hilduin attributes to Dionysius (Hilduin, *Passio Dionysii (metrica)*, fols. 10v, 21v).

The attributes of Sedulius's sheep are too specific for the poem to be a parody of saints in *vitae metricae* in general. Rather, I suggest, Sedulius is having a little fun at the expense of another member of Louis's court, at the incomprehensibility of Pseudo-Dionysian mysticism, and perhaps, by creating his own strange composite (the bishop-mystic-martyr-sheep), at the improbability of St-Denis's patchwork saint. The existence and survival of Sedulius's poem suggest that Hilduin's verse passion was popular enough to be the object of a successful parody.

Like St Cassian and St Eulalia, the ram's skin is pierced and marked by his persecutors. In death, Eulalia's skin becomes a page written on by *purpura sanguinis* (Prudentius, *Per.* 3, lines 136–40). The ram's skin, savaged by thorns and the dogs' teeth, is similarly marked with *sanguis purpureus.* The ram, however, does not have to become a page since he is already the correct surface for writing – vellum. Perhaps Sedulius, in making his hero a sheep, a walking parchment, is subtly mocking yet another element of Hilduin's depiction of Dionysius, namely, his conflation of the saint's codex with his corporeal relics. In Hilduin's letter the Pseudo-Dionysian book functions like a saint's body, and in Sedulius's poem, a similar transformation occurs: the sheep – the source of writing material for books – becomes a martyr. Both vellum objects – the inscribed sheep and the Pseudo-Dionysian codex – are presented in lofty epic verse form. As we have seen, in the ninth century, writers were discussing the relationship of holy words and holy bodies and contesting what in the material realm could be considered *res sacrate.* As Hilduin capitalized on this uncertainty to present the Greek codex and its mystical contents as a holy object, Sedulius, in his subversive little poem, presents a different kind *res sacrata*: a sheep.

NOTES

Thank you to Martha Newman, Alison Frazier, Jorie Woods, Jennifer Ebbeler, and Brian Levack for reading earlier versions of this paper and providing numerous helpful suggestions.

1 Paul converted a man named Dionysius, called the 'Areopagite' after the Areopagus hill in Athens (Acts 17:13–34). In the late fifth or early sixth centuries, an unknown writer claiming to be this Dionysius composed a series of mystical works and letters (Louth, *Denys the Areopagite* 2). Modern scholars call the late antique writer Pseudo-Dionysius, but in the central Middle Ages the

identification of the first-century Pauline convert with the theologian was accepted. On Pseudo-Dionysius in the west, see Jeauneau, 'Denys l'Aréopagite' 1–23, and Luscombe 133–52. For a discussion of the year of the codex's arrival, see Omont 30–2.

2 The Night Office of the saint's feast day, celebrated in the evening or the early hours of the morning, was ornate and featured long readings (Jonsson 11).

3 An example of relics calling out to one another and prompting each other to miracle working is given by Paschasius Radbertus discussing the mass importation of relics into the Carolingian empire (*Vita Walae*, col. 1608).

4 Thus, according to the verse inscription from the mid-ninth-century Gospel book made at Tours at the command of Lothar I, the latter provided the monks with gold ink in order that the book's beauty redound to the monastery's glory: 'he ordered the flock to write the inside of this book beautifully and decorate it reverently with his gold and with pictures, so that it might be known how much influence this place has' ['Hunc pulchreque gregem {the monks of Tours} librum intra scribere iussit / Ipsius ornare auro et picturis venerande, / Ut notum faciat quantum pollet locus ille'] (MGH Poetae 2:671; translated in Diebold, *Word and Image* 134). On Greek learning in the Carolingian world, see Berschin, especially section II; Kaczynski; Herren, ed., *The Sacred Nectar*; and Nees.

5 Important written primary sources for iconoclasm in the west include the *Opus Caroli Regis*, Pope Hadrian's letters to the Byzantine empress Irene and to Charlemagne, Michael's letter to Louis, the *Libellus* of the Paris Synod, and the works of various theologians (see the following note). There are numerous studies on eastern and western iconoclasm. On the Carolingian response to the iconophile Council of Nicaea (787), see Neil, and Freeman's excellent studies on the *Opus Caroli Regis* (formerly known as the *Libri Carolini*), from 1957, proving Theodulf's authorship of the *Opus*, and 1985. For considerations of the issues and background to the debates, see Chazelle's articles from 1986 and 1993. For the different interpretations of the relation of writing and painting in art, see McKitterick, 'Text and Image,' on the one hand, and Diebold, *Word and Image*, especially chapters 3 and 4, and Kessler, *Spiritual Seeing*, especially chapter 7, on the other.

6 Dungal (who spent time at St-Denis) and Agobard of Lyons both wrote treatises against Claudius; see Dungal, *Responsa contra Claudium*; Agobard, *De picturis et imaginibus*. See also Jonas of Orleans, *De cultu imaginum*. On Dungal, see Ferarri, 'In Papia,' and Leonardi, 'Gli Irlandesi'; on Agobard, Bellet; on Jonas, Appleby, 'Sight and Church Reform.'

7 Many of the figures involved in these debates in the eighth and ninth centuries were also poets, for example, Theodulf of Orleans, Angilbert, abbot

of Saint-Riquier, and Dungal. Late eighth- and early ninth-century poets engaged with the iconoclast debates and the value of images in various ways. See, for example, Rabanus Maurus, *Carmen* 38 on the relative value of words and images; Ermoldus Nigellus, *In honorem Hludovici*, lines 2594–9, mentions Claudius of Turin. See also Walafrid Strabo in *De imagine Tetrici*, discussed later in this article.

8 See Luscombe, 136, n. 12 for a summary of scholarly discussion on this matter.

9 Louth notes that Pseudo-Dionysius's preference for images that did not resemble their prototypes and his assertion that the purified mind will go beyond images should have made him problematic for the proponents of images. (In his 2005 article, Louth explicitly rejects his assertion of 1997 that Pseudo-Dionysius supported the iconophile position. See Louth, 'Truly Visible Things' 16, n.1.)

10 The sources for the early history of St-Denis are charters of varying authenticity, chronicles (the *Annales Regni Francorum*, the *Annales* of Einhard, and the *Annales Fuldenses*), and hagiography, as well as architectural remains and manuscripts produced at the abbey. See Levillain 222–58, and Vezin. The numerous secondary sources include the studies by d'Ayzac; Havet; Levillain; Crosby; and the essays in Cuisenier and Guadagnin, eds.

11 For a different interpretation of the relation of Moses to Aaron in this poem, see Herren, 'The *De Imagine Tetrici*' 120, and McCormick 153. See also Godman, *Poets and Emperors* 133–47.

12 The seemingly anomalous address to the sea goddess Thetis refers the reader to the passage in Ovid's *Metamorphoses* where *nuda* (rather than *uda*) Thetis is in her cave, which was made by nature or, more likely, says Ovid, art (whether made by nature or art, it is unclear, but more likely by art ['natura factus an arte, / ambiguum, magis arte tamen'] Ovid, *Met.*, 11.235–6). So the reference to Thetis here alludes to the naked goddess (as opposed to the resplendent Aaron) in her fabricated lair. Is this perhaps a reference to the structure that Hilduin was currently building 'by art,' namely, the elaborate crypta at St-Denis?

13 Walafrid addresses his *Carmen* 29, a poem of thanks for his good fortune, to Hilduin (MGH Poetae 2:383).

14 The MGH prefers the reading *subnixa*, but at least one of the manuscripts, the tenth-century Oxford Bodleian MS 1276 (Laud. misc. 549), contains the variant *subnexa*, which makes better sense.

15 The BHL's online catalogue lists ninety-six manuscripts of Hilduin's prose *Passio Dionysii*. http://bhlms.fltr.ucl.ac.be, viewed 20 May 2006. The passion is printed in Migne, *Patrologiae Latinae* 106; there is no critical edition. There is no printed edition of the verse *Passio Dionysii*.

16 Roughly contemporary 'twinned' works include the prose and verse texts of Rabanus Maurus's *In honorem sancte crucis* and the paired books of Candid's *Vita Eigili* (BHL 2478). On paired works in verse and prose, see Godman, 'The Anglo-Latin Opus Geminatum,' and Wieland.

17 It is unlikely that there were two metric passions of Dionysius, both divided into four books. Only some early medieval *vitae metricae* were divided into books; Heiric's *Vita Germani* (BHL 3458) is composed of six books, Milo's *Vita Amandi* (BHL 333) of four. The anonymous *Vita Eusebiae* (BHL 2737) and Johannes's *Vita Rictrudis* (BHL 7248) are composed of two each.

18 Heiric of Auxerre tells Charles the Bald that it took him ten years to write the verse *Vita Germani* (BHL 3458) (Heiric, *Vita Germani* 429).

19 In his letter to Louis, Hilduin claims that he derived the story of cephalophory, along with other incidents in the narrative, from a 'libellus antiquissimus.' (Louis, in his letter to Hilduin, also refers to a pre-existing work on Dionysius, which he calls a 'libellus passionis.') The identity of this work is discussed by Loenertz ('La légende Parisienne' 221–8). Levillain discusses the relationship between three passions of Dionysius (BHL 2171, 2178 and Hilduin's prose passion) (6–23). On cephalophores see d'Arbois de Jubainville; Stückelberg; Cahier; Saintyves; Coens.

20 Spiegel argues for the originality of Hilduin's conflation of the two saints and the inclusion of the cephalophory. See Spiegel, passim. Not everybody accepted the conflation of the two saints or adopted the cephalophory. For example, Hilduin's student Hincmar makes no mention of Dionysius as the Areopagite until late in his life. See Luscombe 140–2.

21 I am grateful to Giselle de Nie for this reference.

22 On insular book miracles, see Kelly, and on miraculous books more generally, see Diebold, *Word and Image* 28–9. On the symbolic weight of documents in general, see Clanchy 254, and Geary 5. For a fascinating anthropological account of the power of books and writing, see J. Goody, a study upon which Diebold draws (*Word and Image* 28–9).

23 Classical authors describe the ways that a book could substitute for a physical person or a body. In one dramatic example, at the beginning of his *Tristia* written in exile, Ovid addressed his book, telling it to go on its (poetic) feet and visit the sights in Rome that he was no longer able to see. Ovid envisioned his embodied books as his sons, and warned the *Tristia* to avoid its wicked brother, the *Ars Amatoria*, which was the cause of his exile (1.1). Other examples include Seneca the Elder and Pliny who provide different interpretations of the relationship of books and bodies (Seneca, *Suasoriae* 7; Pliny, *Epistula* 9.23).

24 On the intersection of corporeality and poetry in the context of iconoclasm, see the first chapter in my forthcoming book, *Epic Lives*.

25 Heiric employs a less bloody metaphor conflating saints' lives and books. In his verse *Vita Germani* (BHL 3458), completed in the 870s, the poet describes life in the terms of writing or reading a book: 'after completing the chapters {or volumes} of our turbulent life, we can see the true homeland' ['Post inconstantis permensa uolumina uitae / ... patriam donatur cernere ueram'] (Heiric, *Vita Germani* 449).

26 The incident is also recounted in Theophanes of Caesarea's text discussed and edited by Featherstone. For a concise summary of the sources for the *Graptoi* and a fascinating discussion of writing, bodies, and holiness in Byzantine iconoclasm, see Barber 111, n. 1, and passim. Also, see Mullett 156.

27 In the early eleventh century, Bernard of Angers notes that St Foy's reliquary statue was intended to preserve her *memoria*. He calls the statue 'the pious memorial of the holy virgin' ['sancte uirginis pia memoria' (Bernard of Angers, *Miracula* 114; lib. 1:13)].

28 For these inscriptions, Rudolf, *Miracula* 3, 10, 8, 4, 12, 13, 14. They are also printed in MGH Poetae 2:210–14.

29 Rabanus's writings reveal his understanding of the meaning of the Ark as a reliquary. For discussion and references, see Appleby, 'Rudolf' 434–8. See also Bernard of Angers (1:13), who compares Saint Foy's reliquary statue to the Ark of the Covenant, but says that it contains a more precious treasure (Diebold, *Word and Image* 145).

30 The fifteenth-century reliquary of the child proto-cephalophore St Just is in the shape of his head supported by his hands. It thus depicts his miraculous posthumous gesture related in his passion: the martyred Just, sitting with his head in his hands, asked his father and uncle to take his head to his mother so she could kiss it (*Passio Iusti* 338–9; Montgomery 48–64). Montgomery has pointed out how the role of this reliquary in ritual would implicate the viewer in the role of Justus's mother kissing her son's decapitated head, so that this reliquary not only tells a story but also conditions a ritual response (Montgomery 50). St-Denis possessed a similar reliquary head of Dionysius from the thirteenth century, which consisted of a head wearing a bishop's mitre and supported by angels. Montgomery describes this as a 'compressed and simplified' version of Dionysius's cephalophory (Montgomery 55–6).

31 'If anyone wishes to know the abundance of his deeds of virtue, he may take it as a sign that the box in which his most holy body is contained is well decorated with gold and silver from the abundance of gifts, which the devoted hands of the faithful offered and is covered with skilled work' ['Si quis ergo uirtutum illic gestarum copiam, uera inde excipere poeterit indicia, quod arca, qua sacratissimum eius corpus continetur, auro argentoque decenter ornata,

ex oblationum abundantia, quas illi fidelium detulit manus deuota, fabrili opere hactenus contexta cernitur'] (AASS, Jan, vol. 3:161, trans. Diebold, *Word and Image* 118). In the verses that Dungal composed for the altar of St Ambrose, dedicated in the second quarter of the ninth century, the flashy gold and gems of the reliquary cannot compare to the treasures within. 'This nourishing beautiful ark gleams on the outside with a reddish gold decoration of metals; ornamented, it glitters with gems. But inside, this gift is powerful in its sacred bones, more powerful in that treasure than its embellished metal' ['Emicat alma foris rutiloque decore uenusta / Arca metallorum, gemmis que cumpta coruscat. / Thaesauro tamen haec, cumpto potiore metallo, / Ossibus interius pollet donata sacratis'] (Dungal, *Titulus altaris mediolanensis* 665, trans. Diebold, *Word and Image* 130, adapted).

32 'Thus, when – out of my delight in the beauty of the house of God – the multicolored loveliness of the gems has called me away from external cares, and worthy meditation has induced me to reflect on the diversity of the sacred virtues, transferring that which is material to that which is immaterial, then I seem to see myself, by God's grace in an anagogical manner, able to be transported from the inferior to the higher world' ['Unde, cum ex dilectione decoris domus Dei aliquando multicolor gemmarum speciositas ab extrinsecis me curis devocaret, sanctarum etiam diversitatem virtutum, de materialibus ad immaterialia transferendo, honesta meditatio insistere persuaderet, videor videre me ... ab hac etiam inferiori ad illam superiorem anagogico more Deo donante posse transferri'] (Suger 62–5, cap. 33; trans. Panofsky).

33 Hilduin's contemporary, the poet and theologian Dungal, describes the crypt that 'Hilduin, patron of the church, excellent abbot, built' ['Ecclesiae Hilduinus cultor egregias abbas / struxit'] for Dionysius and his two companions using the terms that are frequently used to describe the glittering (*coruscare*) and red-gold metal (*rutilans metallum*) of the saints' final resting places.

34 The verb *claudere* can mean 'to stumble,' and thus Hilduin may be simultaneously expressing a humility topos ('I am allowed to stumble in metric verse').

35 See Diebold on artistic spoliation for a discussion of artists incorporating pagan art into Christian cult objects (Diebold, *Word and Image* 87–95). I argue that Hilduin does something similar using the classical form of epic dactylic hexameter and the different Dionysian traditions to compose his verse *Passio Dionysii*.

36 This letter seems to be an apocryphal Latin addition to the Dionysian corpus, possibly invented by Hilduin himself. Letter 11 is contained in full, in identical prose form, in both Hilduin's passions, but is not included in the Greek codex Paris, BNF, MS grec. 437. Migne in the PG 3, col. 1119–22, classes this letter as *spuria*.

37 For example, in the eleventh century, the monks of St-Emmeram, claiming that Dionysius's body was in their possession, write that the saint performed a mini cephalophory in their church (Coens 31). The monks of St-Emmeram say that they had received the body of Dionysius, secretly stolen from St-Denis. In the *Translatio S. Dionysii Ratisbonam* (BHL 2194), attributed to Otloh, the Regensberg relics prove their authenticity in the following way: the saint's head and body had been placed in separate bags, and the monks assumed that the head had been lost until the bag containing the head moved itself over to join the rest of Dionysius's remains (ed. in Heinemann). The endurance of the doctrine that equated the Parisian bishop and the Areopagite is revealed by the resistance that Abelard encountered at St-Denis when he argued against this version of the Parisian Dionysius's origins (Abelard, *Historia,* 11.941–1037, pp. 89–90). Numerous later saints whose passions drew on the language and model of Dionysius were depicted as cephalophores (Stückelberg 78).

38 According to Odo of Cluny, while visiting St-Denis, Maiolus fell asleep reading a manuscript *de principatu coelesti* (presumably the *Celestial Hierarchy*), and dropped his candle on a page of the book. Amazingly, says Odo, the page was unharmed (Odo, *Vita Maioli Abbatis,* 955C-956A).

39 There are a number of early medieval manuscripts containing metric *passiones* of virgin martyrs. For example, the metric *Passio Agnetis* (BHL 161) in the ninth-century manuscript, Paris, BNF, lat. 14145, fols. 1r–8v; the metric *Passio Benedictae* (BHL 1088) in an eleventh-century manuscript, Paris, BNF, lat. 8431, fols. 5r–20r; the metric *Passio Luciae* (BHL 4994) in a tenth-century manuscript Paris, BNF, MS lat. 989, fols. 41r–53r, as well as two twelfth-century manuscripts. Male martyrs were also represented in early medieval *passiones metricae*. For instance, the *Carmen de S. Quintino* (BHL 7010) in the ninth-century Paris, BNF, MS lat. 14143, fols. 74r–82v.

40 I am thankful to the anonymous reader for suggesting this point. The *uerba* 'baa' and 'bee' – alluding to the etymology of a barbarian (Greek: *barbaros*; Latin: *barbarus*) as someone who makes incomprehensible 'ba' sounds – implies that the ram's *uerba* are unintelligible to the auditors or readers.

WORKS CITED

Primary Sources

Abelard, Peter. *Historia Calamitatum*. Ed. J. Monfrin. Paris: J. Vrin, 1959.

Ado of Vienne. *Miracula Barnardi* (BHL 995). Ed. Socii Bollandiani. *Analecta Bollandiana* 11 (1892): 404–15; rpt in *Bibliotheca hagiographica latina antiquae et mediae aetatis*. 4 vols. Brussels: Society of Bollandists, 1898–1911. 3:157–97.

Adrevald of Fleury. *Miracula Benedicti*. Ed. E. de Certain. *Les Miracles de Saint Benoît*. Paris: Ve J. Renouard, 1858.

Agobard of Lyons. *De picturis et imaginibus*. Ed. L. Van Acker. *Agobardi Lugdunensis Opera Omnia*. CCCM 52. Turnholt: Brepols, 1981. 149–52.

Annales Regni Francorum inde ab A. 741 usque ad A. 829. Ed. G.H. Pertz and F. Kurze. *Monumenta Germaniae Historica Scriptores* (henceforth MGH SS). Hannover: Hahn, 1895.

Annalista Saxo. Ed. G. Pertz. *MGH* SS 6. Hannover: Hahn, 1844. 542–777.

Bernard of Angers. *Liber miraculorum sancte Fidis* (BHL 2942). Ed. Auguste Bouillet. Paris: Alphonse Picard et Fils, Libraires des Archives nationales et de la Société de l'École des Chartes, 1897.

Bios kai marturion tês hagias Anastasias (BHG 81–81a). Ed. François Halkin 'Anastasie la Veuve.' *Subsidia hagiographicorua* 55 (1973): 86–131.

Bobolenus. *Vita Germani Abbatis Grandivallensis* (BHL 3467). Ed. B. Krusch and W. Levison. *MGH Scriptores Rerum Merovingicarum* (henceforth MGH SRM) 5. Hannover: Hahn, 1910. 26–40.

Dado. *Vita Eligii* (BHL 2474). Ed. B. Krusch and W. Levison. MGH SRM 4. Hannover: Hahn, 1902. 669–742.

Dungal. *Responsa contra Claudium. A Controversy on Holy Images*. Ed. and trans. Paolo Zanna. Sismel: Edizioni del Galluzzo, 2002.

– *Titulus altaris mediolanensis*. Ed. E. Dümmler. *MGH Poetae Latini Aevi Carolini* (henceforth MGH Poetae) 2. Berlin: Weidmann, 1884. 665.

Ermoldus Nigellus. *Poème sur Louis le Pieux et épitres au Roi Pépin*. Ed. and trans. Edmond Faral. Paris: Honoré Champion, 1932.

Fortunatus. *Carmina* 1.13, 3.7. *MGH Auctores Antiquissimi* (henceforth MGH AA) 4.1, pp. 15. 57.

Gregory of Tours. *Liber in gloria confessorum*. Eds. B. Krusch and W. Levison. MGH SRM 1. Hannover: Hahn, 1851. 745–820.

Gregory of Tours. *Liber in gloria martyrum* MGH SRM 1. 485–561.

Hadrian I, Pope. *Letter to Charlemagne*. Ed. K. Hampe. MGH Ep. 5. Berlin: Weidmann, 1899. 5–59.

Heiric. *Vita Germani* (BHL 3458). Ed. Ludwig Traube. MGH Poetae 3. Berlin: Weidmann, 1896. 428–517.

Hilduin. *Rescriptum ad Hludovicum* (BHL 2173). Ed. E. Dümmler. MGH Ep. 5. Berlin: Weidmann, 1899. 328–35.

– *Passio Dionysii* (BHL 2175). Ed. J.P. Migne. *Patrologiae Latinae* 106, cols. 13–50.

– *Passio Dionysii (metrica)* (no BHL). Oxford, Bodleian, Bodley, MS 535 (S.C. 2254). Unpublished manuscript.

Hrotsvita. *Passio Sancti Dionisii egregii martyris* (BHL 2186). Ed. Walter Berschin. *Opera Omnia*. Leipzig: Saur, 2001. 104–11.

Jonas of Orleans. *De cultu imaginum*. PL 106. Cols. 305–88.

Libellus Synodalis Parisiensis. Ed. Albert Werminghoff. MGH Concilia (henceforth MGH Conc.) 1.2. Hannover: Hahn, 1908. 480–551.

Life of Michael the Synkellos. Ed. and trans. Mary Cunningham. Belfast: Belfast Byzantine Texts and Translations, 1991.

Louis the Pious. *Epistola* (BHL 2172). Ed. E. Dümmler. MGH Ep. 5. Berlin: Weidmann, 1899. Munich: MGH, 1978. 325–7.

Michael II and Theophilus. *Epistola ad Hludowicum*. MGH Conc. 1.2. 475–80.

Milo. *Vita Amandi* (BHL 333). Ed. Ludwig Traube. MGH Poetae 3. Berlin: Weidmann, 1896. 561–612.

Miracula Barnardi (BHL 995). AASS Jan. Vol. 3. 160–1.

Odo of Cluny. *Vita Maioli Abbatis* (BHL 5182). PL 142. cols. 943B –962B.

Otfrid. *Versus Otfridi*. MGH Poetae 2. 407–8.

Otloh of Saint-Emmeram (?). *Translatio* (BHL 2194). Ed. L. von Heinemann. 'Die älteste Translatio des heil. Dionysius.' *Neue Archiv* 15 (1989): 331–61.

Paschasius Radbertus. *Vita Walae* (BHL 8761). Ed. E. Dümmler. *Philosophische der Wissenschaften zu Berlin*, II (1900): 18–98.

Passio Dionysii ('Post beatam et gloriosam') (BHL 2178). AASS. Oct. vol. 4. 792–4.

Passio Iusti (BHL 4590). AASS Oct. vol. 8. 338–9.

Passio sanctorum martyrum Dionysii, Rustici et Eleutherii ('Gloriosae') (BHL 2171). MGH AA 4.1. 101–5.

Paul I, Pope. *Epistola* 24. Ed. W. Gundlach. MGH Ep. 3. Berlin: Weidmann, 1892. 527–9.

Paulinus of Périgueux. *Versus Paulini de uisitatione nepotuli sui*. Poetae Christiani Minores. Ed. Michael Petschenig. CSEL 16. Vienna, 1888. 161–4.

Pliny. *Epistularum Libri Decem*. Ed. R.A.B. Mynors. Oxford: Clarendon, 1963.

Poleticum of Marchiennes in L'histoire-polyptyque de l'abbaye de Marchiennes (1116/1121), étude critique et edition. Ed. Bernard Delmaire. Louvain-la-Neuve, 1985.

Prudentius. *Peristephanon.* Ed. Maurice P. Cunningham. In *Aurelii Prudentii Clementis Carmina.* CCSL 126. Turnholt: Brepols, 1966.

Rabanus Maurus. *Carmen* 38. MGH Poetae 2. 196–7.

– *In honorem sanctae cruces*. Ed. M. Perrin. CCCM 100. Turnholt: Typographi Brepols Editores Pontificii, 1997.

Rudolf of Fulda. *Miracula sanctorum in Fuldenses ecclesias translatorum*. Ed. G. Waitz. MGH SS 15.1. 328–41.

Sedulius Scottus. *Carmen* 76, MGH Poetae 3. 226–7.

– *Mock Epillyon on a Gelded Ram*. Ed. and trans. Peter Godman. *Poetry of the Carolingian Renaissance*. Norman: University of Oklahoma Press, 1985. 293–301.

Seneca. *Suasoriae*. Ed. and trans. William A. Edward. Cambridge: Cambridge, 1928.

Sigebert. *Catalogus Sigeberti Gemblacensis monachi de viris illustribus*. Ed. Robert Witte. Krit. Ausgabe, Lat. Sprache und Literatur des MA.s 1. Bern: H. Lang, 1974.

– *Chronica*. Ed. G. Pertz. MGH Scriptores 6. Hannover: Hahn, 1844. 300–74.

Suger. *De Administratione*. Ed. Erwin Panofsky. *Abbot Suger: On the Abbey Church of St.-Denis and its Art Treasures*. 2nd ed. Princeton, NJ: Princeton University Press, 1979.

Theodulf of Orleans. *Opus Caroli Regis contra symodum (Libri Carolini)*. Ed. Ann Freeman. MGH Conc. 2, supp. 1. Hannover: Hahn, 1998.

Walafrid Strabo. *De imagine tetrici* and *Carmen* 29. MGH Poetae 2. 370–8 and 383.

Secondary Sources

Appleby, David F. 'Holy Relic and Holy Image: Saints' Relics in the Western Controversy over Images in the Eighth and Ninth Centuries.' *Word and Image* 8 (1992): 333–43.

– 'Instruction and Inspiration through Images in the Carolingian Period.' In *Word, Image, Number: Communication in the Middle Ages.* Ed. John J. Contreni and Santa Casciani. Sismel: Edizioni del Galluzzo, 2002. 85–111.

– 'Rudolf, Abbot Hrabanus, and the Ark of the Covenant Reliquary.' *American Benedictine Review* 46 (1995): 419–43.

– 'Sight and Church Reform in the Thought of Jonas of Orleans.' *Viator* 27 (1996): 11–35.

Barber, Charles. 'Writing on the Body: Memory, Desire, and the Holy in Iconoclasm.' In *Desire and Denial in Byzantium*. Ed. Liz James. Aldershot, UK: Variorum, 1999. 111–20.

Bellet, Paolino. 'El "Liber de imaginibus sanctorum" del nombre de Agobardo de Lyon, obra Claudio de Turin.' *Analecta sacra terraconensia* 26 (1955): 151–95.

Berschin, Walter. *Greek Letters and the Latin Middle Ages from Jerome to Nicholas of Cusa.* Trans. Jerold C. Frakes. Washington, DC: Catholic University of America Press, 1988.

Bozóky, Edina, and Anne-Marie Helvétius, eds. *Les reliques: Objets, cultes, symboles: Actes du colloque international del'Université du Littoral-Côte d'Opale (Boulogne-sur-Mer) 4–6 septembre 1997*. Hagiologia études sur la sainteté en occident – Studies on Western Sainthood, 1. Turnhout, Belgium: Brepols, 1999.

Brown, E.A.R. '*Gloriosae*, Hilduin, and the Early Liturgical Celebration of St. Denis.' In *Medieval Paradigms: Essays in Honor of Jeremy Duquesnay Adams*. Ed. Stephanie Hayes-Healy. New York: Palgrave Macmillan, 2005. Vol. 2: 39–82.

Brown, Peter. *The Cult of the Saints: Its Rise and Function in Latin Christianity.* Chicago: University of Chicago Press, 1981.

Buchner, M. 'Die Areopagitika des Abtes Hilduin von St. Denis und ihr kirchenpolitischer Hintergrund. Studien zur Gleichsetzung Dionysius' des Areopagiten mit dem hl. Dionysius von Paris sowie zur Fälchungstechnik am Vorabend der Entstehung des Pseudoisidorischen Dekretalen.' *Historisches Jahrbuch* 56 (1936): 441–80; 57 (1937): 31–60; 58 (1938): 55–96, 361–403; 59 (1939): 69–117.

Bynum, Caroline Walker, and Paula Gerson. 'Body-Part Reliquaries and Body Parts in the Middle Ages.' *Gesta* 36 (1997): 3–7.

Cahier, C. *Charactéristiques des saints dans l'art populaire*. Brussels: Culture et Civilisation, 1966 [1867].

Canetti, L. *Frammenti di eternità: Corpi e reliquie tra Antichità e Medioevo.* Rome: Viella, 2002.

Chazelle, Celia M. 'Matter, Spirit and Image in the Libri Carolini.' *Recherches Augustiniennes* 21 (1986): 163–84.

– 'Images, Scripture, the Church, and the Libri Carolini.' *Proceedings of the PMR Conference* 16/17 (1993): 53–76.

– '"Not in Painting But in Writing": Augustine and the Supremacy of the Word in the *Libri Carolini*.' In *Reading and Wisdom: The De doctrina Christiana of Augustine in the Middle Ages*. Ed. Edward D. English. Notre Dame, IN: University of Notre Dame Press, 1995. 1–22.

– 'Memory, Instruction, Worship: "Gregory's" Influence on Early Medieval Doctrines of the Artistic Image.' In *Gregory the Great, a Symposium*. Ed. John J. Cavadini. Notre Dame, IN: University of Notre Dame Press, 1996. 181–215.

Clanchy, M.T. *From Memory to Written Record, England 1066–1307*. 2nd ed. Oxford: Blackwell, 1993.

Coens, Maurice. 'Nouvelles recherches sur un theme hagiographique: La céphalophorie.' *Academie Royale de Belgique. Bulletin de la Classe des lettres et des sciences morales et politiques*. 5e série, volume 48 (1962): 231–53. Reprinted in *Recueil d'études Bollandiennes par Maurice Coens.* Brussels: Société des Bollandistes, 1963. 9–31.

Cox Miller, Patricia. '"The Little Blue Flower is Red": Relics and the Poetizing of the Body.' *Journal of Early Christian Studies* 8 (2000): 213–36.

– 'Relics, Rhetoric and Mental Spectacles in Late Ancient Christianity.' In *Seeing the Invisible.* Ed. de Nie, Morrison, and Mostert. 23–52.

Crosby, Sumner McKnight. *The Abbey of St.-Denis.* Yale Historical Publications. History of Art 3. New Haven, CT: Yale University Press, 1942.

Cuisenier, Jean, and Rémy Guadagnin, eds. *Un village au temps de Charlemagne,*

moines et paysans de l'abbaye de Saint-Denis, du viie siècle à l'an mil. Paris: Éditions de la Réunion des musées nationaux, 1988.
d'Arbois de Jubainville, M. 'Saint Denis portant sa tête sur la poitrine.' *Revue celtique* 12 (1891): 166–7.d'Ayzac, Félicie. *Histoire de l'abbaye de Saint-Denis en France*. 2 vols. Paris: Impr. Impériale, 1860–1.
de Nie, Giselle, Karl F. Morrison, and Marco Mostert, eds. *Seeing the Invisible in Late Antiquity and the Early Middle Ages. Papers from Verbal and Pictorial Imaging: Representing and accessing experience of the invisible, 400–1000 (Utrecht, 11–13 December 2003).* Turnhout, Belgium: Brepols, 2005.
Diebold, William J. *Word and Image: An Introduction to Early Medieval Art*. Boulder: Westview, 2000.
– 'The Carolingian Idol: Exegetes and idols.' In *Seeing the Invisible*. Ed. de Nie, Morrison, and Mostert. 443–61.
Dierkens, Alain. 'Du bon (et du mauvais) usage des reliquaires au Moyen Age.' In *Les reliques: objets, cultes, symbols*. Ed. Bózoky and Helvétius. Turnhout, Belgium: Brepols, 1999. 327–8.
Doublet, Jacques. *Histoire de l'abbaye de S. Denis en France*. Paris: J. de Heuqueville, 1625.
Featherstone, J.M. 'The Praise of Theodore Graptos by Theophanes of Caesarea.' *Analecta Bollandiana* 98 (1980): 104–50.
Félibien, Michel. *Histoire de l'abbaye royale de Saint-Denis en France*. Paris: F. Léonard, 1706.
Ferrari, Leonardi. 'In Papia Conveniant ad Dungalum.' *Italia medioevale e umanistica* 15 (1972): 1–52.
Foley, Edward B. *The First Ordinary of the Royal Abbey of St-Denis in France*. Spicilegium Friburgense 32. Fribourg, Switzerland: University Press, 1990.
– 'St-Denis Revisited: The liturgical evidence.' *Revue Bénédictine* 100, no. 4 (1990): 532–49.
Formigé, Jules. *L'abbaye royale de Saint-Denis*. Paris: Presses Universitaires de France, 1960.
Freeman, Ann. 'Theodulf of Orleans and the *Libri Carolini*.' *Speculum* 32 (1957): 663–705.
– 'Carolingian Orthodoxy and the Fate of the *Libri Carolini*.' *Viator* 16 (1985): 65–108.
Freese, Dolores Warwick, and Katherine O'Brien O'Keeffe, eds. *The Book and the Body*. Notre Dame, IN: University of Notre Dame Press, 1997.
Gaborit-Chopin, Danielle. 'Le Trésor de Saint-Denis à l'époque carolingienne.' In *Un village au temps de Charlemagne*. Ed. Cuisenier and Guadagnin. 69–77.
Gajano, Sofia Boesch. 'Reliques et pouvoirs.' In *Les reliques: objets, cultes, symbols*. Ed. Bózoky and Helvétius. 255–69.

Geary, Patrick J. *Furta Sacra: Thefts of Relics in the Central Middle Ages.* Princeton, NJ: Princeton University Press, 1978.

Gerson, Paula, ed. *Abbot Suger and Saint-Denis*. New York: Metropolitan Museum of Art, 1986.

Godman, Peter. 'The Anglo-Latin Opus Geminatum: From Aldhelm to Alcuin.' *Medium Ævum* 50 (1981): 215–29.

Goody, J. *Poets and Emperors: Frankish Politics and Carolingian Poetry*. Oxford: Clarendon, 1987.

Goody, J. 'Restricted Literacy in Northern Ghana.' In *Literacy in Traditional Societies.* Ed. J. Goody. Cambridge: Cambridge University Press, 1968. 198–264.

Hahn, Cynthia. 'The Voices of the Saints: Speaking Reliquaries.' *Gesta* 36 (1997): 20–52.

– 'Metaphor and Meaning in Early Medieval Relics.' In *Seeing the Invisible*. Ed. de Nie, Morrison, and Mostert. 239–63.

– *Portrayed on the Heart: Narrative Effect in Pictorial Lives of Saints from the Tenth through the Thirteenth Century*. Berkeley: University of California Press, 2001.

Havet, Julien. 'Les Origines des Saint-Denis.' *Bibliothèque de l'École des chartes* 81 (1890): 5–62.

Head, Thomas. 'Art and Artifice in Ottonian Trier.' *Gesta* 36 (1997): 65–82.

Herren, Michael W. 'The *De Imagine Tetrici* of Walahfrid Strabo: Edition and Translation.' *Journal of Medieval Latin* 1 (1991): 118–39.

– ed. *The Sacred Nectar of the Greeks: The Study of Greek in the West in the Early Middle Ages.* King's College London Medieval Studies, London: King's College Medieval Studies, 1988.

– 'Walafrid Strabo's *De Imagine Tetrici:* An interpretation.' In *Latin Culture and Medieval Germanic Europe: Proceedings of the first Germania Latina Conference held at the University of Groningen, 26 May 1989*. Ed. Richard North and Tette Hofstra. Groningen: E. Forsten, 1992. 25–41.

Huglo, Michel. 'Les chants de la "missa graeca" de Saint-Denis.' In *Essays presented to Egon Wellesz*. Ed. Jack Westrup. Oxford: Clarendon, 1966. 74–83.

Irigoin, Jean. 'Les manuscrits grecs de Denys l'Aréopagite en Occident, les empereurs byzantins et l'abbey royale de Saint-Denis en France.' In *Denys l'Aréopagite et sa postérité en orient et en occident. Actes du Colloque International Paris, 21–24 septembre 1994.* Ed. Ysabel de Andia. Paris: Institut d'Etudes Augustiniennes, 1997. 19–29.

Jager, Eric. *The Book of the Heart*. Chicago: University of Chicago Press, 2000.

James, Liz, and Ruth Webb. '"To Understand Ultimate Things and Enter Secret Places": Ekphrasis and Art in Byzantium.' *Art History* 14 (1991): 1–17.

Jeauneau, Edouard. 'L'abbaye de Saint-Denis introductruce de Denys en Occident.' In *Denys l'Aréopagite et sa postérité en orient et en occident. Actes du Colloque International Paris, 21–24 septembre 1994.* Ed. Ysabel de Andia. Paris: Institut d'Etudes Augustiniennes, 1997. 361–78.

– 'Denys l'Aréopagite, promoteur du néoplatonisme en Occident.' *Néoplatonisme et philosophie médiévale: Actes du Colloque international de Corfou, 6–8 octobre 1995*. Turnhout, Belgium: Brepols, 1997. 1–23.

Jonsson (Jacobssen), Ritva. *Historia: Études sur la genèse des offices versifiés.* Studia Latina Stockholmiensia 15. Stockholm: Almqvist and Wiksell, 1968.

Kaczynski, Bernice M. *Greek in the Carolingian Age: The St. Gall Manuscripts.* Cambridge, MA: Medieval Academy, 1988.

Kelly, Joseph F. 'Books, Learning and Sanctity in Early Christian Ireland.' *Thought* 54 (1979): 253–61.

Kessler, Herbert L. 'Pictorial Narrative and Church Mission in Sixth-Century Gaul.' In *Pictorial Narrative in Antiquity and the Middle Ages*. Ed. Herbert L. Kessler and Marianna Shreve Simpson. Washington, DC: National Gallery of Art, 1985. 75–89.

– *Spiritual Seeing: Picturing God's Invisibility in Medieval Art.* Philadelphia: University of Pennsylvania Press, 2000.

Kitzinger, Ernst. 'The Cult of Images before Iconoclasm.' *Dumbarton Oaks Papers* 8 (1954): 81–150.

Lapidge, Michael. 'The Lost "Passio Metrica S. Dionysii" by Hilduin.' *Mittellateinische Jahrbuch* 22 (1987): 56–79.

Leclerq, Henri. '*Brandea.*' In *DACL* 14, fasc. 2 (1948) 2294–2359, sec. 13.

Le Mire (Miraeus), Aubert. *Liber de Ecclesiasticis Scriptoribus in Bibliotheca ecclesiastica*. Antwerp: N.P., 1639.

Leonardi, Claudio. 'Gli Irlandesi in Itali: Dungal e la controversia iconoclastica.' In *Die Iren und Europa im früheren Mittelater.* Vol. 2. Ed. Heinz Löwe. Stuttgart: Klett-Cotta, 1982. 746–57.

Levillain, Léon. 'Etudes sur l'abbaye de Saint-Denis à l'époque Mérovingienne.' *Bibliothèque de l'École des chartes* 82 (1921): 5–116.

Loenertz, Raymond. 'Le panégyrique de S. Denys l'Aréopagite par S. Michel le Syncelle.' *Analecta Bollandiana* 68 (1950): 94–107.

– 'La légende Parisienne de S.Denys l'Aréopagite: sa genèse et son premier témoin.' *Analecta Bollandiana* 69 (1951): 217–37.

Louth, Andrew. *Denys the Areopagite.* London: Continuum, 1989.

– 'St Denys the Areopagite and the Iconoclast Controversy.' In *Denys l'Aréopagite et sa postérité*. Ed. de Andia. 1997. 329–39.

– '"Truly Visible Things are Manifest Images of Invisible Things": Dionysios the Areopagite on Knowing the Invisible.' In *Seeing the Invisible*. Ed. de Nie, Morrison, and Mostert. 2005. 15–24.

Lowden, John. 'The Luxury Book as Diplomatic Gift.' In *Byzantine Diplomacy: Papers from the Twenty-fourth Spring Symposim of Byzantine Studies, Cambridge, March 1990.* Ed. Jonathan Shepard and Simon Franklin. Aldershot, UK: Variorum, 1992. 249–60.

Luscombe, David E. 'Denis the Pseudo-Areopagite in the Middle Ages from Hilduin to Lorenzo Valla.' *Fälschungen im Mittelalter: Internationaler Kongreß der Monumenta Germaniae Historica, München, 16–19 September 1986.* Ed. Wolfram Setz. Hannover: Hahn, 1988. Vol. 1. 133–52.

Madan, Falconer, and H.H.E. Craster. *Summary Catalogue of Western Manuscripts in the Bodleian Library at Oxford*. Vol. 2, part 2. Oxford: Clarendon, 1922.

Manitius, M. *Geschichte der lateinischen Literatur des Mittelalters* 2. Munich: C.H. Beck, 1923.

Marchioli, Nicoletta Giovè. 'I libri del tesoro.' In *Tesori: Forme di accumulazione della ricchezza nell'alto medioevo (secoli V-XI)*. Ed. Sauro Gelichi and Cristina La Rocca. Roma: Viella, 2004. 257–88.

McCormick, Michael. 'Textes, images e iconoclasme.' In *Testo e immagine nell' alto medioevo. 15–21 aprile 1993*. Settimane di studio del Centro italiano di studi sull'alto medioevo, 41. Spoleto: Centro italiano sull'alto medioevo, 1994. Vol. 1. 96–162.

McKitterick, Rosamond. 'Text and Image in the Carolingian World.' In *The Uses of Literacy in Early Medieval Europe*. Ed. Rosamond McKitterick. Cambridge: Cambridge University Press, 1990. 297–318.

Montgomery, Scott B. '*Mittite capud meum ... ad matrem meam ut osculetur eum*: The Form and Meaning of the Reliquary Bust of Saint Just.' *Gesta* 36 (1997): 48–64.

Mullett, Margaret. 'Writing in Early Medieval Byzantium.' In *Uses of Literacy*. Ed. McKitterick. 156–85.

Nees, Lawrence. *A Tainted Mantle: Hercules and the Classical Tradition at the Carolingian Court*. Philadelphia: University of Pennsylvania Press, 1991.

Neil, Bronwen. 'The Western Reaction to the Council of Nicaea II.' *Journal of Theological Studies* n.s. 51 (2000): 533–52.

Noble, Thomas F.X. 'The Varying Roles of Biblical Testimonies in the Carolingian Image Controversies.' In *Medieval Transformations*. Ed. E. Cohen and M. de Jong. Leiden: Brill, 2001. 101–19.

Omont, H. 'Manuscrit de S. Denys l'Aréopagite envoyé de Constantinople a Louis le Débonnaire en 827.' *Revues des études grecques* 17 (1904): 230–6.

Rasmussen, Niels Krogh. 'The Liturgy at Saint-Denis: A Preliminary Study.' In *Abbot Suger and Saint-Denis*. Ed. Gerson. 1986. 41–7.

Roberts, Michael. *The Jeweled Style: Poetry and Poetics in Late Antiquity.* Ithaca, NY: Cornell University Press, 1989.

Roberts, Michael. *Poetry and the Cult of the Martyrs: The 'Liber Peristephanon' of Prudentius.* Ann Arbor: University of Michigan Press, 1993.

Ross, Jill. 'Dynamic Writing and Martyrs' Bodies in Prudentius's *Peristephanon.*' *Journal of Early Christian Studies* 3 (1995): 325–55.

Saenger, Paul. 'Silent Reading: Its Impact on Late Medieval Script and Society.' *Viator* 13 (1982): 367–414.

Saintyves, P. 'Les saints céphalophores.' *Revue de l'histoire des religions* 99 (1929): 158–231.

Schmitt, J.-C. 'Les reliques et les images.' In *Les reliques.* Ed. Bozóky and Helvétius. 145–67.

Shortell, Ellen. 'Dismembering Saint Quentin: Gothic Architecture and the Display of Relics.' *Gesta* 36 (1997): 32–47.

Spiegel, Gabrielle M. 'The Cult of St Denis and Capetian Kingship.' In *Saints and Their Cults: Studies in Religious Sociology, Folklore and History.* Ed. Stephen Wilson. Cambridge: Cambridge University Press, 1983. 141–68.

Stock, Brian. *The Implications of Literacy: Written Language and Models of Interpretation in the Eleventh and Twelfth Centuries.* Princeton, NJ: Princeton University Press, 1983.

Stoclet, Alain J. 'La descriptio basilicae Sancti Dionysii. Premiers commentaires.' *Journal des Savants* (1980): 103–7.

– 'Le temporel de Saint-Denis du viie au xe siècle: La constitution du patrimoine foncier dans le Parisis.' In *Un village au temps de Charlemagne.* Ed. Cuisenier and Guadagnin. 94–105.

Stückelberg, M. E.-A. 'Die Kephalophoren.' *Anzeiger für Schweizerische Altertumskunde* 18 (1916): 75–9.

Tardif, Jules. *Monuments historiques, Cartons des Rois.* Paris: J. Claye, 1886.

Théry, Gabriel. 'Contribution à l'histoire de l'Areopagitisme au ixe s.' *Le moyen âge* 35 (1923): 111–53.

– 'Hilduin et le première traduction des écrits du Pseudo-Denis.' *Revue d'histoire de l'église de France* 9 (1923): 23–39.

– 'Le texte intégral de la traduction du Pseudo-Denys par Hilduin.' *Revue d'histoire ecclésiastique du Louvain,* 1925. 33–50.

– 'Recherches pour une édition grecque historique du Pseudo-Denys.' *The New Scholasticism* 1929. 353–442.

– 'L'entrée du Pseudo-Denys en Occident.' In *Mélanges Mandonnet.* Paris: J. Vrin, 1930. Vol. 2: 23–30.

– *Etudes Dionysiennes.* Etudes de Philosophie Médiévale dir. E. Gilson. Vols. 1, 2. Paris: J. Vrin, 1932, 1937.

Vezin, Jean. 'Les faux sur papyrus de l'abbaye de Saint-Denis.' In *Finances, pouvoirs et mémoire: Mélanges offerts à Jean Favier.* Ed. Jean Kerhervé and Albert Rigaudière. Brest: Fayard, 1999. 674–99.

Van Os, Henk. *The Way to Heaven: Relic Veneration in the Middle Ages*. Amsterdam: De Prom, 2000.

Werner, Karl Ferdinand. 'Saint-Denis et les Carolingiens.' In *Un village au temps de Charlemagne*. Ed. Cuisenier and Guadagnin. 40–9.

Wieland, Gernot. '"*Geminus Stilus*": Studies in Anglo-Latin Hagiography.' In *Insular Latin Studies: Papers on Latin Texts and Manuscripts of the British Isles, 550–1066*. Ed. Michael W. Herren. Toronto: Pontifical Institute of Mediaeval Studies, 1981. 113–33.

2 Death Is Not the End: The Encounter of the Three Living and the Three Dead in the Berlin Hours of Mary of Burgundy and Maximilian I

CHRISTINE KRALIK

The Three Living and the Three Dead, a late medieval moralizing story, tells of three young men who are confronted by corpses as they return from an afternoon of hunting. In many versions of this story, the living and dead speak in sequence, and the dead men declare 'As you are, so we once were; what we are now, so shall you become!'[1] This exchange encourages the young men to change their ways and focus more on the fate of their souls than on worldly pleasures.[2]

The earliest manuscript evidence for the story comes from late thirteenth-century France. Several courtly compendia contain the story of the Three Living and the Three Dead in French verse, accompanied by an illumination that presents the young men and the corpses in two groups as though in conversation.[3] Over the course of the following decades, the imagery of the encounter, still most often accompanying one of several different poetic versions of the story, appeared in a variety of manuscript contexts, including Psalters and courtly and theological compendia, all across Europe. By the mid-fifteenth century, the imagery of the story had begun to feature regularly as the pictorial accompaniment to the prayers of Vespers for the Office of the Dead in Books of Hours. As it established a regular new context, the encounter between living and dead began to be presented as more immediate and threatening, with the animated dead often shown pursuing their living targets while wielding weapons.

The representation of the Three Living and the Three Dead accompanying the Office of the Dead in the late fifteenth-century Berlin Hours of Mary of Burgundy and Maximilian I produces a particularly unsettling effect (see fig. 2.1).[4] The image on fol. 220v presents three young aristocratic riders, one of whom is a young woman who has been identified as Mary, Duchess of Burgundy, fleeing three gruesome, blackened, and

Fig. 2.1 The Ghent Associates, 'The Three Living and the Three Dead,' and 'Corpse with a spear and a coffin,' from the *Hours of Mary of Burgundy and Maximilian I*, Ghent, ca 1482. Berlin, Kupferstichkabinett-SMPK, MS 78 B 12, fols. 220v–221r.

decaying corpses who chase after the riders and target them with weapons. The young people, who in early textual treatments of the story had been described as returning from hunting, have here themselves become the hunted. On the adjacent recto, a corpse looks out from the framed illumination and confronts the viewer of the image, while pointing a spear in the direction of the scene depicted on the facing verso. Although the figure is positioned to confront the scene depicted on the verso, the corpse has turned its head so that it directs its empty eye-socketed gaze out towards the viewer of the image.

The contrast between the identification of Mary with the young woman rider in the verso image, which draws her into the devotional space of the book, and the interpellative gaze of the corpse directed to a reader outside the text points to a complex interplay of devotional imagistic and reading practices. Through an exploration of the development and deployment of each of these distinct devotional iconographies, that of the Three Living and the Three Dead, and that of the animated corpse, the effect of their deliberate juxtaposition in the Berlin Hours of Mary of Burgundy and Maximilian I will gain in power and clarity. This essay argues that the heightened drama of the image may be rooted in the function that it served within a private devotional book. The inclusion of the ominous dead within the same pictorial space as a representation of the manuscript's owner and user would have served as a potent reminder of the importance of being always prepared for death; this effect was further intensified, I will argue, by the illustration presented on the opposite recto.

The earliest images of the story of the Three Living and the Three Dead to be found in manuscripts show the living and dead in two groups presented as though in conversation with each other. This iconographic type was employed in many French and English manuscripts, including the well-known Psalter of Robert de Lisle (see fig. 2.2).[5] In this manuscript, the abbreviated text of the poem in Anglo-Norman French, accompanied by rubrics in Latin and additional passages in Middle English, is surmounted on the page by a framed miniature. The young men, richly dressed and bearing royal insignia, stand firmly on mounds of earth, indicating their existence in a worldly and physical space. The three dead, however, are depicted as existing in a completely different realm on the other side of the dividing line. This is suggested not only by the different background, which is bright green and decorated with thistles, but also through the fact that unlike the living, the dead appear to float in space. The interaction between the two groups is suggested through the turning of their bodies to face each other and through the registered response in

Fig. 2.2 The Madonna Master, 'The Three Living and the Three Dead,' from the *Psalter of Robert de Lisle*, English (East Anglian?), ca 1310. London, British Library, Arundel MS 83 II, fol. 127r.

the facial expressions and gestures of the living. The two groups appear to be rigidly separated by a barrier, although the tail of the hawk held by one of the young men breaks the line, suggesting a rupture between two realms. This element of the composition underscores the interaction that occurs between two different worlds.[6]

But this was by no means the only way in which the story of the Three Living and the Three Dead could be presented in its early history. As the tale began to spread across Europe, it was recorded in a number of textual variations in vernacular languages and in Latin, and new pictorial traditions emerged. In Italy, for example, an encounter was depicted that differed in many respects from the tradition of imagery seen most often in French and English manuscripts and wall paintings. A hermit was introduced as an intermediary between the young men, who were often shown on horseback, and the corpses, which were presented lying motionless in their coffins.[7] The figure of the hermit served as a pictorial device to separate but also connect the living and the dead.

While in the thirteenth and fourteenth centuries the imagery of the story had appeared in a number of different manuscript contexts, and still most often accompanied a poem telling the tale, in the early fifteenth century a new context for the visual program was being established across northern Europe. The imagery of the story was beginning to accompany the prayers for Vespers of the Office of the Dead in the Books of Hours, the prayer book of choice for the laity in the late Middle Ages.[8] One of the central texts of Books of Hours, the Office of the Dead was recited for the benefit of the souls of the deceased, but also to prepare oneself for unexpected death.[9] With the establishment of the doctrine of Purgatory at the Second Council of Lyons in 1274, the efficacy of the recitation of prayers for the dead was codified.[10] The *Officium Defunctorum*, from its inception in the early Middle Ages, was intended to be read on a regular basis by the monastic elite (Ottosen, *Responsories* 32). But the urgency of the recitation of this office was enhanced in the early fifteenth century, as the doctrine of Purgatory was reaffirmed at the Council of Florence in 1439 (Boase, *Death* 51). As a result of the belief that the prayers of the living could effect the release of souls from Purgatory, the recitation of these prayers began to play a more significant part in the spiritual life of the laity.[11] The images illustrating those prayers would have played a vital role in enhancing the devotion of the user of the manuscript. While depictions of such real-life moments as the performance of the Requiem Mass or the burial service had long illustrated the prayers of the Office of the Dead, during the fifteenth century such allegorical imagery as that of the Three Living and the Three Dead also became popular.[12] This was at least in part

Fig. 2.3 Master of the Munich Boccaccio, 'The Three Living and the Three Dead,' from the *Hours of Anne de Beaujeu*, Tours, ca 1470. Paris, Bibliothèque Nationale de France, NAL 3187, fol. 139v.

due to its power as an image that confronted the viewer directly with the inevitability of death.

A striking illumination produced to illustrate this text may be found in a manuscript of about 1470 known as the Hours of Anne de Beaujeu (see fig. 2.3).[13] The scene is set just outside a city wall, with three aristocratic riders stopping abruptly before three corpses who approach them in a very unsettling manner.[14] The corpses point and seem to mock the perturbed young riders. One of the young men has already turned his horse around, while another throws his hands into the air as his mount reels. All the while, the dead seem to move towards them. The materiality of the dead is asserted through the shadows that they cast, and also through the way in which the hand of one of the dead cuts in front of the cross. The composition of the image that shows one of the corpses stepping out in front of us cleverly allows us to share the perspective of the dead on the living, and enhances the expectation that we will one day be like the dead, as was suggested in the textual tradition. All of these features heighten the impact and power of the image.

Perhaps even more compelling is the dynamic representation of the tale found in the Berlin Hours of Mary of Burgundy and Maximilian I (see fig. 2.1). The scene is set in a naturalistically rendered landscape, marked as Netherlandish by the windmills depicted in the background.[15] The presence of ravens and dark clouds overhead creates a foreboding atmosphere, appropriate to the theme of death. The only woman in the group, riding her horse at the centre of the image, has been identified as the original owner of the manuscript, Mary of Burgundy, Duchess of Burgundy and wife of the future Habsburg emperor Maximilian I.

A young woman dressed in a very similar fashion appears on fol. 355r of the same manuscript, accompanying a suffrage incipit reading 'Oh angel, who is my guardian' ['Angele qui meus es custos'].[16] This woman, who kneels at a prie-dieu with a visualization of an angel before her, must be the same as the female rider depicted earlier in the same manuscript. The repeated appearance of the initial M on the harness of the horse on fol. 220v suggests that the female rider should indeed be identified as Mary of Burgundy.

Of the three living protagonists, the two male riders have turned away from the road and seem intent on riding into the woods to escape the menacing corpses. One of the men, who might be identified as Mary's husband, Maximilian, beckons her to follow him (König et al., *Berliner Stundenbuch* 36). She takes no notice, however. She has turned her head and seems to direct her gaze in the direction of the dart-wielding corpse chasing after her.

Otto Pächt, in his discussion of the image from the Berlin Hours, suggested that the picture of Mary of Burgundy chased down by a corpse should best be understood as a commemorative image, most likely painted after her untimely death in 1482 following a riding accident. The image must have reflected that event, argued Pächt, because the subject depicted was rare in Flemish illumination and the subject did not usually include a woman as a participant (Pächt, *Mary of Burgundy* 50). However, an examination of an image from another Flemish manuscript, dated circa 1480, undermines Pächt's assertion that the image of the encounter of the Three Living and the Three Dead should be interpreted as a response to Mary's death. The illumination, attributed to the Master of the Dresden Prayerbook, presents a group of riders, here four instead of the usual three, and one of which is a woman, who are assaulted by three dead figures (see fig. 2.4).[17] The frightening dead have cornered the young people and menacingly point arrows at them. The young people respond in different ways; while one turns away and tries to flee, another has stopped and has placed his hands over his face in a gesture of terror.

Anne van Buren also suggested that the image of the Three Living and the Three Dead in the Berlin Hours was most likely executed after Mary's death, due to evidence of a greater degree of personalization on the folio with the image of the Three Living and the Three Dead than elsewhere in the manuscript. The extensive evidence of ownership on this particular page, enhanced with the commemorative initials MM, suggested to van Buren that the page was completed after Mary's death (Van Buren 308). Insignia, mottos, and heraldic imagery were often employed in devotional images including portraits of donors, however, even if this was more common in France than in the Netherlands (König et al., *Berliner Stundenbuch* 31). The decision to include the duchess's initials within the composition of the image could also have been as a result of a desire to personalize the image and to heighten its power as an illumination to be used in devotional practice.

Eberhard König suggested that the representation depicts Mary as fearless in the face of death and that her participation in the action strengthened the image's status as both a *memento mori* and a devotional image (36). The duchess was an avid rider, in fact, and was depicted on horseback for hunting or hawking on a number of occasions during her lifetime. One example is an image found in a manuscript copy of the *Chronik van Vlanderen.*[18] I contend that the representation of Mary was integrated into the composition as one of the aristocratic riders in order to personalize her devotion and make the image a stronger *memento mori* for her own use. But the image might further be interpreted as a pictorial record of an imagined encounter that the duchess and her companions had with death, and that this image employed similar pictorial strategies to those found in other contemporary devotional images, strategies that were intended to enhance the power of devotional images for their beholders.

Fig. 2.4 The Master of the Dresden Prayerbook, 'The Three Living and the Three Dead,' from a Flemish Book of Hours, ca 1480. Berlin, KK-SMPK, MS 78 B 14, fol. 277v.

The visualization of pious thought is one of the striking features of late medieval devotional painting. Images of patrons at their devotions appear quite often in paintings and manuscript illuminations of the late Middle Ages, and many examples include a materialization of a sacred figure to whom the patron directed prayer. It has been suggested that such images were composed in response to the desire of the laity to emulate mystics and members of the monastic elite.[19] Through their visions, mystics were thought to experience union with the divine. Images that depicted lay individuals visualizing the objects of their pious thought as they held devotional images before them contradicted the ideal of imageless devotion, which theologians advocated throughout the Middle Ages (Ringbom, 'Devotional Images' 163). Yet, by the fifteenth century, although this ideal was still applied rigorously to monks, such was not the case for the laity (Ringbom, 'Devotional Images' 165). Images that make manifest the pious thoughts that arise in the mind of the individual at prayer were intended to be used through the medium of corporeal vision, while giving the impression that the devoted beholder was in fact experiencing spiritual vision: that is, internal vision that occurs in the mind but refers to the forms of things seen with the bodily eyes.[20] Internal vision evoked by images in this way could serve to prompt the viewer towards the goal of spiritual vision.

Many images survive that show holy figures appearing to pious donors within the same physical space.[21] A prayer book commissioned by Margaret of York, Duchess of Burgundy, contains a text composed by Nicholas Finet of a dialogue between Margaret of York and Christ, and is accompanied by an image of Margaret kneeling in prayer in her bedroom (see fig. 2.5).[22] As she prays, the resurrected Christ appears before her and reaches out to her, as if to take her hand. Margaret does not look directly at him, but seems to visualize Christ as present with her, the result of her fervent prayer. In a variation on this trend, a patron could also be depicted as a central protagonist in a scene from sacred history. An example of this occurs in an image of the Visitation, with Margaret of Austria presented in the guise of Mary's cousin Elizabeth, in her Book of Hours now in London.[23]

Painters could capture interactions between individuals of different realms in other ways as well, however. An image of Margaret Tudor at prayer in her Book of Hours of circa 1503, now located in London, shows Queen Margaret kneeling at her prie-dieu with her prayer book open before her (see fig. 2.6).[24] As she prays, the Virgin and Child appear above her in the sun above a sickle moon, and the circle of light surrounding the

Fig 2.5 Follower of Dreux Jean, 'Margaret of York and the Risen Christ,' Brussels, shortly before 1468. London, BL Add. MS 7970, fol. 1v–2r.

holy pair mark them as existing in a different space. While the flesh-and-blood queen prayed from her Book of Hours, she would have viewed an image of herself experiencing a vision of the Virgin and Child. The image would have served as a model of devotion, an exemplum of fervent prayer.

Clearly, a variety of pictorial strategies were at the disposal of illuminators in this period as they approached the problem of representing images arising in the minds of the pious at prayer. Similar challenges confronted painters wishing to depict the animated dead in devotional images. The illuminators responsible for the images of the Three Living and the Three Dead in the Hours of Anne de Beaujeu and the Berlin Hours of Mary of Burgundy and Maximilian I could have depicted the dead as existing in a space separate from that of the living, as had been done in the Psalter of Robert de Lisle, for example. And yet the dead were painted as though present in the same space as the young people. I contend that this choice was made in order to heighten the power of the image as an encounter between living and dead and as a devotional image, as well as to suggest the experience of a spiritual vision of the dead on the part of the living.

Fig. 2.6 'Margaret Tudor in Prayer,' from the *Hours of James IV of Scotland*, Ghent, ca 1502–1503. Vienna, ÖNB, MS 1897, fol. 243v.

The images discussed thus far manifest in pictorial terms visualizations experienced by individuals painted on the page, and these were experiences in which the beholders of those images were intended to participate. In other kinds of devotional pictures the depicted visionary was dispensed with, and the image was constructed to evoke the unmediated experience of a vision. Images that simulated a direct confrontation with the Man of Sorrows or the Veronica were popular examples of this trend, but these strategies were put to use in devotional images used in the preparation for death as well.

A particularly compelling example that appeared in late medieval devotional books is the mirror that displays a skull, understood to be a reflection of the future self of the viewer. James Marrow has argued that the meaning of such an image is determined by its function as a reminder of the viewer's mortality and the importance of prayer to prepare oneself for death (Marrow, 'In desen speigell' 154–63). This is achieved through the use of a pictorial strategy identified in other types of devotional images, which is the confrontation of the viewer with an abstracted image, decontextualized in order to serve a powerful devotional function.

Full- or half-length images of animated corpses that confront their viewers also participated effectively in this tradition of representation. An image painted by Jean Colombe in a French Book of Hours made for Princess Anne of France in the 1470s presents a blackened corpse holding an arrow and emerging from a coffin while looking out with a smug expression of triumph (see fig. 2.7).[25] The coffin, made of a pink marble veined in a manner that seems to evoke bodily tissue, is set against the picture plane, while a beautiful northern landscape recedes into the distance. The edge of the coffin, upon which part of the shroud of the corpse rests, recalls the use of the window ledge in contemporary portrait painting. But the presentation of a corpse as a half-length figure may be compared in compositional terms to the type used for representations of Christ and other sacred figures, as well as for portraits of this period.[26] For example, a depiction of the Man of Sorrows in the Très Riches Heures of Jean de Berry, also painted by Jean Colombe, presents Christ, standing in a coffin and facing the viewer (see fig. 2.8).[27] His tortured body, exhibiting the wounds of the Passion, is set against the cross, which still maintains the nails of the Crucifixion. A northern landscape recedes into the distance, which is dotted with castles possibly owned by the patron of the second campaign of the manuscript, Charles of Savoy. Charles and his wife are depicted housed within Colombe's elaborate architectural border of the miniature, praying before the half-length Christ as the Man of Sorrows that appears before them.

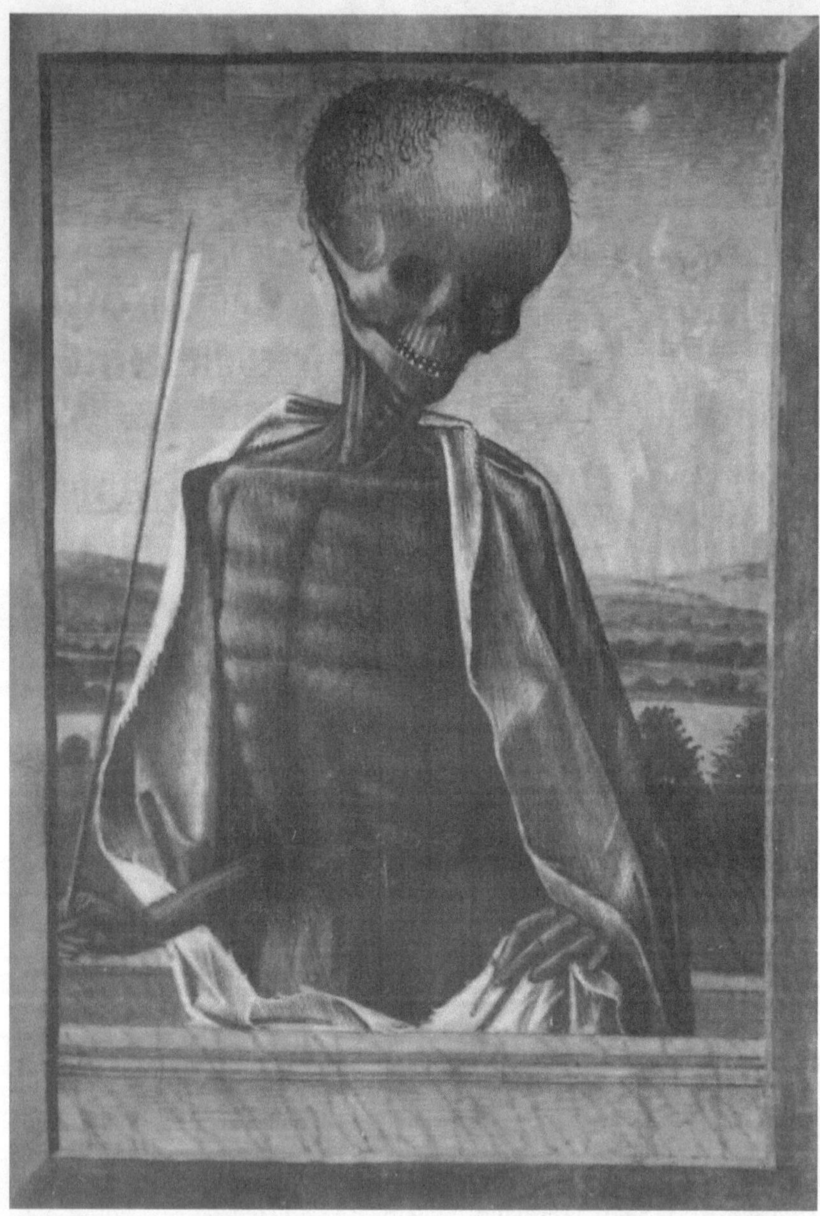

Fig. 2.7 Jean Colombe, 'Death with an Arrow, Rising from a Tomb,' from the *Hours of Anne de France*, Bourges 1473. New York, The Pierpont Morgan Library, M. 677, fol. 245r.

Fig. 2.8 Jean Colombe, 'Man of Sorrows,' from the *Très Riches Heures of Jean, Duke of Berry*, ca 1485. Chantilly, Musée Condé, MS. 65, fol. 75r.

The iconographic type of the Man of Sorrows, purportedly based upon the mosaic of the *Imago Pietatis* housed in the church of Santa Croce in Gerusalemme in Rome,[28] was, from the fourteenth century, visually associated with the vision of Christ experienced by St Gregory the Great as he celebrated Mass. While the pictorial tradition of the Mass of St Gregory recorded the vision of Christ experienced by the Pope during Mass, the tradition of the Man of Sorrows offered the opportunity to the beholder to experience a privileged vision of Christ in the form of a devotional image, often found on panels or within the pages of a Book of Hours.[29] The image of the Man of Sorrows in the Très Riches Heures is enframed by an architectural border, against which representations of Charles of Savoy and his wife may be seen kneeling at prayer. In this context, we might understand the image of the Man of Sorrows as a spiritual vision of Christ experienced by these two pious figures.

There are several striking compositional similarities between Colombe's paintings of the Man of Sorrows and that of Death holding an arrow. The coffin in each image has been oriented lengthwise and has been pushed up against the picture plane, allowing the figure to stand within it and face the viewer. The half-length format has been used in each for the depiction of the main figure, and each image includes a lovely landscape in the background. But a striking contrast may also be found between the two, as the figures of Death and Christ appear as mirror images of one another. While Christ leans to his right, Death leans in the opposite direction. The corpse mimics the posture of the resurrected Christ, but the inherent contradiction of the corpse's animation – that it seems alive but is dead –is highlighted here (Blum 13–27).

A representation of an animated corpse from the Hours of René of Anjou implicates the viewer as directly as does Colombe's image of a corpse with an arrow, but it takes the association with devotional and visionary imagery even further. The illumination accompanying the *Officium Mortuorum* in René of Anjou's prayer book presents a desiccated corpse in an advanced state of decay, its abdomen having been visibly eaten away (see fig. 2.9).[30] The lower half of the figure is obscured not by a coffin, but by a banner that displays the upper half of the coat of arms of René, presenting him as Duke of Anjou, King of Sicily, and King of Jerusalem. The cadaver is set against a lush green landscape, which may display some of René's worldly possessions in the form of his lands. At the centre of the composition is the corpse, wearing King René's crown. This encourages an interpretation of the image as a representation of René's doubled future self as other.[31] The futility of worldly pleasures and the urgency for René to turn

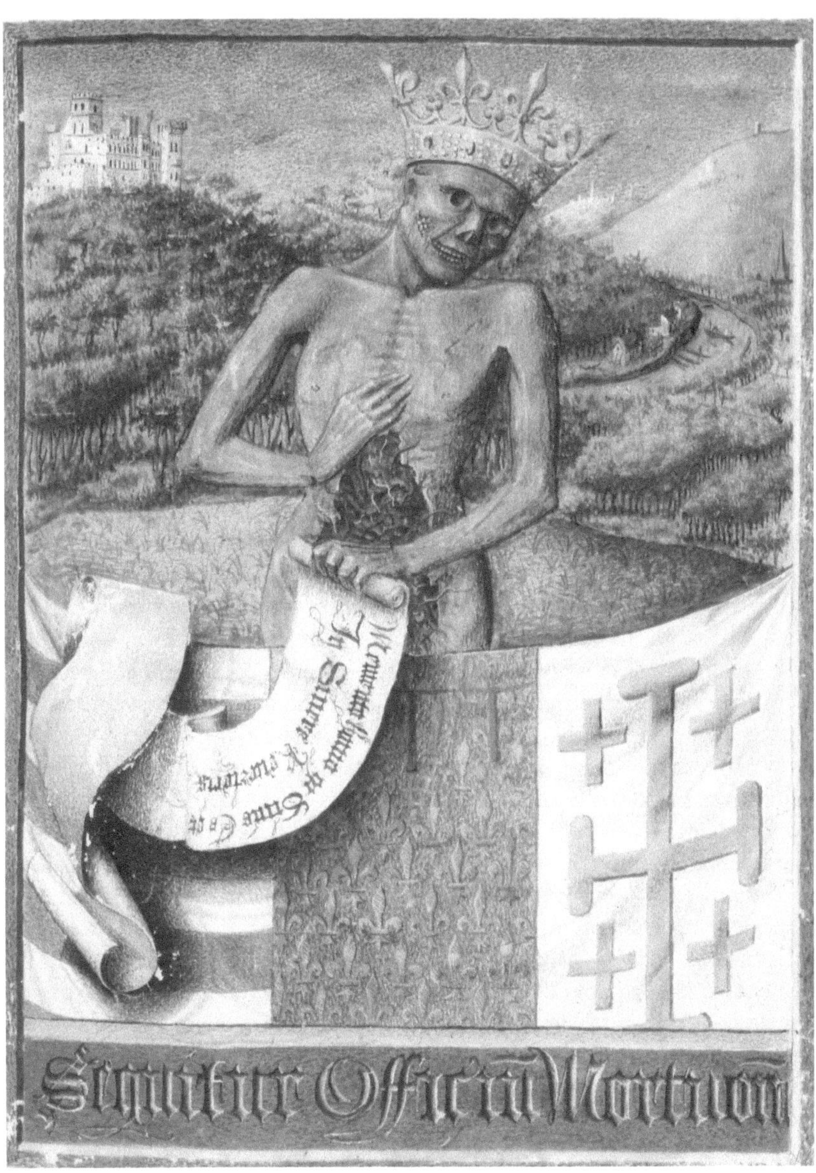

Fig. 2.9 Barthelemy d'Eyck, 'King René as an animated corpse,' from *The Hours of René of Anjou*, ca 1442–3. London, BL, Egerton MS 1070, fol. 53r.

his attention to the cultivation of the soul is underscored not only by the image and the prayers on the adjoining pages, but also in the text in the scroll held in the corpse's left hand, reading 'Remember that you are ash and to ash you will return' ['Memento homo quod sinis (*sic*) es et in sinere reverteris'].[32] The power of this image came from the acknowledgment that the figure reflected on the page represented René's own future self.

While the half-length representations of the animated corpse discussed above are set in a landscape and thus participate in a tradition of portraiture and representation of Christ and the Saints, the full-length corpse depicted on fol. 221r of the Berlin Hours of Mary of Burgundy and Maximilian I is set against an orange foil, suggestive of Purgatorial figures. The corpse here holds a coffin draped with a shroud in its left hand and an arrow in its right (see fig. 2.1). While the corpse is physically turned towards the scene depicted on the verso, the viewer of the image is fixed by the empty eye-socketed gaze that is directed outward from the page. A privileged, personal encounter with death is established through the presentation of this figure before the viewer. I contend that this corpse would have functioned for Mary of Burgundy in a way similar to that in which the crowned corpse in the King René Hours would have functioned for him. Although the corpse on fol. 221r of the Berlin Hours does not appear to be characterized as an alter ego of the viewer as does the corpse in René of Anjou's book, the figure holding the coffin and the dart addresses the viewer in a comparably direct and provocative way.

What sets the image of the animated corpse on fol. 221r in the Berlin Hours apart from the other representations of corpses discussed here is how it works in tandem with the image of the Three Living and the Three Dead on the opposite verso.[33] The representation of Mary of Burgundy in the image of the Three Living and the Three Dead depicts the duchess experiencing an encounter with death, and contemplating her own mortality as she actively participates in the narrative of the image. But unlike the corpse that the painted Mary encountered on the page, the corpse on the recto looks out from the confines of the picture plane to confront the viewer, Mary of Burgundy, in the flesh. The interchange between the *depiction* of Mary of Burgundy and the corpse chasing after her on the verso parallels the encounter that the duchess experienced with the corpse depicted on the recto. The imagery presented on the verso would have served as an exemplum of spiritual vision for which she should strive, while the depiction of the animated corpse directing its gaze directly towards her, on the recto, was constructed in order to suggest the reification of that goal. As she prayed the Office of the Dead and contemplated that very complex pictorial composition, she would in her mind achieve a spiritual vision of death, intensifying her devotional experience and encouraging her to prepare herself for death, and for the life to come.

NOTES

1 I would like to thank Adam Cohen, Jill Caskey, Eileen Jacxsens, Nicole Fallon, and an anonymous reader for their very insightful and helpful comments.

2 See Künstle, *Die Legende der drei Lebenden*; Glixelli, *Les cinques Poèmes*; Servières, 'Les formes artistiques' 19–36; Williams, 'Mural Paintings' 31–40; Rotzler, *Die Begegnung*; Chihaia, *Immortalité*; Binski, *Medieval Death* 134–8.

3 Examples of this imagery are found in late thirteenth-century French compendia of courtly texts such as Bibliothèque Nationale de France, MS Fr. 25566 (fol. 217r, 218r and 223v), MS Fr. 378 (fol. 1r and 7v), and MS Arsenal 3142 (fol. 311v). For Paris, BNF, Bibliothèque de l'Arsenal 3142, fol. 311v, see H. Martin, *Catalogue des Manuscrits de la Bibliothèque de l'Arsenal III*, Paris, 1887, 256–64. For BNF, MS Fr. 378, fol. 1r and 7v, see BNF, *Catalogue des Manuscrits Françaises*, vol. 1, Paris, 1868, 32. For BNF, MS Fr. 25566, fols. 217r, 218r, 223v, see BNF, *Catalogue des Manuscrits Françaises* vol. 13, Paris, 1868, 647–50.

4 The Ghent Associates, *The Three Living and the Three Dead* and *Death*, Berlin, Kupferstichkabinett-SMPK, 78 B 12, fol. 220v–221r, ca 1482. See Pächt, *Master of Mary* 49–50; König et al., *Berliner Stundenbuch* 29–39.

5 The Madonna Master, *The Three Living and the Three Dead*, London, British Library, MS Arundel 83 II, fol. 127r, ca 1310. See Sandler, *Psalter of Robert de Lisle* 44.

6 Examples of this iconographic type may be found in other English manuscripts, including the Taymouth Hours (BL, MS Yates Thompson 13, fol. 123r and 179v–180r, ca 1325–35) and the Smithfield Decretals (BL, MS Royal 10 E IV, fol. 258v–259r, ca 1340). For the Taymouth Hours, see Sandler, *Gothic Manuscripts* 2:107–9. For the imagery of the encounter in the Smithfield Decretals, see Sandler, *Gothic Manuscripts* 1:111–12; Bovey, *The Smithfield Decretals*. See also Fein, 'Life and Death' 69–94.

7 This iconographic motif may be seen in a number of monumental and manuscript contexts. Among the frescoes are the well-known fresco in the Campo Santo in Pisa, attributed to Buffalmacco, and the painting at Sacro Speco at

Subiaco, both dating to the mid-fourteenth century. For the painting in Pisa, see Bolzoni, *Web of Images* 11–40. Manuscript examples include a painting accompanying a *lauda* in a mid-fourteenth century Florentine *Laudario* (Florence, Biblioteca Nazionale Centrale, Banco Rari 18, fol. 134r). Some elements most commonly associated with Italian imagery, such as coffins and mounted riders, were known in France at a fairly early date, as is made evident by the illumination found in the *Psalter of Bonne of Luxembourg* (Cloisters, Inv. 69.86, fol. 321v–322r, ca 1345). See Deuchler, 'Looking at Bonne of Luxembourg's Prayerbook' 267–78.

8 The literature on late medieval Books of Hours is vast. For a general overview, see Harthan, *Book of Hours*; Wieck, *Time Sanctified*.

9 The text of the Office of the Dead as it appeared in the Book of Hours was essentially the same as that found within the monastic breviary. See Ottosen, *Responsories*.

10 See Le Goff, *Birth of Purgatory*, 237.

11 Binski, *Medieval Death* 181–8. For the tradition of depicting (or not depicting) Purgatory, see Binski 188–99.

12 For the types of images chosen to illustrate the prayers of the Office of the Dead, see Meiss, 'La mort et l'Office des Morts' 17–25; Fiero, 'Death Ritual' 271–94; Bartz and König, 'Illustration des Totenoffiziums' 487–527; Wieck, 'Office of the Dead' in *Time Sanctified* 124–48; Wieck, *Painted Prayers* 117–32.

13 Master of the Munich Boccaccio (?), *The Three Living and the Three Dead*, from the Hours of Anne de Beaujeu, Paris, BNF, NAL 3187, fol. 139v, ca 1470. See Avril, ed., *Fouquet* 328–33.

14 Several illuminations in Paris, BNF, NAL 3187, including that of the Three Living and the Three Dead, have recently been attributed to the Master of the Munich Boccaccio. See Avril, *Fouquet* 331.

15 The identification of the illuminator of this image has been much debated. In the early scholarship on this manuscript, the illuminator of the image of the Three Living and the Three Dead was believed to be the same as that of the famous window pages of the Vienna Hours of Mary of Burgundy. See Winkler, *Flämische Buchmalerei* 103–5. In recent decades this has been called into question. Bodo Brinkmann proposed renaming the artist 'the Master of the Berlin Hours of Mary of Burgundy,' to distinguish the artist from the famous Vienna Master. See König et al., *Berliner Stundenbuch* 147–53. Anne van Buren has attributed the image of the Three Living and Three Dead to the Ghent Associates, an attribution that I maintain here; see Van Buren, 'Master of Mary of Burgundy' 286–308.

16 For this image, see König et al., *Berliner Stundenbuch* 108–9.

17 The Master of the Dresden Prayerbook, *The Three Living and the Three Dead*, from a Flemish Book of Hours, Berlin, Kupferstichkabinett-SMPK, 78 B 14, fol. 277v, ca 1480. See Brinkmann, *Flämische Buchmalaeri* 301–5, 383.
18 'Mary of Burgundy as a Hawker,' *Chronik van Vlanderen*, Bruges, Openbare Bibliotheek, MS 437, fol. 372v, ca 1481. See Schenk zu Schweinsberg, *Illustrationen der Chronik von Flanderen* 19.
19 See Ringbom, 'Devotional Images' 159–70; Hamburger, 'Visual and the Visionary' 161–82.
20 Caviness, 'Images of Divine Order' 99–120; Harbison, 'Visions and Meditations' 87–118; Camille, 'Before the Gaze' 197–223.
21 For the different ways in which thoughts could be manifested in pictorial form, see Ringbom, 'Some Pictorial Conventions' 38–69. The problem faced by painters as to how to depict mental images on a two-dimensional surface, in what was a corporeal image, has been explored by a number of scholars, including Jeffrey Hamburger, through an examination of Netherlandish paintings that show such visualizations of pious thought. See Hamburger, 'Seeing and Believing' 49–69.
22 Follower of Dreux Jean, *Margaret of York and the Risen Christ*, illustrating 'Le Dialogue de la duchesse de Bourgogne a Jesus Christ,' Brussels, shortly after 1468. London, BL, Add. MS 7970, fol. 1v. See Kren, *Illuminating the Renaissance* 215–16. This image has recently been interpreted as a representation of the *Noli me tangere*, with Margaret of York in the guise of Mary Magdalene. See Pearson, 'Gendered Subject' 47–66.
23 Gerard Horenbout, *The Visitation*, from *The Sforza Hours*, London, BL, Add. MS 34294, fol. 61r. This manuscript was executed in two campaigns, as it was commissioned for Bona Sforza, Duchess of Milan, in ca 1490, and completed for Margaret of Austria, Regent of the Netherlands, in 1517–21. Gerard Horenbout painted the miniature of the Visitation as part of the second campaign. This miniature introduces the hour of Lauds of the Hours of the Virgin. See Evans, *Sforza Hours* 37; Kren and McKendrick, eds., *Illuminating the Renaissance* 428–31.
24 *Margaret Tudor in Prayer*, *Hours of James IV of Scotland*, probably Ghent, ca 1502–3.Vienna, ÖNB, MS 1897, fol. 243v. See Kren and McKendrick, eds., *Illuminating the Renaissance* 371–3, fig. 110b.
25 Jean Colombe, *Death with an Arrow, Rising from a Tomb*, Bourges, France, 1470s. New York, Morgan Library, M. 677, fol. 245v. See Wieck, *Time Sanctified* 148.
26 See Ringbom, *Icon to Narrative*.
27 Chantilly, Musée Condé, MS 65, fol. 75r. See Cazelles et al., *Illuminations of Heaven and Earth* 112.

28 See Panofsky, 'Imago Pietatis' 261–308; Male, *Religious Art in France* 94–8; Bertelli, 'Image of Pity' 54.
29 See Bynum, 'Seeing and Seeing Beyond' 208–40.
30 *King René of Anjou as a Corpse*, in the *Hours of René of Anjou*, S.E. France, ca 1442–3, London, BL, Egerton 1070, fol. 53r. This illumination, among several others, has been attributed to Barthelemy d'Eyck. See Avril and Reynaud, *Manuscrits à Peintures*, no. 122. These miniatures were later additions to the manuscript, which in large part was produced ca 1410. See also Meiss, *French Painting* 1:328–9.
31 Pächt, 'René d'Anjou,' esp. 89–90, 98, fig. 84.
32 'Remember that you are ash and to ash you will return.'
33 A codicological analysis of the Berlin Hours has shown that fol. 220v is on a single leaf that has been tipped into the manuscript. See König et al., *Berliner Stundenbuch* 167–72, esp. 170. It is therefore possible that the bi-folio on which the image of the Three Living and the Three Dead was painted was altered in some way before the page was sewn into the manuscript. There is no reason to believe that the image was a later addition to the program, however. An examination of the manuscript's program of illustration shows that major textual divisions of the manuscript were all introduced with two facing illuminations, and thus the pairing of the images on fols. 220v and 221r fits nicely with the program of the manuscript as a whole. König et al., *Berliner Stundenbuch* 31.

WORKS CITED

Avril, François, and Nicole Reynaud. *Les Manuscrits à peintures en France, 1440–1520*. Paris: Flammarion, 1993.

– ed. *Jean Fouquet. Peintre et enlumineur du XVe siècle*. Paris: Bibliothèque Nationale de France, 2003.

Bartz, Gabriele, and Eberhard König. 'Die Illustration des Totenoffiziums in Stundenbüchern.' In *Im Angesicht des Todes. Liturgie als sterbe- und Trauerhilfe: Ein Interdisziplinäres Kompendium*. Ed. Hans Jakob Becker et al. Pietas Liturgica 3. St Ottilien: Eos Verlag Erzabtei, 1987. 1:487–528.

Bertelli, Carlo. 'The Image of Piety in Santa Croce in Gerusalemme.' In *Essays in the History of Art Presented to Rudolf Wittkower*. Ed. D. Fraser et al. London: Phaidon, 1967.

Bibliothèque nationale de France. *Catalogue des manuscrits français. Ancien fonds*. 5 vols. 1868–1902.

Binski, Paul. *Medieval Death: Ritual and Representation*. Ithaca, NY: Cornell University Press, 1996.

Blum, Claude. 'Recherches sur les fonctions épistémologiques d'une representation allégorique: L'exemple de l'apparition en Occident de l'allégorie de la Mort en squelette.' *Journal of Medieval and Renaissance Studies* 15 (1985): 13–27.

Boase, T.S.R. *Death in the Middle Ages: Mortality, Judgment and Remembrance*. New York: McGraw-Hill, 1972.

Bolzoni, Lina. *The Web of Images: Vernacular Preaching from Its Origins to St. Bernardino da Siena*. Aldershot, UK: Ashgate, 2004.

Bovey, Alexandra. *Didactic Distractions Framing the Law: The Smithfield Decretals*. PhD diss., University of London, 2000.

Brinkmann, Bodo. *Die Flämische Buchmalaeri am Ende des Burgunderreichs: Der Meister des Dresdener Gebetbuchs und die Miniaturisten seiner Zeit*. Turnhout, Belgium: Brepols, 1997.

Bynum, Caroline Walker. 'Seeing and Seeing Beyond: The Mass of St. Gregory in the Fifteenth Century.' In *The Mind's Eye: Art and Theological Argument in the Middle Ages*. Ed. Jeffrey Hamburger and Anne-Marie Bouché. London: Harvey Miller, 2006. 208–40.

Camille, Michael. 'Before the Gaze: The Internal Senses and Late Medieval Practices of Seeing.' In *Visuality Before and Beyond the Renaissance: Seeing as Others Saw*. Ed. Robert Nelson. Cambridge and New York: Cambridge University Press, 2000. 197–223.

Caviness, Madeleine. 'Images of Divine Order and the Third Mode of Seeing.' *Gesta* 22 (1983): 99–120.

Cazelles, Raymond, and Johannes Rathofer. *Illuminations of Heaven and Earth: The Glories of the Très Riches Heures du Duc de Berry*. New York: Abrams, 1988.

Chihaia, Pavel. *Immortalité et décomposition dans l'art du Moyen-Âge*. Madrid: Fondation culturelle roumaine, 1988.

Deuchler, Florens. 'Looking at Bonne of Luxembourg's Prayerbook.' *Metropolitan Museum of Art Bulletin* 29, no. 6 (February 1971): 267–78.

Evans, Mark. *The Sforza Hours*. New York: Amsterdam, 1992.

Fein, Susanna Greer. 'Life and Death, Reader and Page: Mirrors of Mortality in English Manuscripts.' *Mosaic* 35 (2002): 69–94.

Fiero, Gloria. 'Death Ritual in Fifteenth-century Manuscript Illumination.' *Journal of Medieval History* 10 (1984): 271–94.

Glixelli, Stephen. *Les Cinques poèmes des Trois Morts et des Trois Vifs*. Paris, 1914.

Hamburger, Jeffrey. 'Seeing and Believing: The Suspicion of Sight and the Authentication of Vision in Late Medieval Art and Devotion.' In *Imagination und Wirklichkeit: Zum Verhältnis von mentalen und realen Bildern in der Kunst der frühen Neuzeit*. Ed. Klaus Krüger. Mainz: P. von Zabern, 2001. 46–69.

– 'The Visual and the Visionary: The Image in Late Medieval Monastic Devotions.' *Viator* 20 (1989): 160–82.

Harbison, Craig. 'Visions and Meditations in Early Flemish Painting.' *Simiolus* 15 (1985): 87–118.

Harthan, John. *The Book of Hours*. New York: Park Lane, 1977.

König, Eberhard, et al. *Das Berliner Stundenbuch der Maria von Burgund und Kaiser Maximilians*. Lachen am Zürichsee: Coron, 1998.

Kren, Thomas, and Scot McKendrick, eds. *Illuminating the Renaissance: The Triumph of Flemish Manuscript Painting in Europe*. [Exhibition Catalogue.] Los Angeles: J. Paul Getty Museum / London: Royal Academy of Arts, 2003.

Künstle, Karl. *Die Legende der drei Lebenden und der drei Toten und der Totentanz*. Freiburg: Herdersche, 1908.

Le Goff, Jacques. *The Birth of Purgatory*. Chicago: University of Chicago Press, 1984.

Mâle, Emile. *Religious Art in France. The Late Middle Ages: A Study of Medieval Iconography and Its Sources*. 1949. Trans. Marthiel Mathews. Princeton, NJ: Princeton University Press, 1986.

Marrow, James '"In desen speigell": A New Form of "Memento Mori" in Fifteenth Century Netherlandish Art.' *Essays in Northern Medieval Art Presented to Egbert Haverkamp-Begemann*. Ed. Anne-Marie Logan. Doornspijk: Davaco, 1983. 154–63.

– 'Symbol and Meaning in Northern European Art of the Late Middle Ages and the Early Renaissance.' *Simiolus* 16 (1986): 150–69.

Martin, H. *Catalogue des Manuscrits de la Bibliothèque de l'Arsenal*. Vol. 3. Paris, 1887.

Meiss, Millard. 'La mort et l'Office des Morts à l'époque du Maître de Boucicaut et des Limbourg.' *Revue de l'Art* 1 (1968): 17–25.

– *French Painting in the Time of Jean de Berry: The Limbourgs and Their Contemporaries*. Vol 1. London: Thames and Hudson, 1974.

Ottosen, Knud. *The Responsories and Versicles of the Latin Office of the Dead*. Aarhus, Denmark: Aarhus University Press, 1993.

Pächt, Otto. *Master of Mary of Burgundy*. London: Faber and Faber, 1966.

– 'René D'Anjou-Studien I.' *Jahrbuch der Kunsthistorischen Sammlungen in Wien* 69 [Neue Folge 33] (1973): 85–126.

Panofsky, Erwin. 'Imago Pietatis.' In *Festschrift für Max J. Friedlander zum 60. Geburtstage*. Leipzig: E.A. Seemann, 1927. 261–308.

Pearson, Andrea. 'Gendered Subject, Gendered Spectator: Mary Magdalen in the Gaze of Margaret of York.' *Gesta* 44 (2005): 47–66.

Ringbom, Sixten. 'Devotional Images and Imaginative Devotions: Notes on the Place of Art in Late Medieval Private Piety.' *Gazette des Beaux-Arts* 73 (1969): 159–70.

– *Icon to Narrative: The Rise of the Dramatic Close-up in Fifteenth-century Devotional Painting*. 2nd ed. Doornspijk: Davaco, 1984.

– 'Some Pictorial Conventions for the Recounting of Thoughts and Experiences in Late Medieval Art.' In *Medieval Iconography and Narrative: A Symposium*. Ed. Flemming Andersen. Odense, Denmark: Odense University Press, 1980. 38–69.

Rotzler, Wilhelm. *Die Begegnung der drei Lebenden und der drei Toten: Ein Beitrag zur Forschung über die Mittelalterlichen Vergänglichkeitsdarstellungen*. Winterthur: P.G. Keller, 1961.

Sandler, Lucy Freeman. *Gothic Manuscripts, 1285–1385*. 2 vols. Vol. 5 of *A Survey of Manuscripts Illuminated in the British Isles*. London: Harvey Miller, 1986.

– *The Psalter of Robert de Lisle*. Oxford and New York: Oxford University Press, 1983.

Schenk zu Schweinsberg, Eberhard, Freiherr. *Die Illustrationen der Chronik von Flandern: Handschrift Nr. 437 der Stadtbibliothek zu Brügge und ihr Verhältnis zu Hans Memling*. Strasbourg, 1922.

Servières, Georges. 'Les Formes artistiques du dict des Trois Morts et des Trois Vifs.' *Gazette des Beaux-Arts* 68, vol. 13 (1928): 19–36.

Storck, Willy F. 'Aspects of Death in English Art and Poetry.' *Burlington Magazine* 21 (1912): 249–56.

Van Buren, Anne H. 'The Master of Mary of Burgundy and his Colleagues: The State of Research and Questions of Method.' *Zeitschrift für Kunstgeschichte* 38 (1975): 286–309.

Wieck, Roger. *Time Sanctified: The Book of Hours in Medieval Art and Life*. New York: George Braziller/Baltimore: Walters Art Gallery, 1988.

– *Painted Prayers: The Book of Hours in Medieval and Renaissance Art*. New York: Pierpont Morgan Library, 1997.

Williams, E.C. 'Mural Paintings of the Three Living and the Three Dead in England.' *Journal of the British Archaeological Association* 7 (1942): 31–40.

Winkler, Friedrich. *Die flämische Buchmalerei des XV. und XVI. Jh.: Kunstler und Werke von den Brüdern van Eyck bis zu Simon Bening*. Leipzig, 1925.

3 The Good Death of Richard Whittington: Corpse and Corporation

AMY APPLEFORD

Sometimes the end of the physical body actually extends the body's reach in time and space through 'perpetual' bequests. Even as they become corpses, the bodies of the wealthy give birth to corporations and the urban landscape and its inhabitants are the beneficiaries. This essay explores one such process that helped to shape fifteenth-century London, the process that began, at least for symbolic purposes, with the 'good death' of Richard Whittington: wealthy merchant, important creditor to the crown, and – besides being, under the name Dick Whittington, the owner of the most famous medieval English cat – three times mayor of the city.

An image of this 'good death' forms the frontispiece of the earliest manuscript of the English version of a set of ordinances written for one of the institutions funded by Whittington's massive bequest, the Almshouse of Richard Whittington (see fig. 3.1).[1] The ordinances were first written in Latin and sealed by three of Whittington's executors – John Carpenter, John Coventry, and William Grove – in December 1424, eighteen months after Whittington's death in March 1423 and just after ground had been broken to begin the building both of this establishment and of a related institution nearby, the College of Priests at St Michael Paternoster. The English translation of the ordinances dates from 1442, two decades later, when Carpenter, the most important and longest lived of Whittington's executors, was dead, and when oversight of Almshouse, College, and the Whittington estate had all acceded – as the ordinances required – to the Mercers' Company, the guild to which Whittington and two of his executors had belonged. The frontispiece represents Whittington in the act of commissioning the foundation of the Almshouse and precedes a translation of which this manuscript was likely an official copy, made more or less immediately after the translation was complete.

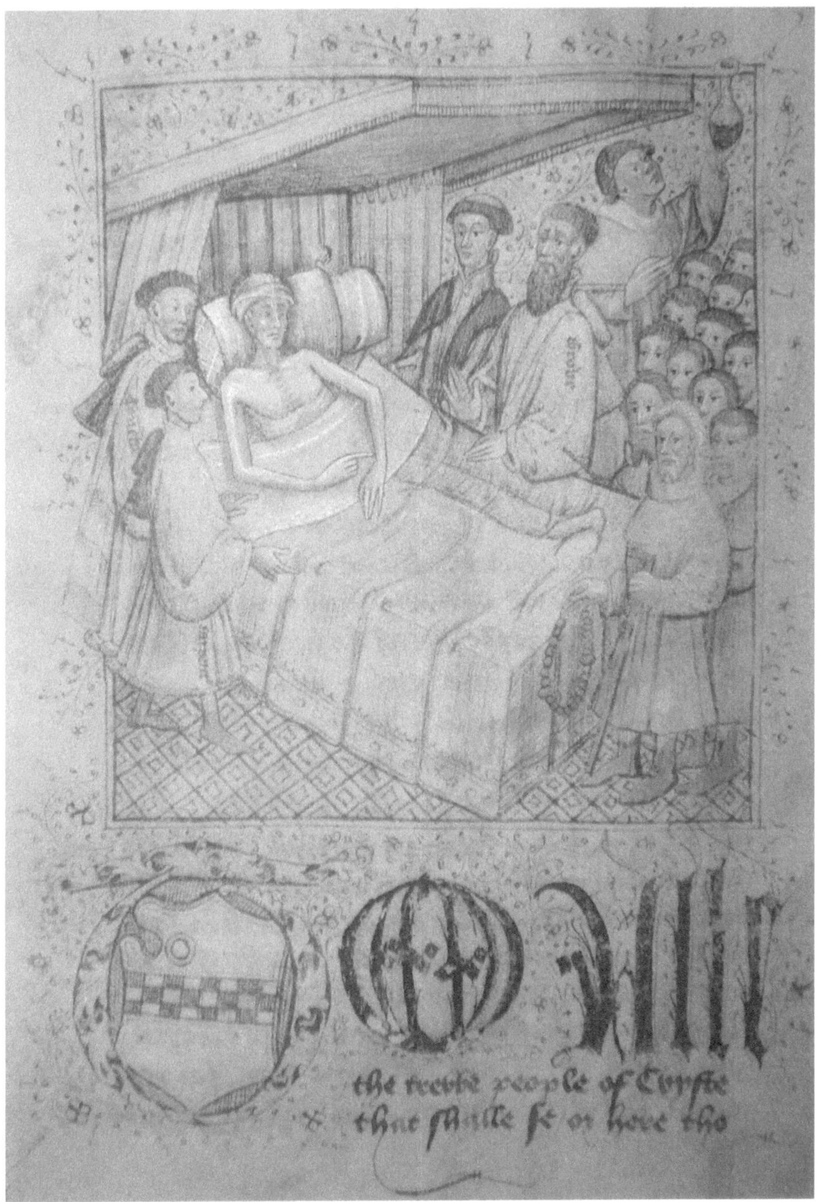

Fig. 3.1 Richard Whittington on his deathbed, Almshouse Ordinances, by permission of the Mercers' Company.

In the frontispiece, Whittington is attended both by a physician, who is checking his urine, and a priest – likely the master of the College of Priests, who was also the rector of St Michael's Paternoster, Whittington's parish church. His witnesses are small bedesmen, representatives of the Almshouse, and two of the three executors who drew up the original Latin ordinances, Carpenter and Coventry, both identified by names on their tunics. The most prominent figure in the frontispiece, however, is the third executor, William Grove, a professional scribe who copied the Latin ordinances but who is pictured here without writing implements, in spoken dialogue with the dying man. Overshadowing the priest – almost as though interrupting or superseding the rituals surrounding the medieval deathbed – Grove, with his right hand, makes a gesture of acquiescence to Whittington's gesture of command, looking sternly across the bed at Carpenter and Coventry, both of whose own right hands in turn gesture towards the thirteen bedesmen and their tutor at the foot of the bed.[2]

The English book of ordinances that follow are enclosed within a plain parchment cover and written on fifteen of the manuscript's twenty folios of narrow vellum, twelve inches high by a four and a quarter inches wide. The text translates the Latin ordinances first copied by Grove closely, at least as to content, making no change to the conditions and rules set down by Whittington's executors in 1423. On the final folio, however, is a dedicatory poem in the form of an envoy, which, like the frontispiece, has no equivalent in the Latin ordinances:

> Go litel boke go litel tregedie
> The lowly submitting to al correccion
> Of theym beyng maistres now of the mercery
> Olney Feldyng Boleyne and of Burton
> Hertily theym besekyng with humble salutacion
> The to accepte and thus to take in gre
> For ever to be a servant with in [þ]eire cominalte. (Imray 121)

This poem plays self-consciously on the metapoetic envoy of Chaucer's *Troilus and Criseyde*, a panegyric on the transcendent idea of poetry often imitated by fifteenth-century writers, including John Lydgate at the end of his own Trojan poem, *Troy Book*:

> Go, litel bok, go, litel myn tragedye,
> Ther God thi makere yet, er that he dye,
> So sende myght to make in som comedye!

But litel book, no makyng thow n'envie,
But subgit be to alle poesye;
And kis the steppes, where as thow seest pace
Virgile, Ovide, Omer, Lucan, and Stace. (5.1786–92)

O moral Gower, this book I directe
To the, and to the, philosophical Strode,
To vouchen-sauf, ther nede is, to correcte
Of youre benignites and zeles goode. (5.1856–9)

However, the names mentioned in the envoy to the ordinances are neither those of the great classical poets nor those of Chaucer's scholarly and poetic contemporaries invoked in *Troilus and Criseyde*, but a group with a very different relation to the text the envoy submits to their 'correccion': the 1442 wardens of the Mercers' Guild and new trustees of the Whittington estate, John Olney, Geoffrey Feldyng, Geoffrey Boleyne, and John Burton.

Together, the deathbed frontispiece and closing envoy of the English ordinances make an unusual and dense semiotic frame for such an apparently utilitarian text. Indeed, when the vernacular ordinances came to be copied by the Mercers' Company a couple of decades later, this frame appears to have been deemed no longer appropriate or necessary: the second, slightly larger presentation book of the English ordinances of ca 1460, although otherwise elaborately decorated, includes neither the frontispiece nor the envoy (Imray 108).[3] Unique to this first copy of the translation, the frontispiece and the envoy are also intriguing in several different ways.

First, the frontispiece describes a complex temporality and chain of authorization, particularly when the historical events it evokes are brought into the picture. Whittington made his will in 1421, two years before his death in 1423. While he was famous for being a 'self-made' man, and, like other wealthy London citizens, prided himself on being a very visible benefactor to the poor, in his will, the former mayor simply instructed his executors to dispose of the residue of his estate in acts of charity for 'the good of his soul and to please God,' making no specific reference to the Almshouse. Although the ordinances assert that Whittington 'charged streitly in his deth bed us his forsaid executours [Coventry, Carpenter, and Grove] to ordeyne an house of Almes after his deth,' the actual conception of the three main charitable foundations built in his name – the Almshouse, the College of Priests, and the Library at Guildhall – was most likely that of his executors (Sutton 162).[4] When Whittington was on his deathbed, the Almshouse had neither been built nor, perhaps, even planned, and the bedesmen pictured attending him had not yet been chosen for their new role and lodging, any more than Whittington's rector was yet master of the College of Priests. The frontispiece implicitly acknowledges all this by representing Grove – whose involvement in the setting up of the Almshouse and other foundations may well have been confined to his activities as a scribe – in a commanding role, as the immediate recipient of Whittington's commission, while keeping any hint of a written document out of the picture. There are no scrolls or papers on the bed in front of Whittington. Thus the figure of Grove here signifies both a perhaps fictitious commission, made orally if at all, and the Latin ordinances he drew up with Coventry and Carpenter in the eighteen months after Whittington's death, which gave the Almshouse legal standing, and from which the English translation the frontispiece introduces has been made.

Second, Whittington's deathbed, as imagined in the frontispiece, is devoid of the traditional iconography of the 'good death.' There are no signs here that the moment of Judgment has come to this rich man or that a mighty battle is about to begin over his soul: no angels, devils, or saintly intercessors crowd this bedside; no miniature humunculus works its way out of the failing body and rises up towards the ceiling as the soul leaves the body. The general placement of the figures instead recalls the traditional iconography of the death of a monarch or saint, with bold, local variations. In place of the dying figure's royal kin or monastic brethren, gathered to ease his parting with their prayers, the community gathered to help this prince among mercers die is civic, made up of those bureaucrats and aldermen who will assure that Whittington's death is 'good' posthumously, in metropolitan terms, through funding spectacular acts of urban charity. Although the image is suffused with religious allusions, its secular figures – from the physician holding up Whittington's urine to show that death is certain to the looming figure of Grove – are far more prominent than its religious ones; and these, the priest and the thirteen bedesmen from the Almshouse, are present more as a public manifestation of charity than as participants at a standard deathbed ritual.

Third, the envoy raises a whole series of questions as to the purpose of the translation. Who, here, is sending the book? Is it Whittington, speaking from his deathbed on the frontispiece, or from beyond the grave? Is it the executors, whose voice is heard in the ordinances themselves? Is it the translator, asking for his work to be corrected by the masters of the Mercers' guild? In which case, would these men be equipped with sufficient Latin to compare the translation with the original? Why, in any case, is the translation into English, not French, in the first place; indeed, why a translation at all? Although English was occasionally used in Guild records, Anne Sutton notes that, '[f]or formal documents Latin was demanded [by the Mercers], and Anglo-French remained the language of the Mercers' accounts until 1458–9' (Sutton 179; Jefferson 1:23–4). Given the use of English, why draw attention to it with an allusion to Chaucer's and Lydgate's vernacular and secular Trojan 'tragedies' in dedicating a set of regulations to a place of prayer? In its explicit fictionality, the envoy, like the frontispiece, encourages us to consider the English ordinances not only in functional terms, but also as a cultural and symbolic artefact and to ask who, precisely, initiated and voiced this vernacularizing project.

Its starting point the image of the dying, but still commanding, body of London's most famous mayor, this essay is an enquiry into the cultural work this image and the historical death it represents performed in the milieu of the city's merchant elite in the second quarter of the fifteenth century, particularly in relation to a second body, the incorporated body of the Almshouse itself. Although it opens onto wider vistas of the contemporary reformist spiritual landscape, the essay's central figure is Whittington's chief executor, the lawyer and common clerk of the City, John Carpenter, the genius behind several civic monuments of the period. Throughout his career, which spanned the twenty-five-year period immediately after the public demise of the Lollard movement, Carpenter appears to have understood himself as shaping the city, materially and discursively, not only as a mercantile power but as a Christian community, working to fashion, in collaboration with others, a particular London religiosity in which profit, politics, and devotion mingled intimately and without apparent strain. As this essay suggests, Whittington's death presented Carpenter with his greatest opportunity to engineer the reorganization of significant areas of public space according to an agenda both reformist and worldly: directed, on the one hand, towards redressing a perceived lack of education of those entrusted with the pastoral instruction of the London laity; and, on the other, to creating a spectacular living monument to his long-time patron and friend, Richard Whittington.

After describing the Whittington foundations and giving an account of Carpenter's worldly and spiritual interests, the essay returns in closing to the manuscript of the English ordinances, with its frontispiece and envoy. Despite the Mercers' preference for Latin and French, it would be natural to assume that translation and manuscript were the commission of a third body, the Mercers' Company itself, made to commemorate its newly gained control over a legacy that so much enhanced its wealth and prestige. The argument here, however, is that the English ordinances were not written for the Mercers but, rather, at them, voicing Carpenter's own concern, through the translator, to safeguard this legacy as it passed permanently beyond his control. What occasions the translation and gives it specific force and urgency is the death of a fourth body: Carpenter's own.

The Whittington Foundations

Like the Guildhall Library, the Whittington Almshouse has attracted the attention of historians of philanthropy because its creation and administration was in lay, rather than ecclesiastic, hands; W.K. Jordan, for example, identifies it as one of England's earliest 'secular' charitable institutions (*Charities* 406; *Philanthropy* 139). But to characterize the innovativeness of the Almshouse, or any of the Whittington foundations, as 'secular' is, in some respects, misleading. The choice of four city bureaucrats – a town clerk, an alderman, a hospital administrator, a scrivener – as Whittington's executors, followed by a guild corporation, can be interpreted as merely enlarging upon a well-established understanding of the guilds as having a spiritual function as collectors of alms. The principles of community and mutual support of the guild structure assured that religious and business interests were intertwined. Whittington and his guild's responsibility for dispensing alms and overseeing funeral arrangements, making sure that even their poorest members had proper Christian burials, would have been assumed (Sutton 196–7; Thomson 178–82; Thrupp 242–8). As R.M. Clay demonstrates in her classic study of medieval hospitals, it was the 'old merchant princes' or prominent townsfolk who were responsible for most of the houses for the poor built in the late medieval period (Clay 81). For their part, the inhabitants of the Almshouse were encouraged to behave as traditional recipients of charity by living like members of a religious community: practising patient poverty, 'intend[ing] to the contemplacioun of God,' attending several services a day, and praying daily for their founders and benefactors. The Whittington Almshouse thus fits into a traditional, and explicitly religious, pattern.

Yet interpreting the Almshouse and its sister College as a new kind of institution – one that negotiates a distinct set of relationships between laity, church, and world – is nonetheless accurate in two ways. First, most pre-fifteenth-century hospitals for the poor were under direct supervision by clergy or Augustinian canons (Rawcliffe 5). The ordinances give various roles to the nearby College of Priests and its master, who say daily services in St Michael's Paternoster, lead the prayers for the souls of Whittington, his wife, Alice, and others, and have the right to fill every seventh vacancy at the Almshouse (115, 113). But full control of the Almshouse remains, first, with John Carpenter as lead executor, and subsequently with the 'Conservatours' and the 'Overseer' – that is, respectively, with the wardens of the Mercers' Guild and the mayor (111). Ecclesiastical involvement, before and after the executors's demise, is kept to a minimum.

Such an arrangement is 'secular' in the medieval sense that it keeps formal responsibility for a religious institution in the hands of the laity, in a fashion reminiscent of the 'Lollard' petitions presented in the Commons in 1410 and 1414, which argued that new almshouses should be under the supervision of 'true and good seculars,' since Church oversight of poor houses had 'well-nigh destroyed all the almshouses in the country' (Thomas and Thornley 88). In the arrangements made for the Almshouse's sister foundation, the College of Priests, it is also 'secular' in a second medieval sense, which contrasts sharply with the anticlericalism evident in the Commons petitions. The College of Priests was notionally under the same structure of oversight as the Almshouse, and its members had the same obligation as the bedesmen to pray for the souls of the founders, celebrating daily Masses to that end. Yet in practice they had far more autonomy than the Almshouse, having the right (at least, formally) to elect both their own master and new members of the college, besides having to exercise care of souls for the whole parish of St Michael's Paternoster (Imray 31). Its members supposedly especially learned and chaste, the College of Priests was, in part, a response to a felt dissatisfaction with the London lower clerisy's pastoral care: an attempt on the part of a major lay foundation to reform and support the city's 'secular' clergy. Rather than signifying a straightforward desire to replace the clergy as custodians of the poor, the Almshouse and College together suggest a desire to sustain – under real, but limited, lay control, a level of control publicly respectful of the specialist and privileged nature of the secular clergy – a new group of competent priests to perform their traditional duties in the cure of souls.

Second, the Almshouse was a new kind of institution in the technical but consequential sense that it was incorporated upon foundation: made into a legal 'person,' empowered to hold property in perpetual succession, one of the first institutions in England to use this particular form of juridical technology (Prescott 49). In 1432, soon after settling its endowment, Carpenter obtained a foundation charter for the Almshouse from the Crown, something he had done seven years earlier for the Mercers' Company, which had been until that time without official corporate status

(Brewer 29; Imray 30, 37). In partial parallel to the steps he took through the ordinances to protect the Almshouse from ecclesiastical oversight, Carpenter's incorporation presumably aimed to protect it from more material kinds of incursion, especially when it passed into the ownership of the Mercers after his death. Had he not taken this still novel, legal step, the Mercers could have sold the Almshouse piecemeal for their own profit; or, alternatively, its properties would have remained vulnerable to alienation by a sovereign strapped for funds.

The perceived importance of the hospital's corporate status is suggested by the care with which both the charter of incorporation and the house's common seal – the symbol of its existence as a legally unified body – were to be treated, according to the ordinances:

> We wille and ordeyne also that the seid Tutor and pour folke have acomyn chest and a Comyn seale in whiche chest thei shalle putte the said Seal. Also their chartres lettres privilegis Escrites and Tresour of theire seid house and other thinges whiche shalle seme ... expedient for the commyn profit of the seid place whiche chest we wille be put in a secreet and a sekir place with ynne the boundes of the seid hous. (117)

This chest was to have three keys: one held by the Tutor, one by the eldest member of the house, the third by 'oon of the othir felawes of the seid Almeshous every yere to be new chosen by us while we lyve and after our discesse by the maisters of the mercerie' (117). The Almshouse was thus constructed as a perpetual body, whose legal standing was equal to that of its future overseers, the Mercers. In this, again, the foundation works within an established tradition (the endowment of a hospital as post-mortem charity), but makes it something new. As the frontispiece to the ordinances recognizes, here the Almshouse, a corporate body, is founded upon the death of the temporal body of Whittington, who ordained its existence as a perpetual extension of his own worldly being. Yet as the frontispiece also implies, Whittington's act of secular charity hopes, above all, to reach beyond the world, in order to ensure the eventual salvation of his own eternal soul.

Despite their lay oversight and organization within a secular, civic world, the Almshouse and its sister foundation thus cannot be understood in separation from their explicitly religious goals, any more than they can be understood as antagonistic towards the clerisy in the fashion of the 1410 and 1414 Commons petitions, with their 'Lollard' disdain for the institutional Church. Rather, their underlying agenda belongs to a decidedly reformist generation, one whose desire for renewal of the Church was expressed not through polemic or anti-ecclesiastical radicalism, but through constructive efforts to establish an innovative lay control and deployment of traditional forms of religious culture. Such control, however, was to be exercised not by just any group of laity, but by a specifically urban and mercantile lay community, one whose sense of itself was intimately bound up with work, mutual self-interest, exchange, negotiation, and profit. Before the fourteenth century, those houses for the poor not founded by religious orders were endowed by gentry or royalty for the perpetual spiritual good of themselves, their ancestors, or their heirs: a situation in which the system of exchange of prayers for money, shelter, and food was occluded within a generalized tradition of aristocratic largesse and patronage. Overseen by a city bureaucrat and a corporation – men who lived by trade and the jostling demands of urban competition – the Whittington Almshouse by contrast makes the exchange economy underlying the traditional practice of securing prayers for the dead from the poor particularly stark. The thirteen bedesmen and their tutor who inhabit and constitute the Almshouse are here explicitly a spiritual workforce, a corporation in the employ of Carpenter and the most powerful of the city's companies, the Mercers. The language of the temporal world of the city and its institutions profoundly interpenetrates the spiritual aspirations expressed by the Almshouse.

London Spirituality and John Carpenter

The mingling of spiritual and temporal, religious and secular, that characterizes the Whittington Almshouse as a civic institution is typical of a number of fifteenth-century urban civic projects that resulted from 'works of charity' like Whittington's. But it is a particular hallmark of the projects associated with his chief executor, Carpenter. Carpenter's work for and with the Whittington estate brings together several concerns that recur throughout his career as common clerk of the City of London (1417–38): his desire to expand the reach of civic power in both temporal and spiritual terms; his at once pietistic and bureaucratic use of texts as an instrument of that expansion; and his exploitation of perpetual, often corporate forms to counter the temporal limitations imposed by human mortality. Carpenter's other major London projects – the composition of the so-called *Liber albus* and the commissioning of a version of Lydgate's *Daunce of the Macabees* as a wall painting around the walls of the Pardon churchyard at St Paul's – are informed by a similar interest in supplementing human frailty as are the Almshouse ordinances, and evoke a similar desire to extend the civic into the realm of the religious.

Begun in 1419, four years before Whittington's death, the *Liber albus* is Carpenter's exhaustive attempt to organize all the archival material surviving since the founding of London; to set down the customs of the city, as they pertain to the distribution and passing on of power in the city's government; and to detail the history and duties of the elected governors and officials that make up the civic hierarchy: all, as his introduction states, in order to circumvent, so far as possible, the unexpected and irresistible power of death. Because 'the fallibility of human memory and the shortness of life do not allow us to gain an accurate knowledge of everything that deserves remembrance,' unless knowledge is recorded in highly codified form, and because death often comes suddenly to the 'aged, most experienced, and most discreet rulers of the royal City of London,' causing disruption to their successors, it is crucial to have in writing how the power structure reproduces itself (3). The *Liber albus* clearly attempts, as Sheila Lindenbaum has argued, to promote and protect the power of the civic government (295), but it should be noted that it does so by *replacing* the minds and memories of members of the city elite with the written technology of the compilation, allowing governance of the city to pass smoothly from one generation of rulers to another, thanks to the forms of authority immortalized in its pages. Focused as it is on the customs and structures of governance that sustain London as a civic entity, the *Liber albus* is not a religious project. But its accounts of the roles of city officials and of the ceremonies so important to performing these roles regularly involve the incursion of the civic into religious spaces and rituals: as the mayor and aldermen, for example, attend major festivities at St Paul's to pray for the soul of Bishop William, 'who by his entreaties ... obtained from his lordship William the Conqueror great liberties for the City of London'; to affirm the Mayor's right to seat himself 'in the stall next to that of the Dean' (Carpenter 26); or to pray in the Pardon churchyard by way of reasserting the City's proprietorial interest in that space and its chantry chapel, dedicated to the parents of Thomas à Becket, London's patron saint.

Similarly, in his other high-profile civic project, the St Paul's Dance of Death, Carpenter embraces the opportunity posed by the death of individuals to create an image of the city as a perpetual entity – intimately connected with, but not subordinate to, the spiritual – and to do so in one of the spaces to which the rituals described in the *Liber albus* most clearly lay civic claim. In John Lydgate's poem, derived from the *Dance macabre* painted on the walls of the Holy Innocents in Paris in 1426, Death unexpectedly summons a member of each estate (mayor, priest, merchant, artisan, labourer) to dance: reifying the social hierarchy in the careful ordering of the dance itself while showing all subject to a single, inevitable fate. As I show elsewhere, Carpenter's canny 1430 commission of a series of panel paintings depicting and illustrating Lydgate's poem in a locale of crucial symbolic significance to the city governors – partly because of its association with the City's patron saint, the Pardon churchyard was the final destination of the new mayor's annual 'riding' – transforms this 'morbid' poem of death into an image of London as a perpetual city: one that endures in its temporal 'dance' as a diverse social structure despite the deaths of individual inhabitants (Appleford). Because poem and wall painting are also clearly didactic – implicitly calling surviving members of the social order to reform their lives in order to avoid dying a *mors improvisa*, an unprepared death – the commission also lays claim to a certain spiritual authority on the part of the civic: a legitimate interest in the eternal, as well as the temporal, fates of its citizens.

If the monuments and documents for which Carpenter was responsible as common clerk and as Whittington's chief executor constitute a public statement of the relation between the civic and the religious, we can gain a sense of the intellectual underpinnings of this statement, and a further demonstration of the care one of London's most skilful fifteenth-century bureaucrats brought to making it, from Carpenter's will. Part of this will makes specific bequests from his private library – 'one of the most extensive ... to be found in fifteenth-century London' – including books in Latin, French, and English, ranging from the pseudo-Aristotelian 'mirror for princes,' the *Secreta Secretorum*, to the ascetical *De miseria conditionis humanae* by Pope Innocent III (a work also carefully studied by Chaucer), to Christine de Pizan's major work of political philosophy, the *Livre du corps de policie* (Barron, *London in the Middle Ages* 306; Brewer 131–65). One work, the sixth-century *De vita contemplativa* of Julianus Pomerius, which Carpenter bequeathed to his opposite number in the Chamberlain's household, the chamber clerk William Chedworth (Barron, *London in the Middle Ages* 183–4), is of particular interest here for its account of the relation between contemplatives who 'receive' the kingdom of heaven as their 'homeland,' and those in the 'active life' who must 'knock at the gate [of heaven] as though with the hands of good works' (Suelzer 33) if they want to be saved, but for whom the acquisition of wealth not gained by 'fraud and thefts' is not an evil but 'a great good' (Suelzer 78). Here, Carpenter might have found a model both for his own charitable works on the part of the Whittington bequest and for the contemplative lives of the inhabitants of the Almshouse and College of Priests.

Much of Carpenter's library, however, is not listed in the will, whose executors are indeed instructed to dispose of the main part of his estate 'in works of piety and mercy' on condition that they do not make 'any inventory of such my goods and chattels' for inspection by the 'ordinary,' the bishop of London, Robert Gilbert; Gilbert even receives the sum of 'twenty shillings sterling' if this clause is honoured (Brewer 142–3). A principal 'work of piety and mercy' the executors, 'Master William Lichefeld and Reginald Pecok,' are to perform is the donation of any books they deem 'good or rare' to be placed and chained in 'the common library at Guildhall, for the profit of the students there, and those discoursing to the common people' (Brewer 143). The Guildhall, the third of Whittington's foundations, in large part established by Carpenter and Whittington's other executors, was in theory open to all, but seems to have been intended primarily as a resource for secular priests in search of materials to use in preaching.[5] With his customary sense of legal nuance and with the aid of two friends – the first a prominent London priest and preacher, the second master of the College of Priests and fifteenth-century England's most prolific vernacular religious writer – Carpenter here enriches a collection that shared the religious aims of the College but excludes the episcopal authorities from oversight so thoroughly that we have no way to reconstruct his donation. Even while drawing on the help of members of the secular clergy – just as, with the Dance of Death, he drew on the services of a Benedictine monk – Carpenter works to protect a civil institution, the Guildhall, from any suggestion of ambiguity as to who controlled its collection.

As his executors in death and trusted friends in life, and despite their different professional backgrounds, Lichfield and Pecock can be assumed to have shared some of Carpenter's complex awareness of the double demands of the spiritual and the temporal that informed projects such as the Almshouse. Lichfield's single surviving vernacular prose work, a rewriting of parts two and three of the important thirteenth-century guide for solitaries *Ancrene Wisse* named *A Simple Tretis* (see Appleford and Watson), offers a model for working with these demands analogous both to Carpenter's own religiosity and to the spiritual life the Almshouse was supposed to encourage (the work's date is uncertain: Lichfield died in 1448 and was active from the 1420s). A discussion of how to keep one's senses pure, followed by an account of the virtues of the solitary life, *A Simple Tretis* expounds a mode of 'secular' living for those who 'haue besines outeward' – householders, priests with 'cure of paryshens ... Sherefes. Maires. And Baylees' – but whose 'intent is euer set on [on] þing. to do right and lawe. of god. kepyng clene. her conscience,' just as solitaries do in their physical removal from the world. While the work has little to say about the secular activities it assumes that its readers pursue, except to insist that, from a spiritual point of view, every worldly thing is 'bot as ... a mene' to 'endles blis,' its reference to specific secular urban professions here (with a clear emphasis on city officials) presupposes their independent, non-religious legitimacy (Baugh 45).

This version of what Walter Hilton, in a late fourteenth-century work widely circulated in London, terms *Mixed Life* (Ogilvie-Thomson) is described in terms more suitable to Carpenter himself, or the members of the College of Priests, than the poor bedesmen in the Almshouse, whose secular responsibilities are negligible. Yet *A Simple Tretis* bespeaks a valorization of the life of solitary reflection and prayer, even on the part of busy urban preachers and civic officials – Lichfield indeed asserts that 'al. men and wymmen shold in party be. solitary' in this way (Baugh 43) – which also seems reflected in the living arrangements made for the 'pouer folk' in the almshouse, or at least in the language the ordinances uses to describe those arrangements:

> Also we woll and ordeyn that every persone of hem now Tutor and pouer folk and successours have a place by him self with in the seid Almeshous. That is to sey a Celle or a litell house with a chymene and a pryvey and other necessaries in the whiche he shalle lyegge and rest ... Whan they be in hir forseid houses or Celles aforeseid and also in the cloistres and other places of the seid almshouse have hem self quietly and pesably without noise or disturbance of his felawes and that they occupie hem self in prayer or reding or in labor of his hondes or in som other honest occupacion. (112)

It is this neo-Carthusian set-up – one in which, nonetheless, the 'pouer folk' have access to the world outside the Almshouse and are fully visible to those who live around them – that Carpenter sought to protect by the very worldly and expensive device of incorporating the institution.

As master of the College of Priests, who had spiritual responsibility for the Almshouse from the year of its formal incorporation in 1432 until two years after Carpenter's death, Reginald Pecock may have been personally nominated for the position by Carpenter (Scase, 'Reginald Pecock, John Carpenter' 267–8) as a person clearly suited to head the new Whittington foundations, with his own creative reforming efforts to contribute to Carpenter's grand experiment in lay spiritual authority. Throughout his career, Pecock's desired 'forto be a profitable procutoure to lay men' (*Reule* 8), 'procuring' and communicating religious truth through books, especially his own productions, many of which were likely written while he was master of the College: *The Rule of Christian Religion*, *The Donet* and its shorter form, *Poor Men's Mirror*, *The Folower*, *The Book of Faith*, and other, now lost, works (Sutton 165). Enabling lay access to books of religious truth was, for Pecock, of crucial importance in the fight against heresy and as a charitable response to 'þe greet nede of oure neighboris soulis.' Indeed, Pecock's vernacular religious projects form a relatively close parallel to the institutional projects undertaken during the same period by his friend Carpenter, and show a similar confidence in the perspicacity of the urban laity (Scase, 'Reginald Pecock, John Carpenter' 267–9). According to Pecock, lack of authoritative books in Middle English, not intellectual ability, was the real barrier to lay theological knowledge, for 'each wise, great mercer in his reckonings and bargains making' must as a matter of professional necessity have a great 'height of wit,' more than enough to read and understand even the most abstract theological discussion if written in the vernacular (*Reule* 21). If, as seems likely, the *Poor Men's Mirror* was written specifically with them in mind, he seems to have had the same high view of the intellectual powers, and theological needs, of the inhabitants of the Almshouse.

Pecock's association with London mercantile culture, not to mention his intimate connection with the Mercers' great charity, the Almshouse, may account for the fact that, for a writer of abstract religious material, he is unusually preoccupied with the cost of learning and devotion. Throughout his writing, he shows a keen sense that books are costly material objects, an awareness implicit in his connections with the devout London lay community behind the John Colop common-profit book scheme (Scase 'Reginald Pecock, John Carpenter'), and explicit in his prologue to his redaction of the *Donet, The Poor Men's Mirror*: 'Not wiþstondyng þat I haue maad þe first parti of þe book clepid "þe donet" ... to be of litil quantite þat welnigh ech poor persoon maye bi sum meene gete coost to haue it as his owne; yit, in to þe moor eese of þe persone poorist in hauer and in witt, I haue drawen þis now folewyng extract' (226). Responsible for the pastoral care of the inmates of the Almshouse, Pecock had, when writing the *Mirror*, many opportunities to judge what a poor person might require as devotional reading. The poor folk of the house may, indeed, have been given the *Mirror* by their parish priest for use in the time they were alone in their rooms, engaged, as the ordinance specifies, in 'prayer or reding or labour of hondes.'

Despite the demotic impulse behind its writing, Pecock's *Mirror* is, like his other works, often difficult and abstruse, suggesting that, like Carpenter and Lichfield, he wished to bring a general audience into an educated conversation about religious matters – his various 'experiment[s] in annexing vernacular territory for orthodox theology' (Bose 217; Campbell) were designed to expand the spiritual reach of the London lay community, not simply to cater to their existing spiritual needs. Pecock's preoccupation with textual access – of opening texts to the widest possible audience – similarly informs another intellectual piecework that he may have undertaken for the Whittington foundations, one that returns this essay to its starting point. As master of the College, Pecock is the most likely person to have undertaken – whether after Carpenter's death or before it – the translation of the Latin ordinances and may have helped to devise, conceivably with Carpenter, the English ordinance book's rich semiotic frame of frontispiece and envoy.

The English Translation: 'Sey openly in Englissh'

The Whittington foundations can therefore be understood as at least in part an experiment in urban lay spirituality, crafted and sustained by a varied group of London citizens (Whittington, Carpenter, and the other executors) and drawing into its orbit, in the 1430s and early 40s, clerical writers deeply interested in thinking in new ways about lay religiosity (Reginald Pecock and William Lichfield). The Almshouse's combination of secular oversight and vigorous clerical involvement points to the way that at least some prosperous and powerful Londoners wanted, on the one hand, ecclesiastical reform, and, on the other, hands-on involvement in nurturing their own spiritual health: control over the works done in this world to ensure their salvation in the next; control over the means by which they could die a good death within the established Church. For this, the most theologically educated generation of laypeople London had seen – the fruits of two centuries of concentrated emphasis on pastoral teaching and the dissemination of books of vernacular theology in a variety of genres – the self-fashioning of religious identity and spiritual autonomy, not the critique or rejection of orthodox beliefs or devotional practice that animated an earlier generation of lay 'Lollards,' may have been of primary concern. As we have seen, these men had the knowledge and the connections to borrow and reshape traditional spiritual identities and modes to suit a commercial sensibility and lifestyle, inflecting late medieval Christianity's traditional focus on the next world and emphasis on the vanity of temporal things with specifically mercantile values such as tangible works of charity, economies of exchange, and juridical models of community.

Read through this understanding of the Almshouse as an innovative experiment in lay spiritual community, crafted by Carpenter and given a theological voice for Londoners by Pecock, the English translation of the ordinances, with its frontispiece and envoy frame, becomes intelligible as a subtle discursive strategy operating on two levels. On the first, fundamentally secular level, translation, frontispiece, and envoy ask to be understood in celebratory terms, as a memento of the moment of final transfer of the Whittington estate to the Mercers' Company: the moment the company must have long anticipated. As noted above, the central position in the frontispiece of the scribe of the Latin ordinances, William Grove, serves to re-present the first act of writing as a point of origin: an origin that goes behind the written Latin document the English ordinances translate to a more potent oral source, Whittington's absent voice and last words, making the pointing figure of Carpenter into one in a chain of unimportant mediators between the glamorous Richard Whittington and the Mercers. Read this way, the use of the Chaucerian envoy on the last folio of the English ordinances makes sense, not only because the envoy is a traditional 'memorializing' and 'eternalizing' form, but also because Chaucer's celebration of Troy through a secular poetics offers a ready parallel to the Mercers' economic and cultural cultivation of a London ruled by the urban laity and their concerns. Where Chaucer rebuilds the Old Troy, the new Mercer 'conservatours' of the Almshouse help to build the New Troy: 'Troynovaunt,' the name late medieval Londoners liked proudly to call their city (Benson; Wallace). Thus, frontispiece and envoy together function in a fashion akin to the authorial presentation miniatures accompanying fifteenth-century literary translations, such as the images of Lydgate presenting *Troy Book*, his translation of Guido delle Colonne's Troy history, to his patron, Henry V (Gillespie 36–40): in the ordinance image and envoy, Whittington is reanimated so that he can 'submit' the Almshouse and all its poor folk 'lowly to all correccion' by the Mercers' Company. Standing in for Homer and his peers in Chaucer's envoy, the wardens of the Company thus assume greater authority, either than the ordinances themselves or, ultimately, than their makers, Whittington and his executors. In other words, we are in the presence of the literary trope of *translatio studii et imperii*, as the Almshouse completes its journey into the hands of the Mercers, and the ordinances undertake a parallel journey, from Latin into the vernacular.

Yet the Almshouse, as we have seen, was only in a specifically religious sense a 'secular' project. On a second, religious level, translation, frontispiece, and envoy are not celebratory of the secular triumph of the Mercers' Company in their 'New Troy,' but protective of the spiritual and religious agenda of the Almshouse's founders – indeed, implicitly admonitory in their concern to ensure this agenda's survival. The translation makes a particular rhetorical move by rendering the Latin rules into English, an apparently demotic gesture, as the text offers itself to a wider, less specialized readership. With its gesture towards the uses of literary English in high-culture poetic productions, the envoy seeks to normalize this move. But whose purposes does English translation of a work of this kind – a non-literary, essentially legal text, serve? As W.M. Ormrod's recent work on the 'deep-seated resistence' to adopting Middle English 'as an authoritative language of record, whether by the Crown, by civic authorities, or by the church' in the fifteenth century suggests, it is unlikely that the Mercers would have sought such a translation for themselves: as noted, the Mercers, like most of the London guilds, preferred their in-house documents to be in Latin or, if in a vernacular, in the more 'formal and authoritative' Anglo-Norman (Ormrod 782, 783, 755; Catto). Whoever its first recipients may have been, the implied audience of the translation – the audience whose presence the translation, by the fact of its existence, reminds any reader – is thus not the Mercers' Company. Rather, the translation announces the public accessibility of the ordinances to a wider audience, with interests not necessarily at all the same as the Mercers: the London community at large, and especially the thirteen members of the Almshouse itself.

The ordinances state that the Almshouse poor folk must gather and listen 'every quarter of þe yere onyse at the leest' as 'this oure present fundacion and ordinaunce and alle and every Chapiter and Statute of the same ... be redde openly and clerely expouned' (Imray 120). The regulations at these occasions were presumably expounded by a member of the College of Priests in English, since elsewhere the ordinances, acknowledging the varying literacies of the bedesmen, identify English as the language of 'openness' – each day, after the bedesmen have said the *De Profundis* at the tomb of Whittington and his wife in St Michael's Church, 'the Tutor or oon of theldest men' is to say, '*openly in Englissh* "God have mercy on oure founders soules and alle cristen"' (116, my italics). In a sense, the 1442 translation project thus simply gives stable form to the practice of public reading of the ordinances in English ongoing since the Almshouse was founded.

Yet the movement of the English ordinances from oral translation into permanent written form suggests that English is here not only the language of community and accessibility but also that of accountability – specifically, the Mercers' accountability to the bedesmen, who, for the first time, have formally set down in their mother tongue not only the rules by which they must live, but the procedures and responsibilities of their new overseers. Read in the light of one last historical detail, the envoy clearly suggests that the translation formed part of John Carpenter's scheme to protect his experiment in lay spirituality after his death: in other words, that he foresaw not just benefits but potential difficulties ahead for his spiritual foundation under lay management. Already by 1431, the year before his attempts to incorporate the Almshouse had met with success, Carpenter had amassed more than sufficient property to secure the annual payments needed to maintain the College and the Almshouse. In order to secure the transferral of the Almshouse and its endowment to the Mercers upon his death – that is, to ensure that its property could be held in mortmain – and to avoid having to obtain permission from the Crown to do so,[6] Carpenter took advantage of 'a custom of the City of London which permitted a freeman of the city to devise lands and tenements in mortmain without any licence' (Imray 28–9) by conveying the Whittington estate to grocer William Sevenoke (sheriff, 1412–13; mayor, 1418–19). Sevenoke, in the same year, made a will bequeathing the College, Almshouse, and their property to the Mercers' Company. But Sevenoke's will also included the provision – obviously written to Carpenter's orders – that any monies left over after the annual payments to the foundations had to be 'deposited in Whittington's chest, near the vestibule of the College' (Imray 28–9). The Mercers were allowed to use this profit from the charities, but only for loans to the needy members of their guild, not to fund the Company's general business ventures or its own rather elaborate and costly ritual celebrations.

Weaving in and out of its note of public submission and celebration, we can hear the echoes in the envoy of just this kind of hard-nosed legal move, or at least of the fear it expresses that the Mercers will try to bend the terms of their great bequest to their own advantage. The anonymous speaker of the envoy (the translator) tells his 'litel booke' to go 'The lowly submitting to al correccion / Of theym beyng maistres now of the mercery / Olney Feldyng Boleyne and of Burton.' Seeming to subordinate the ordinances to the 'corrective' executive authority of the wardens, the apparent gesture of submission here shares the double-edged quality of many humility topoi deployed by fifteenth-century poets such as John Lydgate, its 'self-abnegations' working to 'dampen the force of the possible affront to ... patrons' contained within in its message (Meyer-Lee 53). On a literal level, the envoy imagines the wardens as checking the vernacular translation for accuracy against the original Latin ordinances. Yet, were they to do this in practice, the mercery 'maistres,' as keepers of Whittington's authentic commission, would find themselves going back, and back again, to the original rules written by John Carpenter and the other executors in 1424, in order to 'correct' not only the English translation, but also their own actions regarding the oversight of the house and use of the monies from the Whittington estate. 'Submission' of the vernacular ordinances for the 'correccion' of the Mercery 'maistres' actually entails their submission to the correction of the legally binding Latin text. Spiritual admonishment underlies elegant literary trope.

Conclusion

John Carpenter's work on and for the Almshouse did assure that Richard Whittington made a 'good death' in late medieval Christian terms – and that he did so spectacularly and conspicuously. The results of Whittington's post-mortem charity became a permanent part of the fabric of the London cityscape. In his other public London projects, as we have seen, Carpenter created monuments that played with the relation between mortality, perpetuity, and eternity, the secular and the religious, and the individual's relation to communal structure of the corporation, be it city or guild. The envoy of the translated ordinances, with its clever poetic play, presents a similar thematic.

The wording of the envoy differs in many ways from that of Chaucer's original poem, but retains its first line almost verbatim, 'Go litel boke go litel tregedie,' encoding here the fall not of the heroic lover Troilus, but of the mighty merchant prince, Richard Whittington. A symbol of the turning of Fortune's wheel and the general frailty of even the most powerful, the book, however, is perpetual, sent '*For ever* to be a servant with in [the Mercers' wardens'] cominalte,' not least as a sign and guarantor of the perpetuity of that 'cominalte' itself. As Anne Sutton has recently commented, when Carpenter died and the Company came into the Whittington estate, '[t]he Mercers ... suddenly become a major landlord in the city with greater "lordship" and patronage than any ambitious dream could have envisaged: the company had been handed the means to ensure its own institutional perpetuity as an administrator of charity, whatever time and politics might inflict on the trade of its members and its other functions as a fraternity' (163). The 'tragic' ending of one great, but mortal, man, Richard Whittington, provides the funds necessary to give perpetual existence to an associated collective body, the Mercers' Company, by means of another perpetual corporate entity, the Almshouse poor folk. Implicit, however, in the frontispiece's reminder of the power of Whittington's dying wishes to shape the future and the envoy's charge to the Mercers to 'correct' the translation, and by extension, their own actions, is the warning that this circle of mutual corporate perpetuation works only if the original contract written by Carpenter between the Almsmen and Whittington's executors is honoured: perpetual support of the poor men given in exchange for prayers; perpetual prayers given in exchange for Whittington's eternal salvation and those of the Almshouse's new overseers. Whittington's death can only remain 'good' if the Mercers' Company, the 'cominalte' for whom he has become a founding father, acts in good faith.

NOTES

1 In early modern legend, Whittington is a poor provincial orphan who makes his fortune in the city with the help of his cat, Tommy; in reality, Whittington was of a gentry family, the third son of Sir William Whittington of Pauntley in Gloucestershire, who made his large fortune primarily through trade as a mercer. For Whittington's life and career, see Barron, 'Richard Whittington.' On Whittington's cat, see Newman.

2 For the frontispiece and the Middle English translation of the ordinances, see Imray, Appendix 1, 218–32. All in-text citations are to this edition. The book itself is at Mercers' Hall in London. The frontispiece is thought to have been made by the London illuminator William Abell (Alexander).

3 There are also two early sixteenth-century copies extant; as the religious orientation of the Almshouse would have made it vulnerable to state interference during the reign of Henry VIII, these versions, Imray suggests, 'may well have been working copies made when the revision of the ordinances was under consideration just before the Reformation' (108).

4 But see Imray's account that argues for Whittington's general influence on the executors' building plans, 6–10.

5 The library was built in cooperation with the executors of the mercer William Bury; see Barron, *The Medieval Guildhall* 33.

6 Literally to hold lands with a 'dead hand,' bequeathing lands in mortmain was essential in setting up any 'perpetual' foundation (such as a chantry or, in this case, a charity house for the poor), as it allowed for some 'permanent endowment in the shape of lands or rents' (Chew). If not devised in mortmain to the foundation, the lands or rents would revert to the king upon the death of the individual who owned the land. In the late medieval period, the Crown did

still allow land to be devised in mortmain, but only if a royal licence had been purchased beforehand. Carpenter was not part of a guild and thus presumably not 'free' of the city; therefore, he could not bequeath the estate directly to the Mercers without purchasing a royal licence.

WORKS CITED

Alexander, Jonathan. 'William Abell "lynmour" and English Fifteenth-Century Illumination.' *Kunsthistorische Forschungen Otto Pächt zu seinem 70. Geburtstag.* E.A. Rosenauer and G. Weber. Salzburg: Residenz Verlag, 1972. 166–70.

Appleford, Amy. 'The Dance of Death in London: John Carpenter, John Lydgate, and the *Daunce of Poulys.*' *Journal of Medieval and Early Modern Studies* 38, no. 2 (2008): 285–314.

Appleford, Amy, and Nicholas Watson. 'Merchant Religion: William Litchfield, London Preacher.' *Chaucer Review* 46, nos.1 and 2 (2011): 203–22.

Barron, Caroline. *The Medieval Guildhall of London.* London: Corporation of London, 1974.

– *London in the Middle Ages.* Oxford: Oxford University Press, 2004.

– 'Richard Whittington: The Man behind the Myth.' *Studies in London History Presented to Philip Edmund Jones.* Ed. A.E.J. Hollaender and William Kellaway. London: Hodder and Stoughton, 1969. 197–248.

Baugh, A.C. *The English Text of the 'Ancrene Riwle.'* EETS 232. London: Oxford University Press, 1956.

Benson, C. David. 'Civic Lydgate: The Poet and London.' *John Lydgate; Poetry, Culture, and Lancastrian England.* Ed. Larry Scanlon and James Simpson. Notre Dame, IN: University of Notre Dame Press, 2006. 147–68.

Bose, Mishtooni. 'Reginald Pecock's Vernacular Voice.' *Lollards and Their Influence in Late Medieval England.* Ed. Fiona Somerset, Jill C. Havens, and Derrick G. Pitard. Woodbridge, Suffolk; Rochester, NY: Boydell Press, 2003. 217–36.

Brewer, Thomas. *Memoir of the Life and Times of John Carpenter.* London: Arthur Taylor, 1856.

Campbell, Kirsty. *The Call to Read: Reginald Pecock's Books and Textual Community.* Notre Dame, IN: University of Notre Dame Press, 2010.

Carpenter, John. *Liber Albus: The White Book of the City of London.* Trans. Henry Thomas Riley. London: Richard Griffin and Company, 1861.

Catto, Jeremy. 'Written English: The Making of the Language 1370–1400.' *Past and Present* 179 (2003): 24–59.

Chaucer, Geoffrey. *Troilus and Criseyde.* In *The Riverside Chaucer*. Ed. Larry D. Benson. Boston: Houghton Mifflin, 1987.

Chew, Helena. 'Mortmain in Medieval London.' *The English Historical Review*. 60, no. 236 (1945): 1–15.

Clay, Rotha M. *The Medieval Hospitals of England*. London: Methuen, 1909.

Davies, Matthew. 'The Tailors of London: Corporate Charity in the Late Medieval Town.'*Crown, Government and People in the Fifteenth Century*. Ed. Rowena E. Archer. Fifteenth Century Series 2. New York: St Martin's Press, 1994. 161–90.

Gillespie, Alexandra. *Print Culture and the Medieval Author: Chaucer, Lydgate, and Their Books, 1473–1557*. Oxford: Oxford University Press, 2006.

Imray, Jean. *The Charity of Richard Whittington: A History of the Trust Administered by the Mercers' Company, 1424–1966*. London: University of London; Athlone Press, 1968.

Jefferson, Lisa. *The Medieval Account Books of the Mercers of London: An Edition and Translation*. 2 vols. Farnham, UK; Burlington, VT: Ashgate, 2009.

Jordan, W.K. *The Charities of London, 1480–1660.* London: Kegan, 1959.

– *Philanthropy in England, 1480–1660.* London: Brill, 1960.

Lindenbaum, Sheila. 'London Texts and Literate Practice.' *Cambridge History of Medieval English Literature*. Ed. David Wallace. Cambridge: Cambridge University Press, 2002. 284–315.

Meyer-Lee, Robert J. 'Lydgate's Laureate Pose.' *John Lydgate: Poetry, Culture, and Lancastrian England*. Ed. Larry Scanlon and James Simpson. Notre Dame, IN: University of Notre Dame Press, 2006. 36–60.

Newman, Barbara. 'The "Cattes Tale": A Chaucer Apocryphon.' *The Chaucer Review* 26, no. 4 (1992): 411–23.

Ogilvie-Thomson, S.J. *Walter Hilton's Mixed Life*. Salzburg: Institut für Anglistik und Amerikanistik, Universität Salzburg, 1986.

Ormrod , W.M. 'The Use of English: Language, Law, and Political Culture in Fourteenth-Century England.' *Speculum* 78 (2003): 750–87.

Pecock, Reginald. *'The Donet' ... collated with 'The Poore Mennis Myrrour.'* Ed. Elsie Vaughan Hitchcock. EETS o.s. 156. London: Oxford UP, 1996.

– *The Reule of Crysten Religioun*. Ed. William Cabell Greet. EETS o.s. 171. London: Oxford University Press, 1927.

Prescott, Elizabeth. *The English Medieval Hospital, 1050–1640*. London: B.A. Seaby, 1992.

Rawcliffe, Caroline. 'The Hospitals of Later Medieval London.' *Medical History* 28 (1984): 1–21

Scase, Wendy. *'Piers Plowman' and the New Anticlericalism*. Cambridge: Cambridge University Press, 1989.

– *Reginald Pecock*. Authors of the Middle Ages. Vol. 8, no. 3. Aldershot, UK: Variorum, 1996.

– 'Reginald Pecock, John Carpenter and John Colop's 'Common-Profit' Books: Aspects of Book Ownership and Circulation in Fifteenth-Century London.' *Medium Aevum* 61, no. 2 (1992): 261–74.

Suelzer, Sister Mary Josephine, trans. *Julianus Pomerius: The Contemplative Life*. Ancient Christian Writers 4. New York: Newman Press, 1947.

Sutton, Anne. *The Mercery of London: Trade, Goods and People, 1130–1578*. Aldershot, UK: Ashgate: 2005.

Thomas, A.H., and I.D. Thornley, eds. *The Great Chronicles of London*. London, 1938.

Thomson, J.A.F. 'Piety and Charity in Late Medieval London.' *Journal of Ecclesiastical History* 16 (1965): 178–96.

Thrupp, S.L. 'The Gilds.' *The Cambridge Economic History of Europe*. Vol. 3. Cambridge: Cambridge University Press, 1941–91. 230–79.

Wallace, David. *Chaucerian Polity: Absolutist Lineages and Associational Forms in England and Italy*. Stanford, CA: Stanford University Press, 1997.

PART TWO

Bodily Rhetoric

4 An Epic Incarnation of Salvation: The Function of the Body in the *Eupolemius*

SYLVIA PARSONS

The role of the body in the *Eupolemius* is a function of the poem's own peculiar hybrid anatomy. Neither a biblical epic nor a personification allegory, the *Eupolemius* uses the conventional narrative elements of epic to present a kind of abstract of salvation history. It treats the devil's war against God, recounts the fall of humanity, and traces the fortunes of Judas (the Jewish people) and Ethnis (the gentiles) through the ups and downs of salvation history, culminating in the death of the Messiah. The poem probably dates from the late eleventh century, and its author may possibly have been German, but solid information is so scarce that we do not even know whether 'Eupolemius' is the title of the poem or the pseudonym of its author; I follow Jan Ziolkowski in using *Eupolemius* to refer to the poem (Ziolkowski, 'Eupolemius' 2–5). The work has exercised a certain fascination, and ranks among the fortunate minority of medieval Latin poems that are readily accessible to scholars: an MGH edition by Karl Manitius appeared in 1973, with a good deal of supporting material, and Ziolkowski provided an English translation with introduction in 1991. Ziolkowski offered suggestions and corrections for some textual difficulties in Manitius's edition in a second article in 1992, and both Christine Ratkowitsch (Ratkowitsch 218–30) and Thomas Gärtner have further refined the text, though Gärtner's concern is primarily to extend the *apparatus fontium*. These four scholars – Manitius, Ziolkowski, Ratkowitsch, and Gärtner – have provided among them a sound foundation for the study of the poem, including analysis of the influences that contributed to its multiple strands of genre (Ziolkowski, 'Eupolemius' 3–17; Ratkowitsch 230–50). Despite this solid groundwork, however, the *Eupolemius* remains a curiosity, a kind of genetic freak. It is not the sort of poem that seems an easy fit for wide-ranging critical projects.

Certainly the poem's undeniable eccentricities make it an unlikely starting point for a study working outwards from a particular work of art to establish suggestive connections to the culture that produced it. Indeed, in some ways I offer here less a contribution to our understanding of the body in medieval culture than an attempt to use the focal point of the body as a kind of sampling tool to explore the complex individual nature of the *Eupolemius*. Nonetheless, this exploration has a contribution to make to the more general working out of approaches to the body in medieval culture that this volume represents. Many of the peculiarities of the work arise from a sense that the author is deliberately inciting and maintaining the reader's discomfort at the poem's mixture of categories, its refusal of synthesis. The mind games the author engages in when he simultaneously suggests and refuses the identifications of his characters with their homonymous biblical prototypes (Ziolkowski, 'Eupolemius' 8–10) are symptomatic of the poem's processes in general. The poem's handling of the multiple modes of representation of the body available to it makes dramatic capital out of incongruities and internal culture clashes. In this poem the conflicting elements of which any literary representation of the body is made are not passive categories, artefacts of our analysis, but active protagonists in a debate that is a lively subplot of the poem. The *Eupolemius* is a bizarre piece of literary machinery, but its showcasing of its own workings may suggest to us cogs and wheels that also whir away behind the discreet and polished surfaces of more integrated, less exhibitionistic works.

The body plays distinct and important roles in the ideological matrix of epic, the sign system of allegory, and the realm of biblical symbolism. The *Eupolemius* combines all these modes of signification, and the reader does not always know which code to apply to which message. One might expect the *Eupolemius*'s good guys either to be healers or destroyers, benign biblical physicians or epic heroes. The *Eupolemius* instead insists on both: a character whose name, Doxius (Right Doctrine) suggests allegory, at first appears to defy the military code of epic with his medical garb and bearing, but it turns out that he wields a sword stick. He does not step aside from epic modes of embodiment to present an alternative; instead, he inhabits two worlds of meaning simultaneously. The poem's treatment of the body provides an experimental cross-indexing of its overlapping systems of meaning. The body is one site of the poem's identity crisis, but it is also, I will suggest, a vital term in its solution. If we want to know what sort of thing the *Eupolemius* is, rather than how we should pigeonhole it, then an examination of the function of the body in its mixed messages is a useful diagnostic. An investigation of conflicting and coexisting representations of the body gives the poem the opportunity to enlighten as well as puzzle us, to contribute to, rather than baffle, our understanding.

My exploration of the poem's somatic aspects focuses on its negotiations with the terms of epic: the depiction of violent combat, the establishment of corporeal norms that define appropriate participants in epic interactions, and the fundamental logic whereby the poem equates the destruction of bodies with cultural values worthy of poetic commemoration. These aspects of the genre code of epic inevitably involve the *Eupolemius* in epic codes of values as well. A work that resists both the straightforwardly allegorical working out of the metaphor of spiritual combat and the simple adaptation of the more epic episodes of Old Testament history runs the risk that the insistently oblique relationship it establishes between form and matter will occasionally have the two at cross purposes. It is possible, however, to understand simultaneous meanings at cross purposes as the central drama of the poem. Any biblical epic, and particularly the *Eupolemius*, is a dialogized form in the Bakhtinian sense: the competing languages of biblical and classical culture are in some sense the poem's protagonists (Bakhtin 45, 49).

I will begin by examining the poem's depiction of violence as it is reflected in its use of epic animal similes. By focusing on the imagery that surrounds violence rather than the direct narration of wounding and death I hope to get more precisely at the formal encoding of the action. I will attempt to show that in using an inherited vocabulary of epic simile the *Eupolemius* confronts its readers with cultural homonyms: the same elements, for instance, sheep and wolf, occur in the author's classical and Christian sources, and in the audience's classical and Christian readerly expectations, but with significantly different connotations, creating the opportunity for, or the danger of, irony. The conflicted simultaneity of meanings suggests irony as Linda Hutcheon understands the term: not the subversion of one meaning by another opposite meaning, but the coinherence of two meanings that abut and abrade one another (Hutcheon 59–61). I will then move on to investigate satirical portraits of the body in the *Eupolemius*, both those addressed to the reader in the voice of the narrator and those contained in the exchange of battlefield taunts that make the reading and misreading of the body part of the epic action. Here the poem has a chance to dramatize explicitly some of the culture clash that it implicitly embodies. Finally, I will consider how the *Eupolemius* goes about translating the central bodily transaction of salvation history, the sacrificial death of Christ, into epic terms. Here, if anywhere, the *Eupo-*

lemius presents a transformative conflation, rather than an ironic distancing, of its divergent modes of imagining the body.

Animal Similes

The simile, and more particularly the animal simile, is one of the generic notes of classical epic. As genre markers, epic similes serve a double purpose, situating the narrative within the norms of epic, but also compelling the reader to examine those norms in relation to a set of alternate worlds that dramatize the continuities and contrasts between epic standards and other possible systems of value, as Susanne Wofford elegantly argues. Animal similes, with their implicit questioning of the boundary between natural violence and the socially and artistically formalized violence of epic, are a conventional element that is at once hackneyed and subversive. They are also an important locus in epic's negotiations with the body. Within the corporeal economy of traditional epic, similes that liken the violence of the battlefield to the predatory violence of animals serve to negotiate the distance between violence and the human body. On the one hand, the simile, by diverting the reader's attention to the mediating art rather than the immediate action, distances the bloody content of epic from the human actors who engage in it. At the same time, however, such similes suggest a more intimate physical contact with violence than the conventions and technologies of human combat allow. Warriors within the norms of epic do not maul their opponents with hands and teeth and then devour them, but similes do superimpose on civilized combatants the image of animals with mouths and teeth bloody from their prey. This potential for disturbing incongruities or even more disturbing congruities has been recognized and exploited by epic since the moments in the *Iliad* when the animal aspects of Achilles's violence escape from the poem's carefully bounded imagery into the real world of its characterization and action, most famously in *Iliad* 10.346–7, when he wishes that he could eat Hector raw.

To see how the *Eupolemius* handles animal similes, I will turn not to Greek epic but to a passage our author knew and imitated, from the night raid of Nisus and Euryalus on the sleeping Rutulian camp in *Aeneid* 9. This is far from being a unique example. Similar similes are ubiquitous in the Latin epics to which the *Eupolemius* author had access, as well as in the Homeric template, which he could not have known. Two factors make this particular example apt for my purposes. First, I will shortly be discussing the passage in which the *Eupolemius* author imitated the night raid topos in general and this simile in particular. Second, Vergil himself used the Nisus and Euryalus episode to examine the congruities and incongruities between epic modes and other modes (erotic, lyric) that can be embedded in it; Philip Hardie's introduction to his commentary on Book 9 gives an overview of the complexities of this patch of epic. While the *Eupolemius* poet was experimenting with a combination of elements very different from Vergil's, it is perhaps not a coincidence that he was drawn to and drew from a passage that worked self-consciously with the interplay of tones.

Here is Vergil's simile:

> Just as a famished lion rampaging through the packed sheepfolds – for insane hunger urges him – both bites and drags off the flock soft and mute with fear, he growls with bloody mouth.[1]

> impastus ceu plena leo per ovilia turbans
> (suadet enim vesana fames) manditque trahitque
> molle pecus mutumque metu, fremit ore cruento. (*Aeneid* 9.339–41)

Such similes may seem less worthy of critical attention than those that appear more self-consciously artistic, or that work to establish a deeper rift between the matter of the narrative and the inaccessible parallel world of the images. The potential for distancing contrast between human and animal behaviour in such imagery is delicately undermined by the pervasive location of animal violence within the sphere of human culture: these similes are not nature documentaries, in which exotic wild animals prey on one another in a world carefully distanced from a viewer. Rather, epic predators tend to attack animals domesticated by human agriculture (sheep, goats, oxen), and they frequently encounter human adversaries, either hunters or herdsman attempting to defend their flocks. For a Christian author, moreover, the whole complex of pastoral imagery is further complicated by the literary heritage of the New Testament.

In the *Eupolemius* the imagery of the Bible and Christian tradition shares the animal ecosystem with the epic interactions of predators, prey, and human intervention. In several instances the *Eupolemius* author uses animal similes not only to echo the bodily violence of the action but also to convey the theological event that the epic action represents. When Messiah cuts off the thigh and right hand of Amartigenis (Original Sin), for instance, the image of the wounded snake that follows is not only a vivid picture of the still twitching hand but an interpretation of the event:

the hand jumps, as the wicked tail of a serpent that has been cut in two by a strong stake or a thrown stone often twitches.

Sallit manus, ut sude forti
Aut iacto saxo divise cauda colubre
Improba sepe micat. (*Eupolemius* 2.685–7)

The poet draws on classical precedent for the image of the twitching hand; *Aeneid* 10.395–6 supplies the verb *micare*, and Ovid, as Manitius notes, the source for the snake simile (*Metamorphoses* 6.558–60, speaking of Philomela's severed tongue). Here the function of the image is to point out that the action itself is only an image of Messiah's scotching of sin. In this instance action and imagery are harmoniously dovetailed in the *Eupolemius*, and the Christian content successfully supplements the classical materials. In other cases, however, epic and biblical imagery appear to be at cross purposes.

In the death of Messiah we will see an animal simile that takes this process of reworking epic models to the next level and renegotiates the fundamental logic of the body's role in the text's action. For now, however, I would like to look at a more traditional instance of the imaging of violence, one that reveals some of the unresolved tensions between the *Eupolemius*'s epic form and its salvific content. The scene is a night raid in which Moses, accompanied by Eleimon (Mercy), rescues the captive traitor Judas from the camp of Cacus (the Devil). The subject is Moses:

He himself, having taken along Eleimon, both a fighter and a priest, energetically seeking out by night the enemy camp, while they were all weighed down by wine and sleep and entirely heedless of war, first strikes with his sharp spear sluggish Iereas, Iudas's guard, and the three men with no opposition bloody their swords with dismal gore and trample on the dead and they empty the tents of an additional twenty-three slain enemies. No less energetically than a fierce wolf who breaks by night into the sheepfolds, which a careless shepherd has not defended well, snarls and exercises his accustomed frenzy with bloody teeth and rips apart the tame flock with brutal savagery and does not think to spare any, but insatiate he slaughters the whole flock, so the cruel warrior Moses and his followers rage, slaughtering sleeping men.

Simul hec dicens bellare paratum
Atque renitentem multumque diuque etiamque

Iratum remanere Nomum vix cogit et ipse
Inpiger assumpto pugnaci Eleimone nec non
Levita cunctis somnoque meroque gravatis
Et belli prorsus securis hostica noctu
Castra petens primum preacuta cuspide segnem
Plagat Iercam, Iude vigilem, iugulisque
Innumeris enses funesta cede cruentant
Tres nullo prohibente viri calcantque peremptos
Bisque decem tribus adiectis tentoria cesis
Hostibus evacuant. Non segnius ac lupus acer
Irrumpens noctu caulas, quas non bene pastor
Muniit incautus, ringit solitamque cruentis
Dentibus exercet rabiem laceratque ferina
Mansuetum feritate gregem nec cogitat ulli
Parcere, sed totum necat insaciatus ovile:
Sic bellator atrox Moyses eiusque sequaces
Sopitos cedendo fremunt. (*Eupolemius* 1.581–99)

The motif of the night raid against the sleeping enemy dates back to the beginnings of classical epic, with the expedition of Odysseus and Diomedes in *Iliad* 10; the author of the *Eupolemius* certainly draws on Nisus and Euryalus's slaughter of the sleeping Rutuli in *Aeneid* 9. There, too, the enemy is overcome with wine as well as sleep, and a predatory animal simile that I have already quoted underlines the violence (see Putnam 52, 61–2 for a discussion of the simile's significance). In a poem in which the configuration of sheep, shepherd, and predator must suggest the influence of New Testament parable as well as epic simile, however, the casting here is disturbing: the Devil is the shepherd, his troops the flock, and Moses and Mercy are the bloody predators. In this instance the simile seems to function, or maybe malfunction, as a channel through which the violence of the surface narrative seeps down to contaminate the underlying tenor of the poem. The 'potentially disjunctive structure' (Wofford 46) of epic simile within systems of epic ideology is actively disruptive here because the balance of power between correspondence and separation has been destabilized, with more than one signifying system laying claim to the terms of the image.

If the reversal of expected roles in this simile suggests a structural flaw beyond the ambiguous implications implicit in moral-allegorical violence (on which see the interesting discussion of the legacy of Prudentian allegory in Old English literature in the work of John P. Hermann), we must ask ourselves whether the *Eupolemius* is merely inept, a mechanical application of epic formulae in a situation where the connotations for a Christian audience would be bizarrely inappropriate, or whether the poem reflects, anticipates, and perpetuates an inherently dialogized literary culture. Author, work, and audience all participate in an intertextual community shaped by the competing norms of classical and biblical culture, and, as Linda Hutcheon points out, community enables the possibility of irony (Hutcheon 91–3). I will have to defer a full answer to this question till the end of the paper, but I would suggest that in this poem the late-appearing figure of Messiah represents the solution to literary as well as theological dilemmas. Before I address the problems posed and the solutions offered in the poem's culmination, however, I want to look at another point where epic's relationship with the body is renegotiated to accommodate an experimental adaptation of epic topoi to Christian types.

Reading and Misreading the Body through Satire

An examination of the satirical treatment of the body in the *Eupolemius* will give us a further opportunity to consider the poetic manipulation of the relationship between the surface action of the poem and its underlying content. Satire touching on the body in the *Eupolemius* takes two different forms and emerges in two different contexts. Direct satire, which creates a shared understanding between author and reader concerning the moral significance of the physical traits assigned to a textual body, plays a relatively small part in the *Eupolemius*. Where it does occur it is directed at the army of Cacus and has the effect of tilting the poem's technique more towards traditional psychomachia, in which bodily traits are there to define and emphasize the viciousness of the vices. Unlike Prudentius and his ilk, however, the *Eupolemius* author is not interested in creating a complete portrait gallery of the vices. In so far as it exists, his direct satirical preoccupation with the body focuses on a single feature, the belly. The intent seems to be not to define a particular vice, like gluttony, so much as to invest the characters involved with a scornfully explicit and excessive corporeality. We have already seen a hint of this grossness of corporeality in the drunken sleepers of Moses's night raid, but in that instance the terms were epic. In the *Eupolemius*'s accounts of the greedy Aplestes (Insatiable) and of Judas's degenerate lifestyle after his defection from the party of Agatus (God), the epic author borrows or deploys the motifs and vocabulary of satire. The most elaborate example of this is the portrait of Aplestes, which draws on Horace and Sextus Amarcius[2] to create within epic a non-epic body whose belly is the site of comically mock-epic conflicts:

> Aplestes; this man was in the habit of consuming his abundant wealth in feasts selected from land and sea, and often in his stomach the fish [of uncertain species] used to attack the boar, the turbot the kid, the wolf the bear in secret strife.
>
> Aplestem –
> Mos erat huius opes amplas terraque marique
> Quesitis dapibus consumere et eius in alvo
> Sepe timallus aprum, rombus capream, lupus ursum
> Litibus occultis pressabat. (*Eupolemius* 1.471–5)

This mocking internalization in turn internalizes satire within epic and epic within satire, moving from the world of military action dignified by animal similes to a miniature beast-epic played out in the processes of digestion. Thomas Gärtner has pointed out that this passage draws on Lucan as well as on its satirical sources (Gärtner 553), so that the *Eupolemius* author creates the densest possible interweaving of the two genres, drawing on satire within epic and on satire proper to make his mocking miniature.

Judas's descent into vice, during his first, temporary transfer of allegiance to the camp of Cacus, involves a similar marked and degraded physicality, centred on the belly:

> He [Judas, the Jewish people] becomes as foul as Ethnis [the Gentiles], a glutton, a brawler, an adulterer and idolator, and wantonly he tries out all the pleasures of the flesh. Then the excellent man having now become an apostate undertook all the orders of Cacus and spends the whole day eating and drinking and distends his white belly.
>
> fit turpis ut Ethnis
> Ganeo, rixator, mechus cultorque deorum
> Cunctaque lascive probat oblectamina carnis.
> Ergo vir egregius modo factus apostata, Caci
> Precepta aggressus totum deducit edendo
> Atque bibendo diem ventremque ingurgitat album. (*Eupolemius* 1.514–19)

The 'white belly' is again a phrase with a solid satiric pedigree, appearing in Persius (3.98) and Amarcius (1.375). As we will see in a moment, the vividly realized corporeality of the belly is an element in the vindictively grisly death assigned to one of Cacus's captains, Egon. This type of satire, imposing a ridiculous and disgusting excess of corporeality on the poem's villains, contrasts and sometimes interacts with the dramatizations of bodily satire, in which the satirical elements are voiced by the characters or focalized through their perceptions. These incidents are related to questions of generic propriety. They give the characters the chance to impose and refute accounts of the body that contest the appropriate socio-corporeal image for participants in epic. In the process, the poem recasts the issues at stake in terms that tilt epic norms towards a system of superimposed and subverted values in which the New Testament, rather than the *Aeneid*, is the governing subtext. Or, more riskily, the two systems of meaning coexist, like Hutcheon's duck/rabbit (Hutcheon 59), leaving a quandary of irony without a guaranteed triumph of correct meaning.

Ziolkowski has remarked on the prevalent class tensions in the *Eupolemius*: the armies of Cacus see themselves as knights and their opponents as brutish peasants (Ziolkowski, 'Eupolemius' 10–11). Cacus's warriors read this class identity into their opponents' corporeal self-presentation (clothing, accoutrements, hairstyle, gait) and even the intrinsic properties of their bodies:

> And he [Seon, one of Cacus's captains] when he saw such great bodies of leaders taking their death from Sother's hand and the streams of blood being poured out with impunity by a single man, exclaimed 'Best General, shall we all lose today our bright reputation along with our body? Will we turn our backs on Jebuseian half-men, to whom we were once objects of terror? A rustic swarm attacks our battle lines; look, you would see none among them born from knightly blood. Here they are unsheathing their swords, to whom it would be more becoming to guide the plough and the long mattocks while furrowing. Their necks are fit for buffets, they are shorn from the crown of the head, and they wear short garments that don't cover the knee; you would think that they were dancing like Satyrs.'

> Isque ubi Sotherea letum capiencia dextra
> Corpora tanta ducum rivosque cruoris ab uno
> Fusi inpune viro videt, 'Optime ductor, an omnes
> Claram perdemus hodie cum corpore famam?
> Tergane semiviris, fuimus quibus ante timori,'
> Exclamat 'dabimus Iebuseis? Rustica nostras
> Inpugnant acies examina; prospice, numquem

Inter eos videas ortum de sanguine equestri.
Hic evaginant gladios, quibus esset aratrum
Conveniens regere et longos sulcando ligones;
Apta gerunt colaphis a summo vertice rasi
Colla, breves etiam non tecto poplite vestes
Ut Satiros saltare putes.' (*Eupolemius* 2.105–17)

Ziolkowski rightly suggests, however, that the class placement of Agatus's army has more to do with the social universe of the New Testament and its parables than with any contemporary political commentary. I would add that the aristocratic standards that Cacus and his captains voice are specifically the military class standards of epic.

The battlefield taunt is another venerable epic tradition, and it often addresses the bodily self-presentation of its objects. It is true that the *Eupolemius* author's preoccupation with the markers of class and profession is somewhat atypical. If we take for comparison the taunts that Numanus addresses to the Trojans at *Aeneid* 9.598–620, during the assault on the camp, which, like the speech of Seon, reads the appearance of the enemy to signify their unworthiness as opponents, we find that the classical model is more interested in the norms of gender (intersecting with the cultural otherness of foreigners) than in the corporeal markers of class:

> You have clothing decorated with saffron and bright purple, leisure delights you, you enjoy indulging in dancing, your tunics have long sleeves and your headdresses have ribbons. O truly Trojan women (for you are not Trojan men), range through Dindymon's heights, where the double pipe plays to accustomed ears, and the cymbal and Berecynthian flute of the Idaean mother summon you; leave weapons to men and give up the sword.

vobis picta croco et fulgenti murice vestis,
desidiae cordi, iuvat indulgere choreis
et tunicae manicas et habent redimicula mitrae.
o vere Phrygiae, neque enim Phryges, ite per alta
Dindyma, ubi adsuetis biforem dat tibia cantum.
Tympana vos buxusque vocat Berecyntia Matris
Idaeae; sinite arma viris et cedite ferro. (*Aeneid* 9.614–20)

Numanus is typical of this kind of satirical portrait in that he reads the body through the signifiers of clothing and equipment that define its social presentation. The central attribution of gender (*Phrygiae, neque enim*

Phryges; their foreignness alone is enough to unman them somewhat, but they are in fact Phrygian *women*, not even Phrygian men) comes between the depiction of the Trojans' exotic and effeminate garb and their reassignment to the female (and also foreign) rites of Bacchus. The final adjuration, 'leave weapons to men and give way to iron' ['sinite arma viris et cedite ferro'], with its equation of masculinity with weaponry, is also a territorial marker for epic: by juxtaposing *arma* and *viris*, Numanus's speech takes us back to the first line of the *Aeneid* and manages to suggest that the Trojan hero might be disqualified from his own epic.

By contrast, the *Eupolemius*'s *semiviris* does not segue, as would seem natural, into issues of gender; instead, it leads to issues of class. By redrawing the line that divides the real warriors from the imposters and the real men from the half-men as a distinction between bodies that reflect the appropriate class and bodies that respect their appropriate gender, the author of the *Eupolemius* insists on the difficulties of his own use of form. Figures appear on stage not dressed for epic: their costumes are drawn from other spheres of activity (shepherding, medicine) that serve, in indigenously Christian literature, as analogues to the role of Christ's followers. The contrast is not really between an army of knights and an army of peasants, but between the party that has fully assumed the epic integument and the party that violates integumental decency by letting the concealed meaning show through. What looks like misconstrual by the characters turns out to be miscostuming, or subversively alternative costuming, on the part of the author.

This subversive miscostuming is potentially as disturbing to the reader as it is to the characters, for if members of Agatus's (God's) army break their epic cover by going into battle equipped for other roles, they prove capable of adapting the tools of their unmilitary trades to the service of epic violence. An elaborate single combat illustrates the degree to which the elements that resist assimilation to the epic cover-narrative can nonetheless collaborate with it. As in the case of the animal similes, this collaboration can be as much a contamination of the subversive elements by epic as a contamination of epic by subversive elements. In this encounter, Doxius, champion of orthodoxy, turns the insulting interpretation of his socially marked appearance imposed on him by his opponent to his own advantage, and in the end reduces his enemy from an arrogantly superior reader of bodies to a punctured, whistling paunch. Doxius's opponent, Egon, is speaking:

> 'Where are you rushing, poor wretch, you who have no lance, no wound-dealing sword? What great folly has seized your mind, that you carry into

battle a polished staff more suitable for a pilgrim?' He saw his enemy's staff and he thought his enemy was in want of a sword, but he was not in want of a sword, indeed he was carrying stored away in his staff a sword-stick (called a dolon because this very trick [*dolus*] gave it its name). And he added 'Your pale face shows that you are a medic; either an outlandish medicine chest creates it or it is clearly because as a blood-letter you draw blood from the sick by sucking – it's disgusting even to say it – like a clinging leech.' Then fierce-hearted Doxius said smiling 'His own skill marks or adorns each person; they say that it is proper for the one who doesn't have a horse to go on foot, and I, who lack a sword, carry a staff. But since I am a medic, as a blood-letter I will try with my lancet to pierce for you your veins, black with too much blood.' He spoke and buried his two-edged poniard up to the hilt in his enemy's belly and eviscerated his swollen limbs; the paunch hissed, the fatty innards hissed at the twisted blade with blood boiling up to meet it.

'Quo, miserande, ruis, cui non est lancea, non est
Vulnificus mucro? Que tanta socordia mentem
Cepit, ut ad pugnam peregrino rasile lignum
Apcius afferes?' Fustem videt hostis et hostem
Ense carere putat, qui non caret ense; dolonem
Quod donavit ei nomen dolus ipse, repostum
In baculo gestans. Atque addit 'Pallida monstrat
Te medicum facies, aut hec exotica pixis
Efficit aut certe quoniam sugendo minutor
Elicis egroti – dictu quoque turpe – cruorem
Sicut hirudo tenax.' Tunc pectore Doxius acri
Subridens 'Premit aut ornat sua quemque facultas;
Cui non est sonipes, aiunt, pede pergat opportet,
Et nos adtulimus baculum, quia defuit ensis.
Sed quia sum medicus, nimio tibi sanguine pullas
Flebothemo venas temptabo ferire minutor.'
Fatur et hostili capulo tenus apdit in alvo
Ancipitem sicam crassosque eviscerat artus;
Stridit aqualiculus, stridunt prepinguia sica
Viscera versata ferventi sanguine contra. (*Eupolemius* 2.213–32)

Egon's insult goes beyond the aristocrat's scorn for the professional physician. In the image of the blood-sucking leech he, like the deployers of epic predator similes, likens Doxius to an animal in order to contaminate him in an intimately corporeal way with an intrusion on the body, an intrustion that has been rhetorically stripped of the distancing mediation of technology. Doxius's reply by contrast is emphatically technological. He claims and employs the tools of his trade and reduces Egon to the gross, comic, and exaggerated corporeality of his hissing, fatty belly wound. Within this dialogue of body and equipment, Doxius poses the tricky paradox of identity that his equipment symbolizes, and the trickiness of which it etymologically signals: he is a pilgrim whose staff is a sword-stick, a surgeon whose lancet is a sword.

Like the image of Moses and Mercy as rampaging predators with blood-stained jaws, Doxius's savagely ironic appropriation of the persona of physician is an appropriation-by-hijacking of epic that is at once excessive and jarringly incomplete. If Egon, Doxius's opponent, uses the image of a physician as an insult implying not only unmilitary weakness and a low trade but also the revolting figure of the blood-sucking leech, Doxius claims the role in such a way as equally to strip it of any potentially benevolent connotations. Despite the unmilitary professional role reflected in his face and accoutrements, Doxius is still in the business of destroying, rather than preserving, bodies. This is not an allegory in which the violent soldier conceals the benevolent physician, but one in which the trickily undisguised physician turns out to be an efficient soldier. It remains to see how the author of the *Eupolemius* will integrate the salvific passivity of Messiah's sacrificial death into this world of epic destruction and epic exertion.

The Death of Messiah

The death of Messiah contains all the elements I have been discussing: it hinges on an animal simile, it features an insulting reading of the class identity of a body, and it employs and reverses standard epic technique, for Messiah's death is the culmination and surprise ending of an *aristeia*. But in order to get his hero onto the battlefield in the first place the *Eupolemius* poet must first find a way to incarnate the Incarnation within the epic terms of his narrative. Ziolkowski has remarked on certain startling aspects of the *Eupolemius*'s solution to this literary problem: the *Eupolemius* author, he observes, depicts the incarnation of Messiah as an act of cross-dressing (Ziolkowski, 'Eupolemius' 8). Without downplaying this aspect of the two brief accounts of the Incarnation – once as it is proposed by the prophetic counsellor Eleimon, once as it actually takes place – I would see a more complex manipulation of gender and epic in these brief vignettes. Here is Eleimon's proposal:

> 'There is in Bethlehem a poor woman of chaste reputation, Parthenie ... if Messiah covers his limbs with her clothing (and may there be no shame about

it) and if he rushes to death of his own free will, believe for a certainty that a triumph of no small distinction will be granted to his side.'

'Est Bethlem caste paupercula fame
Parthenie ...
... Cuius, nec sit pudor, artus
Messias si veste suos obduxerit inque
Mortem sponte ruit, pro certo credite, parti
Illius haut modico continget honore triumphus.'
(*Eupolemius* 2.581–2, 583–6)

'In her clothing,' however, can be read as 'clothing consisting of her' as well as 'clothing belonging to her.' Messiah is putting on not just Mary's outfit, but Mary herself. The borrowing of clothing is infused with, as well as acting as a metaphor for, the assumption of Mary's flesh in the Incarnation.

The narrative in which the Incarnation is actually carried out is even briefer and more interesting: 'Messiah having assumed the womanly covering, clothes himself and takes up the shield covered with a triple hide' ['Messias sumpto muliebri tecmine sese / Vestit et umbonem membrana triplice tectum / Sumit' (*Eupolemius* 2.598–600)]. *Tegmen* is used of armour and of shields, as well as clothing; what this passage does is conflate the Incarnation with the hero's arming. This sense of *tecmine* is confirmed when the poet moves on immediately to show Messiah taking up his shield. Seen in this light the covering associated with a woman is profoundly congruent, as well as strangely incongruous, with the norms of epic. If a warrior does not normally go to battle in drag, it is altogether proper for the hero to go forth arrayed in armour wonderfully provided by his mother.

Eleimon proposes the incarnation as a military strategy – Messiah's death is the prerequisite for their side's victory. In Eleimon's speech, however, the poet of the *Eupolemius* is simultaneously working out a poetic strategy, positioning Messiah's death halfway between atonement and epic. The choice of the Roman heroes Eleimon invokes as examples for Messiah underlines this:

'Weigh what Decius and Regulus did; both, not wishing to be stingy with their short life, of their own free will, so fame relates, underwent destruction to take away the death of their people.'

'Decius, perpende, quid egerit et quid
Regulus; ambo brevi nolentes parcere vite

Sponte sua, sic fama refert, pro clade suorum
Tollenda letum subiere.' (*Eupolemius* 2.588–91)

The first of these, Decius, performed a well-known *devotio*, sacrificing himself to bring victory to his side and a curse on his enemies, while Regulus was famous for martyr-like endurance rather than for heroic violence. Stretching without breaking the military cover of his narrative, Eleimon, and the poet through him, prepare the reader to accept and interpret the epic fate of being killed as sacrificial dying. In doing so he draws on Augustine, who featured both the Decii and Regulus in the long list of Romans whose behaviour might shame Christians into heroic endurance in *De Civitate Dei* 5.18. This is another of the *Eupolemius* author's disconcerting hermeneutic reversals, as exempla that are, in Augustine, entirely subordinate to the ruling exemplum of Christ are used as motivating examples *for* Christ. Christ, it seems, is being motivated to effect not only the reconciliation of Agatus and humankind but the bridging of some of the tricky faultlines between classical epic and Christian adaptation.

Messiah is attacked and killed by Judas, the personification of the Jewish people, who has decisively defected to the party of Cacus. The *Eupolemius* interprets this attack as insanity, as Judas turns on his kinsman and rescuer. Messiah, unwilling to fight him, holds back and pleads with Judas to recognize him: 'I am Messiah; I have come to free you from wars; you see my hands and my face' ['Messias ego sum, veni te solvere bellis; / Aspicis ora, manus' (*Eupolemius* 2.710–11)]. This encounter develops into the last and most significant of the scenes of the misreading of bodies in the *Eupolemius*. The misreading of Messiah that the author of the *Eupolemius* attributes to Judas repeats the familiar Christian charge that the Jews were culpably blind to Jesus's identity as Messiah. It is also the last and most original example in the poem of a body being read and rejected according to class standards explicitly based in the values of epic.

Here is how the *Eupolemius* has Judas answer Messiah's appeal:

'I do not know who you are, while fighting I wish to learn who you are. "I am the son of Agatus (God)" you say; you lie, surely Agatus is not your begetter, from the witness of your face you might be believed to be the son of a carpenter; you are the son of a carpenter. Whoever you are, you will find out that this day is your last.'

Cui Iudas ore minaci
'Nescio, tu qui sis, pugnans volo discere, qui sis.

"Agatides sum" inquis, mentiris; non tibi certe
Agatus est genitor, credi poetes indice vultu
Filius esse fabri, fabri es filius. Istam,
Quisquis es, esse tibi lucem experiere supremam.' (*Eupolemius* 2.710–16)

Several biblical passages lie behind this exchange between Messiah and Judas, notably the scenes in Matthew and Mark in which Jesus's audience rejects his claim to be the son of God because they already know who he is, the son of Joseph the carpenter (Matt. 13:55; Mark 6:3). Messiah's plea for recognition also suggests the encounter with doubting Thomas after the resurrection, when Jesus shows the unconvinced apostle his hands (John 20:27). Judas, however, claims no knowledge of Messiah's origins; he merely reads his social status from his appearance, like other characters in the poem, and proposes the thoroughly epic view that trial by combat is the appropriate proving ground of identity. In this decisive instance the author of the *Eupolemius* does not simply translate the norms of epic into their spiritual equivalent, peopling the battlefield with noble virtues and base vices. Instead he suggests that the radically different transaction of salvation leaves Judas's epic standards of judgment at a loss.

Messiah at first flees from Judas, wishing to spare him the crime of killing a kinsman, but at the walls of Jerusalem he remembers Eleimon's prophecy that he will win victory by a voluntary death. He turns to face his opponent, refusing to defend himself with his weapons, and he receives from Judas's spear the emblematic five wounds of the passion. Messiah wins as allegorical warrior by playing the part of symbolic victim. Here the author of the *Eupolemius* deploys his last animal simile: 'a guileless lamb is not more silent when it is carried to the holy altar to be sacrificed for the sin of the people' ['Simplex, cum geritur sacram mactandus ad aram / Pro populi noxa, non est taciturnior agnus' (*Eupolemius* 2.728–9)]. This biblical imagery, adapted from the suffering servant passages in Isaiah (Isaiah 53:7), here decisively displaces the thoroughly epic and sometimes incongruous animal similes for human violence that I discussed above. Messiah's death, interpreted in this image, puts a sacrificial body in place of a heroic one; in so doing Messiah solves the literary dilemma of finding a congruous place for the body in the poem as well as the tactical problem of how to achieve human salvation. Ratkowitsch is surely right to read this passage as pivotal to the question of the poem's identity (Ratkowitsch 235). It is an identity that hinges on the role of the body.

The difficulty of categorizing the *Eupolemius* suggests a poem that is more experiment than synthesis. The representation of the body in this hybrid epic has featured some startling juxtapositions. The reader may well ask whether the whole poem is a collection of imperfectly assimilated parts that add up to no coherent whole. Is the *Eupolemius*'s strangeness a symptom of artistic failure? I will not attempt to argue that some unifying harmony underlies the *Eupolemius*'s flaunting of its own piecemeal nature. However, if we consider the *Eupolemius* as consciously experimental (an experiment conducted, perhaps, by a mad scientist), and if the success of an experimental literary work lies in an intelligent representation of the process of testing rather than the harmonious and invisible integration of elements, the *Eupolemius* can ultimately be classed as a success. Or, to return to the Bakhtinian terms I invoked near the beginning of this study, if we consider that the true protagonists of the poem are not so much the named figures who oscillate so disconcertingly between values and levels of meaning but rather the poem's multiple languages, the sacrificial death of Messiah allows both languages to survive in a moment of integrated meaning.

If an analysis of the function, or rather the functions, of the body in the *Eupolemius* has been of some value in clarifying the poem's nature and achievement, it remains to be asked whether so atypical an example has indeed contributed to our modellings of cultural constructions of the body in the Middle Ages. The solution the *Eupolemius* poet developed for the inherent tensions of working with competing literary and cultural modes for representing the body was, as I have suggested, experimental, *sui generis*. But the visible joins in the *Eupolemius* are a reminder of processes of assimilation that go on in some form in every work of literature. No theoretically informed reading of the representation of the body in literature is so naive as to ignore the elaborate interweaving of competing, polysynchronous systems of literary convention and cultural construction. We do not look to the *Eupolemius* to hold up a mirror to the late eleventh-century body, the body in salvation history, the body in allegorical-biblical epic, or any other such reified entity. What is both exciting and disconcerting about the *Eupolemius* is that it seems to anticipate and explicitly repel such demands. For the critical reading of the body in medieval literature the *Eupolemius* is a workshop and a workout as well as a fascinating object of study.

NOTES

1 All translations from Latin are my own unless otherwise noted.

2 It is not impossible that the *Eupolemius* author was Sextus Amarcius; see

Manitius 10–11. Ratkowitsch, however, treats them as separate writers and argues convincingly for the priority of Amarcius (Ratkowitsch 262–71).

WORKS CITED

Bakhtin, Mikhail. *The Dialogic Imagination: Four Essays*. Ed. Michael Holquist. Trans. Carlyn Emerson and Michael Holquist. Austin: University of Texas Press, 1981.

Gärtner, Thomas. 'Zu den dichterischen Quellen und zum Text der allegorischen Bibeldichtung des Eupolemius.' *Deutsches Archiv für Erforschung des Mittelalters* 58 (2002): 549–62.

Hardie, Philip, ed. *Aeneid Book IX*. Cambridge: Cambridge University Press, 1994.

Hermann, John P. *Allegories of War: Language and Violence in Old English Poetry*. Ann Arbor: University of Michigan Press, 1989.

Hutcheon, Linda. *Irony's Edge: The Theory and Politics of Irony*. London and New York: Routledge, 1994.

Manitius, Karl, ed. *Sextus Amarcius: Sermones. Monumenta Germaniae Historica Quellen zur Geistesgeschicte des Mittelalters* 6. Weimar: Hermann Böhlaus, 1969.

– *Eupolemius: Das Bibelgedicht. Monumenta Germaniae Historica Quellen zur Geistesgeschicte des Mittelalters* 9. Weimar: Hermann Böhlaus, 1973.

Putnam, Michael C.J. *The Poetry of the Aeneid*. Cambridge, MA: Harvard University Press, 1965.

Ratkowitsch, Christine. 'Der Eupolemius: Ein Epos dem Jahre 1069?' *Filologia mediolatina: Revista della Fondazione Ezio Franceschini* 7 (2000): 215–71.

Wofford, Susanne. *The Choice of Achilles: The Ideology of Figure in the Epic*. Stanford, CA: Stanford University Press, 1992.

Ziolkowski, Jan. 'Eupolemiana.' *Mittellateinisches Jahrbuch* 26 (1992): 117–32.

– 'Eupolemius' (trans. with intro.). *Journal of Medieval Latin* 1 (1991): 1–45.

5 Losing Face: Heroic Discourse and Inscription in Flesh in *Scéla Mucce Meic Dathó*[1]

SARAH SHEEHAN

Early Irish sagas are celebrated for their terse narrative style, concreteness of imagery, and forthright portrayal of bodily realities. *Scéla Mucce Meic Dathó* ('The Story of Mac Dathó's Pig'), one of the best-loved Irish sagas,[2] typifies these qualities. This short tale occupies just over four columns in the earliest manuscript, the twelfth-century Book of Leinster. The dating of the text is uncertain: because the text is in Old Irish[3] with some later forms, its most recent editor posits a tenth- or eleventh-century common source for the surviving manuscripts (Thurneysen, *Scéla Mucce* iv), but other scholars would date the text a century or two earlier. *Scéla Mucce*'s humorous approach to saga heroes has led critics to read it as either a parody or a satire;[4] yet the ongoing categorization debate has deflected attention from the text's complex representation of the heroes' behaviour. The saga's central feast scene features a heroic contest whose black humour relies on mutilation and violence. The heroes who dominate signify their dominance in resolutely corporeal terms,[5] using mutilated male bodies to affirm their position at the top of the warrior hierarchy. The warriors Cet mac Mágach and Conall Cernach successively establish their pre-eminence by presenting themselves as the inscribers of other men's flesh, whether that flesh belongs to the opponent himself or to the opponent's male kin. *Scéla Mucce* thus represents warriors gaining honour and producing shame by manipulating a semiotics of the body. In defining degrees of honour and heroic entitlement according to bodily integrity, the contest sequence constructs a masculine hierarchy that links honour directly to the (male) body; in the saga's heroic discourse, warrior honour is specifically grounded in the materiality of the body and is consequently as vulnerable as the body itself.

Like other early medieval societies, early Irish society considered honour and shame to be important components of identity. As anthropological studies of honour and shame demonstrate, the identity secured by honour (and eroded by dishonour) is a *masculine* identity; patriarchal cultures are especially likely to emphasize honour as a crucial attribute for any self-respecting man, while also requiring that it be constantly maintained and defended against (male) competitors (see Peristiany and Gilmore). In the honour-based culture of medieval Iceland, for example, honour defined a man's identity in relation to his peer group; Icelandic honour thus functioned to create fluid, often provisional social hierarchies among men of equal status, who worked to maintain their honour at their peers' expense (see Miller, *Bloodtaking* 26–34, and *Humiliation* 93–130). Honour, then, is deeply implicated in masculinity and thus in a culture's gender system.

Like the medieval Icelanders, *Scéla Mucce*'s warriors also create hierarchies in which masculinity figures prominently – indeed, in one instance a warrior shames his opponent by impugning his literal manhood. It is worth noting that *Scéla Mucce* arguably thematizes gender relations in the broader narrative that frames the contest sequence in ways that implicate gender in the tale's conception of honour and insult. The hosteller Mac Dathó devises his plan to host his feast as the result of his wife's advice; the text highlights the conjugal conversation by presenting it in the form of a verse dialogue in which the hosteller repeats a misogynist proverb that he attributes to a male authority, Cremthann Nia Náir (Poppe 4–9). Although Mac Dathó's proverb warns against confiding in women, the narrative effectively contradicts the proverb when the wife's advice enables the hosteller to resolve his dilemma and so preserve his honour. In the tale's closing episode, a charioteer comically obtains his demand for female adulation as the result of threatening the Ulster king in a feminizing posture (Dooley 189–90).[6] The text thus frames its account of the feast with confrontations characterized by an ambivalent stance towards male authority figures (Cremthann Nia Náir and the king of Ulster). *Scéla Mucce*'s central sequence, however, is strictly male homosocial; the heroes' performance of masculinity takes place before an exclusively male audience. The palpable irony in the saga's descriptions of boasting, brawling warriors also works to destabilize heroic masculinity in the text,[7] and further complicates our reading of the shame and mutilation to which the competing men are subject.

Studies of honour and shame in early Irish literature emphasize their reliance on publicity and tangible evidence: honour and shame are attained through public acts such as praise and insult (Charles-Edwards, 'Honour and Status' 123; O'Leary 115). The Old Irish words for honour and shame demonstrate the exteriority – and perhaps even the corporeal basis – of these concepts. The word for honour, *enech*, has the primary meaning 'face,' and although the noun *tár* serves to convey the abstract meaning of 'insult, disgrace, shame,' two further terms denoting a physical blemish, *ainim* and *on*, also convey the figurative sense of 'blot, disgrace' (DIL s.vv. 'enech,' 'tár,' 'ainim,' 'on').[8] In a society where an individual's identity depends on their remaining honourable, 'the devastating consequences of public shame are clear: as shame deprives high status of practical value so does it humiliate a man's whole social personality: he ceases to be the person he was' (Charles-Edwards, 'Honour and Status' 130).[9] To shame another was to strike a powerful blow indeed, depriving the shamed person of their previous identity. In many ways, *Scéla Mucce*'s contests dramatize the exteriority of honour and shame in early Irish culture: as Philip O'Leary notes, honour in this saga is 'a purely external honour based on public display and inextricably linked with the dishonouring of the defeated foe' (119). The shaming public display described in *Scéla Mucce* is unambiguously linked to the body: in the majority of the contests, dishonouring or shaming involves the public declaration of deficient bodily integrity.

Honour and the public perception of bodily integrity are also linked in a variety of non-literary texts including law tracts, penitentials, and an early Patrician document. Two early Irish legal texts, *Bretha Déin Chécht* ('Judgements of Dían Cécht') and *Bretha Crólige* ('Judgements on Blood-Lyings'), provide the only clear surviving evidence of medical learning in early medieval Ireland (see Binchy, 'Bretha Déin Chécht' 5, and 'Sick-Maintenance'). Both texts are concerned with compensation due for unlawful bodily harm and discuss the classification of injuries (cf. Davies 47); although they are preserved in a single fifteenth-century medical manuscript, both are in Old Irish and may thus be considered roughly contemporary with *Scéla Mucce*.[10] *Bretha Déin Chécht*, which codifies the physician's portion of the fine for injury, contains detailed information on the classification of wounds, specifying higher fines for disfiguration and visible wounds (§24).

As Binchy notes, a third, fragmentary legal text corroborates *Bretha Déin Chécht*'s emphasis on the visibility of wounds when it states that a bloodless injury is compensated 'if the disfigurement [can] be seen' ['dia naicestar aisc' (Binchy, 'Bretha Déin Chécht' 14)].[11] The noun *aisc* has the primary meaning of 'disgrace'; DIL cites only the passage from the fragmentary legal text for the sense 'blemish, disfigurement' (s.v. 'aisc'). *Bretha Déin Chécht*'s references to shame, blushing, and the public context of assemblies indicate a concern to compensate the dishonour incurred through the public witnessing of disfigurement. When the text states that the penalty for larger wounds increases according to 'the fear of death, the gravity of the sickness, and the extent of the blemish' ['omna bais 7 trumai galuir 7 mete anme' (§10)], the ambiguity of *ainim* causes *mete anme* to convey a hint of the meaning 'extent of the disgrace.' Shame (*tár*) is associated with a 'conspicuous' injury when the text stipulates a heavy fine for causing 'shame on the countenance [by] raising a conspicuous lump' ['tar nenech ard gnodad' (§26)]. The text also levies fines for publicizing a person's disfigurement: fines are specified for 'every mouth that publishes it [the blemish] in the presence of an assembly' ['cach mbel nodifoclatar fib firdal'] as well as for 'every assembly ... [and] for every advertisement for which [his] cheek blushes' ['cech aonuig ... cach aidbriuda ima ruide rus' (§31; see Binchy, 'Bretha Déin Chécht' 18)].[12] *Bretha Crólige*, which codifies laws related to the institution of *othrus*, 'sick-maintenance,'[13] states that a permanently injured person is entitled to 'fines for blemish and loss [of limb]' ['fiachu huin 7 esbuide' (§41; see Binchy, 'Sick-Maintenance' 95)] and lists one way of classifying wounds as 'according to blemish' ['fo on' (§63)]. Operating in both texts is a clear legal principle: when visible or publicized, disfigurement provokes shame, and reparation must be made for this damage to honour. Further, as Binchy notes ('Sick-Maintenance' 106n2), the boy Cú Chulainn refers to *othrus* in the version of the *Táin Bó Cúailnge* ('Cattle-Raid of Cooley') found in the Book of Leinster,[14] separated by a few folios from *Scéla Mucce*. That a literary text can refer to *othrus* through the voice of a precocious boy-hero suggests these legal concepts had a broader currency during the period of *Scéla Mucce*'s earliest manuscript witness.[15]

Other early Irish sources show a similar concern with blemishes and bodily integrity. Ecclesiastical texts in both Latin and the vernacular show a concern that bishops be free of physical blemish. A vernacular document in the Book of Armagh describes Patrick requesting a candidate for episcopacy who, among other things, is 'without defect, without blemish' ['cen on, cen anim' (Bieler, *Patrician Texts* 176; trans. Bieler)].[16] A Latin penitential text fixes fines for spilling the blood of a bishop and 'for the embarrassment of his bruise or wound in a meeting or in any crowd to the third year or longer' ['pro eius liuoris uel uulneris admiratione in conuentu uel in qualibet multitudine usque ad tertium annum aut eo amplius' (Bieler, *Irish Penitentials* 170; trans. Bieler; see discussion in Ó Corráin,

'Irish Law' 164–6)].[17] Further, as many scholars have noted, bodily integrity is viewed in a broad range of contexts as a requirement for the ideal king. In the legal text *Bechbretha* ('Bee-Judgements'), a king who is blinded in one eye loses his kingship; in the saga *Echtra Fergusa maic Leiti* ('The Adventures of Fergus mac Leti'), however, King Fergus mac Leti continues to reign after suffering a facial blemish, but must keep out of public view (Jaski 82–8; and Eichhorn-Mulligan, 'Politics of Anatomy' 5). Both the early Irish Church and secular society, then, appear to have shared a view of honour as vulnerable. The frequent emphasis on the public visibility of bodily integrity, rather than bodily integrity in itself, suggests the fear that a defective body will face shaming public exposure – a vulnerability inappropriate for men in positions of public authority.

Scéla Mucce reflects cultural views of honour and bodily integrity while also portraying literary, discursive uses of their negative aspects – shame and mutilation – in its representation of heroic action. To summarize the saga up to its central feast scene: Mac Dathó, the king of Leinster (or, in some versions, its chief hosteller),[18] has promised his famous hound to both Ulster and Connacht, and the rulers of both provinces have arrived at his hostel with large retinues to claim the animal. Mac Dathó avoids mentioning the hound and instead ushers everyone in to the feast he has prepared for his guests, a feast whose pièce de résistance is a huge, magnificent pig with forty oxen lain across it. The two hosts regard each other darkly from either side of the hostel, for the Ulaid and Connachta are enemies who have been at war, as the text reminds us, for three centuries before the birth of Christ (§5.10–11).[19] The pig is served; Ailill, king of Connacht, asks Conchobar, king of Ulster, how they should divide it; and the Ulster warrior Bricriu jumps in with a typically mischievous question: how else but 'by contests' ['ar chomramaib' (§6.9)], since previously everyone present had given everyone else 'a punch in the nose' ['builli dar sróin' (§6.10)]. The assembled heroes exchange boasts and insults until finally a warrior of the Connachta, Cet mac Mágach,[20] dominates and sits down to carve the pig.

Instead of carving the pig right away, Cet invites the other warriors to challenge him for the privilege, and so begins the contest sequence proper. Seven Ulstermen step forward to challenge Cet. The text's description of each 'contest' follows the same basic pattern: the challenger makes a statement disputing Cet's right to carve the pig; the challenger is identified by name; Cet tells a story with humiliating implications for the challenger; and the challenger responds by simply taking his seat. Cet does most of the talking in these verbal contests.[21] Cet does not specify what wound he dealt his first challenger, Lóegaire – who is traditionally (and for the tale's contemporary audience, ironically) known as Lóegaire Búadach, 'the Victorious' (see, e.g., *Táin Bó Cúailnge* [hereater cited as TBC] I 3366–7 and TBC II 4386) – telling Lóegaire only that he escaped their encounter with 'a spear through you' ['gaí triut' (§9.8)]. The tales Cet tells concerning the remaining six challengers, however, all centre on an act of mutilation, giving explicit accounts of wounds and lost body parts (cf. Sayers 40, 42). Each warrior's silence and immediate retreat in response to Cet's story indicate that the meaning conveyed to them by Cet's corporeal signs is unambiguous and beyond dispute. The text does not refer to abstract concepts such as honour or shame until the end of the contest sequence, when it states, 'In this way he brought *shame* on the whole province' ['Do·rat *tár* fon n-indas-sin forsin cóiced n-uile' (§14.9–10)]. With the exception of this statement, it is not narrative commentary but mutilated bodies that convey the sense of Cet's, and later Conall's, right to dominate.

In view of *Scéla Mucce*'s insistent use of corporeal signification, the concept of inscription in flesh is useful in examining the discursive role of mutilation in the saga's contest sequence. Inscription in flesh refers to the violent marking of bodies through acts such as tattooing, scarification, and mutilation that form the basis for what Gilles Deleuze and Félix Guattari term the territorial order of inscription (*Anti-Oedipus* 144, 203).[22] In this mode of representation (which may be understood as the tribal mode), the subject construes meaning by extracting it from painfully marked bodies (Deleuze and Guattari, *Anti-Oedipus* 211): because signification results from violence, interpretation entails reading the signs of violence. Thus inscription in flesh refers to violence that creates meaningful bodies or body parts, 'literal signs' in one critic's helpful reformulation (Overing 89). The corporeal signs that injured bodies represent, however, have no inherent meaning, and *Scéla Mucce* bears this out when it makes its contest of honour hinge on interpretive performance. A mutilated warrior is not disqualified from the contest until his mutilation is publicly proclaimed, 'read' by his opponent. We can also consider the saga's emphasis on interpretation, on reading wounds, in light of Elaine Scarry's analysis of the function of wounded bodies in the discourse of war. As Scarry argues, martial discourse exploits injured bodies' 'compelling reality' in order 'to lend the aura of material reality to the winning construct' (20, 21); injuring produces powerful 'abiding signs' that are nevertheless ambiguous and thus open to interpretation (115). In *Scéla Mucce*, inscribed bodies, or corporeal signs, are the primary means by which heroic discourse operates. While Cet mac Mágach shames his six remaining challengers through boasts centred on corporeal signs, Conall Cernach displaces Cet by pairing a more ambitious boast with a corporeal sign that is physically present. For the purposes of discussion the key passages from these contests will be grouped according to type of mutilation, progressing from wounds to lost body parts.

According to Cet's boasts, the bodies of his sixth and seventh challengers bear debilitating wounds that Cet himself inflicted by piercing them with his spear. Cet tells his sixth challenger, Celtchair mac Uithechair, how on one occasion, when he had invaded the old warrior's territory and Celtchair had thrown a spear at him, he threw his own spear at Celtchair and injured him in the groin:

> I threw another spear at you so that it went through your thigh and through the upper part of your testicles. You have had a *galar fhúail* [lit. sickness of urine[23]] since that time, and neither son nor daughter has been born to you. What could bring you to me?

> Ro·lécus-sa gaí n-aill cucut-su co·ndechaid tret shlíasait ocus tre húachtar do macraille. Ataí co ngalur fhúail ónd úair-sin, nicon·rucad mac na ingen duit. Cid dot·bérad cucum-sa? (§13.7–10)

Cet gives this account of Celtchair's wounding and its consequences in merciless detail. According to Cet, Celtchair's body bears lasting evidence of their encounter in the disability Celtchair suffers; the absence of further children proclaims his emasculation to the community at large. Cet thus claims responsibility for Celtchair's infertility and infirmity. *Bretha Déin Chécht* groups wounds causing Celtchair's ailment, *galar fhúail*, with nineteen other injuries for which physicians were the most highly compensated; these injuries were potentially mortal.[24] The legal text equates *galar fhúail* with haemorrhage, stipulating the highest leech-payment for '[a wound that causes either] a haemorrhage from the belly over the lips with constant vomiting of blood and passing (?) of blood or *galar fhúail*, for the latter is reckoned as blood' ['toidecht fola a bru for beolu combithochur fola. combi fuil dobeir no galar fuail – is meass fola teite for sodain' (§17; trans. adapted from Binchy's)]. The evidence of *Bretha Déin Chécht* suggests that *galar fhúail* was understood as a form of haemorrhage (but cf. Binchy, 'Bretha Déin Chécht' 57).[25] However, near the end of the Book of Leinster *Táin*, *fúal* is used to refer to menstruation when Medb is described as getting 'her *fúal* of blood' ['a fúail fola' (TBC II 4825; see discussion and references in Dooley 175–81)]. The ambiguity of *fúal* suggests that the *galar fhúail* Cet attributes to Celtchair could refer not to urinary disease but rather to a reproductive disorder. Its precise nature aside, the disability Cet claims to have caused in Celtchair compounds the emasculation effected by Cet's injury to Celtchair's reproductive organs. Cet's sardonic closing question – what could bring you to *me*? – encourages us to read his story as an attack on Celtchair's masculinity, with the old warrior's body bearing the proof of his now-deficient manhood. At the same time, Cet effectively (and publicly) implies a flattering comparison with his own masculinity through the sign of Celtchair's wounded thigh and genitals.

Cet's seventh challenger is a son of Conchobar, the king of Ulster. When the assembly identifies Cúscraid Mend Macha mac Conchobair to Cet, they also add that his physical appearance makes him an appropriate candidate for kingship, saying, 'he is fit to be king on account of his appearance' ['is adbar ríg ar deilb' (§14.3)]. The phrase *adbar ríg* (lit. material of a king) occurs in technical contexts to denote eligibility for kingship (Charles-Edwards, *Early Irish and Welsh Kinship* 106–8; and Jaski 236–47). Cet responds by telling the young man how he met him when he was out on his first foray to the border:

> I acted thus: a spear through your throat so that you do not get a word out of your head properly; for the spear wounded the sinews of your throat. And you have been called Cúscraid Mend ['the Stammering'] since that time.
>
> is samlaid do·cúadaiss ocus gaí tríat brágit conna·étai focul fort chenn i córai; ar ro·loitt in gaí féthi do brágat. Conid Cúscraid Mend atot·chomnaic ónd úair-sin. (§14.6–9)

Cet thus claims responsibility for Cúscraid's nickname Mend, 'stammering, inarticulate' (DIL s.v. 'menn'). As he did with Celtchair, Cet again gives the precise details and consequences of his spear wound: the pierced sinews of Cúscraid's throat (*brágit*) – his damaged vocal chords – render him unable to control his speech. As a result, Cúscraid also acquires a humiliating epithet that identifies him as the victim of this injury. As Charles-Edwards observes, Cúscraid's neck would also bear a visible blemish (*Early Irish and Welsh Kinship* 107), publicly testifying to his ineligibility for kingship. Cet signals the young man's loss of vocal control and ability to wield royal power through the sign of Cúscraid's wounded throat.

In these last two contests Cet speaks of wounds, shaming his challengers by publicizing their 'blemish' before the hosts of Ulster and Connacht.

In the first four contests, Cet's boasts involve the violent removal of parts of the body. The mutilated body in question, however, is not necessarily the challenger's. More often, Cet claims to have mutilated men connected to the challenger by bonds of loyalty or kinship; in only one instance does he boast of mutilating the challenger himself. Cet tells his third challenger, Éogan mac Durthacht, king of Fernmag, how he disfigured him by depriving him of an eye. Cet describes how he invaded Éogan's territory on a cattle raid; Éogan threw a spear at Cet, but it lodged in his shield; and, as Cet says to Éogan, 'I threw the same spear at you so that it went through your head and took your eye out of your head. The men of Ireland see you with one eye. I myself gouged the other eye out of your head' ['Do·llécimse duit-siu in ngaí cétna co·lluid tret chenn ocus co·mbert do shúil as do chiunn. Atot·chiat fir Hérenn co n-oínshúil. Messe thall in súil n-aili as do chinn' (§11.8–11)]. Cet's mockery is reinforced in the text by repetition of forms of the verb *ad·cí*, 'to see,' (with Éogan as the grammatical object) in the preceding dialogue (cf. Martin, 89): when Éogan steps forward to challenge him, Cet says he has *seen* Éogan before ['At·chondarc-sa riam'], and Éogan asks, 'Where have you *seen* me?' ['Cairm indom·acca?' (§11.4–5)], thus prompting Cet to relate the tale of their encounter. With its pointed reference to the watching men of Ireland, Cet's boast exploits the greater shame of a visible disfigurement in medieval Irish society. The emphasis on the visibility of Éogan's mutilation can also be read in Deleuze and Guattari's terms: interpretation in tribal discourse privileges the visibility of the marked body, with the eye 'extracting' meaning from an inscribed body by measuring the visible evidence of pain (*Anti-Oedipus* 204). Every man in Ireland can read the meaning of Éogan's disfigured face. It is also interesting to note that Cet refers not to Éogan's lost sense of sight, but to the loss and absence of an organ, to that organ's removal. The opposition Cet sets up between the 'one eye' ['oínshúil'] visible to the men of Ireland and 'the other eye' ['in súil n-aili'] that he himself has taken emphasizes the virtual transfer of the eye from Éogan to Cet, pairing inscription with accumulation, as though the balance of organs was tipped towards Cet – lack versus surplus.[26] As the contest continues, one almost imagines Cet assembling a grotesque collection of human trophies as he stakes his claim to honour.

Cet's exchange with his fourth challenger, Muinremor mac Gerginn, appears to feature an instance of the infamous Celtic practice of headhunting. When Muinremor challenges Cet's right to carve the pig, Cet boasts of a triple inscription of the bodies of Muinremor's dependants in Muinremor's own territory: 'I'm the one who has just cleaned my spears,

Muinremor ... It is not three days since I took three warrior-heads from you including the head of your first son – from your land' ['Is mé ro·glan mo goo fodéoid, a Muinremuir[27]... Ni·fuilet trí thráth and ó thucus-sa trí laíchcenn úait im chenn do chétmeic ast fherunn' (§12.3–5)]. Wordplay on Muinremor's name may have prompted the text to associate him with the head and thus with decapitation: the name Muinremor mac Gerginn translates as 'Thick-neck son of Short-head.'[28] As he did with Éogan's eye, Cet again phrases his mutilation in terms of removal, as though his raid had been on the men's bodies. Further, Cet accentuates the warriors' connection with Muinremor to such an extent that their heads are regarded as belonging to Muinremor: Cet says he took these heads away from Muinremor himself. Even here, after hearing this proclamation of homicide, Cet's challenger does not swear vengeance. Muinremor simply responds to the inscribed bodies in Cet's boast as the other warriors do – by sitting down, tacitly assenting to Cet's dominance.

Cet boasts to Muinremor of having decapitated Muinremor's son; in Cet's exchanges with his second and fifth challengers, he boasts of having mutilated the challengers' fathers. Interestingly, these two contests feature the most complex wordplay. When each of these two challengers is identified by name, Cet self-consciously interprets his challenger's patronymic as encoding the father's mutilation. Cet thus reads each name as pointing to a corporeal sign indicating the shame of the challenger's father. Cet's second challenger is called Óengus mac Láme Gábaid. Why is Óengus's father called Lám Gábaid? Cet asks, paving the way for a boast. *I* know ['Ro·fetar-sa' (§10.5)], he says, and he describes how he met with Óengus' father during a border raid:

> Everyone came. Then Lám came. He cast a great spear at me. I threw the same spear at him so that it took his hand [*a láim*] off him, and it was on the ground. What could bring his son to a contest against me?
>
> Do·roich cách. Do·roich dano Lám. Tárlaic urchor do gaí mór form-sa. Dos·léicim-se dó in ngaí cétna co·mbert a láim de, co·mboí for lár. Cid do·bérad a mac do chomram frim-sa? (§10.6–10)

Elsewhere in the literary tradition Óengus's patronymic is 'mac Óenláma' 'son of One-hand';[29] the text's use of the name 'Lám' rather than 'Óenlám' facilitates Cet's mockery of Óengus's father by deferring the revelation of Lám's eventual one-handedness. In Cet's boast, the hapless father starts out as 'Hand,' only to have his hand removed by his own spear. Cet leaves it to the audience to construe Lám's loss of his hand as the reason for his current name, Lám Gábaid. Cet's reading of the second element of this name seems to play on the noun *gábait*, meaning 'a piece or section, a division of the body,' generally a piece made by violent division (see DIL s.v. 'gábait'), so that Lám Gábaid conveys a meaning like 'Mutilated Hand,' a hand that has become a separate piece.[30] The father's new name becomes Óengus's patronymic and thus marks Óengus himself as deficient, even though it is not his own body but rather his father's that Cet claims to have mutilated. Cet's boast makes a shameful mutilation – the father's chopped-off hand – part of Óengus's identity through his father's name.

Cet's fifth challenger is called Mend mac Sálchada.[31] When the crowd identifies Mend, Cet mocks his name and parentage, asking whether he must now compete with 'the sons of herdsmen with nicknames' ['meic na mbachlach cusna lesanmannaib' (§12.8)]. Like Conchobor's son Cúscraid, this challenger has the name Mend ('Stammerer'); after briefly drawing attention to Mend's name, obliquely drawing attention to its meaning, Cet shifts his attention to the father's name. Cet appears to read the name of Mend's father, Sálchad, as an indication of labourer status through play on the verb *salchaid*, 'to soil, dirty, defile' (DIL s.v. 'salchaid').[32] After this initial mockery, Cet claims responsibility for Mend's father's name:

> For it was I who was the priest who baptized his father with that name: I hacked off his heel with a sword so that he went away from me with only one foot. What could bring the son of the one-footed man to me?

> Ar ba mese ba sacart oc baistiud ind anma-sin fora athair, messe thall a sháil de co claidiub conna·ruc acht oínchois úaim. Cid do·bérad mac ind oínchoisseda cucumsa? (§12.9–12)

Cet abandons his reading of Sálchad as 'dirty' and substitutes a new interpretation of the name capitalizing on its first element, *sál* 'heel': Cet himself cut off Sálchad's heel, mutilating his foot, to the extent that (as Cet claims with some stretching of his own meaning) he left the encounter with a single foot. In this parsing of Sálchad, Cet construes the name as a compound of *sál* + *cath* 'battle, fight' (see Uhlich 191): 'Heel-Fight.' The variant form of Mend's father's name, Sálcholgan, allows similar punning on 'heel' by combining *sál* with *colg*, a noun whose primary meanings 'point; sword' become extended to 'stab, thrust; act of piercing, stabbing' (DIL s.v. 'colg').[33] As he did with Óengus, Cet ends the contest by referring to his opponent as the son of a mutilated father, calling Mend 'the son of the one-footed man' ['mac ind oínchoisseda']. Even the sons of such men, Cet implies, must suffer the humiliating consequences of their fathers' wounds. Most importantly, in his startling formulation of mutilation as baptism, with himself as the priest, Cet explicitly links his inscription in flesh with naming and thus with the identity of the mutilated subject. By designating himself as 'baptizing priest' ['sacart oc baistiud'], Cet frames his power to wound and mutilate as the power to alter identity through shame.

To maintain his precedence, Cet consistently enlists corporeal signs in speech: a pierced throat and groin, a severed hand, an eye, a heel, three severed heads. He claims for himself the honourable, inscribing role when he boasts of his mutilations, and thus designates his opponents as inscribed, dishonoured. Conall Cernach, the Ulster warrior who finally displaces Cet, also refers to corporeal signs in speech, but he wins the right to carve the pig by surpassing Cet's purely verbal performance. Conall Cernach is a late arrival at Mac Dathó's feast, making an outrageously dramatic entrance by leaping into the hostel. In the contest between Cet and Conall Cernach, Conall swears that since he took up arms, he has slain Connachtmen every day and pillaged every night, and he has never slept 'without a Connachtman's head under my knee' ['cen chenn Connachtaig fom glúin' (§16.7)]. This boast prompts Cet to admit defeat, but Conall uses yet another corporeal sign to clinch his victory:

> 'It's true,' said Cet, 'you are a better warrior than I. If Ánlúan were in the hall, he would give you one contest after another. It is a shame[34] for us that he is not in the hall.' 'But he is,' said Conall, taking Ánlúan's head out of his girdle; and he threw it at Cet, at his abdomen, so that a [lit. his] mouthful of blood burst forth over his lips. He [Cet] got up from the pig, and Conall sat down by it.

> 'Is fír' ol Cet, 'at ferr do láech indó-sa. Mad Ánlúan no·beth is'taig, do·bérad comram ar araile duit. Is anim dún nad·fil is'taig.' 'Atá immurgu' ol Conall, oc tabairt chinn Ánlúain assa chriss; ocus do·léici do Chet dara bruinni co·rróemid a loim fola fora béolu. Ro·gab side immurgu ón muic, ocus dessid Conall acci. (§16.8–13)

Although Conall Cernach's statement concerning severed heads wins him Cet's concession, it is his revelation of Ánlúan's severed head that causes Cet to leave the pig. Cet does not give Ánlúan a patronymic, but he is elsewhere called Ánlúan mac Mágach (see TBC I 4–5; TBC II 151–3): tradition considers him to be Cet's brother,[35] connecting the sign of Ánlúan's head with the signs involving fathers and sons in Cet's boasts. As Cet's brother, Ánlúan is a Connachtman; his severed head thus instantiates Conall's boast of collecting heads from the Connachta. No one challenges Conall Cernach; his display of this corporeal sign ends the contests. In revealing Ánlúan's head Conall Cernach 'display[s] the ultimate public confirmation of his own pre-eminence' (O'Leary 118). Conall produces a corporeal sign, visible to all, and it is this that trumps Cet's retrospective discourse of mutilated men's bodies. While the wounds borne by Cet's challengers or their kin must be interpreted and publicized before they can confer honour and shame – in itself '[t]he wound is empty of reference' (Scarry 118) – the severed head's significance is self-evident in its unmediated materiality. Compounding this is the fact that, when Conall strikes Cet in the abdomen with Ánlúan's head, he causes blood to issue from Cet's lips,[36] thus performing the only publicly witnessed inscription in flesh in the contest sequence.

During the contest, Cet and Conall vie for the heroic privilege of 'dividing' or carving Mac Dathó's pig. Ironically, the resolution of this contest prompts the feast's descent into chaos, calling the whole competitive enterprise into question. Having won the place of honour, Conall Cernach enjoys his dominance by devouring the pig:

> Then Conall set about dividing the pig. He took the end of the belly in his mouth, and the dividing of the pig was done. He sucked the belly – a burden for nine men – so that he didn't leave a speck of it. He gave nothing to the Connachta but two of the pig's feet out of his throat. The Connachta found their share small. They got up, then the Ulaid got up, and they fell upon one another.
>
> Luid íarum Conall do rainn na-mmucce. Ocus gebid dano cenn in tarra ina béolo, co·tairnic dó rann na-mmucce. Ro·súig in tairr .i. ere ind nónbair cona·farcaib bannai de. Ni·tarat immurgu do Chonnachtaib acht dá chois na-mmucce foa brágit. Ba becc dano la Connachta a cuit. At·ragat sidi, at·ragat dano Ulaid, co·rroacht cách araile. (§17.5–18.3)

The ensuing brawl becomes a massacre, with bodies piling up in the hostel and streams of blood flowing out of its doors. Outside the hostel, Fergus uproots an oak tree in sheer belligerence. The fighting spreads into the surrounding countryside and, finally, a lowly charioteer decapitates the famous hound that was the reason for the feast. The behaviour of the pre-eminent warrior, as determined by the boasting contest, causes this eruption of violence. Conall Cernach makes a mockery of his role of apportioning meat, descending to a level of bestial appetite; his gargantuan excess renders the preceding competition meaningless. The contest's ironic failure to establish a winner who can perform his duties appropriately opens up the possibility for a critical readerly stance vis-à-vis heroic honour and masculinity.[37] Conall Cernach does not simply undo the work of the heroic contest: he pushes its principles of mutilation and accumulation to their logical limit. If heroic masculinity demands the assertion of honourable wholeness by reducing other men to shameful deficiency, *of course* the winner of the heroic contest will eat the whole pig. By incorporating the animal in its entirety, Conall conveys both a potent insult and a final bodily gesture signifying his dominance.

Scéla Mucce Meic Dathó's contest sequence and its aftermath reflect early Irish ideas concerning honour, shame, and the body while also destabilizing these ideas through irony and excess. Cet mac Mágach and Conall Cernach's use of corporeal signs as the currency of warrior competition shows an early medieval semiotics of the body at work in a literary context. The saga's masculine, honour-based hierarchy is grounded in the public perception of bodily integrity; mere association with a deficient body renders a warrior ineligible for heroic privilege. Yet the vulnerability of the body upon which this external honour depends makes shame an imminent threat to identity. The exteriority of Irish sagas can perplex modern readers; as *Scéla Mucce* shows, reading bodies opens early Irish literature to new interpretations.

NOTES

1 Many thanks to Ann Dooley, David Townsend, Markus Stock, E. Ruth Harvey, and the conference participants for helpful comments on earlier versions of this essay. I am indebted to the editors and anonymous reader for their careful reading and many useful suggestions.

2 Texts of *Scéla Mucce* survive in a comparatively large number of manuscripts, and references to the tale appear in a variety of contexts in medieval and early modern Irish. The medieval tale survives in four manuscripts, and two early modern versions of the tale also survive in manuscript form. References to the story are found in sources including the tale lists (see note 4 below), several poems (see Thurneysen, *Scéla Mucce* iv–vi), and the later tract *Cóir Anmann* ('Fitness of Names'). See Breatnach for discussion of the early modern version of *Scéla Mucce*.

3 The Old Irish period is conventionally considered to be prior to ca 900 CE.

4 For a survey of critical views on *Scéla Mucce*, see Poppe 1–3. On *Scéla Mucce* as 'a sophisticated parody of the heroic genre as represented by *Táin Bó Cúalnge*,' see Ó Corráin, 'Irish Origin Legends' 85–6; for discussion of the issue of parody and *Scéla Mucce*, see Tristram 211–12; and Dooley 189–90. On *Scéla Mucce* as didactic Christian fable, see Buttimer; McCone 77–9; and Martin. That the saga's classification may also have been a matter for medieval debate – *scéla*, 'story,' or *orgun*, 'slaughter'? – is suggested by its designation by the alternate title *Orgain Meic Dathó* ('Mac Dathó's Slaughter') in the tale lists, including the Book of Leinster list (Best and O'Brien 4:836; Thurneysen, 'Scél mucce' 494; Mac Cana 47, 61); see Toner for a recent discussion of the tale lists.

5 There has been limited discussion of the body or embodiment in medieval Irish literature; notable exceptions are the discussions of heroic and gendered bodies in Dooley 34–6, 175–82, and two recent articles by Eichhorn-Mulligan. I thank Prof. Mulligan for sharing with me several chapters of her DPhil dissertation (Oxford, 2003), including earlier forms of her articles.

6 The charioteer jumps 'íar cúl Conchobair' 'behind Conchobar' (§20.7); the word *cúl*, 'back, rear,' is glossed by Latin *terga* (DIL s.v. 'cúl').

7 I am indebted to the work of Clare Lees and David Townsend on masculinity in Germanic heroic literature, particularly their insights concerning male competition and irony.

8 See also note 34 below.

9 Although Charles-Edwards makes this point during his discussion of the Four Branches of the *Mabinogi* and Welsh *wyneb*, 'face; honour' (cognate with Irish *enech*), his remarks are also applicable to shame and identity in Irish contexts.

10 Both texts are edited by Binchy; all translations of the legal texts are Binchy's. As Binchy notes, the first section of *Bretha Déin Chécht* is in eighth-century Old Irish, while the second section (from §25) is in Archaic Old Irish, i.e., seventh-century or earlier ('Bretha Déin Chécht' 3–4). Binchy views *Bretha Crólige* as part of the *Senchas Mar*, which Thurneysen dates to the first half of the eighth century ('Bretha Crólige' 1).

11 Binchy provides an edition and translation of this fragmentary tract in his introduction to *Bretha Déin Chécht*. *Bretha Crólige* also appears to emphasize the distinction between a visible wound and a wound that can be shielded from view. Although the text's 'a wound of eye, a wound of "non-eye"' ['fuil ruisc, fuil amruisc' (§63)] is obscure, Binchy suggests a translation of *ruisc* and *amruisc* as 'visible' and 'invisible' ('Bretha Crólige' 76).

12 Because this section is obscure, the precise nature of the shaming blemishes is uncertain. See also the discussion in Ó Corráin, 'Irish Law' 164–6.

13 'Nursing' or 'sick-maintenance' in legal contexts; the primary meaning is 'illness' (DIL s.v. 'othrus'; Binchy, 'Sick-Maintenance' 78–9).

14 In the *Macgnímrada* ('Boyhood Deeds') Cú Chulainn declares that his opponent Túachall mac Nechtain will never receive from him 'a house of healing or sick-maintenance' ['teg legis nó othrais' (TBC II 1125)]. Citations from the *Táin Bó Cúailnge* are from O'Rahilly's editions, designated TBC I (Recension 1) and TBC II (Recension 2).

15 The Old Irish Penitential, a short penitential text organized around the seven deadly sins, introduces penance into the system of compensation for injury codified in *Bretha Déin Chécht*: under the heading of *Ira*, this text demands sick-maintenance and the payment of a penalty for blemish [*ainim*] combined with penance, stipulating that if the offender cannot pay the fine due for the blemish, he can perform twice the penance (ch.V §8, Gwynn, 'An Irish Penitential' 168; cf. Bieler, *Irish Penitentials* 272). Binchy, whose translation of the Old Irish Penitential forms an appendix to Bieler's work, dates the text to the late eighth century at the latest (Bieler, *Irish Penitentials* 258). The Irish text is edited in Gwynn, 'An Irish Penitential' (see also Gwynn, 'Notes').

16 The dating of the group of documents to which this one belongs is uncertain; the group would appear to date from the eighth or ninth century (Bieler, *Patrician Texts* 47–9).

17 Bieler observes that this text, one of a group known as *Canones Hibernenses*, 'fixes punishments of a secular nature for offences or attacks on ecclesiastical personages'; its dating is uncertain, but is likely no later than the mid-seventh century (*Irish Penitentials* 8, 9). This section of the penitential provides important evidence for inter-borrowing between vernacular Irish law and Latin canon law (Ó Corráin, 'Irish Law' 165–6).

18 For discussion of the legal and historical context for hostels, hostellers, and the cultural significance of hospitality in medieval Ireland, see Mac Eoin and O'Sullivan.

19 Citations are from the standard edition by Thurneysen, with some alterations to indicate lenition and word division; a diplomatic edition of the Book of Leinster text can be found in Best and O'Brien, 2:418–24. See Quin, Gleasure, and Lindeman for corrections to Thurneysen's edition. All translations are my own unless otherwise noted.

20 As one of the sons of Mágu, Cet is a high-status warrior who is elsewhere linked by kinship to Connacht's royal couple: in the Book of Leinster *Táin*, Ailill identifies his mother as Máta Muirisc, daughter of Mágu (Máta Murisc ingen Mágach, TBC II 50), making Ailill sister's son to Cet, his maternal uncle.

21 For comparative discussion of verbal contests in Irish and Icelandic saga literature, see Sayers and Frotscher.

22 The territorial order of inscription corresponds to the 'presignifying' semiotic regime in Deleuze and Guattari's later thought ('On Several Regimes of Signs' 117). Although Deleuze and Guattari's earlier schema assigns each order of inscription to a stage of social development (while betraying a certain nostalgia for the 'primitive'), their later remarks eschew a developmental model, emphasizing instead the plurality and coexistence of 'regimes of signs' ('On Several Regimes of Signs' 119).

23 According to DIL, *galar* means 'sickness, disease, physical pain,' while *fúal* refers to both 'urine' (it is glossed by Latin *urina*) and 'water (foul water, a puddle?)' (s.vv. 'galar,' 'fúal').

24 The other injuries in this group are blows to the twelve 'doors of the soul/portals of life' ['dorus anma' (§2A)] and the seven most serious fractures (§2B). Impotence ['etracht' (§30)] is also mentioned later in the text, grouped with disfigurement, blemish, and loss of limb.

25 According to E. Ruth Harvey, *Scéla Mucce*'s apparent linking of male infertility and urinary disease is not consistent with later medieval urological knowledge. Although blood in the urine was a well-known symptom of internal bleeding (as *Bretha Déin Chécht* attests), medical authorities from the twelfth century on do not connect urinary disease with infertility or impotence (E. Ruth Harvey, personal communication).

26 A similar accumulative logic is evident in the later text *Cóir Anmann* (short version), which explains the name of the Fenian character Lugna Fer Trí by relating a story of how Lugna removed one of Oscar's testicles, thus 'gaining' a third testicle and his epithet Fer Trí 'Man of Three' (cf. long version §237, Stokes 382). See Arbuthnot, ed., *Cóir Anmann* 181, and discussion in Arbuthnot, 'On the Name Oscar.'

27 But cf. the alternate reading proposed by Quin (96).

28 Muinremor is a compound of *muin-*, '-neck,' + *remor*, 'stout, thick'; Gerginn is a compound of *gerr-*, 'short-,' + *cenn*, 'head' (DIL s.vv. 'muin,' 'remor,' 'gerr').

29 Óengus mac Óenláma Caíme (TBC I 2489); mac Óenláime Gábe (TBC II 2440).

30 DIL offers no translation of the hapax *gába* in the patronymic mac Óenláime *Gábe*, the form of Lám Gábaid found in TBC II (s.v. 'gába'; see note 29 above). In the account of the combat between Cet and Lám in *Cóir Anmann* (long version), however, 'Lámh Ghábhaidh' is read as 'Hand of Danger' (§280, Stokes 404–6), taking the second element as the genitive form of *gábud* 'danger, peril, stress' (DIL s.v. 'gábud'). Cet appears to exploit a potential *gábud-gábait* pun offered by Gábaid.

31 Although the initial element 'Sál-' remains constant, the father's name varies between manuscripts of *Scéla Mucce*. The Book of Leinster text has 'Salcholgan,' (cf. 'Sal colgg' in the long version of *Cóir Anmann* [§278, Stokes 404]); Trinity College, Dublin H.3.18 has 'Salchadai'; and the Harley manuscript and Rawlinson B.512 both give two versions of the name, 'Salc-a no Salcalgai' or 'Salca or Salcalgai' and 'Salcada no -calccu' or 'Salcada or [Sal]calccu,' respectively (Thurneysen, ed., *Scéla Mucce* 12). See discussion in Thurneysen, 'Scél mucce' 497n2. Mend appears in the Book of Leinster *Táin* as the warrior Mend mac Sálcholgán (TBC II 3837–55, 4077, 4516), whereas in the earlier version of the *Táin* he is called both Mend mac Sálchada (TBC I 3337, 3792) and mac Sálcholca (TBC I 3481–2); no mention is made of Mend's herdsman parentage in either version.

32 Although *sál* and *salchaid* (adj. *salach* 'dirty') differ in vowel quality, the aural association may have been sufficient for punning purposes: there appears to be wordplay on *sál-salach* (likewise with the goal of insult) in the early modern saga *Altromh Tighi Da Medar* ('The Fosterage of the House of the Two Goblets,' §6; Dobbs 204–5; cf. Duncan 193, 213). Thanks to Ann Dooley for this reference. We can also construe Cet's initial reading of Sálchad as a compound of *sál* + *cáide* (genitive sg. *cáda*), a noun meaning both 'dirt, filth; blemish' and 'holiness' (DIL s.v. 'cáide') – a reading that would perhaps account for the religious terms later in the contest with Mend.

33 See note 31 above.

34 On this idiomatic use of *anim*, 'blemish, disgrace,' see DIL s.v. 'ainim.'

35 Cet also gives Ánlúan the patronymic 'mac Magach' in the fifteenth-century Rawlinson B. 512 version of the text (Thurneysen, ed., *Scéla Mucce* 16).

36 Cet's bleeding indicates that the blow to his abdomen caused internal bleeding, providing a further correspondence with *Bretha Déin Chécht*'s wounds causing haemorrhage ['fola a bru for beolu' (§17)].

37 Viewing the narrative from the Leinster perspective, however, removes many of its ironies (cf. Buttimer 64–6; Tristram 210–11; Poppe 8–9): Mac Dathó succeeds in preserving his honour by orchestrating the Ulster-Connacht confrontation and thus evading his obligation to give away his hound.

WORKS CITED

Arbuthnot, Sharon J. 'On the Name Oscar and Two Little-Known Episodes Involving the *Fían*.' *Cambrian Medieval Celtic Studies* 51 (2006): 67–81.

– ed. and trans. *Cóir Anmann: A Late Middle Irish Treatise on Personal Names.* Part 1. London: Irish Texts Society, 2005.

Best, R.I., and M.A. O'Brien, eds. *The Book of Leinster, Formerly Lebar na Núachongbála*. Dublin: Dublin Institute for Advanced Studies, 1956.

Bieler, Ludwig, ed. and trans. *The Irish Penitentials*. Dublin: Dublin Institute for Advanced Studies, 1963.

– ed. and trans. *The Patrician Texts in the Book of Armagh*. Dublin: Dublin Institute for Advanced Studies, 1979.

Binchy, D.A., 'Sick-Maintenance in Irish Law.' *Ériu* 12 (1938): 78–134.

– ed. and trans. 'Bretha Crólige.' *Ériu* 12 (1938): 1–77.

– ed. and trans. 'Bretha Déin Chécht.' *Ériu* 20 (1966): 1–66.

Breatnach, Caoimhín. 'The Early Modern Versions of *Scéla Mucce Meic Da Thó–Tempus, Locus, Persona et Causa Scribendi*.' *Ériu* 41 (1990): 37–60.

Buttimer, Cornelius G. '*Scéla Mucce Meic Dathó*: A Reappraisal.' *Proceedings of the Harvard Celtic Colloquium* 2 (1982): 61–73.

Charles-Edwards, T.M. 'Honour and Status in Some Irish and Welsh Prose Tales.' *Ériu* 29 (1978): 123–41.

– *Early Irish and Welsh Kinship*. Oxford: Clarendon Press, 1993.

Davies, Wendy. 'The Place of Healing in Early Irish Society.' In *Sages, Saints and Storytellers: Celtic Studies in Honour of Professor James Carney*. Ed. Donnchadh Ó Corráin, Liam Breatnach, and Kim McCone. Maynooth, Ireland: An Sagart, 1989. 43–55.

Deleuze, Gilles, and Félix Guattari. *Anti-Oedipus: Capitalism and Schizophrenia*. Trans. Robert Hurley, Mark Seem, and Helen R. Lane. New York: Viking, 1977. Rept. Minneapolis: University of Minnesota Press, 1983.

– '587 B.C.–A.D. 70: On Several Regimes of Signs.' *A Thousand Plateaus: Capitalism and Schizophrenia*. Trans. Brian Massumi. Minneapolis: University of Minnesota Press, 1987. 111–48.

Dictionary of the Irish Language: Based Mainly on Old and Middle Irish Materials. Compact ed. Dublin: Royal Irish Academy, 1983.

Dobbs, M.E., ed. and trans. 'Altromh Tighi da Medar.' *Zeitschrift für celtische Philologie* 18 (1930): 189–230.

Dooley, Ann. *Playing the Hero: Reading the Irish Saga* Táin Bó Cúailnge. Toronto: University of Toronto Press, 2006.

Duncan, Lilian, ed. and trans. 'Altram Tige Dá Medar.' *Ériu* 11 (1932): 184–225.

Eichhorn-Mulligan, Amy C. '*Togail Bruidne Da Derga* and the Politics of Anatomy.' *Cambrian Medieval Celtic Studies* 49 (2005): 1–19.

– 'The Anatomy of Power and the Miracle of Kingship: The Female Body of Sovereignty in a Medieval Irish Kingship Tale.' *Speculum* 81, no. 4 (2006): 1014–54.

Frotscher, Antje G. 'Old Irish *Curad-Mír* and Old Norse *Mannjafnaðr*: Two Forms of Literary Man-Comparison in Early Medieval Literature.' *Comitatus* 33 (2002): 19–36.

Gilmore, David D. *Manhood in the Making: Cultural Concepts of Masculinity.* New Haven, CT: Yale University Press, 1990.

Gleasure, James W. 'The Rawlinson B512 Version of *Scéla Mucce Meic Dathó* Revisited.' *Scottish Gaelic Studies* 17 (1996): 143–5.

Gwynn, E.J., 'Notes on the Irish Penitential.' *Ériu* 12 (1938): 245–9.

– ed. and trans. 'An Irish Penitential.' *Ériu* 7 (1914): 121–95.

Jaski, Bart. *Early Irish Kingship and Succession.* Dublin: Four Courts Press, 2000.

Lees, Clare A. 'Men and *Beowulf.*' In *Medieval Masculinities: Regarding Men in the Middle Ages.* Ed. Clare A. Lees, with Thelma Fenster and Jo Ann McNamara. Minneapolis: University of Minnesota Press, 1994. 129–48.

Lindeman, Fredrik Otto. 'Varia IV: On *Scela Mucce Meic Datho* §16, 9f.' *Ériu* 31(1980): 167.

Mac Cana, Proinsias. *The Learned Tales of Medieval Ireland.* Dublin: Dublin Institute for Advanced Studies, 1980.

Mac Eoin, Gearóid. 'The *Briugu* in Early Irish Society.' *Zeitschrift für celtische Philologie* 49–50 (1997): 482–93.

Martin, B.K. 'The Medieval Irish Stories about Bricriu's Feast and Mac Dathó's Pig.' *Parergon* n.s. 10.1 (1992): 71–93.

McCone, Kim. *Pagan Past and Christian Present in Early Irish Literature.* Maynooth: An Sagart, 1990. Rept. Maynooth, Ireland: Dept. of Old Irish, National University of Ireland, Maynooth, 2000.

Miller, William Ian. *Bloodtaking and Peacemaking: Feud, Law, and Society in Saga Iceland.* Chicago: University of Chicago Press, 1990.

– *Humiliation: And Other Essays on Honor, Social Discomfort, and Violence.* Ithaca, NY: Cornell University Press, 1993.

Ó Corráin, Donnchadh. 'Irish Law and Canon Law.' In *Irland und Europa: Die Kirche im Frühmittelalter. Ireland and Europe: The Early Church.* Ed. Próinséas Ní Chatháin and Michael Richter. Stuttgart: Klett-Cotta, 1984. 157–66.

– 'Irish Origin Legends and Genealogy: Recurrent Aetiologies.' In *History and Heroic Tale: A Symposium.* Ed. Tore Nyberg et al. Odense, Denmark: Odense University Press, 1985. 51–96.

O'Leary, Philip. 'Contention at Feasts in Early Irish Literature.' *Éigse* 20 (1984): 115–27.

O'Rahilly, Cecile, ed. and trans. *Táin Bó Cúalnge from the Book of Leinster.* Dublin: Dublin Institute for Advanced Studies, 1967.

– ed. and trans. *Táin Bó Cúailnge, Recension I.* Dublin: Dublin Institute for Advanced Studies, 1976.

O'Sullivan, Catherine Marie. 'Hospitality and the Irish Guesthouse-Keeper.' *Hospitality in Medieval Ireland: 900–1500.* Dublin: Four Courts Press, 2004. 120–63.

Overing, Gillian R. *Language, Sign, and Gender in* Beowulf. Carbondale and Edwardsville: Southern Illinois University Press, 1990.

Peristiany, J.G., ed. *Honour and Shame: The Values of Mediterranean Society*. London: Weidenfeld and Nicolson, 1965.

Poppe, Erich. '*Scéla Muicce Meic Da Thó* Revisited.' *Studia Celtica Japonica* 9 (1997): 1–9.

Quin, E. Gordon. 'Textual Notes: *Scéla Mucce Meic Dathó*.' *Éigse* 18, no. 1 (1980): 95–7.

Sayers, William. 'Serial Defamation in Two Medieval Tales: The Icelandic *Ölkofra Þáttr* and the Irish *Scéla Mucce Meic Dathó*.' *Oral Tradition* 6, no. 1 (1991): 35–57.

Scarry, Elaine. *The Body in Pain: The Making and Unmaking of the World*. Oxford and New York: Oxford University Press, 1985.

Stokes, Whitley, ed. and trans. '*Cóir Anmann*: Fitness of Names.' *Irische Texte: mit Übersetzungen und Wörterbuch*. Vol. 3, part 2. Ed. Whitley Stokes and Ernst Windisch. Leipzig: S. Hirzel, 1897. 285–444.

Thurneysen, Rudolf. '"Scél mucce Maic Dathó": Die Geschichte vom Schwein des Mac Dathó.' *Die irische Helden- und Königssage bis zum siebzehnten Jahrhundert*. Halle: Max Niemeyer, 1921. Rept. Hildesheim: Georg Olms, 1980. 494–500.

– ed. *Scéla Mucce Meic Dathó*. Dublin: Dublin Institute for Advanced Studies, 1935.

Toner, Gregory. 'Reconstructing the Earliest Irish Tale Lists.' *Éigse* 32 (2000): 88–120.

Townsend, David. 'Ironic Intertextuality and the Reader's Resistance to Heroic Masculinity in the *Waltharius*.' In *Becoming Male in the Middle Ages*. Ed. Jeffrey Jerome Cohen and Bonnie Wheeler. New York: Garland, 1997. 67–86.

Tristram, Hildegard L.C. 'Feis und Fled: Wirklichkeit und Darstellung in mittelalterlichen irischen Gastmahlserzählungen.' In *Medialität und mittelalterliche insulare Literatur*. Ed. Hildegard L.C. Tristram. Tübingen: Gunter Narr, 1992. 183–220.

Uhlich, Jürgen. *Die Morphologie der komponierten Personennamen des Altirischen*. Witterschlick and Bonn: M. Wehle, 1993.

6 The Dazzling Sword of Language: Masculinity and Persuasion in Classical and Medieval Rhetoric

JILL ROSS

Oratory in the Roman world was an important vehicle for establishing social and political dominance. Trumping the traditional battlefield where *virtus*, or Roman martial valour, is forged and displayed, the law courts became, by the late Republic, the new arena in which Roman manliness was negotiated. As Thomas Habinek has put it, rhetorical training and competition was the crucible from which emerged the 'transformed, or newly formed, elite male subject, possessed of a distinctive linguistic, sexual, political and intellectual identity' (Habinek 78). The crafting of a suitably active and authoritative masculinity that embraces the Roman values of impenetrability, muscularity, bodily control, martial valour, and mastery over self and others can be seen clearly in the advice provided by theoretical treatments of rhetoric that counsel appropriately virile posture and gesture, modulation of the voice, and especially for my argument, subjection and direction of language to the aggressive, bellicose necessities of the case at hand.

The infusion of gendered corporeality into the dictates of stylistic formulation is a phenomenon common to the classical rhetorical theory of Cicero and Quintilian and is taken up by later antique Christian writers such as St Augustine, whose representation of a linguistically embodied masculinity makes its way into medieval arts of preaching, poetry, and letter writing, where the constellation of language and martial masculinity, now shaped by clerical written culture, shifts its valences in fascinating ways. Preaching becomes infused by an ethos of aggressive violence directed against the sins colonizing the souls of the passive listeners, while the medieval writer of poetry or letters turns his aggression to the language and ideas he is attempting to shape and directs the radiance of figurative language to the revelation of truth or meaning, thereby granting to the reader the virile, active power of penetrating the veils of language and constructing meaning. By the late Middle Ages, the sword of language is used to unleash a form of desire that so overwhelms its victims that it leads to social chaos and death.

Roman theoretical writing on rhetoric conveys the need to project an authoritative masculinity most clearly in advice on how to master the body's posture and gestures in order to deliver a suitably masculine performance. In Cicero's *De oratore* (3.59.220), Catulus counsels that the orator's gestures ought to be manly and restrained, not stagy, theatrical, or over-the-top. Rather than engaging in mimicry, the speaker should use his body obliquely, conveying his *virtus* (prowess and excellence) by means of manly gestures such as the throwing out of the chest that typifies the posture acquired through training with weapons or on the wrestling mat. Such martial posturing ought to be matched by the appropriate voice. The anonymous author of the *Rhetorica ad Herennium* counsels 'manly dignity' in speaking rather than sharp exclamation that smacks of 'feminine outcry' ['muliebris vociferatio' (3.12.22)].

The language deployed by the male orator should be infused with the kind of virile dignity and vigour that characterize the modulation of his body and voice. The orator's words must be as taut, controlled, and sculpted as his battle-ready muscles and finely tuned responses. Cicero describes verbal training and effectiveness in overtly muscular terms:

> Then finally our orator must be shaped in regard to both his words and his thoughts in the same way as persons whose business is the handling of weapons are trained in style, so that just as people who practice fencing or boxing think that they must give consideration not only to avoiding or striking blows but also to the grace of movement, similarly he may aim on the one hand at neatness of structure and grace in his employment of words and on the other hand at impressiveness in expressing his thoughts.
>
> Tum denique hic nobic orator ita conformandus est et verbis et sententiis ut ei qui in armorum tractatione versantur ut quemadmodum qui utuntur armis aut palaestra non solum sibi vitandi aur feriendi rationem esse habendam putant set etiam ut cum venustate moveantur, sic verbis quidem ad aptam compositionem et decentiam, sententiis vero ad gravitatem orationis utatur. (*De oratore* 3.52.200; trans. Rackham)[1]

Cicero, here, in his distinction between the employment of words and the expression of thought, is invoking, not coincidentally, the division of the *figurae* into those of diction and those of thought. The idea of figurality is, perhaps, the primary vehicle for the translation of body into language. The Greek word *schema*, on which the Latin *figura* is calqued, refers to the positioning of the body in wrestling formation and thus already incorporates the muscular, martial connotations that Cicero views as conditioning the proper manly use of language and thought by the speaker (Fantham, *Comparative Studies* 164, and *Roman World* 282; Dugan, *Making a New Man* 160–1, 276).

This effort of tying troping and other figures to the virile arts of war or athletics is a two-edged sword, if you pardon the pun, for these 'gestures of language' ['gestus orationis' (Cicero, *Orator* 83; Quintilian, *Institutio oratoria* 9.1.10–11; Dugan, *Making a New Man* 147–8)], as they are explicitly termed by both Cicero and Quintilian, may also slip into the unseemly, excessively effeminate movements of dancers, actors, or even the monstrous if they enact an overly violent twisting of language away from the literal. The problem of maintaining hard and fast distinctions between the masculine and the feminine is one that has haunted the history of rhetoric, and especially the treatment of linguistic form and style, from the beginning. Greek rhetoricians like Demosthenes responded to deeply ingrained cultural notions of manliness as consisting solely of actions rather than 'mere' words by vehemently defending the use of legal recourse in the face of an affront, insisting such a response was just as manly as physical retribution would be (Roisman 78). The personification of Peitho (Persuasion) as a seductive assistant to Aphrodite whose rhetorical power played on male desire in order to deprive men of the reason, discretion, and independence of Athenian manhood also conditions Roman attitudes towards oratory (Roisman 140).

In his extensive writing on rhetorical style, Dionysius of Halicarnassus, the Greek rhetorician working in Rome in around 30 BCE, splits the feminine personification of rhetoric into two figures, the virgin and the harlot. Each of these figures embodies the stylistic virtues and vices represented by the opposing aesthetic movements of Asianism and Atticism, with the virgin exemplifying the Attic stylistic restraint and simplicity that eschews showy ornamentation for the smooth, seamless flow of harmonious structure and language, and the harlot exemplifying the gaudily decked out language dripping with provocative *figurae* supposedly typical of Asianism (Leidl 42–8). The competing aesthetic ideologies of Atticism, a literary movement central to Roman rhetorical culture in the middle of the first century BCE, and Asianism, a style attributed to Hellenistic orators from Asia Minor, maps the tension between the simplicity, restraint, and purity of the Attic prose style and the overly emotional and ornate oratory of the Asianist onto gendered bodily behaviour as it is manifested in the orator's physical bodily presence and voice and in the gendered inflections of his linguistic style. In other words, as John Dugan has discussed, the body (in both its literal and metaphorical capacities) was 'the central vehicle through which the Atticist/Asianist discourse was articulated' ('Preventing Ciceronianism' 409). Attempts to define and control the gendered body, whether constituted literally through the appropriate physical training and reinforcement of its physiological tendencies, or produced in the texture and tone of corporealized notions of style as 'healthy,' 'robust,' 'full of blood,' or as 'loinless' (*elumbis*), and 'lacking sinews' (*enervis*), are what animate the often vehement struggles between Asianists and Atticists.

The projection of anxieties about gender roles and identity onto the screen of rhetorical stylistic terminology paradoxically reveals that rhetorical performance, both linguistic and gestural, not only attempts to reinforce firm boundaries between what is manly and what is effeminate, but also problematizes the very possibility of constructing any such boundaries since the very training in masculine performance exposes the artificial, 'performative nature of ideal masculinity' (Habinek 66; Connolly). One of the sites where this tension about gender definition is most acute is, not surprisingly, the *figurae* whose cosmetic, supervenient nature has been the object of suspicion since Plato's condemnation of rhetoric in the *Gorgias*, and whose embodiment of gendered physical movement and mannerism make them into almost literal gendered performances. Cicero, having to defend himself against accusations of an excessively Asianist, 'womanish' oratorical style, uses the *figurae* as a strategic tool in promoting a vigorously masculine ethos that manages to marry both force and beauty, and thus to undercut any simplistic opposition between the masculine and the feminine, the Attic and the Asian.

The use of a profusion of figures ornamenting a speech as flowers beautify gardens or fields and appeal to the senses of sight and smell, or as jewels attract the eyes by their colour and brilliance, is part of an aesthetic, sometimes called 'the jeweled style' (Roberts), that became increasingly normative in later antiquity. However, in the late Republic, such an aesthetic was more typically associated with an overly flashy, unrestrained, unmanly style. Aware of the ambivalent connotations of such stylistic exuberance, Cicero and other rhetorical authors who favoured a more robust style, like the anonymous author of the *Ad Herennium* manual, conflate the eye-catching brilliance of flowers and jewels, but locate them in the most masculine symbols of martial aggressiveness and assertion: the sword or spear. In *De oratore* (2.78.317), Cicero discusses the effectiveness of the opening passage of a speech as akin to a fight to the death between two gladiators. The winning combatant knows that death will be determined by the blade ('ferro'), but before going in for the kill delivers a number of strokes that are not intended 'ad vulnus' ('to wound'), but 'ad speciem' ('for show or beauty'), in the same way that the orator's opening verbal feints are intended more for pleasure ('delectatio') than for pure, deadly force ('vis'). Later on (*De or.* 3.54.206), Cicero equates stylistic diction with arms that are employed to threaten and attack, but that also are brandished simply for their beauty. The association of deadly beautiful force with *figurae* comes across more explicitly in the *Ad Herennium*. When comparing the figure of diction called *articulus*, or 'comma, or phrase,' which consists of single words being set apart by pauses in staccato speech (4.19.26), with that of *membrum* ('colon or clause'), the author describes the action of *membrum* as a drawing back of the arm while the hand whirls about to bring the sword ('gladius') to the adversary's body, while in *articulus* the sword pierces the body with quick and repeated thrusts.

Quintilian, writing later in the Empire (first century CE), in a gesture of deference to his Ciceronian model of oratorical perfection (Kennedy 117), brings together the deadly penetrative force of such figures, with their sensually appealing performance, in a remarkable metaphor. For Quintilian, the very essence of eloquence, *elocutio* or 'style,' the communicative act of drawing out thought from the mind in the form of speech (*eloqui*), is figured by the drawing of a sword out of its scabbard:

> The word *eloqui* means to bring out the thoughts you have formed in your mind and strike (*perferre*) the blow home to an audience. Without this, everything that has gone before is useless, like a sword that has been put up and will not come out of its scabbard.
>
> Eloqui enim est omnia quae mente conceperis promere atque ad audientis perferre, sine quo supervacua sunt priora et similia gladio condito atque intra vaginam suam haerenti. (*Institutio oratoria* 8.pr.15–16; trans. Russell)

The very act, then, of styling thought in persuasive, ornate language epitomizes Roman manliness and power: to wield the sword of language is to be a man. Quintilian goes even further, however, homing in not only on the deadly penetrative potential of this sword of eloquence, but also on its dazzling ability to beguile an audience with its potent brilliance. Effective and powerful language should compel the listener's attention and understanding in the same way that sunlight streams into the eyes. This light is best delivered by means of ornamented, figurative language for, as Quintilian says, it enables the orator to fight 'with weapons that are not only effective but polished and gleaming' ['nec fortibus modo sed etiam fulgentibus armis proeliatur' (8.3.2–3)]. The flash of the sword is supposed to captivate the listener's attention and goodwill by means of the pleasure (*delectatio*) it induces, while at the same time threatening a kind of thrilling violence: 'The sword strikes terror also to the eye; even lightning would not dismay us so much if it was only the force that we feared, and not the flash as well' ['Nam et ferrum adfert oculis terroris aliquid, et fulmina ipsa non tam nos confunderent si vis eorum tantum, non etiam ipse fulgor timeretur' (8.3.5)]. The unsheathed, dazzling sword, or the polished thought that is brandished, compels attention both by the violence it threatens as well as by its flashy beauty. The yoking together of ornate beauty and violence goes a long way toward dispelling anxieties of gender inherent in the spectacle of men indulging in pleasures of language as they wield words instead of swords.

Immediately after Quintilian has drawn out his drop-dead-gorgeous sword, he betrays unease with the possible confusion between the gendered valences of supervenient beauty and those of strength and utility. He reaffirms that *ornatus* should be 'manly, strong and chaste' ['virilis et fortis et sanctus'] and that it should 'shine with health and vigour' ['sanguine et viribus niteat'] rather than with the artificial, effeminate smoothness effected through cosmetics (8.3.7). He also openly admits that 'vices and virtues in this area are particularly close neighbours' ['cum in hac maxime parte sint vicina virtutibus vitia' (8.3.7)], suggesting that the boundaries between the masculine and the feminine are porous and artificially constructed. Eric Gunderson has written about the culturally potent symbolism of swords in the stories staged as role-playing exercises in Roman declamation (*Declamation* 154–86). These invented pieces of rhetoric provide an arena not only to hone one's oratorical skill, but also to explore and question central problems of Roman identity, culture, and status. The question of what it meant to be an upper-class Roman male was of central concern to the identity formation of the young men who were trained by means of these exercises. In some of the situations rehearsed by these stories, the sword becomes a symbol of phallic mastery that is exercised both on the battlefield and in the bedroom, as well as a way of figuring the relationship between men (Gunderson 179). In one particularly striking declamatory situation, a tribune's homosexual overture towards one of his soldiers is initiated by the tribune's order that the soldier 'put on' his sword, thereby putting the soldier in the uncomfortable position of either being rendered a passive, penetrated male (i.e., more akin to a powerless woman), or of actually using his sword to kill his superior, thereby making him into both a murderer and, paradoxically, a paradigm of Roman manhood and honour where masculinity is predicated on remaining inviolate and exercising one's mastery over others (Gunderson 167; Williams; Walters). The soldier chooses to 'be a man' and the issue to be decided is whether the soldier is guilty or innocent of murder. The sword as emblematic of potential loss of manhood if one is subject to its penetrative power or of the assertion of masculine power in the context of men contending against other men, be it in the law court or on the battlefield, clearly haunts Quintilian's ambivalent use of the dazzling sword of language.

The association of rhetoric with deadly martial force as exemplified in the threatening, but beautiful, sword became so utterly conventional by late antiquity that the allegorized figure of Lady Rhetoric in Martianus Capella's *The Marriage of Philology and Mercury* (early sixth century), spouting the ossified doctrine of rhetoric devoid of any innovation or originality, sports the weaponry expected of impressive rhetorical performance: 'in her hands the arms with which she used either to defend herself or to wound her enemies, shone with the brightness of lightning' ['arma in manibus quibus se vel communire solita vel adversarios vulnerare, fulminea quadam coruscatione renidebant' (5.426, p. 148)]. Like the terrible power attributed to the menacing flash of Quintilian's sword of figural language, Martianus's description of rhetoric exploits the violence inherent in the sword in his assimilation of Lady Rhetoric to Jove, the omnipotent sender of storms:

> When she clashed her weapons on entering, you would say that the broken booming of thunder was rolling forth with the shattering clash of a lightning cloud; indeed it was thought she could hurl thunderbolts like Jove. For like a queen with power over everything, she could drive any host of people where she wanted and draw them back from where she wanted; she could sway them to tears and whip them to a frenzy and change the countenance and senses not only of cities but of armies in battle.

> haec cum in progressu arma concusserat, velut fulgoreae nubis fragore colliso bombis dissultantibus fracta diceres crepitare tonitrua; denique creditum quod instar Iovis eadem posset etiam fulmina iaculari. Nam veluti potens rerum omnium regina et impellere quo vellet et unde vellet deducere et in lacrimas

> flectere et in rabiem concitare et in alios etiam vultus sensusque convertere tam urbes quam exercitus proeliantes, quaecumque poterat agmina populorum. (5.427, 148–9; trans. Stahl, 5.427, 156)

However, unlike the persuasive beauty of ornamented language, Martianus's view of martial rhetoric emphasizes the raw power of rhetorical force that one medieval commentator associated not with the decorative nature of figural expression, but rather with the 'argumenta rhetorum' (Remigius 64; 211.6), and even the gems decorating Rhetorica's belt are linked with the topoi of argumentation (Remigius 65; 211.15) instead of the more conventional stylistic adornments so constitutive of the jewelled style. Martianus's placing of the arms of rhetoric in the hands of a woman of 'outstanding beauty' (5.426, p. 156) perhaps preserves some of the ambiguity of gender evinced in the classical fusion of deadly force and dazzling sparkle, but the feminizing potential of rhetorical ornament is clearly subordinated to the bellicose function of aggressive attack and self-defence.

By the fifth century, one might imagine that the values of military masculinity embodied in the linguistic strategies and texture of oratorical speech would have undergone a major shift given that the Empire's military supremacy was in great doubt (Rome was sacked in 410), and that the Empire's Christianization implied a devaluing of bellicose aggression in favour of an ideal of manly strength in passive victimhood, an ideal most perfectly exemplified by those *milites Christi*, the martyrs (Kuefler, ch. 4). However, in the fourth book of St Augustine's *On Christian Doctrine*, often referred to as a Christian rhetorical manual for would-be preachers, we find Augustine using the very same language and imagery that had resonated so deeply in Cicero's and Quintilian's constructions of the muscular, male speaker. Augustine recasts the three levels of style (the subdued, the middle, and the grand) by severing them from the nature of the material and linking them, instead, to the impact each style will have on the listeners. Since the Christian truth that is the *materia* of the preacher is always of the utmost importance, the stylistic mode adopted by the speaker should depend on whether his primary aim is to teach (the subdued style), to please (the middle style), or to cause radical change in the listener's behaviour (the grand style). In his treatment of the grand style, which Augustine views as leading to the victory of persuasion, he evokes the jewelled sword of classical Roman rhetoric, but in order to reject it rather than embrace it:

> It is enough for the matter being discussed that the appropriateness of the words be determined by the ardor of the heart rather than by careful choice.

For, if a strong man is armed with a gilded and bejeweled sword, and he is fully intent on battle, he does what he must with the arms he has, not because they are precious, but because they are arms.

Satis enim est ei propter quod agitur, ut verba congruentia, non oris eligantur industria, sed pectoris sequantur ardorem. Nam si aurato gemmatoque ferro vir fortis armetur, intentissimus pugnae, agit quidem illis armis, quod agit, non quia pretiosa, sed quia arma sunt. (4.20.42; trans. Robertson, 150)

Here, Augustine is concerned to restrain and minimize the sword's aesthetic appeal, to break the bond between beauty and power, and return the sword to its properly virile, martial function. Clearly, for Augustine, the dazzling nature of the sword serves only as an artificial, unnatural distraction that in no way enhances the power of the speaker's message.

In fact, such superficial decoration is firmly elided with the vice of feminine cosmetics and ornamentation. It is surely not coincidental that Augustine's choice of topic in order to exemplify the features of the grand style is the, by now, traditional Christian condemnation of the adulteration of God's handiwork by women who use cosmetics or dye their hair. Augustine cites excerpts from both Cyprian's and Ambrose's treatises dealing with the proper conduct for women and virgins, where language in the grand style is used in order to dissuade women from adulterating nature through their use of rouge (*De doctrina christiana* 4.21.49–50). Echoing Plato's association of rhetoric with a cosmetic use of language that only leads to a superficially pleasing appearance (*Gorgias* 463b, 465b; 100–1), Augustine's directing of grandly ornamented style to the condemnation of the very technique animating it is, to say the least, profoundly ambivalent.

While Augustine grudgingly acknowledges the need for a grand style in order to bring about obedient action on the part of the listener, his preference is for the subdued style that 'pertains to understanding' ['ad submissum intellegenter … pertineat' (4.26.56)] as he accords to it twice the space allotted for his summary of the moderate and grand styles combined (4.26.56–8). In his outline of the advantages of the subdued style whose goal is to teach or explain, Augustine emphasizes that its 'natural' mode of showing can bring as much light and dazzle as the grand style: 'it brings to light and sets forth most acute principles from I know not what caverns, as it were in an unexpected way' ['dum sententias acutissimas de nescio quibus quasi cavernis, unde non sperebatur, eruit et ostendit' (4.26.56; trans. Robertson 163)]. However, it accomplishes this in a way quite distinct from the flashy mode of the grand style. The subdued style should only be leavened with minimal linguistic adornment, such as a few rhythmic closings that grow naturally out of the subject matter and that do not draw attention to themselves out of a desire for ostentation. Augustine accords the most martial, virile presence and power to the naked body and muscles of the speech, and in a stripping away of the *figurae* and tropes that brought virile corporeal vitality into Roman rhetoric, he thoroughly privileges this power over that of the body decked out in weapons and armour. The subdued style 'does not come forth armed or adorned, but, as it were, nude, and in this way crushes the sinews and muscles of its adversary and overcomes and destroys resisting falsehood with its most powerful members' ['Non enim quia neque incedit ornate neque armata, sed tamquam nuda congreditur, ideo non adversarium nervis lacertisque conlidit et obsistentem subruit ac destruit membris fortissimis falsitatem' (4.26.56; trans. Robertson 163)]. The necessity of arms is treated as a mere ornament, a distraction from the true manly power of the Christian orator. The reliance on sheer muscle power harks back to the Greek etymology of 'troping' as 'wrestling,' yet here it is tied to the unadorned style, leaving the grand style curiously dependent on the 'real' muscle power of its subordinate.

This Augustinian recasting of the construction of the speaker's rhetorical body and gender in Christian terms also repositions the listener. Unlike the feminizing threat of being pierced by the orator's dazzling sword, here, the Christian listeners are not positioned as passive or penetrated. What Augustine is presenting is more akin to a situation of hand-to-hand combat in which the struggle for power is much more graphic and vehement. Augustine does not just want to 'stick it to' his opponent, he wants literally to pound listeners into submission with the force of truth.

The constellation of imagery involving radiance, troping, bodies, and violence is one that continues into the Middle Ages. However, the tracing of its trajectory must follow the multiple paths that medieval rhetoric takes in the arts of preaching, letter writing, and poetry. Medieval arts of preaching are perhaps the best vehicles for the transmission of classically based ideas about performance and delivery given their emphasis not only on the strategies for inventing copious sermon material and on the arrangement of this material in clearly marked divisions and subdivisions, but also on the crucial elements of the preacher's voice, manner, gestures, clothing, and relationship to his listeners. While Augustine's privileging of unadorned, raw, masculine power in effecting victory is conveyed in the traditional language of classical rhetorical *agon*, medieval arts of preaching, according to Claire Waters, attempted to restrain and deflect the problematic relationship of language and effeminizing adornment by foregrounding the most technical aspects of rhetoric at the expense of openly engaging with rhetoric's more sensual implications (Waters 74). Some preachers, though, like the fourteenth-century Franciscan Francesc Eiximenis, follow Augustine's embrace of the violent potential of the preacher and his ambivalence about the potential of rhetorical adornment to unman the power of the preacher. Eiximenis constructs the figure of the preacher as a warrior for truth wielding the sword of God's word fearlessly against all vice, and whose determination to achieve victory is unmoved by either love or fear (305), but whose manly status is in danger if he adorns God's word – the *gladium Dei* to which he has just referred – with the colours of rhetoric:

> Those who, in their windy sermons, do not aim for the aforesaid ends [i.e., glory, honour, and praise of God; salvation of the people; salvation and merit of the preacher] prostitute the word of God, and in contempt of the word of God and as a scandal to their listeners, they turn themselves towards painted, rhymed and rhetorically adorned words. (306)

> meretricantes uerbum Dei, qui in suis uentosis predicacionibus nullum finem de predictis intendunt ... Et ad hoc in contemptum uerbi Dei et in scandalum audiencium conuertunt se ad uerba picta, rimata et rhetorice ornate.

Clearly, for Eiximenis, the potential of rhetorically ornate language to unman the body and language of the preacher, and to corrupt the audience, was very real.

However, most preaching manuals choose to sidestep or suppress the gendered ambiguity of language that was so powerfully embodied in the figure of the jewelled sword, and to emphasize the threatening power of the preacher's discourse, which is often cast in militaristic and violent imagery. Thomas Waleys, writing in the fourteenth century, harks back to Vegetius's late classical manual on military organization and strategy for his likening of preachers to novice soldiers who should practise their battlefield manoeuvres and weapons prior to actual combat when there is no danger and opportunity to correct any defects or clear up any confusion (Waleys 340). While the martial imagery inherent in the jewelled sword of language is still retained in medieval arts of preaching, what has changed is the shift of the sources of such imagery away from the world of classical oratory to that of the scriptures, a shift that also reflects an awareness on the part of the authors of medieval preaching texts that 'modern' preaching is directed more at moral instruction of the faithful than at the radical aim of conversion as it was in the early days of Christianity as Thomas Chobham, writing in the early thirteenth century, observed in his *Summa de arte praedicandi* (Chobham 15, ll. 18–25).

Preachers, as the embodiment of the forces of God's truth and power, are represented as fully engaged in a ferocious war against the devil and vice, a war whose intensity and violence would be familiar to any reader of Prudentius's *Psychomachia*. According to Humbert of Romans, preachers are 'soldiers of Christ' since 'for them, to preach is to fight, for they make war on the errors against faith and morals' (Humbert 11), an identification that is rooted in scriptural precedents drawn from Paul, Maccabeans, the Psalms, and Zachary (Humbert 11–12). Basing himself on the Pauline dictum in Ephesans 6.17 ('et gladium Spiritus quod est verbum Dei' ['and the sword of the Spirit which is the word of God'], Alexander Ashby, in his *De artificioso modo predicandi* (early thirteenth century), asserts an important distinction between the priest who possesses (*habere*) the word of God in the form of knowledge of scripture, but who fails to use it (*tenere*) to draw blood (902, ll. 27–30), and those priests who 'soli gladios tenent qui instanter verbum Dei predicant, qui quod ore docent opere complent' ['alone wield swords and who right away preach the word of God, who fulfil in deed what they teach orally' (Ashby 926, ll. 821–6)]. According to many preachers, the weapons of language should be used not only to cut vice out of one's own soul, but also to assault the vice inhabiting the souls of the listeners. Thomas of Chobham and Humbert of Romans recognize that the extirpation of vice requires violent means. For Thomas, if gentle persuasion fails to eliminate vice, the preacher needs to resort to more drastic measures like a hammer, axe, or even fire to vaporize the evil in men's hearts (21, ll. 73–3, 89), and for Humbert, 'inspired preaching can shatter them [hard hearts] with the sureness of a hammer' (26).

Like in the rhetorical treatises of antiquity, the metaphorical battering of the audience by the violent onslaught of the preacher's powerful words constructs the listeners as passive subjects of the verbal onslaught directed at them. There is, however, another model for the relationship of the bodies of speaker and listener that arises out of a context deliberately divorced from the tenets of classical rhetoric. Gregory the Great, in his *Pastoral Care*, employs the extended metaphor of the preacher as *artifex* who creates harmony by playing the minds and hearts of his listeners as if they were the strings of a musical instrument, touching each one with the force necessary to produce the proper melody (*Regula pastoralis*, pars 3, prol., *PL* 77 49C–D). Gregory links this sensitivity on the part of the preacher to the skill a physician must exercise in the healing process, a connection that Augustine had also articulated in *On Christian Doctrine* (1.14.13, 4.16.33). In one of the earliest medieval preaching texts, Alan of Lille's *De arte praedicatoria* (ca 1199), the preacher is cast as a physician who must know how to administer the correct cure depending on the nature of the audience he faces. If preaching to the lustful, for example, he must adduce appropriate authorities and exempla against this vice. One of the tools in the preacher's medicine bag is none other than the sword of language, whose efficacy lies in its threatening healing violence, in the possibility of excising disease: 'Nunc ferro secet per comminationem, nunc foveat per consolationem' ['sometimes, menacing with his sword, let him amputate, at other times let him be encouraging through consolation' (*PL* 210, ch. 39, col. 184D)]. While the tailoring of the preacher's words to the needs of the individual listener's body and soul is often referred to as the subjection of the audience to the sword or plectrum wielded by the speaker, the performative power of such imagery is underscored in the formulation of Thomas Waleys, who refers to the preacher's tongue and mode of speaking ['modus dicendi' (333)] as the bow that plays the chords of the viola that can be equated both with the sermon itself and with the listeners (Waleys 333). Here, the phallic verbal power of the sword has becomes the stick required for the playing of a femininely shaped instrument, a process that was often understood in sexualized terms in many medieval popular puns and stories (Ross 161–4). Unlike the orator, whose masculine prowess was threatened by figural adornments of the sword, the preaching manuals betray no anxiety about the assertive dominance of the speaker over and above the feminized 'body' of listeners arrayed before him.

Like medieval theoretical writing on preaching, the arts of letter writing provide an arena for the writer to wield the Roman sword of persuasive power and beauty. Alberic of Montecassino, eleventh-century author of treatises on letter writing, mirrors both the Roman oratorical ethos and the combative stance of preachers against vice and sin when, at the outset of his *Flowers of Rhetoric*, he refers to the progression of the student from the basics of grammar as a move from preliminary training (*praeludium*) to 'the battle of composition' ['ad pugnam compositionum fiat transitus' (1.1, p. 33)], a transition that he views as constitutive of an appropriate male gender identity since it is an entrance into 'the full manly power of knowledge' ['in virile robur scientiae transitur' (1.1, p. 33)]. Alberic models this hyper-masculine mode of discourse and the effect it should have on its audience by affirming that, with this treatise, he himself seeks the kind of victory (*palma*) that will leave his adversary (his reader?) 'mute, agape, stunned with admiration' ['sileat, obmutescat, miretur, obstupeat' (1.1, p. 33)]. The desire to overwhelm the reader by means of powerful, virile language is an impulse that has remained consistent in rhetorical theory since Cicero.

The arts of letter writing and of poetry, less concerned with the charisma and oral power of a speaker before an audience, make the radiance of the figural sword into a means of creating clarity, in both a visual and intellectual sense, of the figural language employed and of the writer's own mind. In the shift from the orally based arena of rhetorical performance and reception to the medium of the written page, the engagement in verbal combat with a passive audience is also translated into an aggression that is turned to the language and ideas that the writer is attempting to shape. Instead of treating troping and figuration as flashing weapons in the arsenal of the orator, Alberic of Montecassino directs the radiance of figurative language to the revelation of truth or meaning, thereby granting to the reader the virile, active power of penetrating the veils of language and constructing meaning.

Alberic initially associates the key trope of metaphor with the negative, femininely charged connotations of both seduction and deceit when he describes metaphor's functioning as the dressing up of an old object in a 'fresh new wedding garment' in order to pass it off as nobler (and more virginal) than it really is (*Flowers* 6.1, p. 146). Like Cicero and Quintilian, whose use of the imagery associated with the dazzling sword enabled them to marry metaphor's effeminate beauty with deadly virile force, Alberic adds to his discussion of metaphor by associating it with *radius*, a phallic[2] beam of light that illuminates self-reflexively the mechanisms required for its interpretation: 'Added on to metaphor is the colour we call "light beam" and it truly is one since, like a kind of light, it penetrates, uncovers, illuminates the darknesses of metaphor' ['Subiungitur vero metaphorae color quem radium dicimus et vere radium quippe qui quasi quadam luce, si qua sunt obscura metaphorae penetrat, detegit, illustrat' (6.2, p. 147)]. Instead of slaying the listener with its persuasive force, this ray of light is a tool provided by Alberic as an accessory to his metaphor making, thereby providing both writer and reader with the tools to take possession of and undress the meanings that lie at the heart of figuration. Such a tool lends agency to both writer and reader, enabling the writer to remain in control of the unruly potential of metaphor, and the reader to divest meaning of the distorting layers of metaphorical language.

In the *Poetria nova*, Geoffrey of Vinsauf examines the various ways in which metaphorical words ['vox transsumpta' (5.886; trans. Nims

48)] glow. Here, the light that is cast upon the workings of *transumptio* is achieved by the poet's skilled use of adjectives that illuminate the transposed nature of the verb they accompany. For Geoffrey, many verbs used metaphorically are 'in a darkness' ['caligine' (v. 853)] that can only be dispelled by the light cast by appropriate adjectives. The illumination afforded by such adjectives can also serve to 'elucidate the verb's meaning still more fully by shedding clear light upon it' ['illuminet illud plenius et plenum lumen transfundat in ipsum' (vv. 848–9, Faral 223; trans. Nims 46)].

Not only is the luminosity of *figurae* turned onto the writer and his *materia*, but so is the violence involved in producing the poem. Whereas Augustine and later medieval preachers viewed persuasion or conversion as the battering of the listener's soul, mind, and heart into submission, writers hoping to produce effective poetry constructed the artistic process as one involving the brutal imposition of the writer's will and mastery upon the unruly *res* (Faral, v. 1611). Instead of the preacher's verbal weaponry or muscular speech uprooting sin, for a poet like Geoffrey of Vinsauf, the writer engages in an inner, mental conflict that is fundamental to the artistic process. The poet's mind is the arena where a struggle takes place to discipline the raw poetic matter that the writer subjects to repeated attacks like a blacksmith raining blows on hot iron: 'Hammer it out with a will on the forge of the understanding, pound it again and again, and at last pound out what is suitable' (Faral, vv. 1615–16; trans. Nims 73–4). This intense working of language by the poet is reminiscent of the core concept of physical struggle that is inherent in the turning and twisting of language into tropes, a kind of wrestling with words and thought that the classical orators were keen to portray as a masculine, virile enterprise. Here, Geoffrey of Vinsauf styles the poet as possessing a mind that is 'as eager as a wrestler to enter the combat. Its struggle, indeed, is with itself ... Tormented by its labours, it is in anguish; and at last, by violent effort, it wrings out from itself what it wishes. So it exults, victor over itself and self-vanquished' (Faral, vv. 1751–6; trans. Nims 78–9). The desire of the poet's mind to exercise mastery over the material stuff of language that may be resistant to control suggests the uncomfortable possibility that the poet might be unmanned by the sensuality of his *materia*. By the late Middle Ages, the dazzling sword of language wielded to such great virile effect by classical and medieval technicians of language has become literalized as a woman whose sensual power deprives her victims of all agency.

The late medieval Spanish sentimental romance, *Cárcel de amor* (*Prison of Love*), written in 1492 by Diego de San Pedro, opens with a scene that represents a striking conflation of desire, the feminized dazzling sword, and its hapless male victim. The narrator of the story (who is also identified as the Auctor), while travelling through the mountains on his way home, is confronted by the sight of a fierce-looking hairy wildman carrying an iron shield in his left hand and wielding in his right hand, in place of the expected sword, an image of a beautiful woman engraved on shiny stone, which is emitting flaming rays that blind the narrator and burn the body of the unfortunate captive whom the wildman is dragging by a rope behind him. In the explanation of this opening allegory, both the reader and the Auctor discover that the wildman is Desire personified and the brilliant, dangerous image is the weapon with which he causes 'aficiones' ['passion' (*Prison* 5)] that burn and destroy men's lives (*Cárcel* 84). Despite the best efforts of the Auctor on behalf of the unfortunate prisoner of love, Leriano, the consuming effects of love leave him defeated and lead to his suicide.

Critics have wondered about the sword-like image of flashing feminine beauty wielded by Desire, positing its provenance in a combination of the iconographical conventions of the Virgin Mary and Venus, the goddess of love (Sharrer), or, explaining its significance as a way of figuring the extent to which the feminine is bound up with desire and its unsettling impact on the phallocentric positioning of language (Gilkison 115–17). However, given the extent to which Diego de San Pedro, author of the *Cárcel de amor*, was steeped in the study and practice of classical, medieval, and humanist rhetoric, the dazzling, purely feminine sword in the hand of Desire can be viewed as a late medieval distillation of the long tradition of rhetorically ornate language intended to unman its opponent by means of its force and beauty. Like the pliable, inert stuff of language mastered by the orator, preacher, or poet, the shining image of the woman held by Desire disturbs the Auctor's sight ['me turbava la vista' (*Cárcel* 81)] to the extent that his eyes deprive him of the power of speech. While looking upon the woeful state of love's captive seated upon a chair of fire within the castle, the Auctor states that this sight so disrupts the other senses that his eyes are forced to exercise the function of the tongue that is too paralyzed to ask the necessary questions about the bizarre scene arrayed before him ['con la turbación, descargava con los ojos la lengua' (86)]. The transformation of linguistic expression into vision whereby the eyes work instead of the tongue is a direct effect of the deadly beauty of the woman-sword. Robert Folger has likened the shining *imagen femenil* to the kind of striking image that the orator forms in his mind as a mechanism for retaining the contents of his speech in the memory (Folger 623). The power of the mnemonic image so aptly described in the pseudo-Ciceronian *Rhetorica ad Herennium* (3.21.35–6) functions in a way similar to that of ornate figures of speech intended to unman the audience. The lover, Leriano, once penetrated by the sight of the feminine image, is ultimately unmanned by the passion that invades his mind, while Laureola, in her resistance to passion and marshalling of reason, is more closely aligned with the cultural construction of masculinity (Folger 633–4).

It is significant that in the *Cárcel* the sword no longer belongs to the hyper-masculine speaker or writer, but rather to the figure of Desire, an allegorization of the power of the senses to overwhelm reason, to deprive the victim of agency and language. One wonders, then, whether there is a crisis of rhetoric and its effect on the body that are being explored in the text. One critic of the *Cárcel*, Maureen Ihrie, views the text as 'a literary dramatization of rhetoric, of how rhetoric could and should be used in Renaissance Spain' (1). Reading the role of the savage figure of Desire as the embodiment of the Ciceronian myth of the orator as the founder of civilization who uses rhetoric as spur to social cohesion and organization, and the contrasting role of Laureola's father as the evil king who relies on fixed, scholastic notions of truth that are resistant to circumstance and moral nuance, Ihrie argues that the text explores the conflict between the humanistic embrace of a renewed Ciceronian emphasis on the virtue and morality of rhetoric and the rigid, dry, 'barbarian' rejection of pagan rhetoric characteristic of reactionary, scholastic rhetoric (Ihrie 2–4). However, the dazzling feminine image wielded by the disruptive figure of Desire certainly complicates such an optimistic view of the fortunes of Renaissance rhetoric and its corporeal effects. While Ihrie's perceptive point about the metatextual role of rhetoric in the novel is valid, the substitution of Desire for the manly, powerful orator suggests that the yoking of the power of love to that of rhetoric is fraught with anxiety, an anxiety that is played out in the realm of language.

The role of the Auctor is to restore language to both himself and Leriano, bringing desire back into language in the form of the epistolary exchange between Leriano and his beloved Laureola, with his own words fulfilling an intermediary function between the two lovers. What is striking in the *Cárcel*, though, is the trouble caused by the introduction of gender into the process of the generation of language and desire. Although the male persona of the wildman, a figure who, by definition, is located outside the bounds of human social discourse, wields the dazzling woman-sword to deadly effect, no human user of language in this text is rhetorically effective. Leriano's words fail to truly persuade Laureola to love him (her replies make clear that she is only answering out of pity or duty), and Laureola's minimal use of language suggests a refusal to be drawn into the battlefield of words (Gilkison 117). The marshalling of merely human words, although carried out in proper oratorical, dictaminal form (Corfis 33–6; Whinnom, intro. 52–4), is no match for the phallic, yet feminine, weapon of beauty wielded by desire upon vulnerable men.

The inefficacy of rhetorically crafted language is also conveyed visually in the opening tableau of the novel that, in fact, constitutes a reversal of iconographic norms in medieval and Renaissance depictions of the power of rhetoric. The representation of the seductive power of rhetoric is commonly depicted as a woman wielding the iconic sword of language. In a medieval illustration of *rhethorica* from Thomasin von Zerklaere's *Der welsche Gast* (ca 1215), Rhethorica is seated on a dais opposite a standing Tullius (Plett 506, 528 fig. 70). Both figures are holding onto a large shield in the middle of which extends a large sword that Tullius grips by the handle and Rhethorica grips by the end of the blade. In a later early modern image on a playing card designed by Andrea Mantegna (1431–1506), Rhetorica is displayed in imperial majesty, wearing a crowned helmet and a jewelled breastplate, and holding up a large, very sharp sword in her right hand, a sword that Heinrich Plett surmises is 'a symbol of the penetrating sharpness of judicial oratory' (508, 530 fig. 72).

In addition to this iconographic convention of Lady Rhetoric and the sword of language, we also find in the early modern period another representation of the irresistible pull and power of rhetoric. The opening of one of the most basic rhetorical handbooks in the Middle Ages, the Ciceronian *De inventione*, casts the invention of rhetoric as a civilizing force, creating a structured, harmonious society out of wild chaos. Early modern representations of the civilizing power of rhetoric often use the mythological figure of Hercules, whose traditional physical force had liberated the world from the terror of monsters. Hercules's physical power is now displaced from his club to his tongue. Issuing from Hercules's tongue are the golden chains of eloquence by which he subdues his enemies, who are drawn behind him by these chains attached to their ears (Plett 513–16).

The opening scene of the *Cárcel de amor* combines both of these iconographic motifs, but with subversive or ludic intent. The monstrous wildman who identifies himself as Desire to the Auctor stands in for the regal, powerful figure of Rhetorica, who is now reduced to a feminized, corporealized instrument wielded by Desire. Instead of the civilizing force of the orator who binds his captives with his golden chains of language, the hairy savage forcibly drags his captive behind him, and unleashes social and political chaos when the love that is sparked by Desire produces suffering, war, familial discord, destruction, and ultimately the death of the lover. The violence that is so enmeshed in the history of rhetoric's attempts to harness the deadly beauty of language to a phallic, agonistic principle of masculine aggression has now come full circle. The *Cárcel* plays with these norms and demonstrates the consequences of rhetoric's violent turning against its own gendered principles. When language is provoked and produced in and through sensual desire, it is drained of its rhetorical efficacy and loses its masculine agency as a force for social good.

The *Cárcel*'s implicit critique of the potency of flashy, sensual language appears to go against the grain of much early modern thinking about the aesthetic power of *figurae*. While there is little research on the approach to figuration in late fifteenth- and early sixteenth-century Spanish rhetorical theory, according to Brian Vickers, figures in English and French literary aesthetics constitute the 'basic principle of Renaissance literary language' whose organic relationship to subject matter is a source of emotional or intellectual conviction, or simply of beauty (Vickers 332). The *Cárcel de amor*'s conflation of deadly, dazzling sword of language and blinding, incapacitating love points to a thorough familiarity with the conventions of rhetorical theory and practice, as well as to a crisis of confidence in the efficacy of language, a crisis that challenges the gendered assumptions of masculine power and figural beauty.

NOTES

1 All translations are my own unless otherwise noted.
2 The base meaning of *radius* is 'staff' or 'rod.' Lewis and Short, *A Latin Dictionary*.

WORKS CITED

Alan of Lille. *De arte praedicatoria*. *Patrologia Latina* 210, cols. 52–198.

Alberic of Montecassino. *Flores rhetorici*. Ed. D.M. Iguanez and H.M. Willard. *Miscellanea Cassinense* 14 (1938): 33–59.

– *Flowers of Rhetoric*. Trans. Joseph M. Miller. In *Readings in Medieval Rhetoric*. Ed. Joseph M. Miller, Michael H. Prosser, and Thomas W. Benson. Bloomington: Indiana University Press, 1973. 131–61.

Ashby, Alexander. *De artificioso modo predicandi*. Ed. Franco Morenzoni. 'Aux origins des *Artes praedicandi*. Le *De artificioso modo predicandi* d'Alexandre D'Ashby.' *Studi medievali*, 3a series, 32, no. 2 (1991): 887–935.

Augustine. *De doctrina christiana*. Ed. Joseph Martin. Corpus Christianorum Series Latina, vol. 32. Turnhout, Belgium: Brepols, 1962. 1–167.

– *On Christian Doctrine*. Trans. D.W. Robertson, Jr. Indianapolis: Bobbs-Merrill, 1958.

Chobham, Thomas de. *Summa de arte praedicandi*. Ed. Franco Morenzoni. Corpus Christianorum Series Latina, vol. 82. Turnhout, Belgium: Brepols, 1988.

Cicero. *De Oratore*. Ed. and trans. H. Rackham. *De oratore in Two Volumes*. Loeb Classical Library. Cambridge, MA: Harvard University Press, 1960.

– *Orator*. Trans. H.M. Hubbell. Loeb Classical Library. Cambridge, MA: Harvard University Press, 1988

Connolly, Joy. 'Virile Tongues: Rhetoric and Masculinity.' In *A Companion to Roman Rhetoric*. Ed. William Dominik and Jon Hall. Malden, MA: Blackwell, 2007. 83–97.

Corfis, Ivy A. 'The *Dispositio* of Diego de San Pedro's *Cárcel de Amor*.' *Iberromania* 21 (1985): 32–47.

Dugan, John. *Making a New Man: Ciceronian Self-fashioning in the Rhetorical Works*. Oxford: Oxford University Press, 2005.

– 'Preventing Ciceronianism: C. Licinius Calvus' Regimens for Sexual and Oratorical Self-Mastery.' *Classical Philology* 96, no. 4 (2001): 400–28.

Eiximenis, Francesc. 'L'*Ars Praedicandi* de Francesc Eiximenis.' In *Homenatge a Antoni Rubió i Lluch. Miscellània d'estudis literaris, històrics i linguistics*. Ed. P. Martí. Vol. 2. Barcelona, 1936. 301–40.

Fantham, Elaine. *Comparative Studies in Republican Latin Imagery*. Toronto: University of Toronto Press, 1972.

– *The Roman World of Cicero's 'De Oratore.'* Oxford: Oxford University Press, 2004.

Folger, Robert. '*Carceles de amor*: "Gender Trouble" and Male Fantasies in Fifteenth-Century Castile.' *Bulletin of Spanish Studies* 83, no. 5 (2006): 617–35.

Geoffrey of Vinsauf. *Poetria nova*. In *Les arts poétiques du XIIe et du XIIIe siècle*. Ed. Edmond Faral. Paris: Champion, 1962. 194–262.

– *'Poetria Nova' of Geoffrey of Vinsauf*. Trans. Margaret F. Nims. Toronto: Pontifical Institute of Mediaeval Studies Press, 1967.

Gilkison, Jean. 'Language and Gender in Diego de San Pedro's *Cárcel de Amor*.' *Journal of Hispanic Research* 3 (1994–5): 113–23.

Gregory the Great. *Regula pastoralis*. *Patrologia Latina* 77, cols. 12–125.

Gunderson, Erik. *Declamation, Paternity and Roman Identity: Authority and the Rhetorical Self*. Cambridge: Cambridge University Press, 2003.

Habinek, Thomas. *Ancient Rhetoric and Oratory*. Malden, MA: Blackwell, 2005.

Humbert of Romans. *Treatise on Preaching*. Ed. Walter M. Conlon. Trans. Dominican Students of the Province of St Joseph. London: Blackfriars, 1955.

Ihrie, Maureen. 'Discourses of Power in the *Cárcel de amor*.' *Hispanófila* 125 (1999): 1–10.

Kennedy, George A. *Classical Rhetoric and Its Christian and Secular Tradition from Ancient to Modern Times*. 2nd ed. Chapel Hill: University of North Carolina Press, 1999.

Kuefler, Mathew. *The Manly Eunuch: Masculinity, Gender Ambiguity, and Christian Ideology in Late Antiquity*. Chicago: University of Chicago Press, 2001.

Leidl, Christoph G. 'The Harlot's Art: Metaphor and Literary Criticism.' In *Metaphor, Allegory and the Classical Tradition: Ancient Thought and Modern Revisions*. Ed. G.R. Boys-Stones. Oxford: Oxford University Press, 2003. 31–54.

Martianus Capella. *Martianus Capella*. Ed. James Willis. Leipzig: Teubner, 1983.

– *Martianus Capella and the Seven Liberal Arts. Volume II: The Marriage of Philology and Mercury*. Trans. William Harris Stahl with E.L. Burge. New York: Columbia University Press, 1977.

Morenzoni, Franco. 'Aux origins des *Artes praedicandi*. Le *De artificioso modo predicandi* d'Alexandre d'Ashby.' *Studi medievali*, 3a series, 32, no. 2 (1991): 887–935.

Plato. *Gorgias*. Trans. Donald J. Zeyl. In *Plato on Rhetoric and Language: Four Key Dialogues*. Intro. Jean Nienkamp. Mahwah, NJ: Hermagoras Press, 1999. 83–162.

Plett, Heinrich F. *Rhetoric and Renaissance Culture*. Berlin: Walter de Gruyter, 2004.

Quintilian. *The Orator's Education*. Ed. and trans. Donald A. Russell. 5 vols. Loeb Classical Library. Cambridge, MA: Harvard University Press, 2001.

Remigius of Auxerre. *Remigii Autissiodorensis Commentum in Martianum Capellam, Libri III–IX*. Ed. Cora E. Lutz. Leiden: Brill, 1965.

Rhetorica ad Herennium. Trans. Harry Caplan. Loeb Classical Library. Cambridge, MA: Harvard University Press, 1954.

Roberts. Michael. *The Jeweled Style: Poetry and Poetics in Late Antiquity*. Ithaca, NY: Cornell University Press, 1989.

Roisman, Joseph. *The Rhetoric of Manhood: Masculinity in the Attic Orators*. Berkeley: University of California Press, 2005.

Ross, Jill. *Figuring the Feminine: The Rhetoric of Female Embodiment in Medieval Hispanic Literature*. Toronto: University of Toronto Press, 2008.

San Pedro, Diego de. *Cárcel de amor*. Ed. Keith Whinnom. Madrid: Castalia, 1982.

– *Prison of Love*. Trans. Keith Whinnom. Edinburgh: Edinburgh University Press, 1979.

Sharrer, Harvey L. 'La *Cárcel de amor* de Diego de San Pedro: La confluencia de lo sagrado y lo profano en "la imagen femenil entallada en una piedra muy clara".' In *Actas del III Congreso de la Asociación Hispánica de Literatura Medieval (Salamanca, 3 al 6 de octubre de 1989)*. Ed. María Isabel Toro Pascua. Salamanca: Biblioteca Española del Siglo XV; Departamento de Literatura Española e Hispanoamericana, 1994. Vol. 2. 983–96.

Vickers, Brian. *In Defence of Rhetoric*. Oxford: Clarendon, 1988.

Waleys, Thomas. *De modo componendi sermones*. In *Artes praedicandi: Contribution à l'histoire de la rhétorique au moyen-âge*. Ed. Thomas M. Charland. Paris: J. Vrin, 1936. 328–403.

Walters, Jonathan. 'Invading the Roman Body: Manliness and Impenetrability in Roman Thought.' In *Roman Sexualities*. Ed. Judith P. Hallett and Marilyn B. Skinner. Princeton, NJ: Princeton University Press, 1997. 29–43.

Waters, Claire M. *Angels and Earthly Creatures: Preaching, Performance, and Gender in the Later Middle Ages*. Philadelphia: University of Pennsylvania Press, 2004.

Whinnom, Keith. 'Introducción.' In *Cárcel de amor*. Ed. Keith Whinnom. Madrid: Castalia, 1982. 7–66.

Williams, Craig A. *Roman Homosexuality: Ideologies of Masculinity in Classical Antiquity*. Oxford: Oxford University Press, 1999.

PART THREE

Performing the Body

7 Amputating the Traitor: Healing the Social Body in Public Executions for Treason in Late Medieval England

DANIELLE M. WESTERHOF

It is a well-established anthropological axiom that for human beings the body is the 'first and most natural instrument' to give meaning to and conceptually structure their environment and social interactions (Mauss 104). Body metaphors for abstract notions have always been part of social and cultural discourse, and as for example Mary Douglas in *Natural Symbols* has argued, the ways in which the human body is perceived by society will be informed by how it is used to render visible these abstractions. This is particularly evident in the perception of the social body as a regulator of individual corporeal behaviours in social interaction.

In the past twenty years or so, the 'historiography of the body' has become increasingly popular. Often engaging with modern theoretical stances and with studies focusing on the perception of the body in other historical eras, medieval scholars have also turned towards the study of the body (Porter). The function of the somatic in medieval religious experience and eschatology has been systematically mapped (e.g., Brown; Bynum, *Resurrection of the Body*). Danielle Jacquart, Miri Rubin, and Joan Cadden, amongst others, have called attention to the fact that notions of physiology, gender, and disease served to define, maintain, and on occasion subvert patterns of social interaction and hierarchy. Additionally, political historians still draw inspiration from Ernest Kantorowicz's 1957 study on the 'king's two bodies,' in which notions of the body politic were for the first time systematically explored by a modern historian.

In general, however, the focus has been on constructions of the human body in literature and art, while less attention has been paid to the slippage of these discursive bodies into everyday practice. The ways in which the human body appears in text and image may allow us to make tentative observations about how medieval men and women saw their own and others' bodies, and how educated notions and metaphors of the body filtered through and were shaped by day-to-day experience and observation; as at least one sociologist has remarked: we *are* our bodies as much as we *have* them (Turner 232).[1]

It is my intention in this article to examine how medieval ideas on the body, disease, and treatment fused with notions of society and betrayal in the work of political commentators of the twelfth and thirteenth centuries in England, in particular in John of Salisbury's *Policraticus*, and how this complex slipped into English judicial practice later in the thirteenth century in the elaborate public deaths of traitors. My argument will centre on how the body of the traitor came to *represent* the corrupted body social while at the same time *being* a corruption to be expelled from it during the process of the public execution, whereby the notion of 'amputation' acquired a double signification of dismembering and beheading a physical body as well as of cutting away a rotten 'limb' from society.[2]

This approach will allow us to read the traitor's body as more than the object of communal or royal revenge, or its treatment as one means of *surveillance* in a Foucauldian sense (Foucault; Cohen; Royer). Instead, one also has to take into account that for executions to be politically meaningful, they would have to be couched in terms understood by those for whom the executions were staged. These terms related as much to the ways in which treason was understood as a crime, as to the ways in which it was rendered visible during the punishment. This is not to say that public executions were not meant to be educational, not staged as a show of political force, and not enacted out of ordinary lust for revenge, but what they reveal above and beyond all is the constant interplay of the somatic and the conceptual that served to explain everyday social interaction.

John of Salisbury's *Policraticus*, written in the late 1150s, is generally hailed as the first comprehensive medieval treatise on political theory, although, as Cary Nederman has observed, it is perhaps better 'described as the philosophical memoir of one of the most learned courtier-bureaucrats of twelfth-century Europe' (*John of Salisbury* 51).[3] In its eight books, John unfolds a vision of ideal government based on a combination of ancient moral philosophy and Christian theology. He draws his material from a wealth of sources, although some in the digested format of florilegia and some through indirect transmission (Nederman, *John of Salisbury* 53–4). Professing himself a follower of Cicero in spirit, he maintains that the fundamental prerequisites for good government are 'honesty' and 'usefulness' (Liebeschütz 80). This, as we shall see, has significant consequences for John's ideas on treason. However, the *Policraticus* is perhaps best known for its extended discussion of society as a body, cloaked in a fictitious letter of instruction to Emperor Trajan by Plutarch.

The idea of society as a body did not originate with John and can be traced back, via the Pauline notion of the Church as a body of Christians, to Greek and Latin philosophers. Despite the fact that only a relatively small selection of ancient philosophy was known to John and his contemporaries, the idea of the body social or religious was relatively widespread (Struve). The novelty of John's approach lies in his vision of a society in which each member exists in a hierarchical yet interdependent and cooperative relationship with other members towards the single purpose of maintaining harmony (*Policraticus* Lib. IV, Cap. 1). As there are different organs within the body with different functions, so there are different social groups with different tasks: those who are destined to toil the land, for example, should not aspire to more wealth or a higher status. At the same time, John stresses that this does not mean that the lowest social groups should be treated with contempt; because the peasants (or the feet) sustain the rest of society with their toil, the king (or head) should take care of their well-being: 'The feet coincide with peasants perpetually bound to the soil ... those who erect, sustain and move forward the mass of the whole body ... Remove from the fittest body the aid of the feet; it does not proceed under its own power, but either crawls shamefully, uselessly and offensively on its hands or else is moved with the assistance of brute animals' (Lib. V, Cap. 2). Thus, although adherence to a hierarchy still lies at the basis of John's vision of society, cooperation and mutual respect are equally essential to maintain a harmonious collective, so that whatever happens to one part of the body will have a potentially detrimental effect on the rest of the organism (Nederman, 'Physiological Significance' 214–15).

John develops this point further in his version of the fable of the man, his belly, and his limbs: the stomach (the treasury) appears to swallow up all profit, which angers the limbs since they feel they do not benefit from their hard work. They decide to starve the stomach but only manage to endanger the whole body with their hunger strike. The limbs repent just in time and the body is restored. As John's contemporary Marie de France maintained in the moral to her version of the fable: 'If either one [person] fails the other / Evil befalls them both' (Nederman and Forhan 25). The implications are evident: people should not aspire to a different position to the one they have, but trust that those whose function it is to oversee the running of society (the king and his advisors) will maintain the common good. Moreover, justice cannot be dispensed by anyone other than the king, who receives his guidance, powers, and superior moral virtue from

God (Lib. IV, Cap. 1–2). For the limbs to take justice into their own hand is to disrupt the natural harmony of society.

Widely circulating ideas about health and the prevention of disease appear to inform John's thinking. The early encyclopedist Isidore of Seville saw medicine as the art of moderation geared towards maintaining the balance of the four humours, which could be affected by internal and external factors. Effective treatment of disease meant being aware of the variables that had led to the imbalance and direct the treatment towards restoring harmony (*Etymologiae* Lib. IV, Cap. 2, 5). Although limited compared to the medical advances of the fourteenth century and beyond, this system was common knowledge within the monastic milieu in which John moved (Siraisi 115–18).

Sometimes, however, the affected body part was beyond gentle treatment or cure: it was dead, corrupt, fetid, useless, and thus a danger to the rest of the body. After proscribing a progressively severe treatment of the diseased part with 'iron and fire' (i.e., cauterisation), the author of the early tenth-century *Leechbook of Bald* suggests that 'the dead and the unfeeling flesh' should be amputated as soon as possible (Lib. I, Cap. 35). The French surgeon Henri de Mondeville (fl. 1300–20) concurs and adds that the 'corruption' should be taken away, 'so to defend the patient against death' (*Chirurgie* Tract. III, Doctr. I, Cap. 6). Amputation can therefore be necessary to save the patient's life, but only after all else has failed.

To John of Salisbury, following common physiological ideas, any excess, deprivation, or injury disrupts the internal harmony of the body social, and it is therefore the moral duty of the ruler (*medicus rei publicae*) to restore society's health by administering the law like a medicine (*medicinaliter*; *Policraticus*, Lib. IV, Cap. 8). This does not come without a price, however, and sometimes the ruler will have to resort to more painful measures, which will hurt the *medicus* as much as the patient:

> It is above all the habit of physicians [*medicorum ... consuetudo*] that when they are not able to cure an affliction with palliatives and gentle medicines, *they employ harsher cures, as for example fire or iron* ... And thus, when mild power does not suffice for the ruler to cure the vices of inferiors, he properly administers painful blows of punishment ... But who is so strong as to amputate [*amputare*] a part of his body without pain? ... In tormenting the parts of the body of which he is the head, he serves the law mournfully and with groans. (Lib. IV, Cap. 8; my emphasis)

John's apparent ignorance of medical procedure may be reflected in a conflation of cauterisation and amputation, but the effect remains a powerful invocation of images of judicial corporeal punishment in which the criminal may be subjected to iron and fire with deadly consequences if he poses a persistent danger to the health of the body social. Moreover, it is evident that John's 'cure' is directed towards society rather than the 'unfeeling' or straying limb.

This is nowhere more sharply thrown into relief than in John's discussion of the nature of treason. Echoing contemporary attempts to define treason, influenced by Roman law, and found in legal tracts such as *Glanvill* (ca 1180) and *Bracton* (ca 1220), John lists a number of crimes that are primarily intended to cause disruption to society. Treason (*crimen majestatis* – this is a term found in Roman law) thus encompasses anything from contemplating regicide to fleeing from battles; helping the enemies of the realm with money, military supplies, or information; and inciting rebellion (Lib. VI, Cap. 25).[4] Moreover, he equates treason with sacrilege. Both crimes contain a decidedly moral dimension (dishonesty, secrecy, apostasy) and both indicate the spiritual death of the perpetrator: by committing treason or sacrilege, the perpetrator acts against the greater good of the collective and is therefore no longer of use (Lib. VI, Cap. 25).

Treason thus does not only affect the ruler but the whole of society, and John's list emphasizes the threat to public security inherent in the crime. Therefore, although John maintains that the ruler is by ordination 'a sort of deity on earth, and that any attack on him is an attack on God,' he argues above and beyond that as a consequence of the interdependence of head and members, 'a blow to the head [*lesio capitis*] ... is carried back to all the members and a wound unjustly inflicted upon any member whomsoever [i.e., outside the bounds of justice] tends to the injury of the head' (Lib. VI, Cap. 25). Treason thus reverberates throughout the social body and like a corrupted wound will destroy the body if left to fester. John, invoking Christ's metaphor of removing offending members from the body of the religious community (Matthew 18:8: 'If your eye or your foot offend you, root it out and cast it away from you'), concludes that in order to preserve the safety of the body, the corrupt body part ought to be removed: '[T]his is to be observed by the prince in regard to all of the members to the extent that not only are they to be rooted out, broken off and thrown far away, if they give offence to the faith or public security, but *they are to be destroyed utterly so that the security of the corporate community may be procured by the extermination of the one member*' (Lib. VI, Cap. 26; my emphasis).[5] The painful procedure of the death penalty, therefore, is for the good of the community since the perpetrator is corrupted, spiritually dead, and beyond cure through the very nature of his crimes.

The practice of amputating corrupt and deadened body parts thus takes on a decidedly moral dimension in John's vision of ideal society. Although the ruler is advised only to consider harsh punishment in moderation lest he be branded a tyrant (Lib. IV, Cap. 8), there is to be no mercy for habitual offenders or for those who commit crimes that bring society into moral danger; they are utterly useless. Following contemporary legal treatises, John asserts that the one crime which falls within the latter category is treason (both temporal and spiritual). But where legal tracts restrict themselves to providing a definition of treason and stipulate what punishment should follow, John uses powerfully emotive language and metaphors taken from medical discourse to stress the effects of social disruption and dishonesty on society and to advocate the removal of members acting against the common good.

It is not possible to digress *in extensio* on the problems surrounding the definition of treason in this period. What constituted treason was inevitably informed by political circumstances and opinions, or personal enmity. Punishments could differ accordingly and could be influenced by the social position of the accused. Therefore, although death and dismemberment had been advocated as punishments for treason by Anglo-Saxon and Anglo-Norman legal theorists, before the middle of the thirteenth century these were hardly ever enacted (e.g., Alfred, Intro. 49.7; V Æthelred, 28–30; II Cnut 64; *Leges Henrici primi*, C.10.1, 12.1a, 64.2).[6] Until this time, treason was a crime committed mostly by those below the level of the aristocracy. With the notable exception of Earl Waltheof of Northumbria in 1076, rebellious barons were fined, exiled, or imprisoned; their followers were often killed or maimed (e.g., Orderic 2:322–3 and 6:352–5; Gillingham, *Richard I* 50 and 269). This clemency towards the aristocracy can of course be partially explained in terms of financial gain, the risk of retribution, or the weakness of the royal position. As William Rufus was advised after the 1188 rebellion: 'The man who does injury today may perhaps serve as a friend in the future' (Orderic 4:133); Stephen was likewise unable to act against his rebellious barons, although he threatened to hang both Geoffrey de Mandeville and Ranulph of Chester if they failed to hand over their estates to him (*Gesta Stephani* 162–3, 195–9). Moreover, as Judith Green rightly points out, to punish aristocratic rebellion would be an act of hypocrisy for rulers such as William Rufus and Stephen since 'in taking the throne they had perjured themselves' (264).

By the late 1230s the royal attitude towards aristocratic treasonous acts had begun to change.[7] In 1238, according to Matthew Paris, an anonymous 'literate knight' was executed for trying to kill the king. Rather than imposing exile or even the more common punishment of hanging, Henry III had the knight drawn, hanged, quartered, and displayed in public (*Chronica majora* 3:497–8). In 1242 it was William de Marisco's turn. Son of a justiciar of Ireland, he had been implicated in the murder of Richard Marshal, earl of Pembroke; upon being outlawed he became a pirate with some companions in 1235 and had allegedly sent the *armiger literatus* in 1238 to kill Henry III. After his capture in 1242, William was drawn, hanged, eviscerated, and quartered. His comrades, however, were simply drawn and hanged (*Chronica majora* 4:193–7; *Historia Anglorum* 2:462–3). Although in the case of the anonymous knight the charge was plotting to kill the king, William de Marisco was more prominently accused of crimes against king and kingdom; in other words, he had intentionally endangered the health of the social body. These executions thus appear to mark a turning point in the history of royal relations with the aristocracy as well as a change in the perception of crimes directed against the body social. The real impact of these changes in attitude can only be fully understood from the events of 4 August 1265.

On this day, Simon de Montfort, earl of Leicester, his eldest son, and several of his followers were deliberately killed on the battlefield of Evesham. If that was not outrageous enough (Robert of Gloucester referred to the battle as the 'murder' of Evesham; 2:764), the earl's corpse was dismembered, emasculated,[8] and beheaded by some unknown members of the royal army. Echoing the telling image of William de Marisco's sword and shield broken in half in Matthew Paris's autograph copy of the *Historia Anglorum* (BL Royal 14.C.VII, f. 133v), we find an arresting depiction of de Montfort's mutilation in the early fourteenth-century *Flores historiarum* continuation by an anonymous monk from Rochester (BL Cotton Nero D.II, f. 177r). The scene centralizes the dismembered corpse of the earl, which is identified by the arms on the shield and hauberk displayed alongside the body. The only other identified figure is de Montfort's eldest son, fully clothed but disarmed, in a pose reminiscent of the 'cross-legged' knightly effigies popular at the time (Tummers 1980). To the left, a number of anonymous knights are depicted in the act of 'amputating' the earl's limbs and head (Rishanger 2:37; Wykes 173), while to the right, barely visible in the present state of the manuscript, one can make out a number of bodies, presumably representing de Montfort's followers, in a disorderly heap on the ground. A recently discovered account of de Montfort's final hours tellingly states that after Roger de Mortimer, a member of the death squad assembled for the purpose by Prince Edward, had struck the fatal blow that killed the earl, 'all worthy nobles turned away from him' ['tote la gent de value de luy se turnerent'] while unidentified 'others' ['puis autres'] conducted the dismemberment (Laborderie, Maddicott, and Carpenter 408). When Simon de Montfort the younger finally arrived on the scene, he was confronted with his father's head being carried around on a spear (Wykes 175). In light of de Montfort's posthumous popularity and the suspected royal hand in the affair, it is not surprising that no one came forward to claim responsibility for the act and that the narrative shies away from implicating any aristocratic participants.[9]

What is significant about Simon de Montfort's post-mortem dismemberment, beheading, and subsequent display of body parts is that these are punitive elements only found in association with treason in legal treatises and in the executions earlier in Henry III's reign. De Montfort was generally considered a traitor by royalists. Before the Battle of Lewes in 1264 both Henry III and his brother Richard of Cornwall had renounced the Montfordians as traitors to the king and kingdom (*Flores historiarum* 2:493–4; Carpenter, 'From King John' 32). De Montfort was hailed by the royalist army at Evesham as an 'old traitor' who should not expect to survive the day (*Annales de Oseneia* 170). Similarly, the *Song of Lewes* suggests that the barons did not act to maintain the 'peace and common customs' of the kingdom, and were in fact guilty of treason (l. 604). It is obvious that in the eyes of the royalists, de Montfort was a traitor who deserved to meet a traitor's fate. For Henry III and Edward it was probably enough to remove the earl permanently from the political stage; for their followers it was not. By deliberately amputating the limbs from the earl's body, the royalist knights drew attention to the fact that he had endangered the well-being of the polity, that he had become corrupted and was therefore to be 'rooted out' from the body social. Significantly, in a letter to Pope Alexander IV written in 1258 de Montfort explained his actions in words that appear to be lifted straight from John of Salisbury's *Policraticus*: '[T]he republic is a sort of body, which grows through the benefit of divine gifts, and is driven by the command of the highest equity and ruled by a sort of rational government, and it is not useful that in one body of members there is discord' (*Chronica majora* 6:402–3; cf. *Policraticus*, Lib. V, Cap. 2). The metaphor of the body politic had thus entered the political arena; with the earl's death and dismemberment by the royalist army it seems that the concept of amputating corrupt body parts had arrived as well.[10]

This is not to say that all traitors and rebels were treated in the same way from this point onwards. With the death of Simon de Montfort, the leader of the rebellion had gone; his followers could be dealt with more leniently in the re-established peace. They lost their possessions, but were allowed to live, and under the provisions of the Dictum of Kenilworth (31 October 1266), the survivors of Evesham were allowed to reclaim their social position and their estates after paying a hefty fine (in accordance to their status and financial circumstances). Moreover, the king was urged not to harbour any resentment towards those who had strayed. After the prolonged state of war in the kingdom, it was expedient to refill the royal coffers and to move on (art. 5, 12–17).

The gruesome physicality of treason punishments did not stop, however. During the reigns of Edward I and Edward II, aristocratic men accused of treason faced the prospect of a public death accompanied by various forms of dismemberment. Moreover, despite initial unease in chronicles about the corporeal punishment of aristocrats, their authors generally condoned them when it was evident that crimes had been committed to endanger the stability of the polity. Although their non-English birth will have weighed against them in public opinion, men such as David of Wales (d. 1283), William Wallace (d. 1305), Simon Fraser, and John earl of Atholl (both d. 1306) were considered traitors of the people of the whole realm, as Edward I was keen to point out. David of Wales was accused of spilling 'vast quantities of innocent blood' (*Foedera* 1:630); William Wallace had committed a range of crimes against the people of England and Scotland, including robbery, raping and killing innocent women and children, and sacrilege, as well as having committed treason (*Annales Londonienses* 142). Thomas of Lancaster and Andrew Harclay were both sent to their deaths for treason against the king and the kingdom (*Rotuli parliamentorum* 2:3; *Foedera* 2:509) In 1326 Hugh Despenser the younger was sent to his execution with the words 'traitor,' 'renegade,' and 'evildoer' firmly ringing in his ears. According to the surviving text of his judgment, he had been convicted by the whole kingdom ['bones gentz du Roialme, greindres et meindres, riches et poures'] since he was an 'enemy of the Realm' (Taylor 73, 77).

The last years of Edward II's reign stand out as particularly bloody. By the 1320s it had become easier to accuse one's political opponents of disrupting the balance of power by assuming royal authority and depriving the king of his dignity. In this atmosphere of overheated treason rhetoric, those who rebelled against the king (whether or not for just reasons) stood to die if caught (Fryde). Without fail, however, convicted traitors died because they had disrupted the internal harmony of the kingdom.

The main instigators of the alleged treason were without fail condemned to a bloody death on the scaffold. Like Simon de Montfort in 1265, David of Wales, William Wallace, Simon Fraser, John of Atholl, Gilbert Middleton (d. 1318), Andrew Harclay (d. 1323), and the Despenser father and son (both d. 1326) were killed, beheaded, and in nearly all cases quartered for subsequent display of their body parts. Some were in addition eviscerated. All of them underwent the same humiliating procedure of being drawn, dressed in sackcloth or sewn into an oxhide, to the site of execution where they were hanged until unconscious before the dismemberment and beheading took place (Westerhof, 'Aristocratic Executions' 160–208).[11]

The changing perception of treason accompanied by a prominent increase in the number of treason accusations against the aristocracy from the later thirteenth century onwards are evidence of a shift in the relations between kings and their barons, but also of a shift in thinking about the unity of the realm, in which treason was a crime committed against all and not just against the king. From the Anglo-Saxon notion of *hlafordsearwe* ['betrayal of one's lord'], the concept of treason gradually came to encompass a betrayal of the kingdom as well as the king, however, without defining exactly *what* acts of treason involved under what circumstances. This development was paralleled by an increase in corporeal punishments of traitors, whereby the emphasis was on the public death and post-mortem mutilation of the main perpetrators.[12]

In 1352 the Statute of Treasons was drafted in response to a request by the Commons to have more clarity on what treason actually was, mainly to limit the number of treason cases in the local courts. As the text of the statute makes clear, the reasons for this request were essentially financial: in cases of treason, forfeited lands would fall to the king; if the crime was judged a felony, estates would go to the immediate superior of the culprit. The definition of treason in the statute, although it left a loophole for king and parliament to decide on individual cases whether or not treason had been committed, is interesting. More limited than earlier definitions, the list of crimes considered treason concerned threats to the safety of the king, his family, his government officials, and his justices. In other words, treason came to refer to the deliberate sabotage of the vital systems of the polity (which in John of Salisbury's metaphor equated to the head and its eyes, ears, and mouth, the heart and the stomach; *Policraticus* Lib. V, Cap. 2), signalling a more political view on the concept of treason possibly influenced by the body politic metaphor (*Statutes of the Realm* 25 Edward III, c. 2). Significantly, on the punishment of traitors the statute is conspicuously silent; the death and dismemberment of convicted traitors seems generally accepted as a just means of removing them from society.

Following in the footsteps of legal theorists and moral philosophers such as John of Salisbury, later thirteenth-century English society came to view treason as the crime most disruptive to society, a corrupting disease which would spread if left to fester. Death and post-mortem dismemberment were necessary to eradicate the traitor from society and heal the internal imbalance caused by his actions. The public executions of traitors were thus an act of cleansing the social body from disease, whereby the traitor came to embody the corrupted member painfully amputated from the body through his physical and social death, while simultaneously his unconscious body came to signify the body social itself, which was symbolically purged through the act of amputation.

NOTES

1 This also accounts for the impossibility of defining the 'body' or 'the body' (Kay and Rubin 1–9; Bynum, 'Why All the Fuss' 3).

2 Although in the twelfth century in England, corporeal punishments included mutilation such as blinding, castration, and cutting off individual limbs for felonies, and occasionally treason, these were not normally intended to kill the criminal. In the course of the thirteenth century, mutilation for treason becomes most definitely aimed towards killing the traitor, while lesser felonies are punished with hanging. For mutilation punishments, see Hyams, Hollister, and von Eickels. Von Eickels argues that castration and blinding in Germanic and Norman societies were common punishments for treason and other crimes. However, Gillingham ('Introduction of Chivalry') presents a different picture of Norman society becoming increasingly 'polite' in the course of the eleventh century.

3 Although a modern Latin edition of the first four books has recently appeared, I will use the older edition by Webb throughout. Translations are taken from Nederman (ed.), *Policraticus*.

4 I address the apparent difficulties of defining treason in this period more fully in Westerhof, 'Aristocratic Executions' 160–208. The standard discussion on the law of treason is Bellamy. See also Pollock and Maitland for the development of the concept of treason before the thirteenth century in England. The study of Roman law was well established by the time John of Salisbury wrote the *Policraticus*. Richardson and Sayles 71–4.

5 It is obvious that John was influenced here by Cicero, *De officiis*, iii.6, where he argues that just as body parts are amputated if they appear lifeless and thus jeopardize the health of the body, so is it allowed to kill those who endanger the well-being of society. See also Geraldus Cambrensis, *De principis instructione*, Dist. I, Cap. 32.

6 The standard edition for the Anglo-Saxon law codes is Liebermann.

7 According to David Carpenter, this is partly a consequence of the loss of Normandy in 1204 (Carpenter, 'From King John' 33–4).

8 Both images are reproduced in Westerhof (2008). The image from the Matthew Paris manuscript can also be found in the British Library's online catalogue of illuminated manuscripts (http://www.bl.uk/catalogues/illuminatedmanuscripts/). The scene of Simon de Montfort's mutilation is also displayed on the web pages for Kenilworth Castle, which is cared for by English Heritage (www.english-heritage.org.uk/).

9 Afterwards, de Montfort's head was allegedly sent to Roger de Mortimer's wife as a trophy (Rishanger 37).

10 It is significant that it was also around this time that we find the first evidence of John of Salisbury being considered an authority on the subject of legitimate resistance to tyrants, which forms another theme of the *Policraticus* (Linder 276–82).

11 For an analysis of Hugh Despenser the Younger's execution as an exercise in public humiliation and stigmatization, see Westerhof, 'Deconstructing Identities.'

12 Although any breach of the king's peace could result in either death or mutilation according to the circumstances or severity of the crime, treason is the only crime for which the two punishments are combined.

WORKS CITED

Primary Sources

Annales de Oseneia 1016–1347. *Annales monastici*. Ed. H.R. Luard. Vol. 4. Rolls Series 36. 5 vols. London: Longman, 1864–9.

Annales Londonienses. *Chronicles of the Reigns of Edward I and Edward II*. Ed. W. Stubbs. Vol. 1. Rolls Series 76. 2 vols. London: Longman, 1882–3.

Bracton. *On the Laws and Customs of England*. Ed. G.E. Woodbine and trans. S. Thorne. 4 vols. Cambridge, MA: Belknap Press, 1968.

Cicero, Marcus Tullius. *De officiis/On Obligations*. Ed. and trans. P.G. Walsh. Oxford: Oxford University Press, 2000.

Dictum of Kenilworth. *Documents of the Baronial Movement of Reform and*

Rebellion 1258–1267. No. 44. Ed. R.F. Treharne and I.J. Sanders. Oxford: Clarendon Press, 1973.
Downer, L.J., ed. *Leges Henrici primi*. Oxford: Clarendon Press, 1972.
Flores Historiarum. Ed. H.R. Luard. Rolls Series 95. 3 vols. London: Eyre & Spottiswoode, 1890.
Geraldus Cambrensis. *De principis instructione*. Ed. G.F. Warner. *Opera*. Gen. ed. J.S. Brewer et al. 8 vols. Vol. 8. Rolls Series 21. London: Longman, 1861–91.
Gesta Stephani: The Deeds of Stephen. Ed. and trans. K.R. Potter and R.H.C. Davis. Oxford: Clarendon Press, 1976.
Henri de Mondeville. *Die Chirurgie des Heinrich von Mondeville (Hermondaville) nach Berliner, Erfurter und Pariser Codices*. Ed. J.L. Pagel. Berlin: Hirschwald, 1892.
Isidore of Seville, *The Etymologies of Isidore of Seville*. Ed. and trans. S.A. Barney et al. Cambridge: Cambridge University Press, 2006.
John of Salisbury. *Policraticus; Of the Frivolities of Courtiers and the Footprints of Philosophers*. Ed. and trans. C.J. Nederman. Cambridge: Cambridge University Press, 1990.
– *Policraticus sive de nugis curialium et vestigiis philosophorum libri VIII*. Ed. C.C.I. Webb. 2 vols. Oxford: Clarendon Press, 1909.
Leechbook of Bald. Leechdoms, Wortcunning and Starcraft of Early England. Ed. O. Cockayne. Vol. 2. 3 vols. London: Rolls Series, 1864–6.
Liebermann, F. *Gesetze der Angelsachsen*. 3 vols. Halle: M. Niemeyer, 1898–1916.
Matthew Paris. *Chronica majora*. Ed. H.R. Luard. Rolls Series 57. 7 vols. London: Longman, 1872–83.
– *Historia Anglorum*. Ed. F. Madden. Rolls Series 44. 3 vols. London: Longman's, Green, Reader, and Dyer, 1866–9.
Nederman, C.J., and K. Langdon Forhan, eds. *Medieval Political Theory: A Reader. The Quest for the Body Politic 1100–1400*. London: Routledge, 1993.
Orderic Vitalis. *Historiae ecclesiasticae: The Ecclesiastical History of Orderic Vitalis*. Ed. M. Chibnall. 6 vols. Oxford: Clarendon Press, 1969–80.
Rishanger, William. *Chronica*. Ed. H.T. Riley. Rolls Series 28.2. London: Longman, 1865.
Robert of Gloucester. *Metrical Chronicle*. Ed. W.A. Wright. Rolls Series 86. 2 vols. London: Eyre & Spottiswoode, 1887.
Rotuli Parliamentorum. 6 vols. London, 1783.
Rymer, T., ed. *Foedera, Conventiones, Litterae et Acta Publica*. 4 vols. London, 1816–69.
Song of Lewes. Ed. C.L. Kingsford. Oxford: Clarendon Press, 1890.
Statutes of the Realm. 11 vols. London, 1810–28.

Taylor, J. 'The Judgement on Hugh Despenser, the Younger.' *Mediaevalia et Humanistica* 12 (1958): 70–7.

Tractatus de legibus et consuetudinibus regni Angliae qui Glanvilla vocatur. Ed. G.D.G. Hall. London: Nelson, 1965.

Wykes, Thomas. *Chronicon. Annales monastici*. Ed. H.R. Luard. Vol. 4. Rolls Series 36. 5 vols. London: Longman, 1864–9.

Secondary Sources

Bellamy, J.G. *The Law of Treason in England in the Later Middle Ages*. Cambridge: Cambridge University Press, 1970.

Brown, P. *The Body and Society: Men, Women and Sexual Renunciation in Early Christianity*. New York: Columbia University Press, 1988.

Bynum, C.W. *The Resurrection of the Body in Western Christianity 200–1336*. New York: Columbia University Press, 1995.

– 'Why All the Fuss about the Body? A Medievalist's Perspective.' *Critical Inquiry* 22 (1995): 1–33.

Cadden, J. *Meanings of Sex Difference in the Middle Ages*. Cambridge: Cambridge University Press, 1993.

Carpenter, D. 'From King John to the First English Duke, 1215–1337.' In *The House of Lords: A Thousand Years of British Tradition*. London: Smith's Peerage, 1994. 28–43.

Cohen, E. '"To Die a Criminal for the Common Good": The Execution Ritual in Late Medieval Paris.' In *Law, Custom and the Social Fabric in Medieval Europe: Essays in Honour of Bryce Lyon*. Ed. B.S. Bachrach and D. Nicholas. Kalamazoo, MI: Medieval Institute Publications, 1990. 285–304.

de Laborderie, O., J.R. Maddicott, and D.A. Carpenter. 'The Last Hours of Simon de Montfort: A New Account.' *English Historical Review* 115 (2000): 378–412.

Douglas, M. *Natural Symbols: Explorations in Cosmology*. 1970. London: Routledge, 1996.

Foucault, M. *Discipline and Punish: The Birth of the Prison*. Harmondsworth, UK: Penguin, 1977.

Fryde, N. *The Tyranny and Fall of Edward II, 1321–1326*. Cambridge: Cambridge University Press, 1979.

Gillingham, J. '1066 and the Introduction of Chivalry into England.' In *Law and Government in Medieval England and Normandy: Essays in Honour of Sir James Holt*. Ed. G. Garnett and J. Hudson. Cambridge: Cambridge University Press, 1994. 31–55.

– *Richard I*. New Haven, CT: Yale University Press, 1999.

Green, J. *The Aristocracy of Norman England*. Cambridge: Cambridge University Press, 1997.

Hollister, C.W. 'Royal Acts of Mutilation: The Case against Henry I.' *Albion* 10 (1978): 330–40.

Hyams, P. 'Feud in Medieval England.' *The Haskins Society Journal* 3 (1992): 1–21.

Jacquart, D., and C. Thomasset. *Sexuality and Medicine in the Middle Ages*. Cambridge: Polity Press, 1988.

Kantorowicz, E.H. *The King's Two Bodies: A Study in Medieval Political Theology*. 1957. Princeton, NJ: Princeton University Press, 1997.

Kay, S., and M. Rubin. *Framing Medieval Bodies*. Manchester: Manchester University Press, 1997.

Liebeschütz, H. *Mediaeval Humanism in the Life and Writings of John of Salisbury*. London: Warburg Institute, University of London, 1950.

Linder, A. 'John of Salisbury's *Policraticus* in Thirteenth-Century England: The Evidence of MS Cambridge Corpus Christi College 469.' *Journal of the Warburg and Courtauld Institutes* 40 (1977): 276–82.

Mauss, M. *Sociology and Psychology: Essays*. London: Routledge and Kegan Paul, 1979.

Nederman, C.J. 'The Physiological Significance of the Organic Metaphor in John of Salisbury's *Policraticus*.' *History of Political Thought* 8 (1987): 211–23.

– *John of Salisbury*. Tempe: Arizona Center for Medieval and Renaissance Studies, 2005.

Pollock, F., and F.W. Maitland. *The History of English Law before the Time of Edward I*. 2nd ed. Cambridge: Cambridge University Press, 1968. 2 vols.

Porter, R. 'History of the Body Reconsidered.' In *New Perspectives on Historical Writing*. Ed. P. Burke. 2nd rev. ed. Cambridge: Polity Press, 2001. 232–60.

Rawcliffe, C. *Medicine and Society in Later Medieval England*. London: Sandpiper Books, 1995.

Richardson, H.G., and Sayles, G.O. *Law and Legislation from Aethelberht to Magna Carta*. Edinburgh: Edinburgh University Press, 1966.

Royer, K. 'The Body in Parts: Reading the Execution Ritual in Late Medieval England.' *Historical Reflections/Reflexions Historiques* 29 (2003): 319–39.

Rubin, M. 'The Person in the Form: Medieval Challenges to the Bodily "Order."' In *Framing Medieval Bodies*. Ed. S. Kay and M. Rubin. Manchester: Manchester University Press, 1977. 100–22.

Siraisi, N. *Medieval and Early Renaissance Medicine: An Introduction to Knowledge and Practice*. Chicago: University of Chicago Press, 1990.

Struve, T. *Die Entwicklung der organologischen Staatsauffassung im Mittelalter.* Stuttgart: Hiersemann, 1978.

Tummers, H.A. *Early Secular Effigies in England: The Thirteenth Century.* Leiden: Brill, 1980.

Turner, B. *The Body and Society: Explorations in Social Theory.* 2nd ed. London: Sage Publications, 1996.

van Eickels, K. 'Gendered Violence: Castration and Blinding as Punishment for Treason in Normandy and Anglo-Norman England.' *Gender and History* 16 (2004): 588–602.

Westerhof, D.M. 'Aristocratic Executions and Burials in England c.1150–c.1330: Cultures of Fragmentation.' PhD diss., University of York, 2004. [Published as: *Death and the Noble Body in Medieval England.* Woodbridge: Boydell, 2008.]

– 'Deconstructing Identities on the Scaffold: The Execution of Hugh Despenser the Younger, 1326.' *Journal of Medieval History* 33 (2007): 87–106.

8 'A Defect of the Mind or Body': Impotence and Sexuality in Medieval Theology and Canon Law

CATHERINE RIDER

Medieval attitudes to sex have received a great deal of attention in recent decades. Historians have examined canon law, theology, medicine, hagiography, and other sources in order to understand how medieval people thought about their bodies and about sexual behaviour.[1] As might be expected, several of these recent studies discuss sexual impotence. In particular, among historians of theology and canon law, James Brundage (*Law, Sex, and Christian Society* and 'Impotence') has outlined how twelfth- and thirteenth-century canon lawyers developed the rules for when marriages could be annulled on grounds of impotence, and Pierre Payer (73–5) has discussed theological attitudes to impotence. In addition to establishing rules for annulment cases, however, medieval canonists and theologians also talked about why impotence happened at all, and their comments on this have not been looked at in detail. These discussions offer an interesting perspective on medieval churchmen's views of the body.

Medieval legal and theological writing about the causes of impotence is particularly interesting because it emphasizes different aspects of the condition from those described by one of the greatest influences on medieval ideas about the body and sex: St Augustine. Augustine described impotence as something that could happen unpredictably to any man at any time, whereas medieval canonists and theologians focused on long-term forms of impotence that had identifiable causes. This difference in emphasis had wider implications for how these writers wrote about the body in general. Augustine had presented the body, and sexual desire in particular, as something that was not under rational control. Medieval canonists and theologians did not repudiate this view, and indeed reproduced it in some contexts, such as when they wrote about sexuality in a theoretical way, or when they discussed the difficulties that clerics might experience in remaining celibate (Payer 47–9; Murray 12–18). When they wrote about impotence, however, they described the body as working in ways that were not irrational, but predictable, sometimes even mechanical. The unspoken assumption behind their writing on this subject was often that a man or woman who had nothing physically wrong with them should be able to have sex with any partner at any time.

I will begin by summarizing Augustine's view of impotence, before jumping ahead to examine how twelfth- and thirteenth-century canonists and theologians discussed the subject. Their views can be found in the commentaries on three texts in particular. Two were collections of canon law rulings: the *Decretum* of Gratian, compiled between 1139 and the mid-1150s, and the *Decretals* of Gregory IX, also known as the *Liber Extra*, promulgated by Pope Gregory IX in 1234. Both of these works became standard canon law textbooks and were commented on in universities for the rest of the Middle Ages. The third text was the *Sentences* of Peter Lombard, compiled in the 1150s, which was from the 1220s onwards the standard university textbook on theology. I will first outline the basic framework used by the canonists and theologians to analyze impotence and formulate a set of legal rules, and then examine the more detailed discussions of the causes of impotence offered by a number of thirteenth-century writers, focusing particularly on the canonist Henry of Susa, better known as Hostiensis, and the theologian Albertus Magnus, a Dominican writing at Paris in the late 1240s who went on to produce many scientific and philosophical works. When these writers discussed impotence, they did not do so in the same terms as Augustine had, but instead developed a different model that fitted their own concerns better.

Augustine on Impotence

Augustine's view of impotence was closely linked to his interest in what sex would have been like if Adam and Eve had not disobeyed God in the Garden of Eden. Michael Müller (19–32) and Peter Brown (399–423) have described how, after exploring several different views of sex, Augustine eventually settled on the idea that God had always intended Adam and Eve to reproduce sexually. However, Augustine argued that before the Fall, sex would have been a completely different experience from how it was in his own day. In Paradise, Adam and Eve would have had orderly bodies that were fully subject to conscious control. This would have included sex: moving the sexual organs would have been no different from moving a hand or foot. This ordered sexuality was disrupted when Adam and Eve disobeyed God by eating from the Tree of Knowledge, and, as a punishment, their own bodies began to disobey them. Sexual desire became tainted by concupiscence (*concupiscentia*), a form of intense desire that overwhelmed the mind, and so became a force outside rational control. This belief that sexual desire was now fundamentally uncontrollable was also reflected in Augustine's writing on impotence. In the *City of God*, he described how the uncontrollability of desire could manifest itself either as an unwanted erection, or as impotence: 'Sometimes the impulse is an unwanted intruder, sometimes it abandons the eager lover, and desire cools off in the body while it is at boiling heat in the mind ... although on the whole it is totally opposed to the mind's control, it is quite often divided against itself' (Augustine 14.16, 577).

Elements of this view can be found in earlier sources: for example, some pagan classical writers had similarly presented impotence as unpredictable and outside conscious control (Rider 19–20). Augustine's ideas were also shaped by the debates that preoccupied many ecclesiastical writers in the late fourth and early fifth centuries about how virtuous marriage was, compared to virginity (which led Augustine to argue that sex was part of God's plan for humanity), and about how original sin could be transmitted from generation to generation (which caused him to formulate his idea of concupiscence). Nonetheless, Augustine's presentation of sex as originally good but tainted by the Fall seems to have been a departure from earlier Christian attitudes, and Peter Brown argues (406–7) that his emphasis on the uncontrollability of sexual desire stemmed from the difficulties that he personally experienced in giving up sex. It is possible that his view of impotence as mysterious and unpredictable also came from his own experience.

Augustine's view of how sex would have taken place in Eden without concupiscence was very influential, and Michael Müller has shown that it was well known in theology and canon law until at least the thirteenth century. Gratian was influenced by Augustine when he mentioned in the *Decretum* that in Paradise, Adam and Eve would have conceived children 'without heat' ['sine ardore'], and that only after the Fall did 'illicit motion' ['illicitum motum' (Gratian, C. 32, qu. 2, d. p. c. 2; ed. Friedberg 1:1120)] become a problem. In the *Sentences*, Peter Lombard took the same view in his discussion of why God had instituted the sacrament of marriage: 'If the first men had not sinned, they and their successors would have come together without the incitement of the flesh and raging lust' ['sine carnis incentivo ac fervore libidinis' (Peter Lombard, Bk. 4, Dist. 26, Ch. 2; ed. Collegium S. Bonaventurae 2:417)]. When he discussed how sex would have been in Eden, Peter Lombard also used Augustine's image of moving the genitals just like other body parts: 'And we would move [the genitals] just like other parts of the body, as [we move] a hand to our mouth, without the heat of lust ...' ['sine ardore libidinis' (Peter Lombard, Bk. 2, Dist. 20, Ch. 1; ed. Collegium S. Bonaventurae 1:427–8)].

When they commented on these passages, later theologians and canonists continued to argue that sex was tainted with concupiscence by the Fall. For example, two twelfth-century commentators on Gratian's *Decretum*, Paucapalea and Rufinus, described how marriage had been created by God in two stages: first in Paradise, for reproductive purposes, and then again after the Fall, as a remedy against concupiscence (Paucapalea, C. 27, ed. von Schulte, 110; Rufinus, C. 27, ed. von Schulte 382–3). Likewise, in the 1250s Thomas Aquinas discussed in his commentary on the *Sentences* of Peter Lombard how concupiscence was a punishment for Adam and Eve's disobedience against God: 'the shamefulness of concupiscence that always accompanies the marriage act is a shamefulness not of guilt, but of punishment inflicted for the first sin, inasmuch as the lower powers and the members do not obey reason.' To this Augustinian argument he also added the words of Aristotle, stating that 'there is always excess of pleasure in the marriage act, so that it overcomes reason ... hence the Philosopher says in *Ethics* book seven, chapter twelve, that it is impossible for a man to understand anything at the same time' (Thomas Aquinas, Bk. 4, Dist. 26, art. 3; ed. *Commento* 9:188; trans. *Supplement* 82).

The idea that sexual desire had been rendered uncontrollable by the Fall was thus well known to medieval theologians and canonists. By contrast, the way in which Augustine linked impotence to this view does not seem to have been preserved in the same way. A search of the *Patrologia Latina*, *Corpus Christianorum*, and *Acta Sanctorum* databases reveals no later writer who echoed the passage on impotence from the *City of God*, quoted above. Nor do medieval canonists and theologians seem to have drawn the same parallel as Augustine between irrational sexual desire and impotence independently. This is perhaps because as members of a clerical elite that was from the twelfth century onwards expected to be celibate, they were more worried about the body's uncontrollability manifesting itself in unwanted erections than in impotence (Murray 11). Nevertheless, it meant that when they came to discuss impotence, they were free to discuss it in a different way.

Gratian's *Decretum* and Annulment Rules for Impotence Cases

Both canonists and theologians from the twelfth century onwards took their basic ideas about impotence from Gratian's *Decretum*, Causa 33, Question 1. This contained four texts that discussed impotence, all of which date originally from the eighth and ninth centuries. All four texts stated that if a man was unable to have intercourse with his wife, then the couple could separate, although they differed over whether the man should then be allowed to marry someone else. Commenting on these texts, Gratian distinguished between two kinds of impotence:

> See that the impossibility of rendering the [marriage] debt dissolves the bond of marriage. But this is the rule for natural impossibility [*naturali inpossibilitate*]. But in this case [the hypothetical case that Gratian was discussing at this point] the marriage debt is prevented by a magical impediment [*maleficii inpedimento*], not by natural coldness [*frigiditate naturali*]. (Gratian, C. 33, Qu. 1, d. p. c. 3; ed. Friedberg 1:1150)

Gratian did not go into detail about what *frigiditas naturalis* was, but heat had long been used by Christian writers as a metaphor for sexual desire, so it was logical to describe impotence in terms of coldness. The language of heat and coldness was also well established in medical writing, which argued that a man needed a sufficient quantity of heat in his body to enable him to have sex (Cadden 63).

In contrast to Augustine, Gratian did not link impotence to the way in which sexual desire worked more generally. Indeed, his collection of legal rulings leaves little space for Augustine's view of impotence as a failure that could happen randomly to any man at any time, presumably because this kind of one-off impotence was unlikely to lead to annulment cases. Instead Gratian focused on long-term impotence, suggesting two specific causes: the man's natural *frigiditas*, or magic. Once the cause was known, Gratian also assumed that an accurate prognosis could be made about whether the man would recover. The man who had *frigiditas* was assumed to be impotent permanently with all women. Gratian did not say this explicitly, but this was surely the reasoning behind his comments on remarriage: 'If [the impotent man] accepts another spouse, then those people who have sworn [that the man was impotent] should be held accountable for the crime of perjury, and after penance, the [original] couple should be forced to resume the first marriage' (Gratian, C. 33, Qu. 1, Ch. 2; ed. Friedberg 1:1149). In other words, if the man subsequently proved able to have sex with another woman, he could not have had true *frigiditas* in the first place, and so the original annulment had been made in error. The theologian Alexander of Hales put it more succinctly in the 1220s: 'if someone is naturally *frigidus* with one woman, he is *frigidus* with all' (Alexander of Hales, Bk. 4, Dist. 34, Ch. 5; ed. Collegium S. Bonaventurae 4:539). Only in cases of impotence caused by magic did Gratian permit the man to remarry, because a bewitched man might be impotent with one woman but not with others (Gratian, C. 33, Qu. 1, Ch. 4; ed. Friedberg 1:1150).

The twelfth-century commentators on the *Decretum* followed Gratian's approach to impotence, dividing the condition into natural *frigiditas* and magic, without discussing how sexual desire worked in detail. Rufinus explained that 'inability to have intercourse sometimes stems from coldness of nature [*frigiditate naturae*], sometimes from magic' (Rufinus, C. 33, Qu. 1; ed. von Schulte 432–3). Gradually, however, the canonists introduced further ways of categorizing impotence, the most important of which was according to whether it was temporary or permanent. Only permanent impotence was a ground for annulment (Brundage, *Law, Sex, and Christian Society* 290–1). When they mentioned temporary impotence, the canonists were probably thinking of the kind of unpredictable, one-off impotence that Augustine had described in the *City of God*, but because this was not a ground for annulling a marriage, they said little about it, concentrating instead on permanent *frigiditas* and magic.

The canonists continued to focus on long-term forms of impotence with identifiable causes in the early thirteenth century, when Tancred of Bologna defined impotence as 'a defect of the mind or body, or both, by which someone is impeded from having sexual intercourse with another person' (Tancred, Title 30; ed. Wunderlich 61). This description of impotence as a 'defect' suggests that the problem was seen not as a symptom of the body's inherent uncontrollability (as Augustine would have it), but instead as something that was not expected to happen if the man's body was working normally. Tancred's definition proved very influential, and was quoted by the later canonists Raymond of Peñafort and Hostiensis (Raymond of Peñafort, Bk. 4, Title 16, p. 558; Hostiensis, Bk. 4, Title 16, Ch. 1, fol. 214r). Thirteenth-century canonists thus continued to discuss impotence in terms of definite causes, and to relate those causes to the rules that should be followed in annulment cases.

Twelfth- and early thirteenth-century theologians were not so concerned with formulating the legal rules for annulment cases, but they presented impotence in similar ways to the canonists. Peter Lombard, discussing impotence in Book Four, Distinction 34 of the *Sentences*, reproduced the same four texts that Gratian had included in the *Decretum* (ed. Collegium S. Bonaventurae, 2:463–5), and commentators on the *Sentences* also tended to follow canon law. This is especially true of the earliest *Sentences* commentators, writing between the 1220s and the 1240s. In this period Alexander of Hales and Hugh of St Cher in Paris, and Richard Fishacre in Oxford, all reproduced Tancred of Bologna's definition of impotence as 'a defect of the mind or body or both' (Alexander of Hales, Bk. 4, Dist. 34, Ch. 3; ed. Collegium S. Bonaventurae, 4:538; Hugh of St Cher, Bk. 4, Dist. 34, fol. 113r; Richard Fishacre, Bk. 4, Dist. 34, fol. 359ra). Later *Sentences* commentators followed the canonists less closely and added their own questions about impotence (Rider 137), but they still kept the distinction between *frigiditas* and magic, and copied the annulment rules that went with this distinction. Therefore, like the canonists, they continued to focus on long-term impotence, and discussed it as a comprehensible and predictable ailment.

Detailed Discussions of the Causes of Impotence

Although the annulment rules for impotence relied on the basic distinction made by Gratian between natural *frigiditas* and magic, Gratian himself did not discuss how either physical problems or magic could actually cause impotence. During the thirteenth century, as canon law and *Sentences* commentaries became ever longer and more detailed, the commentators attempted to fill this gap in two different ways. The canonists discussed a range of physical problems that might cause impotence, while the theologians were interested both in the physical problems that caused impotence and in how impotence could be caused by magic. This more detailed focus on the causes of impotence had the potential to disrupt Gratian's neat scheme that distinguished between *frigiditas*, which rendered a man impotent with all women, and magic, which rendered him impotent with one woman only, because some types of impotence did not seem to fit into either of these categories. For the most part, however, the canonists and theologians used the additional information to reinforce Gratian's emphasis on forms of impotence that had specific causes, and continued to suggest that the man's chances of recovery could be predicted if those causes were known.

As early as the twelfth century, several canonists began to consider how impotence could be caused by physical injuries or deformities not mentioned by Gratian. In the 1180s Sicard of Cremona noted that 'impossibility of having intercourse proceeds sometimes from *frigiditas*, sometimes from magic, sometimes from castration' ['impossibilitas coeundi aliquando ex frigiditate, aliquando maleficio, aliquando ex sectione provenit' (Sicard of Cremona, C. 33, fol. 61rb)]. In around 1190, Bernard of Pavia mentioned *arctatio*, a kind of impotence found in women, in which the woman's vagina was too narrow for sexual intercourse (Bernardus Papiensis, Bk. 4, Title 16; ed. Laspeyres 176). In the early thirteenth century Alanus Anglicus suggested that either childhood or old age constituted a kind of natural impotence equivalent to *frigiditas*: 'impossibility of having intercourse either stems from nature [inborn], or from an accident [that is, it happens to a person later in life]. Natural impotence is either because of age or because of natural *frigiditas*' ['Impossibilitas coeundi aut est a natura, aut est ex accidenti. A natura vel ex etate, vel ex naturali frigiditate' (Alanus Anglicus, C. 33, fol. 49r)]. Tancred of Bologna also said that old age could be a cause of impotence, because old people lacked the heat necessary for sexual intercourse, but he believed that this problem was often curable: 'although an old man lacks natural heat, nonetheless sometimes he can be moved to intercourse with the help of diet or of some medicine' (Brundage, 'Impotence' 417).

Castration, *arctatio*, and old age soon became part of the regular discussion of impotence, additional categories to put alongside natural *frigiditas* and magic. However, some canonists did not stop there. Henry of Susa, better known as Hostiensis, included even more kinds of impotence in his *Summa* on the *Liber Extra*, completed in around 1253. He claimed to have encountered a wide range of sexual problems in both men and women when judging impotence cases:

> What if the man is not bewitched or naturally *frigidus*, but like a naturally *frigidus* man feels desire and can get an erection, but in no way completes [intercourse]? Or if he has two penises and one impedes the other? Or if as soon as he puts his penis in place he ejaculates, or if he can penetrate the woman but cannot complete intercourse [presumably, he cannot ejaculate]? I have had many cases like this and similar ones come before me, and you can encounter this yourself every day both in court and in the confessional. And you should say in cases like this that if the man can be helped by certain electuaries or medicines, then the matter is clear. If he cannot [be helped] by some of these things, the pope should be consulted.
>
> Quid si vir non est maleficiatus nec naturaliter frigidus, sed quasi naturaliter frigidus movetur et erigitur, sed nullatenus perficit? Vel habet duas virgas una

> impedit reliquam? Vel quam cito apponit virgam semen spargit, vel bene immittit sed non perficit? Multa talia et consimilia de facto habui coram me, et tam in iudiciis quam confessionibus quotidie poteris experiri. Et dicas in talibus quod si potest iuvari electuariis vel medicinis aliquibus planum est. Si non potest in aliquibus ex his consulendus esset papa. (Hostiensis, Bk. 4, Tit. 15, Ch. 13, fol. 215r)

And for women:

> What if she is so fat that she cannot be known, as in fact happened in Grasse [in the south of France]? Or what if she bears dead children because of some defect in her vulva? Or what if she is naturally sterile, or in some other way physically defective? Or if because of some defect in her bladder she cannot hold the humour collected there but urinates in the bed or between her hips when she should render the marriage debt? Do not be disturbed, for similar and even more disgusting things are heard of, and doctors of souls should not be ignorant of such things. And it seems that these things impede and invalidate a marriage because two goods of marriage are lacking, both the principal and final causes for which marriage is contracted, that is, fidelity and the avoidance of fornication, and the begetting of children ... You should say that if she is impotent to render the marriage debt for whatever reason, the marriage is impeded.

> Quid si ita lata sit quod non possit cognosci, ut de facto fuerit apud Grassam? [text emended from London, British Library MS Royal 10.E.VIII, fol. 180ra; 1548 edition reads 'ut de facto fuit Grasse'] Item quid si vitio vulve mortuos pariat? Item quid si naturaliter sterilis sit, vel alias vitiosa corpore? Vel si vitio vesice collectum humorem continere non potest, sed in lecto mingit vel inter coxas quando debet reddere debitum? Non turberis, nam similia et turpiora audiuntur, nec sunt talia ab animarum medicis ignoranda. Et videtur quod hec impediant et dirimant cum duo bona matrimonii deficiant: et cause principales et finales propter quas matrimonium contrahitur, scilicet fides et evitatio fornicationis et susceptio prolis ... Dicas quod qualitercunque impotens sit ad carnale debitum reddendum matrimonium impeditur. (Hostiensis, Bk. 4, Tit. 15, Chs. 4–6, fol. 214r)

Here Hostiensis draws on what he claims are his own observations of real cases to give a very broad picture of problems that might be classed as impotence. His list also suggests that the canonists' model of impotence was to a large extent gender neutral. Although canonists and theologians devoted most space to discussing male impotence, Hostiensis describes physical problems that render women unable to have sex in very similar terms. It is strange, however, that he includes sterility and bearing dead children as reasons for annulment, because canon law usually emphasized that infertility was not an impediment to marriage (Brundage, *Law, Sex, and Christian Society* 201). In this picture, not every sexual problem corresponds with Gratian's original classification of impotence as either caused by *frigiditas* or by magic – and Hostiensis expects his readers, too, to find cases where the neat schemes of theoretical canon law do not apply. Nevertheless, his reference to medicine implies that even in anomalous cases such as these, the impotence has a physical cause that should be identifiable. Moreover, cases where this does not apply are sufficiently unusual to require a papal judgment.

Thirteenth-century theologians also went into more detail about the causes of impotence than their earlier counterparts, but they approached the subject in a different way. Instead of discussing physical deformities, they asked what was meant by *frigiditas*, and how exactly an excess of coldness in the man's body could cause impotence. For example, a number of theologians expanded on Tancred's suggestion that old age could be a cause of *frigiditas*, but that 'warming' medicines could often solve the problem. Albertus Magnus in the 1240s and Thomas Aquinas in the 1250s suggested that old people might have sufficient heat at least to have sex, even if they were infertile (Albertus Magnus, Bk. 4, Dist. 34, Art. 4; ed. Borgnet 30:332; Thomas Aquinas, Bk. 4, Dist. 34, Art. 2; ed. *Commento* 9:532; trans. *Supplement* 255–6). In the 1290s, John Quidort of Paris even suggested a particular warming medicine: 'To the argument that is argued about old people, I say that that impotence can be relieved by medicines, such as ... by ginger and similar things' ['Ad argumenta quod arguitur de senibus dico quod illa impotentia potest relevari per medicinas sicut ... per gingenbratum et talia' (John Quidort, Bk. 4, Dist. 34, fol. 166r)].

Although the idea that impotence had something to do with coldness was an old one, much of this theological discussion of how, exactly, heat and cold in the man's body caused impotence was the work of Albertus Magnus. Albertus seems to have been the first theologian to suggest that if too little heat in the man's complexion could cause impotence, then so could too much heat, a condition he called '*caliditas*.' However, Albertus believed that '*caliditas* is hardly ever a permanent impediment' because it was naturally diminished by age, or could be remedied by a special diet (Bk. 4, Dist. 34, Art. 4; ed. Borgnet 30:332).

Albertus also suggested heat-based explanations for various other forms of impotence. Some men's heat might evaporate too quickly, giving them only the 'first impetus' required to have sex. This would not be enough to deflower a virgin, but would be sufficient to have sex with a wife who was not a virgin:

> Finally it is asked here about those who are weak in heat: for it is sufficient to move the members to desire, but it quickly evaporates, and [he] relaxes weakly. Therefore, if such a man has a wife who is a virgin, because he only has the first impetus, he cannot deflower her; but nonetheless he can have intercourse with a woman who is not a virgin, if he has her as a wife. What should be done about them? (Bk. 4, Dist. 34, Art. 4; ed. Borgnet 30:331)

Albertus suggested that the woman's hymen could be broken by hand; and, in case this sounded too much like a dubious sexual practice, he emphasized that it was not a sin to do it for medical reasons: 'it is different to apply a hand to medicate [*ut medicantem*] than to pollute [*ut polluentem*]' (Bk. 4, Dist. 34, Art. 4; ed. Borgnet 30:331–2).

Similarly, Albertus asked what happened if a man had enough heat to have sex with a woman he desired, but not with all women: 'One woman is more loveable [*amabilior*] than another. Therefore we suggest that someone who does not have sufficient heat in his complexion for intercourse, can nonetheless be aroused by 'accidents of the soul' [emotions] such as love, desire, and similar things'(Bk. 4, Dist. 34, Art. 6; ed. Borgnet 30:334). Albertus's response to this problem is interesting. On the one hand, he suggests that couples in this situation might be able to help themselves: 'the woman should be advised to make herself clean [or 'elegant': *mundam*] and loveable for her husband, using adornments and courtesy. And the man should be advised to think of the things that make women more loveable.' On the other hand, he also suggested that this case was similar to cases of magic, because 'one kind of magic is a detestation [*abominatio*] that [the man] conceives towards the woman' (Bk. 4, Dist. 34, Art. 6; ed. Borgnet 30:334). Here is a situation for which modern readers might be tempted to offer a psychological explanation (that the man simply did not desire his partner), but which Albertus interpreted as a physical problem caused by a lack of heat in the body, or as the result of bewitchment.

Albertus's extension of ideas about heat and coldness to cover forms of impotence that earlier writers had not considered is probably the result of his interest in medical and scientific topics more generally. In particular, he may have been influenced by a medical text newly translated from Arabic, Avicenna's *Canon of Medicine*, which was being read at Paris in the 1240s (Jacquart 72–3). Avicenna mentioned several of the same ideas as Albertus: that emotions such as 'horror of sex' or 'shame' could affect a man's sexual desire (although he did not mention dislike of one particular partner), and that too much heat, as well as too much cold, in a man's body could cause impotence (Avicenna, Bk. 3, Fen 20, Ch. 15, fol. 353v).

Albertus Magnus's statements also throw interesting light on what he believed to be the normal workings of the body. The implication, both in the case of the man who cannot deflower a virgin, and in the case of the one who does not desire his wife enough, is that a man with a normal level of heat should be able to have sex with any woman. Psychological factors like desire only seem to become a problem if the man already lacks sufficient heat. Other *Sentences* commentators did not go into the same detail as Albertus did, however. The influential Franciscan theologians Bonaventure and Duns Scotus, for example, did not give detailed accounts of the relationship between heat and impotence, preferring simply to list the categories of impotence discussed by canon lawyers: *frigiditas*, magic, *arctatio*, and sometimes castration (Bonaventure, Bk. 4, Dist. 34, Art. 2, Qu. 1, p. 771; Duns Scotus, Bk. 4, Dist. 34, p. 403). Nonetheless, although Albertus says more about the causes of impotence, his views are not incompatible with theirs. In all of these theologians' discussions of impotence, the body, and sexual desire, appear as predictable, even mechanical.

Albertus also went into great detail about how magic could cause impotence (Rider 138–41). He agreed with earlier canonists that unlike the man who was *frigidus* or castrated, the man who was bewitched had nothing physically wrong with him, and so his impotence did not have to operate in predictable ways. In particular, a bewitched man might be impotent with one woman but not with others, although Albertus did also claim that spells existed in magical texts that could make a man impotent with everyone (Bk. 4, Dist. 34, Art. 10; ed. Borgnet 30:338). One of the functions of magic in discussions of impotence thus seems to have been to provide an explanation for cases of impotence that lasted long enough to lead to annulment cases, but which did not follow the predictable pattern of *frigiditas*, which was believed to make a man impotent with everyone.

The other function of magic was to explain cases in which the man was impotent but did not seem to have anything physically wrong with him. As Duns Scotus put it in the early fourteenth century, 'It is difficult to see [the difference between natural impotence and *maleficium*] except by physical inspection, if any necessary disposition required for the act is lacking in that part, or by the physicians' judgement as to *frigiditas*, if some signs manifestly show that he has that complexion. But if neither the one nor the other applies, and yet he is simply impeded, it should be presumed that it is magic' (Duns Scotus, Bk. 4, Dist. 34, p. 404). Magic thus functions as an explanation for otherwise mysterious events. The same idea can be found in medieval accusations of love magic, which were sometimes used to explain why a person might behave irrationally. For example, in a case in Florence in 1375, when a man became so devoted to his mistress that he neglected his wife, children, and business affairs, the mistress was accused of using magic on him (Brucker 9).

In twelfth- and thirteenth-century canon law and theology, then, we can see impotence becoming polarized into two different conditions. *Frigiditas*, castration, *arctatio*, and the other physical causes of the problem expressed the idea that the body was rational and predictable and that, given the right stimulus and sufficient heat, sex should always be possible. Magic was used to explain the cases in which this model did not work, and why men could suffer from long-term impotence despite good health and adequate stimulus. Neither of these conditions corresponded to the one-off impotence described by Augustine, but it is possible that Augustine had not needed to make such firm distinctions: if sexual desire was by nature irrational and uncontrollable, then there was no need to resort to a magical explanation for mysterious impotence.

Conclusion

When they discussed impotence, medieval canonists and theologians focused on long-term impotence that had specific causes, and they assumed that if the cause was known, the future of the condition could be predicted with enough certainty to formulate legal rules. Nor was this view of impotence just a theoretical system: it also had practical consequences in the way in which cases were dealt with in the Church courts. Although the canonists were aware that allegations of impotence were difficult to prove, several writers suggested that in some cases, the man's sexual organs should be inspected. Sometimes these inspections showed that the man had a physical deformity (Pedersen 117–18), but when this was not the case, the idea that the body was predictable could be used to judge whether or not a man was impotent. Richard Helmholz has uncovered an English case from 1433, in which the Church court enlisted a woman to try to stimulate the allegedly impotent man sexually. When she failed to do so, he was judged to be impotent (Helmholz 89). This method of proof makes sense in the light of the view in canon law and theology that a man whose body was working 'normally' should be able to be aroused by any woman.

This way of thinking about impotence implied that the body worked in different ways from the account given by St Augustine. It did not amount to a rejection of Augustine's model, which could still be found elsewhere in legal and theological writing. Instead, the canonists and theologians simply thought about kinds of impotence that Augustine did not discuss, and used a different framework to do so. This may have been because they were unaware of Augustine's comments on impotence, which do not seem to have been widely copied by later writers, but other reasons are also likely to have played a part. First, new ideas about nature and causation probably encouraged them to focus on the causes of impotence. From the twelfth century onwards, a number of theologians and writers of natural philosophy began to seek natural explanations for previously unexplained phenomena, and the search for explanations was given a further boost in the thirteenth century, with the translation of many works of Aristotle into Latin (Chenu 11–15). Second, the translation of Arabic medical texts into Latin probably also encouraged some writers to think about the causes of impotence, as these texts discussed impotence as a physical problem with specific causes that could be treated. Avicenna's *Canon*, for example, listed many causes of impotence, and may have influenced Albertus Magnus.

Another important reason for the change is probably that Augustine's view of impotence would not have been very helpful when dealing with the legal problems that interested Gratian and subsequent canon lawyers. From the twelfth century onwards, churchmen had established that marriage cases should be judged by the ecclesiastical courts, according to canon law. It therefore became necessary for canonists to formulate clear rules to deal with sexual matters, in a way that Augustine had not envisaged. Only impotence that was deemed to be permanent was a ground for annulment, and so the one-off impotence that Augustine described would never have come to their attention. This new legalism also changed attitudes to sex and marriage in other ways. For example, John Gillingham has argued that the development of the canon law rule that consent, rather than consummation, was sufficient to make a valid marriage, combined with the growing importance of heiresses in the twelfth century, gave a new prominence to the idea that husband and wife should love each other, and that love included sexual compatibility (Gillingham 297). Conversely, canonists and theologians also responded to what they found in the world around them: for example, canonists and theologians from the thirteenth century began to take a more positive view of marital sex than had been the case earlier, and one reason for this was probably the need to counter the claims of contemporary Cathar heretics that all sex was sinful (d'Avray, 169; Brundage, *Law, Sex, and Christian Society* 431).

It is interesting to compare this new, more positive valuation of love and sex within marriage with the canonists' and theologians' writing on impotence, because the comparison shows how the same factors could lead medieval writers to formulate different ideas of the body when different situations required it. On the one hand, the new emphasis on the role of sex in marriage can be found in discussions of impotence: it is expected that a healthy man will naturally be able to have sex given the right stimulus. On the other hand, the emphasis on love and consent might have been expected to encourage the canonists and theologians who wrote about impotence to emphasize the emotional aspects of the problem, as well as the physical ones. As we have seen, however, this was not the case. Many writers did not mention emotional factors at all and Albertus Magnus, who did, classed them as a kind of physical problem, or as magic. One reason for this lack of interest in the emotional side of impotence may have been that, despite the emphasis on consent in canon law, many marriages were still arranged, and the partners were expected to manage sexually without necessarily loving each other.[2] Certainly many aristocratic marriages were arranged, although for lower social levels, the evidence suggests the existence of both arranged and unarranged marriages, and it is difficult to know which were more common (Hughes 17, 22–3; Donahue 356–66).

Another reason why the canonists and theologians did not emphasize either one-off, unpredictable impotence or the emotional causes of the problem is probably connected to the canon law itself. To have their marriage annulled on grounds of impotence, a couple had either to demonstrate that one of the parties had an obvious physical problem, or else to live together for three years and try to have sex. Only after three years was the impotence judged to be permanent. It is possible that many cases of impotence solved themselves within this time, especially as there were other remedies that the couple could try. A number of medical writers gave advice on sexual techniques and aphrodisiacs, for example (Jacquart and Thomasset 130–3). Other couples may have separated informally, without seeking an annulment (Brundage, *Law, Sex, and Christian Society* 458). Therefore, it seems likely instead that a disproportionately high number of the cases that canon lawyers encountered concerned men or women with serious, long-term physical problems that could not be overcome by other means.

Thus we can see that the way in which medieval canonists and theologians imagined the body varied considerably, according to what they wanted to do with the models they created. In the case of impotence, the development of canon law made it necessary to formulate clear rules to deal with sexual matters in a way that Augustine, writing in the fourth century, had not needed to. Although much medieval writing on sex and marriage drew on earlier writers, these sources were not used uncritically. When circumstances required it, the canonists and theologians of the twelfth and thirteenth centuries were prepared to adapt their existing sources or depart from them altogether to formulate new models of the body and sex.

NOTES

1 I would like to thank David d'Avray and Giles Pearson for comments on earlier drafts of this paper. All translations are mine unless otherwise specified. I have also quoted the original Latin for texts that are not available in a modern edition.

2 I am grateful to Isabelle Cochelin for suggesting this.

WORKS CITED

Primary Sources

Alanus Anglicus. Commentary on Gratian's *Decretum*. Paris: Bibliothèque Nationale MS lat. 3909.

Albertus Magnus. *Commentarium in IV Sententiarum*. In *Opera Omnia*. Ed. Auguste Borgnet. 38 vols. Paris, 1890–9.

Alexander of Hales. *Glossa in Quatuor Libros Sententiarum Petri Lombardi*. Ed. Collegium S. Bonaventurae. 4 vols. Quaracchi, Italy: Collegium S. Bonaventurae. 1951–7.

Augustine. *City of God*. Trans. Henry Bettenson. Harmondsworth, UK: Penguin, 1972.

Avicenna. *Liber Canonis*. Venice, 1507; repr. Hildesheim, Germany: G. Olms, 1964.

Bernardus Papiensis. *Summa Decretalium*. Ed. E.A.T. Laspeyres. Ratisbon, 1860.

Bonaventure. *Commentaria in Quartum Sententiarum*. In *Opera Omnia*. Ed. Collegium S. Bonaventurae. Vol. 4. Quaracchi, Italy: Collegium S. Bonaventurae, 1889.

Duns Scotus. *Quaestiones in Quartum Librum Sententiarum*. In *Opera Omnia*. Ed. Lucas Wadding. Vol. 19. Paris, 1894; repr. Farnborough: Gregg Press, 1969.

Friedberg, Emil, ed. *Corpus Iuris Canonici*. 2 vols. Leipzig, 1879.

Hostiensis. *Summa Aurea*. Lyons, 1548.

– *Summa*. London, British Library MS Royal 10.E.VIII.

Hugh of St Cher. Commentary on the *Sentences* of Peter Lombard. Evreux, Bibliothèque Municipale, MS 15L.

John Quidort. Commentary on the Fourth Book of the *Sentences* of Peter Lombard. Basel Universitätsbibliothek MS B.III.13.

Paucapalea. *Die Summa des Paucapalea über das Decretum Gratiani*. Ed. Johan Friedrich von Schulte. Giessen, 1890.

Peter Lombard. *Sententiae in IV Libris Distinctae*. Ed. Collegium S. Bonaventurae. 2 vols. Grottaferrata, Italy: Editiones Collegii S. Bonaventurae, 1971–81.

Raymond of Peñafort. *Summa de Penitentia et Matrimonio*. Rome, 1603; repr. Farnborough, UK: Gregg Press, 1967.

Richard Fishacre. Commentary on the *Sentences* of Peter Lombard. London, British Library MS Royal 10.B.VII.

Rufinus. *Die Summa Magistri Rufini zum Decretum Gratiani*. Ed. Johan Friedrich von Schulte. Giessen, Germany, 1892.

Sicard of Cremona. Commentary on Gratian's *Decretum*. London, British Library MS Add. 18367.

Tancred. *Summa de Matrimonio*. Ed. Agathon Wunderlich. Göttingen, 1841.

Thomas Aquinas. *Commento alle Sentenze di Pietro Lombardo*. 10 vols. Bologna: ESD, 1999–2001.

– *The Summa Theologica of Thomas Aquinas: Supplement*. Vol. 19, qq. XXXIV–LXVIII. Trans. Fathers of the English Dominican Province. London: Eyre and Spottiswoode, 1932.

Secondary Sources

Brown, Peter. *The Body and Society: Men, Women, and Sexual Renunciation in Early Christianity*. New York: Columbia University Press, 1988.

Brucker, Gene A. 'Sorcery in Early Renaissance Florence.' *Studies in the Renaissance* 10 (1963): 7–24.

Brundage, James. 'Impotence, Frigidity and Marital Nullity in the Decretists and the Early Decretalists.' In *Proceedings of the Seventh International Congress of Medieval Canon Law*. Ed. Peter Linehan. Monumenta Iuris Canonici C.8. Vatican City: Bibliotheca Apostolica Vaticana, 1988. 407–23.

– *Law, Sex, and Christian Society in Medieval Europe*. Chicago: University of Chicago Press, 1987.

Cadden, Joan. *Meanings of Sex Difference in the Middle Ages*. Cambridge: Cambridge University Press, 1993.

Chenu, M.-D. *Nature, Man and Society in the Twelfth Century*. Trans. Jerome Taylor and Lester K. Little. Chicago: University of Chicago Press, 1968.

d'Avray, David. *Medieval Marriage: Symbolism and Society*. Oxford: Oxford University Press, 2005.

Donahue, Charles, Jr. 'English and French Marriage Cases in the Later Middle Ages: Might the Differences Be Explained by the Differences in the Property Systems?' In *Marriage, Property and Succession*. Ed. Lloyd Bonfield. Berlin: Duncker and Humblot, 1992. 339–66.

Gillingham, John. 'Love, Marriage and Politics in the Twelfth Century.' *Forum for Modern Language Studies* 25 (1989): 292–303.

Helmholz, Richard. *Marriage Litigation in Medieval England.* Cambridge: Cambridge University Press, 1974.

Hughes, Diane Owen. 'Urban Growth and Family Structure in Medieval Genoa.' *Past and Present* 66 (1975): 3–28.

Jacquart, Danielle. 'La réception du "Canon" d'Avicenne: Comparaison entre Montpellier et Paris aux XIIIe et XIVe siècles.' *Histoire de l'Ecole Médicale de Montpellier: Actes du 110e Congrès National des Sociétés Savantes*. Paris: CTHS, 1985. 2:69–77.

Jacquart, Danielle, and Claude Thomasset. *Sexuality and Medicine in the Middle Ages*. Trans. Matthew Adamson. Cambridge: Polity Press, 1988.

Müller, Michael. *Die Lehre des hl. Augustinus von der Paradiesesehe und ihre Auswirkung in der Sexualethik des 12. und 13. Jahrhunderts bis Thomas von Aquin*. Regensburg: F. Pustet, 1954.

Murray, Jacqueline. 'The Law of Sin That Is in My Members: The Problem of Male Embodiment.' In *Gender and Holiness: Men, Women and Saints in Late Medieval Europe.* Ed. Samantha J.E. Riches and Sarah Salih. London: Routledge, 2002. 9–22.

Pedersen, Frederik. *Marriage Disputes in Medieval England*. London: Hambledon Press, 2000.

Payer, Pierre J. *The Bridling of Desire: Views of Sex in the Later Middle Ages.* Toronto: University of Toronto Press, 1993.

Rider, Catherine. *Magic and Impotence in the Middle Ages*. Oxford: Oxford University Press, 2006.

9 Bodily Performances and Body Talk in Medieval Islamic Preaching

LINDA G. JONES

'Bodies (are a means of) saving souls, and by this I mean salvation through good deeds' (Anonymous, fol. 1).[1] This is but one of the numerous maxims and motifs featuring the body that appear in medieval Islamic sermons. The saying, spoken by a thirteenth-century anonymous Mudejar preacher,[2] epitomizes a moral theology that envisages the body as partner, rather than foe or obstacle, in the spiritual path towards God. It will serve as my point of departure to explore the representation, function, and cultural import of the body in medieval Islamic sermons delivered before Muslim audiences in the Iberian Peninsula and the Maghreb between the thirteenth and fifteenth centuries. An examination of these homiletic sources, along with theological and juridical texts, and eschatological literature will demonstrate the ubiquity and centrality of the body in medieval Islamic articulations of piety and morality that shaped the individual self and communal identity.

References to the body appear in a myriad of themes and images within the sermon: Whatever the homiletic topic, be it the celebration of festivals, the repentance of sins, or warnings of the Last Judgment, the preacher customarily fills his homilies with exhortations of rituals that must be performed, prayer formulas that must be uttered, and warnings that body parts must be managed. I will suggest that Muslim preachers emphasize carnal imagery in conveying the message to their audiences because of scripturally based dogmas affirming a monistic unity of soul and body and the physical continuity of the body in the afterlife. These dogmas warn that the fate of one's soul depends on one's *habitus* – bodily dispositions, actions, and gestures – which reveal the true intention of the heart and belie the hypocrisy of speech. Consequently, I shall argue that constructions of Muslim personhood and communal identity, as well as of spiritual dispositions – faith or infidelity, moral virtue or sinfulness, the search for God or spiritual alienation, and so forth – are of necessity imagined as embodied.

To test this premise, this essay will explore medieval Islamic attitudes towards the body and its relation to soul, mind, or spirit as reflected in three different specimens of Islamic sermons. The sources in question include a collection of canonical sermons [pl. *khutab*, s. *khutba*] composed by the venerable Sufi mystic Ibn 'Abbad of Ronda (d. 1390); a collection of extra-canonical moralistic sermons [*mawa'iz*] by the aforementioned anonymous Mudejar preacher from Aragon; and a tractate of pious exhortations entitled *Consolation for the Eyes and Relief for Saddened Hearts* [*Qurrat al-'uyun wa mafrah al-qalb al-mahzun]* by the theologian Abu 'l-Layth al-Samarqandi (d. ca 983), whose work widely circulated in Muslim Spain and the Maghreb. Despite the different genres and contexts of these sources, they all share in common an adherence to traditional monistic discourses underscoring the essential unity and codependence of body and soul, and hence, the capacity of the body to reveal the true inner states of the mind, soul, or spirit. This view of the symbiosis of body and spirit or soul reflects the orthodox Sunni position against Neoplatonist or Aristotelian dualisms that oppose body to soul and posit the superiority of the latter to the former.[3] Two issues in particular rise to the fore in Islamic homiletic discussions about the body and the soul: the body as the primary instrument in this life for engendering religious identity, morality, and the salvation of the soul, and the reality of the material continuity of the body in the hereafter.

Body Talk: Images of the Body in Islamic Sermons

The three major medieval Islamic sermon genres, liturgical sermons [*khutab*], extra-canonical homiletic exhortations [*mawa'iz*], and homiletic stories [*qisas*], share certain core themes in common.[4] These core messages include exhortations to fear and obey God and the Prophet Muhammad; to remain humble, steadfast, and patient in joy and adversity; to eschew the trappings of the mundane world and yearn for the Return to God and the delights of Paradise; to ponder with trepidation the Last Judgment; and to dread the torments of the hellfire. The analysis of how these topics are developed reveals that medieval preachers neither considered such virtues as humility, piety, asceticism, patience, obedience, moral probity, and eschatological desire solely as mental states, nor implied that their acquisition and cultivation could be attained solely through mental processes. Instead, the theme of embodiment looms large in homiletic discourse. Preachers portray ritual acts, gesture, and bodily praxis as culturally constructed signifiers of one's inner states. The fundamental message they convey to their audiences is that bodily *habitus* signifies religious and moral identity.

Muslim preachers employ a variety of rhetorical strategies to this end; however, here I shall confine the following discussion to three major themes: the ritualization of the body as the medium of drawing nearer to God; the body as a classification system for defining and differentiating Muslim personhood, virtue, and communal identity from those of non-Muslims; and the emphasis on the body as a means of making credible the material reality of the Last Judgment and the hereafter. Drawing upon the words of sociologist Marcel Mauss, we shall see that Islamic homiletic discourse extols the body as the Muslim's 'first and most natural instrument ... [or] technical object' of his or her subjectivity as a Muslim (Mauss 104; cited in Hollywood 111). This avowal of the necessity of the body is a far cry from the Christian reinterpretation of Neoplatonist dualistic motifs that regard the body as intrinsically evil and an impediment to spiritual fulfilment. The sermons to be considered below consistently depict body and soul as united in constituting personhood and religious identity in the mundane world and in the hereafter.

Ritualization and Spiritual Experience

The first sermon to be considered comes from a collection of *khutab* that the fourteenth-century Sufi mystic and preacher [*khatib*] Ibn 'Abbad of Ronda delivered for the feast days and sacred months of the Islamic calendar (Ibn 'Abbad of Ronda, fols. 1–22).[5] Ibn 'Abbad of Ronda was one of the most revered Sufi masters of the Maghreb and one of its most prominent preachers. He served as chief prayer leader [*imam*] and *khatib* of the Qarawiyyin congregational mosque in Fez from 1375 until his death in 1390. Ibn 'Abbad delivered a *khutba* for the month of Rajab, the seventh month in the Islamic calendar, which was regarded as a sacred month even in pre-Islamic times, when sacrificial rituals were performed in gratitude for the increase in flocks and herds and warfare was prohibited.[6] The transformation of Rajab into an Islamic sacred month and the heated juridical debates about the appropriate way of celebrating it are beyond the scope of this paper.[7] Here it suffices to note that Ibn 'Abbad was among those members of the religious elite who believed that Rajab was endowed with special blessings that Muslims could garner by performing specific gestures and rituals, notably fasting and prayer. After uttering the obligatory liturgical formulas praising God, testifying to His oneness and to Muhammad's status as a Messenger of God, and invoking the blessing upon the Prophet that must initiate every *khutba*, Ibn 'Abbad then exhorted his audience as follows:

> Servants of God! Hasten to the greatest victory and seize the opportunity [to gain] the spiritual graces of this month. Know that God Almighty has amply bestowed his blessings upon us and has abundantly rewarded to us with his favor in it. He has made the pious deed during it praiseworthy of the Return and has redoubled [its] reward and the recompense. That is Rajab the unique, possessed of merits so numerous that they cannot be counted. (Ibn 'Abbad of Ronda, fol. 5)[8]

Despite Ibn 'Abbad's hyperbole that the spiritual merits of Rajab 'cannot be counted,' the preacher in fact goes on to meticulously enumerate for his audience the rewards that they will accrue from fasting successive days of the month. Basing himself on the authority of Abu Darda' (d. 652), a younger contemporary and possibly a Companion of the Prophet Muhammad who was particularly revered by Sufis as a paragon of pious asceticism, Ibn 'Abbad related the belief that the person fasting the first day of the month

> aspires through it to encounter God Almighty. His fast exempts him from the wrath of God and it shall close off from him one of the doors of the Inferno ... Whoever fasts three days shall have likewise and God shall forgive him his past sins. Whoever fasts for four days shall have likewise and the Book inscribing his fate in the hereafter shall place him among the first to be saved. (Ibn 'Abbad of Ronda, fol. 5)

The narrative climaxes with the promise that whoever fasts Rajab entirely shall have likewise thirty times as much and a divine herald shall summon him with the good tidings, 'Oh friend of God,' the greatest honour (Ibn 'Abbad of Ronda, fol. 6, op. cit.). (In Sufi parlance a 'friend of God' may be compared with a Christian saint.[9]) Ibn 'Abbad is enticing his audience with the extraordinary promise that fasting the entire month of Rajab confers the closest proximity to God.

He then relates a narrative recorded from another Companion of the Prophet, Anas b. Malik (d. 711),[10] who equates the spiritual rewards for fasting one day of Rajab with fasting an entire year. Hence, 'whoever fasts a single day, it is as if he had fasted a year. Whoever fasts two days, it is as if he had fasted for two years,' and so forth until the sixth day. But if he fasts seven days, 'God shall close off from him the seven doors of hell and whoever fasts for eight days, God shall open to him the eight doors of Paradise. If he fasts for ten days, God shall transform his evil doings into good deeds' (Ibn 'Abbad of Ronda, fol. 6).

It is important to note that fasting any day during the month of Rajab is a supererogatory act of devotion, since Islamic law only mandates the fast of the month of Ramadan.[11] Sunni legal schools concur that it is legally desirable [*mandub ilayhi*] for one to fast certain days of the months of Muharram, Shawwal, Dhu 'l-Qa'da, and Dhu 'l-Hijja, which the Islamic tradition designates as sacred. The Rajab fast is a completely voluntary and joyful gesture of renouncing food and the appetites of the flesh in order to gain greater consciousness of and closer proximity to God.

The greater God-consciousness that fasting provokes is enhanced further by the performance of rituals such as recitation of the Qur'an, litanies in praise of God and the Prophet, and prayer exercises. Ibn 'Abbad proceeds to relate a lengthy Hadith that the Sunni theologian Abu Hamid al-Ghazali (d. 1111) attributed to the Prophet Muhammad on the merits of combining fasting with performing supererogatory prayers when done at a precise time and in a fixed order: the ritual must be undertaken by one fasting the first five days of Rajab during the period between the two evening prayers. Such fasting Muslims must pray twelve cycles of prostrations. At every prayer cycle they should recite the 'Fatihah' (the first chapter of the Qur'an), the chapter, 'We have indeed revealed this message in the Night of Power' (Q 97) three times, and the chapter, 'Say: He is God, the One and Only' (Q 112) twelve times. After each two prayer cycles they are to utter the blessing upon the Prophet, and when they complete the twelve prayer cycles, they must again invoke the prophetic blessing seventy times, prostrate once more, and say seventy times, 'Glory to God, the Most Holy, the Lord of the Angels and the spirits,' then raise their heads and say seventy times, 'Lord, forgive and have mercy, disregard what you know [of our sins]. Verily you are the Most High, the Most Mighty' (Ibn 'Abbad of Ronda, fol. 7).

Ibn 'Abbad concludes the Hadith related by al-Ghazali with his own narrative commentary[12] in the form of a promise that assures his audience of the veracity of these statements and reaffirms the eschatological rewards for performing the supererogatory prayers: 'There is no one who has prayed this ritual prayer whom God has not forgiven all of his sins, even if they were as the drops of the ocean, the number of grains of sand, the weight of the mountains, the leaves of a tree, and he shall intercede on the Day of Resurrection for 700 of those who deserve the Inferno' (Ibn 'Abbad of Ronda, fol. 7). The *khutba* ends with a final supplication to God, thanking him for 'including us among his party of the fortunate and of his righteous servants and granting us success in following him and pleasing him in every time and circumstance,' and beseeching him to 'unite our hearts in obedience of you, our minds [or resolve] in the renunciation of disobedience ... to constrain our limbs from mortal sins, and to immunize us against what you have forbidden' (Ibn 'Abbaḍ of Ronda, fol. 7).

This sermon demonstrates that the journey towards God is envisaged as a journey whose medium of transport is the physical body and not only the somatized soul. Despite the final allusions to the mind and resolve (and a previous exhortation to the audience to mark the observation of the month of Rajab also with good deeds such as giving charity to prisoners of war, orphans, and the poor, and showing kindness and comprehension towards those who have suffered misfortunes [Ibn 'Abbad of Ronda, fol. 7][13]), the emphasis throughout the sermon has been on the power of the purified and disciplined body to overcome and eradicate sin. Practices like fasting and prayer allow the pious Muslim, male or female, to aspire to 'encounter God,' elude the torments of hell, and attain a place among the highest ranks of heaven. The sayings related on the authority of Abu Darda', Anas b. Malik, and al-Ghazali instil in the audience the capacity of the body itself to become a 'focusing lens'[14] marking off not so much the sacred from the profane as 'the successful' (i.e., the saved) from the damned ('the losers') (Ibn 'Abbad of Ronda, fol. 7)[15] through their persistent and disciplined performance of supererogatory prayers and fasting during the sacred month of Rajab. Corporeal discipline and ritualization are inherent in the stipulation that in order to be spiritually efficacious, supererogatory prayer prostrations and utterances must be performed at a specific time, in a precise order, and repeated an exact number of times by bodies that have been ritually purified. The net effect or objective of such sermons delivered during the 'sacred times' is to create Muslims whose hearts, minds, and bodies are united and disciplined in the obedience of God, and whose bodies are constrained from committing mortal sin, immune to temptation, and divinely inspired to draw nearer to God through good works. Still, this idealized transformed body is contingent upon time, specifically upon the distinction between sacred and normative time, since the gist of the sermon is to underscore that fasting and prayer have greater effect when performed *at these times*. The next section will explore sermons in which the body is depicted as a perpetual focusing lens or a classification system *habitually* demarcating faith and infidelity, obedience and disobedience, morality and sin irrespective of time.

The Remembrance of God or the Somatization of Morality and Identity

Ibn 'Abbad's sermon for Rajab exhorted his audience to fast and perform supererogatory rituals at this sacred time to discipline their bodies in the obedience of God and the avoidance of sin in the hopes of attaining salvation. Such pious deeds are common rituals through which pious Muslims 'remember' God, death, and the Last Things. Indeed, one of the most frequent themes in Islamic hortatory sermons is 'the remembrance of God,' a scriptural command that may have polemical connotations. The Qur'an identifies the People of Israel as those who 'forgot' or 'neglected' their duties towards God in contrast to Muslims who recall and fulfil their spiritual obligations.[16] As I have argued elsewhere, this polemical sense of the remembrance of God inspired the anonymous thirteenth-century Mudejar preacher, whose sermons sought to vindicate the piety and religious identity of the Mudejar community in Aragon vis-à-vis its Christian oppressors.[17] In the very first sermon, he portrays the remembrance of God not as a mental process but rather as bodily praxis and ethical responsibilities, in which the bodily and the ethical are closely intertwined. While he initially defines the remembrance of God as faith and religious obligations, he goes on to discuss these exclusively in terms of a classification system that associates each body part with a specific virtue or vice:

> As for faith, it too is divided into three parts: the utterances of the tongue, the beliefs in the heart, and the actions of the members of the body. As for the tongue and the heart, they share in the same concern. As for the deeds of the members of the body, they are a witness because actions reveal what the tongue says and the heart believes. (Anonymous, fol. 2)

The preacher likewise compartmentalizes the sins that every Muslim must avoid. The 'avoidance of the forbidden things' is divided into nine parts and seven groupings: six concern the tongue, three concern the ears, and there is a group that concerns the eyes, a group that concerns the stomach, a group that concerns the genitalia, a group that concerns the heart, a group that concerns the two hands, a group that concerns the two legs, and a group that concerns the tongue (Anonymous, fols. 2–3). The sins of the tongue include blasphemy and slander, the sins of the stomach include consuming forbidden foods and wine, the sins of the ears include listening to gossip and 'petty trifles,' while the sins of the hands include unlawful murder, theft, and sowing dissent and corruption (Anonymous, fol. 3).

The preacher self-consciously refers to his own role in inculcating the necessity of embodying one's belief and faith. Quoting the Qur'an, he states that it is the preacher's duty to remind Muslims of their religious obligations and of the consequences of forgetting or neglecting them: 'Do not forget them, lest you be counted among those of whom God said, "Whoever turns away from My Message, verily for him is a life narrowed down and We shall raise him up blind on the Day of Judgment"' [Q 20:124]' (Anonymous, fol. 3). The immediate context of this verse is the narrative of Adam and Eve's expulsion from the Garden of Paradise (Q 20:116–30). The allusions to being 'narrowed down' and risen up blind prefigure the punishments of the grave that unrepentant sinners will face. Previous verses of sura 20 narrate the fate of the Pharaoh of Egypt, who stubbornly 'rejected and refused' all the Signs of God (cf. Q 20:56), and the People of Israel, who broke their promises to God (cf. Q 20:87). The preacher thus offers exempla about God's awesome power to punish those who disbelieve and disobey his Signs and fail to repent their sins. The recitation of Q 20:124 issues a warning that disbelieving and disobedient Muslims will share the same fate as the wayward Children of Israel and the infidel Pharaoh. Of particular relevance is the fleshliness of those eschatological punishments.

Several notions about the body may be inferred from the Mudejar preacher's discussion of the remembrance of God. The body emerges first and foremost as a primary classification system that distinguishes the true Muslim from the hypocrite and the unbeliever. It is a mnemonic device for recalling and inscribing God's ethical prescriptions and prohibitions. It is the focusing lens or central site upon which righteous behaviour and religious identity are demarcated and publicly displayed in this world and the next. And it is the Muslim's primary instrument in determining whether he or she will be prosecuted or acquitted at the Last Judgment. Hence the preacher enjoins his audience to routinely scrutinize each part of his or her body: each act, gesture, and bodily disposition (or *habitus*) is an exterior sign of his or her internal state, beliefs, intentions, and sentiments, knowing that all will be revealed on the Last Day.

This conception of the body may be situated within the context of Sunni Islamic debates regarding the relative importance of faith [*iman*] and works ['*amal*] in the economy of salvation,[18] and the affirmation of the material continuity of the body at the Resurrection, a fundamental dogma of the Qur'an and the Hadith, which graphically describe the horrors of the grave, the trials of the Day of Reckoning, and the fate of the 'triumphant' and the 'losers' in heaven and hell.[19] I will leave the eschatological considerations for the final section and limit my comments here to analysing the Mudejar preacher's exposition of the actions of the body in relation to faith.

The key phrase, in my opinion, is his assertion that the tongue and the heart 'share in the same concern' and that the 'deeds of the members of the body ... are a witness because actions reveal what the tongue says and the heart believes' (Anonymous, fol. 2). The statement harks back to medieval theological and legal discussions about the definition of faith. The general consensus among the men of religion was that faith has three components: the internal conviction, the verbal expression, and the performance of the prescribed works [*al-i'tiqad bi 'l-qalb*, *al-i'tiqad bi 'l-lisan* (or *qawl*), and *al-i'tiqad bi 'l-'amal*, respectively]. The various schools of law and even theologians within a single school debated the relative importance and weight of each aspect of *iman*.[20] The anonymity of this sermon manuscript makes it virtually impossible to affirm where our preacher stood in this debate. What does seem clear is the Mudejar preacher's conviction that the body is essential and determinative in defining and proving faith or infidelity, a stance that conforms with Qur'anic verses recounting the weighing of one's good and bad deeds on Judgment Day (cf. Q 21:47, 101:6–9), and which approximates the views held by theologian Abu Hamid al-Ghazali, whom the preacher cites on many occasions.[21]

The Mudejar preacher's portrayal of the body as the discloser of the person's true beliefs and intentions aims to caution against the dangers of hypocrisy [*nifaq* or *riya'*]. The semantic range of *nifaq* as employed in the Qur'an also includes apostasy and lying.[22] The term *riya'* or its cognate *ri'a* appears several times in the Qur'an (Q 2:264, 4:38, and 8:47). It is also treated extensively in the Hadith, in al-Ghazali's magnum opus on theology, *Ihya' 'ulum al-din* [*Revival of the Religious Sciences*], as well as in numerous Sufi texts.[23] Derived from the Arabic verb '*ra'a*,' meaning 'to see,' the word *riya'* suggests ostentatious hypocrisy, whereby the outer form conceals the true inner disposition. Typically, the literature on the topic contrasts hypocritical ostentation with sincerity or purity of intention [*ikhlas*], and places great emphasis on the somatization of ostentation in 'the body, external appearance and dress, speech, and action.'[24] This notion that hypocrisy and sincerity may be somatized accords with the Mudejar preacher's conviction that the deeds of the members of the body bear 'witness' to what the 'tongue says and the heart believes.' Additionally, the preacher introduces the imagery of illness and disease to refer not only to sin or immorality, but especially to hypocrisy, understood as the disjuncture between bodily praxis and internal belief.

The Mudejar preacher pursues these themes in the third and the eighth sermons of the collection. The third sermon begins with the exordium, 'God Almighty Most Sublime said, "Hasten to the forgiveness from your Lord; and a Garden, the extensiveness of which is (as) the heavens and the earth, it is prepared for those who guard (against evil)"' (Q 3:133, 57:21; Anonymous, fols. 8–12). The preacher develops this sermon around the Qur'anic injunction to 'command right and forbid wrong' (Q 3:104), a sort of 'golden rule' of Islam that encapsulates for the Mudejar preacher the compliance with all the obligations and the avoidance of all the prohibitions. He invokes the metaphor of the sick body to explain the dangers of failing to fulfil all the positive commandments and to avoid all the taboos imposed by God. He observes, for instance, that the full recovery of the sick body requires equally the consumption of nourishing food and the appropriate medicine, on the one hand, and the avoidance of all that is harmful to it, on the other. Similarly, the Muslim 'yearning for Paradise' must persevere in the ritual prayers, giving charity, fasting the month of Ramadan, reciting the Qur'an, and the 'sum total of the religious obligations.' Nor must the Muslim ignore the prohibitions but strive to avoid all sinful acts such as drinking wine, fornication, disobedience to one's parents, slander, envy, and contempt (Anonymous, fol. 8). The Mudejar preacher warns that those who fail to resist temptation and shun sin 'will gain nothing from [their nightly vigils of] prayer except sleeplessness and distress, nothing from their fasting except hunger and thirst, and they shall be struck with blindness because they were not sincere before the face of God Almighty' (Anonymous, fol. 8).

To reinforce the imperative of the sincerity of one's actions, he narrates a Hadith stating that those whose ritual prayer does not impede them from committing 'the abominations' increase in distance from rather than in proximity to God (Anonymous, fol. 8).[25] A subsequent saying that he cites on the authority of al-Ghazali is even more ominous: 'And those who are knowledgeable about God, all of them are doomed except for those who do good deeds. And those who do good deeds, all of them are doomed except for those who are sincere. And those who are sincere are in the gravest danger' (Anonymous, fol. 8). The text is damaged and partly illegible at this point, but there seems to be an extraordinary comparison being made between the sincere Muslim who makes the slightest infraction and the worst of sinners: 'the sincere Muslims will resemble the polytheists who worship a god other than God and those who practice usury in their transactions' (Anonymous, fol. 8).

In the eighth sermon, also devoted to the 'remembrance of God' (Anonymous, fols. 28–38), the Mudejar preacher draws upon images of physical illness to speak of the spiritual perils of failing to remember God by avoiding the conduct He has forbidden. Thus we read that the sick body may be treated by the use of the 'appropriate medicine and the avoidance of harmful foods.' Yet 'if he uses the beneficial nourishment and medicine but also uses the harmful thing which was the cause of his decay, then he is closer to utter destruction than to prolonging his life.' Similarly, the treatment of the soul has two parts: 'the acceptance of everything that God has commanded and imposed as a religious duty from among the divine precepts and acts of devotion in word, belief, and deed, and the avoidance of all that he has forbidden' (Anonymous, fol. 31). Even mixing a 'smidgeon' of wrongdoing with obedience to God 'contaminates' body and soul and 'nullifies' the heavenly recompense of the good deed (Anonymous, fols. 31–2). In the same vein, he admonishes those who attend hortatory preaching assemblies against imagining that they will be saved by such public displays of piety if they have committed by word, deed, or praxis any of the forbidden things:

> And so it is with humanity. For if one does not concern oneself with the pious deeds that salvation and the plentiful hereafter require, then of what use will be listening to a hortatory sermon [*maw'iza*]? On the contrary! Listening to that while renouncing good works is an increment in sinfulness, deviation, and disobedience and that is a manifest proof and a clear evidence of one's guilt after having heard what God has commanded and forbidden. (Anonymous, fol. 32)

The Mudejar sermons considered thus far marshal a considerable arsenal of Qur'anic texts, Hadith, and sayings of respected Sufi theologians to warn the audience that their every deed, gesture, and bodily disposition should be in accordance at all times – not solely during special, sacred times – with obeying God and following the Prophet Muhammad in fulfilling all the religious obligations and resisting all sin and temptation. The preacher evokes repeatedly the image of bodily illness to describe the discord between body, soul, and faith. The underlying message is that verbal professions of faith alone are deficient as an indicator of sincere Muslim faith because people are capable of saying or doing what they do not believe. The true beliefs and intentions lodged within the heart are somatized and disclosed in the attendant actions and gestures. The sinful and immoral Muslim will be recognized in the present world and the afterlife by the defects in his or her deeds and bodily *habitus*: stomachs that have consumed forbidden foods and wine rather than adhering to the proscriptions against them; ears that preferred to listen to gossip than to the word of God; hands that have stolen, lashed out in anger, committed usury, or sown corruption on the earth instead of performing prayer and acts of charity; mouths that have spoken lies and brought false testimony against others instead of praising God and speaking the truth; and legs that have walked in the disobedience of God and illegality rather than abide by the divine laws (Anonymous, fol. 3, op. cit). Moreover, those who have committed such sins will not be saved by ostentatious displays of piety, such as performing ritual or supererogatory prayers and attending preaching assemblies. On the contrary, such hypocrisy will magnify their punishment. We have already glimpsed the eschatological consequences of sin in one of the Qur'anic exhortations that the Mudejar preacher cited: 'Do not forget them, lest you be counted among those of whom God said, "Whoever turns away from My Message, verily for him is a life narrowed down and We shall raise him up blind on the Day of Judgment"' (Q 20:124; Anonymous, fol. 3). The final section will explore in greater detail homiletic discussions of the body in Muslim eschatology, where graphic corporeal images are deployed to support a literal interpretation of the sacred texts concerning the Last Things.

The Body in Muslim Eschatology

Eschatology is an important theme in the Qur'an. The earliest Qur'anic verses issued urgent warnings about Judgment Day and of the convulsions that will take place at that time.[26] Many verses, but particularly Q 2:177 and 4:136, place belief in the Last Day as second only to belief in God in the list of essential beliefs necessary for being considered a Muslim.[27] Indeed, it would not be an exaggeration to state that in Qur'anic discourse human life finds its maximum significance in the hereafter [*al-akhira*]. The most striking feature of Islamic eschatology is its fleshliness. The carnal delights of the Islamic heaven are well known: the whole of heaven is a garden beneath which rivers flow. There, the triumphant consume sumptuous meals, they savour the once forbidden wine, they adorn their bodies with silk and precious jewels, and men enjoy the sensual pleasures of numerous beautiful women [*houris*]. The torments of the Islamic hell are likewise infamous: it is a place inhabited by gigantic snakes, scorpions, and other hideous creatures that inflict the bodies of the damned with unimaginably horrific and painful castigations before roasting in the hell-fire. Fazlur Rahman observes that there is nothing purely spiritual about heaven or hell or the souls inhabiting them in Islamic eschatology. 'The Qur'an, unlike Muslim philosophers, does not recognize a hereafter that will be peopled by disembodied souls – in fact, it does not recognize the dualism of the soul and the body and man, for it is a unitary, living, and fully functioning organism' (Rahman 112).

The anonymous Mudejar preacher and Ibn 'Abbad of Ronda adhere closely to the Qur'anic discourses on the material reality of the hereafter, and they frequently quote the pertinent scriptural passages throughout their sermons. In this they follow the trend of orthodox Sunni theological teachings imparted to the masses[28] emphasizing that the eschatological events described in the Qur'an truly indicate what will happen at the end of time and must be understood literally rather than allegorically.[29] A fundamental duty of the preacher, therefore, is to impress upon the community the realities of the Last Things in the most palpable and tangible way possible. And indeed, both preachers have striven to make the realities of death and the Last Judgment resemble real life as far as possible. As William Chittick explains, 'reality of death can only be known through reality of life, "imitation (*taqlid*) and tradition (*sama'*)"' (Chittick 390). The Qur'an and the canonical Hadith furnish ample material on the body in Muslim eschatology from which preachers liberally quote. Yet in their attempts to achieve verisimilitude in their descriptions of the hereafter, preachers often resort as well to extra-canonical texts on eschatology[30] and a subgenre of Muslim homiletic literature known as the 'books of warnings and delights' ['*kutub al-mawa'iz wa 'l-raqa'iq*'][31] to embellish their sermons with terrifying graphic images of the tortures of hell and enticing descriptions of the sensual delights of paradise.

It will be recalled from the previous discussion of the sermon on the 'remembrance of God' that the Mudejar preacher defined faith from the perspective of the tongue, the heart, and the members of the body, referring to the latter as a 'witness' to what 'the tongue says and the heart believes' (Anonymous, fol. 2). He proceeded to illustrate his teachings on the somatizing of faith with a stern warning from the Qur'an:

> And this is why, on the Day of Resurrection, as God Almighty has said, 'They will not utter a sound nor will it be permitted to them and they will have no excuse. Rather their hands and their legs shall testify against them

> regarding what they have done.' On that day, as God Almighty has said, 'we shall seal up their mouths' [Q 77:35]. (Anonymous, fol. 2)

This Qur'anic verse and its parallel Q 41:19–24, which threatens that 'their ears and eyes and skins will give evidence against them of what they have done,' provide a chilling image of the futility of using the mouth to conceal the truth from God about one's deeds and beliefs. Pitting the members and actions of the body against the tongue and the heart obviates any attempt to lie or conceal one's hypocrisy or insincerity. The Mudejar preacher may have had in mind Qur'anic verses declaring that on Judgment Day everyone will be subjected to the weighing of the scales (Q 21:47–8) and the Reckoning of all their acts (Q 15:92–3), and will be forced to face the accusations against them recorded in their book of deeds (Q 59:18–26). Yet he cited most often the homilies of a celebrated tenth-century Hanafi theologian, Abu 'l-Layth al-Samarqandi,[32] to which I shall now turn my attention.

The text in question is entitled *Consolation for the Eyes and Relief for Saddened Hearts* [*Qurrat al-'uyun wa mafrah al-qalb al-mahzun*].[33] *The Consolation* is a collection of ten homilies, each of which deals with the eschatological punishments that will accrue for committing a specific sin, beginning with the worst, the abandonment of the ritual prayer, and ending with music and singing.[34] Each homily on the eschatological torments for sin is paired with a homily on the heavenly rewards for righteous conduct. The text thus conforms to the aforementioned homiletic subgenre of 'books of warnings and delights,' which aims to inspire repentance by appealing to the sentiments of fear and desire. The *Consolation* was widely diffused and frequently cited in the Muslim Middle Ages, including, as mentioned, by the Mudejar preacher. A key theme throughout the sermon collection is the correlation between the deeds of the body in the here and now and the physical torments one will face in the hereafter, according to one's acts and *habitus*.[35] The first homily on the worst sin, the neglect of prayer, sets an ominous tone, accusing those who abandon the ritual prayer of wholly abandoning their religion:

> And God Almighty said, 'Woe to the worshippers who are negligent in their prayer.' Ibn 'Abbas said, 'By the oasis of hell! ... This is the resting place of those who deferred the prayer from the appointed time.' The Prophet said, 'Nothing stands between the believer and the unbeliever except the abandonment of ritual prayer. Whoever abandons or rejects prayer is an unbeliever [*kafir*].' (Abu 'l-Layth al-Samarqandi 128)

The author reaffirms persistence in ritual prayer as the quintessential marker of Muslim identity. Obliged to be performed five times a day every day, the ritual prayer exhibits more than any of the other pillars of Islam the power of repetition in creating a bodily *habitus*. Al-Samarqandi portrays the one who persistently prays as spiritually transformed; he or she attains the spiritual ideal of habitually preferring the sacred to the mundane. The association of the Islamic ritual prayer with Muslim identity justifies the hideous castigation of those who abandon it, delay it for their own mundane purposes, or otherwise belittle its significance. A clear and unequivocal line exists between belief and unbelief, and these binary opposites are inscribed upon the body.

Al-Samarqandi upholds the Qur'anic view of the continuity of the physical body in the afterlife in specifying that one who abandons prayer will face 'six punishments in this world, three upon death, three in the tomb, and three upon the resurrection from the grave' (Abu 'l-Layth al-Samarqandi 128–9). The punishments in this world constitute a deconstruction of the person as an individual and a social being, and a negation of the deeds of an entire life. One reads that 'God will strike off [*yanza'u*] the blessing from his life; God will blot out [*yamsahu*] from his face his resemblance to the pious; God will not reward any of his good deeds.' God will not answer any of his prayers, and he shall be despised by his fellows (Abu 'l-Layth al-Samarqandi 129).

Corporeal imagery becomes increasingly graphic and terrifying with each passage of the eschatological journey from death, to the grave, to the resurrection. Speaking of the punishments at death, al-Samarqandi tersely warns that the neglecters of prayer will die 'lowly and despised, hungry, and thirsty' (Abu 'l-Layth al-Samarqandi 129). The punishments to be faced in the grave and at the awakening presuppose bodily integrity and psychological consciousness. Al-Samarqandi's description of these torments greatly embellishes canonical Hadith motifs of the 'narrowness (or confinement)' of the grave. He informs his audience that

> the grave will squeeze him until his ribcage is torn out. A fire will be ignited in his grave and he will be turned over in its embers day and night. He will be tormented by a hydra whose iron fangs will pierce though his body, biting him continuously. Its eyes are of fire and its fangs of iron. The length of every claw is like roaring thunder. And he will say, 'My Lord commanded me to bite you for neglecting the morning prayer from the morning till the afternoon, and to bite you for neglecting the afternoon prayer from the afternoon to the evening prayer, and to bite you for neglecting the evening prayer

> from the evening till the sunset, and to bite you for neglecting the sunset prayer from the sunset till the nightly prayer from the night until the morning.' (Abu 'l-Layth al-Samarqandi 129–30)

So terrifying are these events that al-Samarqandi interrupts his narrative to utter a prayer: 'God spare us from the torments of the grave!' (Abu 'l-Layth al-Samarqandi 130). On the Day of the Arising, God will sentence the neglecter of prayer to the hellfire. During the reckoning of his sins, 'God will look upon him with intense hatred ... and the flesh of his face will fall off' (Abu 'l-Layth al-Samarqandi 130). Al-Samarqandi cites the Prophet Muhammad, who declared, 'Verily, in hell there is an oasis filled with vipers whose poison will boil over onto the body of the abandoner of prayer ... Then it will consume his flesh and his bones will be hacked to pieces' (Abu 'l-Layth al-Samarqandi 135).

Images of bodily pain, violent piercings and perforations, burning, disfiguration, destruction, and obliteration pervade the narratives of the punishments of the grave and the Day of the Arising. By contrast, a presumption of bodily wholeness prevails in the descriptions of heavenly rewards for righteous conduct. Abu 'l-Layth cites a Hadith from the Prophet Muhammad: 'Whoever prays the morning prayer for forty days straight without missing a single prostration, God will spare him from the hellfire ... The Prophet said, "Whoever prays the morning prayer in its entirety then sits to invoke God's name [*dhikr*] until the sun rises, God will build for him a castle in the highest level of paradise, yeah seventy castles, each one having seventy doors of gold and silver"' (Abu 'l-Layth al-Samarqandi 131).

For al-Samarqandi, Muslim identity and personhood emanate from the assiduous performance of the ritual prayer, while its abandonment or neglect literally effaces the identity of the Muslim *qua* Muslim. Hence the graphic images of eschatological punishment as fragmentation and disfiguration. If ritual prayer is understood as the means by which the Muslim redefines himself or herself as Muslim and reconstructs the Muslim self as one who recognizes the sovereignty of God, the punishment for neglect or abandonment of prayer represent an inversion, an unmaking of the Muslim self. Thus, the signs of piety will be obliterated from the negligent Muslim's face, meaning that God will not recognize him or her as pious, but rather as condemned. The neglectful Muslim will also lose his or her social identity, dying 'despised' by his or her fellows – a terrible punishment in societies which honour and shame are critical. Nor will God hear or answer prayers nor reward any other good works. Returning like for like, God wilfully ignores and neglects the Muslim who has wilfully ignored and neglected him by abandoning prayer. These are powerful images of the obliteration of personhood and identity.

Conclusion

This study of the body in Islamic preaching has drawn attention to the revelatory power of the body to signify religious identity and interior states. The individual body's *habitus*, gestures, and ritual acts are never devoid of meaning; they always signify something, be it morality or vice, faith or unbelief, spirituality or profligacy, sincerity or hypocrisy, and so forth. The discourses about the body encountered in the sermons surveyed for this essay emphasize that *all* the gestures and the very *habitus* of the Muslim somatize his or her interior states and dispositions, revealing and authenticating (or discrediting) the sincerity of his or her deeds and words. The possibilities of a discrepancy, conflict, or separation between the body and the mind or soul appear to dissipate in the ethos that 'the body *reveals* what the tongue says and the heart believes.'

Such an understanding of the body is consistent with monistic conceptions of the body and the soul. Both the Qur'an and the Prophet's *sunna* advocate this body-soul unity in discourses postulating that the sincere faith of the heart and mind are manifested through the actions, gestures, and praxis of the disciplined, ritualized body. The preachers' emphasis on the body's capacity to construct faith, sincerity, and orthodoxy – or their opposites – in each and every ritual act, gesture, and disposition challenges, in my opinion, scholarly assertions regarding the 'misrecognition' of how ritual does what it does.[36] On the contrary, the severe warnings of the even worse eschatological torments awaiting hypocrites who purify their bodies, perform the ritual prayers, and attend hortatory preaching sessions and yet persist in sinful behaviour evince a lucid understanding of the role of the ritualized body, bodily praxis, gestures, and strategic speech acts in engendering the inner qualities and states that define the ideal Muslim.[37]

Ibn 'Abbad of Ronda and the anonymous Mudejar of Aragon may well have been aware of competing Sufi discourses privileging the esoteric and the spiritual over the exoteric and the material, or of the Aristotelian body-soul dualism of Avicenna and other Muslim philosophers. Yet for both preachers, as well as al-Samarqandi, such elitist discussions had no place in sermons delivered before 'the masses,' who must be instructed in the duties of canonical worship and the obedience of the divine prohibitions, which they deemed best articulated in terms of embodiment. This explains, in my view, the emphasis on carnality in Islamic homiletic discourse. Medieval Islamic preachers do not invoke binary opposites between body and soul, but rather between drawing nearer to and straying from God, the remembrance of God and forgetting God, purity or impurity, showing gratitude or ingratitude towards God. The body itself is the 'focusing lens' in which these binary opposites are played out. Body talk is deployed in sermons as a mnemonic device to classify vice and virtue or belief or unbelief; as an instrument to obtain spiritual states; and as the locus of eschatological reward and punishment. In all cases, the treatment of the body is informed by an eschatology that presupposes the necessary continuity of body and soul following death and beyond to Resurrection Day.

No less remarkable is the fact that the revelatory power of the body not only continues after death but reaches it zenith on the Last Day when mouths will be sealed and eyes, ears, hands, legs, genitalia, stomachs, and skin will testify against the person as to what they have done and believed. The Qur'anic verses, Hadith, and the treatises on eschatology that preachers cite in their sermons uphold the presupposition that the post-mortem body retains its integrity, consciousness, and capacity to feel; hence the preacher's stress upon the literal interpretation of the Last Things. Although there were theological texts available advancing metaphorical and spiritual interpretations of the events of the afterlife,[38] medieval preachers went out of their way to select those narratives that supported a literal understanding of these events in the belief that this would be the best strategy to incite right conduct and to deter sin among their audiences. The vivid imagery of compartmentalization, whereby the individual members of the body will testify against the person at the Last Judgment, the rhetorical use of powerful words such as 'blotting out' and 'effacing' the sinner's face, together with the images of eschatological bodily fragmentation and destruction were intended to persuade audiences of the physical realities of the Last Things. It may not be gratuitous to add that in a religious tradition that forbids the iconographic representation of the Last Judgment such as one would find depicted in Christian churches, powerful words and graphic language emphasizing the body, embodied suffering, and bodily fragmentation constitute the most potent rhetorical tools at the preacher's disposition to convey his message. Surely such descriptions were more compelling and more likely to induce the desired effects of repentance and moral reform than any abstract discourse about the Islamic system of rewards and punishments.

NOTES

This is an expanded version of a talk given at the conference 'The Body in Medieval Culture' held at the Centre for Medieval Studies, University of Toronto (March 2006). I wish to thank Dr Carolyn Muessig and Dr Dwight F. Reynolds for their comments and suggestions.

1 The manuscript remains unedited.
2 Arabic manuscripts containing religious texts in addition to this sermon collection were found hidden in a house in Zaragoza (Aragon). Palaeographic and internal evidence points to the late twelfth or early thirteenth century, while the preacher's own comments regarding being 'oppressed and prey to the polytheists' (fol. 39) confirm the Mudejar origins of the text. See J. Ribera and M. Asín (i–xxix, 255–6).
3 The question of whether or not preachers or other members of the religious establishment denied or ignored the dualistic theories of the soul postulated by the Muslim philosophers is beyond the scope of this paper. On this, see T.A. Druart. The main point is that such dualistic theories of anthropology are not reflected in the homiletic sources. The survival of Neoplatonist dichotomies between the body and the soul in Christian thought has recently been challenged by a number of medievalists. See Bynum, *Fragmentation* and 'Why All the Fuss about the Body?'; Elliott; and Butler. Regarding Christian preaching, see d'Avray.
4 The medieval Islamic *khutba* remains understudied in Western scholarship. A typology of the *khutba* and the other preaching genres is presented in detail in Jones, 'The Boundaries of Sin' 106–254. See also Wensinck, 'Khutba'; Vadet. On the *mawa'iz* and *qisas*, see Swartz; Pedersen, 'The Islamic Preacher' and 'The Criticism of the Islamic Preacher;' 'Athamina; and Berkey.
5 The manuscript is unedited. On Ibn 'Abbad, see the study by Paul Nwyia.
6 This synopsis of the merits of the month of Rajab follows the article by M.J. Kister, 'Radjab'; and idem, 'Radjab is the Month of God.'
7 See the previous footnote for a succinct analysis of the issues under discussion.
8 All translations from Arabic are mine unless otherwise noted.
9 Such comparisons have their limitations, however. See J. Wasim Frembgen.
10 See J. Robson and A.J. Wensinck, 'Anas b. Malik.'
11 On the traditions regarding the obligatory and supererogatory fasts, see A.J. Wensinck, *Concordances*.
12 On the function of narrative commentary in religious discourse, see Witten, esp. pp. 22–30.

13 The exhortations referred to occur in the paragraph that immediately precedes the final supplications to God.

14 J.Z. Smith defines ritual space as a 'focusing lens, marking off and revealing significance.' It is a space where the 'ordinary ... becomes significant, becomes sacred ... by having our attention directed to it in a special way.' See Smith 54–5. I am suggesting, following Mauss's discussion of body techniques, that J.Z. Smith's notion of a 'focusing lens' may be applied to the body itself, the human being's primary ritual space.

15 Here Ibn 'Abbad uses the terminology most frequently employed in Qur'anic discourse to speak of those who attain salvation or suffer damnation as the 'successful and the losers,' respectively, cf. Q 10:45, 22:11, 40:78, and 91:7–10.

16 For instance, Q 20, which presents Adam and the People of Israel as examples of those who neglected their duties towards God or, in the case of Pharaoh, who stubbornly refused to see the truth of the divine Signs. The Mudejar preacher often cites this sura and Q 50 in his sermons.

17 See notes 1 and 2 above regarding the manuscript and Jones, 'Boundaries of Sin' 410–21 and 453–96 for a discussion of the underlying polemical motives of the sermons.

18 A brief introduction to the issues involved is found in L. Gardet. For an exhaustive exposition of the different schools of thought on faith [*iman*] and deeds ['*amal*], see the eponymous chapters in the classic study by A.J. Wensinck, *The Muslim Creed.*

19 As Fazlur Rahman points out in his *Major Themes of the Qur'an* (108), the Qur'an speaks less of salvation and damnation than of success [*falah*] and loss [*khusran*].

20 L. Gardet, 'Iman.'

21 Al-Ghazali defines faith as the sum total of belief [*tasdiq*], word [*qawl*], and action ['*amal*], *The Revival of the Religious Sciences [Ihya 'ulum al-din]* (vol. I, 103). By way of contrast, see Coope. The author concludes that for Ibn Hazm of Cordoba (d. 1064) 'the work of the limbs is valuable in and of itself, and [is] not simply ... a product of belief in the heart' (108), and that 'works bear a relationship to belief, but they are not identical with it' (109).

22 A. Brockett, 'al-Munafikun.' The Qur'an devotes an entire chapter [*sura*] to 'the hypocrites' ['*al-Munafiqun*' (Q 63)], and in that *sura* and elsewhere the hypocrites are equated with the infidels [*al-kuffar*] and share the same fate of condemnation to the eternal hell-fire (cf. Q 4:140–5, 48:4, 57:13–15, and 59:11–17).

23 Wensinck's *Concordance* of Hadith includes twenty-three entries for the term *ra'a*. The discussion of *riya'* is based upon Deladrière.

24 Deladrière, 'al-Riya',' 547.
25 I have not been able to identity or locate the source of this Hadith.
26 For instance, Q 92, 96, 101, etc.
27 The Qur'anic proof text mentions five essential beliefs: belief in God, the Last Day, the angels, Scripture, and the prophets: 'righteous is he who believeth in Allah and the Last Day and the angels and the Scripture and the prophets' (Q 2:177).
28 Muslim theologians differentiate between the elites [*al-khawass*] who have acquired expertise [*'ilm*] in the orthodox sciences (Qur'an, scriptural exegesis, hadith, and law) and the masses [*al-'awamm*] whose knowledge is more rudimentary. The Mudejar preacher explicitly distinguishes between the duties of the elites ('warning and reminding the people'), and the duties of the masses ('professing faith in the oneness of God, carrying out the religious prescriptions, and avoiding the prohibitions') (Anonymous, fols. 1 and 28).
29 Chittick, 383, where the author argues that most theologians and Sufis subscribe to the literal interpretation of these events; only the philosophers prefer allegorical interpretation. Chittick, citing Fazlur Rahman, affirms the indispensability of the body to the soul at all stages of existence. Rahman explains that in the Qur'an the term *nafs* [soul] refers to the whole of human existence and not a disembodied spirit, and is more aptly translated as 'person' or 'inner person.' The individual existence of the soul depends upon the locus (body) within which it becomes manifested (Chittick 390).
30 See al-Ghazali. Other popular treatises on eschatology include Ibn Abi 'l-Dunya, *The Book of Graves* [*Kitab al-Qubur*]; idem, *The Book of Death* [*Kitab al-Mawt*]; and Muhammad b. Ahmad al-Qurtubi, *Reminders of the States of the Dead and the Matters of the Afterlife* [*Al-Tadhkira fi ahwal al-mawta wa umur al-akhira*].
31 The Maliki jurist al-Wansharisi (d. 1508) records numerous juridical *responsa* [*fatawa*] from previous centuries of people in al-Andalus and the Maghreb gathering together in assemblies to 'listen to readings from the books of warnings and delights.' Al-Wansharisi, vol. XI, p. 105, and vol. XI, pp. 61–2.
32 The date of Abu 'l-Layth al-Samarqandi's death ranges from 983 to 1003 CE. See J. Schacht, 137.
33 I have not located a critical edition of this text. The text I am using is located in the margins of the homiletic work, Shu'ayb al-Hurayfish, *Al-Rawd al-fa'iq fi 'l-mawa'iz wa'l-raqa'iq [The Exquisite Garden of Warnings and Delights*], ed. unknown (Rabat: Dar al-Fikr, n.d.), 128–261.
34 The other punishments in ascending order are for drinking wine, fornication, homosexuality, consuming carrion, contracting a female wailer for funerals,

obstructing the obligatory tithe [*zakat*], unlawful murder, disobeying one's parents, ending, as noted, with music and dance.

35 The measured recompense for evil deeds contrasts with the manifold rewards for even one good deed, as seen above in Ibn 'Abbad's sermon for Rajab, in which the person who fasted one day was promised the recompense of fasting an entire year, etc.

36 An allusion to Bell 108–17, where the author follows the assertions of Althusser, Burridge, and others that ritualization does not see how it transforms people and creates distinction and hierarchies of power.

37 This applies to both the preacher and his audience. Ibn al-'Attar rebuked those *khatib*s who 'enjoined piety upon the people, but neglected to do so themselves.' See Ibn al-'Attar 92, where he cites a Hadith of the Prophet from the occasion of his visions of heaven and hell in which he saw 'men whose mouths were being cut to shreds with scissors made of fire.' The angel Gabriel informed Muhammad that these were hypocritical, impious preachers.

38 See Chittick 379–90 for a survey of the significant Sufis and theologians who wrote on this topic, including al-Ghazali.

WORKS CITED

Ali, Abdullah Yusuf. *The Meaning of the Holy Quran*. 10th ed. Beltsville, MD: Amana Publications, 2001.

Anonymous. *Maw'iza li dhikr Allah Akbar (A Warning to Remember God Is Great)*. Madrid, Biblioteca de la Junta, MS C no. 3.

'Athamina, Khalil. 'Al-Qasas: Its Emergence, Religious Origin, and Its Socio-Political Impact on Early Muslim Society.' *Studia Islamica* 76 (1992): 53–74.

Bell, C. *Ritual Theory, Ritual Practice.* Oxford: University of Oxford Press, 1992.

Bériou, Nicole, and David L. d'Avray, eds. *Modern Questions about Medieval Sermons: Essays on Marriage, Death, History and Sanctity*. Spoleto: Centro Italiano di Studi sull'alto Medioevo, 1994.

Berkey, Jonathan P. *Popular Preaching and Religious Authority in the Medieval Islamic Near East.* Seattle: University of Washington Press, 2001.

Brockett, A. 'al- Munafikun ff.' *The Encyclopaedia of Islam*. Rev. 2nd ed. Vol. 7. 561.

Butler, Judith. *Bodies that Matter: On the Discursive Limits of 'Sex.'* New York: Routledge, 1993.

Bynum, Caroline Walker. *Fragmentation and Redemption: Essays on Gender and the Human Body in Medieval Religion*. New York: Zone Books, 1992.
– 'Why All the Fuss about the Body? A Medievalist's Perspective.' *Critical Inquiry* 22 (Autumn 1995): 1–33.
Chittick,William C. 'Eschatology.' In *Islamic Spirituality I: Foundations*. Ed. Seyyed Hossein Nasr. New York: SCM Press, 1989. 378–409.
Cook, David. 'Moral Apocalyptic in Islam.' *Studia Islamica* 86 (1997): 37–70.
Coope, Jessica A. 'With Heart, Tongue, and Limbs: Ibn Hazm on the Essence of Faith.' *Medieval Encounters* 6, nos. 1–3 (2000): 101–13.
d'Avray, D.L. 'Some Franciscan Ideas about the Body.' In *Modern Questions about Medieval Sermons: Sermons on Marriage, Death, History and Sanctity*. Ed. Nicole Bériou and David L. d'Avray. Spoleto: Centro Italiano di Studi sull'Alto Medioevo, 1994. 155–74.
Deladrière, R. 'al-Riya'.' *The Encyclopaedia of Islam*. Rev. 2nd ed. Vol. 8. 547.
Druart, T.A. 'The Human's Soul's Individuation and its Survival after the Body's Death: Avicenna on the Causal Relation between Body and Soul.' *Arabic Sciences and Philosophy* 10, no. 2 (2000): 259–73.
Elliott, Dyan. *Fallen Bodies: Pollution, Sexuality, & Demonology in the Middle Ages*. Philadelphia: University of Pennsylvania Press, 1999.
Frembgen, J. Wasim. *The Friends of God: Sufi Saints in Islam, Popular Poster Art from Pakistan*. Karachi: Oxford University Press, 2006.
Gardet, L. 'Iman.' *The Encyclopaedia of Islam*. Rev. 2nd ed. Vol. 3. 1170.
Al-Ghazali, Abu Hamid. *Ihya' `ulum al-din*. 4 vols. Cairo: al-Matba`ah al-'Uthmaniyah al-Misriyah, 1933.
– *The Remembrance of Death and the Afterlife. Kitab Dhikr al-mawt wa-ma ba'duhu. Book XL of The Revival of the Religious Sciences, Ihya 'ulum al-din*. Trans. T.J. Winter. Cambridge: Islamic Texts Society, 1989.
Hollywood, Amy. 'Performativity, Citationality, Ritualization.' *History of Religions* 42, no. 2 (Nov 2002): 93–115.
Ibn 'Abbad of Ronda. *Khutab Ibn 'Abbad al-Rundi*. Rabat: al-Khizana al-Malikiyya, MS no. 2688.
Ibn Abi al-Dunya, Abd Allah ibn Muhammad. *Kitab al-Mawt wa-Kitab al-Qubur*. Ed. Leah Kinberg. Haifa: Qism al-Lughah al-Arabiyah wa-Adabiha. Jamiat Hayfa, 1983.
Ibn al-'Attar, 'Ali ibn Ibrahim Dawud. *Kitab Adab al-khatib* (*The Craft and Manners of the Preacher*). Ed. M.H. al-Sulaymani. Beirut: Dar al-Gharb al-Islami, 1996.
Jones, Linda G. 'The Boundaries of Sin and Communal Identity: Muslim and Christian Preaching and the Transmission of Cultural Identity in Iberia and

the Maghreb (12th to 15th Centuries).' Unpublished PhD thesis, University of California, Santa Barbara, 2004.

Kienzle, Beverly M. 'Medieval Sermons and their Performance: Theory and Record.' In *Preacher, Sermon, and Audience.* Ed. Carolyn Muessig. Leiden: Brill, 2002. 89–124.

Kister, M.J. 'Radjab in the Month of God ... A Study in the Persistence of an Early Tradition.' *Israel Oriental Studies* 1 (1971): 191–223; rpt. in *Studies in Jahiliyya and Early Islam.* London: Variorum, 1980.

– 'Radjab.' *The Encyclopaedia of Islam.* Rev. 2nd ed. Vol. 8. 373.

Mauss, Marcel. 'Techniques of the Body.' In *Sociology and Psychology: Essays.* Trans. B. Brewster. London: Routledge and Kegan Paul, 1979.

Nwyia, Paul. *Un mystique prédicateur a la Qarawayin de Fes: Ibn 'Abbad de Ronda (1332–1390).* Beirut: Imprimerie Catholique, 1958.

Pedersen, J. 'The Criticism of the Islamic Preacher.' *Die Welt des Islams* 2 (1953): 215–31.

– 'The Islamic Preacher, *Wa'iz, Mudhakkir, Qass.*' In *Ignace Goldziher Memorial Volume.* Part I. Ed. S. Lowinger and J. Somogyz. Budapest, 1948. 215–31.

al-Qurtubi, Muhammad b. Ahmad. *Al-Tadhkira fi ahwal al-mawta wa umur al-akhira (Reminder of the States of the Dead and the Matters of the Afterlife).* Ed. Ahmad Hijazi al-Saqa. Vol. 1. Cairo: Dar Ihya' al-kutub al-'arabiyya, 1980.

Rahman, Fazlur. *Major Themes in the Qur'an.* Chicago: Biblioteca Islamica, 1980.

Ribera, J. and M. Asín. *Manuscritos árabes y aljamiados de la Biblioteca de la Junta.* Madrid: Ibérica, 1912.

Robson, J., and A.J. Weinsinck. 'Anas b. Malik.' *The Encyclopaedia of Islam.* Rev. 2nd ed. Vol. 1. 482.

al-Samarqandi, Abu'l-Layth. *Qurrat al-'uyun wa mafrah al-qalb al-mahzun (Consolation for the Eyes and Relief for Saddened Hearts).* In Shu'ayb al-Hurayfish, *Al-Rawd al-fa'iq fi'l-mawa'iz wa'l-raqa'iq (The Exquisite Garden of Warnings and Delights).* Ed. unknown. Rabat: Dar al-Fikr. 128–367.

Schact, J. 'Abu 'l-Layth al-Samarkandi, Nasr b. Muh. B. Ahmad b. Ibrahim.' *The Encyclopaedia of Islam.* Rev. 2nd ed. Vol. 1. 137.

Schmitt, J.-C. *La raison des gestes dans l'occident médiéval.* Paris: Gallimard, 1990.

Smith, J.Z. *Imagining Religion: From Babylonia to Jonestown.* Chicago and London: University of Chicago Press, 1982. 53–65.

Sudyam, Mary A., and Joanna E. Zeigler, eds. *Performance and Transformation: New Approaches to Late Medieval Spirituality.* New York: St Martin's Press, 1999.

Swartz, Merlin L. 'Arabic Rhetoric and the Art of the Homily in Medieval Islam.' In *Religion and Culture in Medieval Islam.* Ed. R.G. Hovannisian and G. Sabagh. Cambridge: Cambridge University Press, 1999. 36–65.

Vadet, J.-C. 'L'éloquence d'une sermonnaire hanbalite du XIIe siècle, Abd al-Qadir al-Jilani.' In *Prédication et propagande au Moyen Age, Islam, Byzance, Occident.* Ed. G. Makdisi, D. Sourdel, and J. Sourdel-Thomine. Paris: Presses Universitaires de France, 1983.

al-Wansharisi, Ahmad. *Kitab al-Mi'yar [The Criterion].* Ed. M. Hajji. 11 vols. Rabat: Nashr Wizarat al-Awqaf wa-al-Shu'un al-Islamiyah, 1981–.

Wensinck, A.J. 'Khutba.' *The Encyclopaedia of Islam.* Rev. 2nd ed. Vol. 5. 74–5.

– *Concordances et indices de la Tradition musulmane.* Leiden: Brill, 1936–.

– *The Muslim Creed: Its Genesis and Historical Development.* London: Frank Cass, 1932, rpt. 1965.

Witten, Marsha. 'The Restriction of Meaning in Religious Discourse: Centripetal Devices in a Fundamentalist Christian Sermon.' In *Vocabularies of Public Life.* Ed. Robert Wuthnow. London: Routledge, 1992. 19–38.

PART FOUR

Material Body

10 The Leprous Body in Twelfth- and Thirteenth-Century Rouen: Perceptions and Responses

ELMA BRENNER

Leprosy was a significant problem in the central Middle Ages, as reflected by the establishment of numerous leper houses across Western Europe between the late eleventh and the mid-thirteenth centuries, and by the fact that the words 'leper' and 'leprosy' retain strong associations for us even today. Historians such as Saul Brody (60–1) have argued that, in the Middle Ages, the healthy responded to the leprous with fear and revulsion. The belief that leprosy was contagious, and constituted a divine punishment for sin, resulted in the isolation of lepers from society, with lepers forming a subgroup among the mass of the marginalized 'poor.' However, recent studies, in particular those of François-Olivier Touati and Carole Rawcliffe, have questioned this interpretation of medieval responses to the disease. Touati (*Maladie* 188–201) argues that lepers were viewed as a religious group, specially chosen by God to suffer in this life in order to be redeemed in the next. Rawcliffe (*Leprosy* 9 and chapter 1) underlines the variation in medieval attitudes to leprosy, and suggests that the modern-day image of the medieval leper was to a large extent constructed in the nineteenth and early twentieth centuries.

This chapter will discuss the evidence regarding the lepers of Mont-aux-Malades, a prominent leper house outside Rouen, the chief city of Normandy, founded between 1106 and 1135, probably ca 1130. It will argue that, at Rouen in the twelfth and thirteenth centuries, not all leprous bodies were rejected from society. Indeed, Mont-aux-Malades quickly became a focus of lay piety, and its community retained strong links with the healthy citizens of Rouen. However, the lepers admitted to Mont-aux-Malades were a privileged group: there were other communities of lepers at Rouen, ranging from those within smaller leper houses to poor, wandering lepers. This suggests that, while the physical aspects of leprosy undoubtedly shaped attitudes towards its sufferers, bodily characteristics were neither the only, nor the most important, factor in determining social perceptions in the Middle Ages. The social and religious status of individual lepers, in particular the fact that they were Christians whose souls needed to be cared for, was equally crucial in determining their fate. Although some lepers were marginalized, therefore, others remained members of Rouen's society.

Leprosy in Medieval Western Europe

Leprosy is an infectious bacterial disease that takes a variety of forms. The most serious variant, Hansen's disease or low-resistant lepromatous leprosy, manifests itself in large, disfiguring skin sores and, ultimately, degeneration of the facial features, particularly the nose, and destruction of the nerves at the extremities of the body, such as the fingers and toes, resulting in loss of sensation and thus damage to these areas (Richards xv, xvi; Rawcliffe, 'Learning to Love the Leper' 232; Marcombe 135–6). The sufferer's voice may become 'hoarse and rasping,' and the face may take on 'a classic, heavy leonine appearance' (Rawcliffe, *Leprosy* 3). In contrast to Hansen's disease, the second main form of leprosy, the high-resistant tuberculoid strain, often 'heals spontaneously' and leaves the skin relatively unscathed (Marcombe 136; Rawcliffe, 'Learning to Love the Leper' 232). However, it too entails nerve damage at the extremities and, like the lepromatous form, may result in blindness (Richards xvi; Rawcliffe, *Leprosy* 2–3).

The bacterium responsible for leprosy, *Mycobacterium leprae*, enters the body through the nose, throat, and skin: it is thus inhaled as air or water droplets, or admitted through 'cuts, scratches or insect bites' (Richards xv, xvi; Marcombe 135). Individuals who contract the disease must therefore have come into contact with other carriers of the bacterium. Furthermore, they must do so repeatedly, making it likely that leprosy will cluster within a family or small community (Jacquart and Thomasset 185; Marcombe 135). Those living in a poverty-stricken environment may be particularly susceptible, since they reside in close proximity to other persons and, through their daily activities, risk suffering cuts or bites to the skin (Richards xvi). In today's India, for example, there are approximately one hundred thousand new cases of leprosy each year (Rawcliffe, *Leprosy* 1). Nonetheless, the disease has a long incubation period, taking over two years, perhaps even ten years or longer, to manifest itself. The development of leprosy in those exposed to the bacterium is relatively rare (Jacquart and Thomasset 185; Rawcliffe, *Leprosy* 2; Richards xv, xvi).

Discussing twelfth-century England, Max Satchell (v) stresses that leprosy did not represent a crisis of epidemiological proportions in the country. Thus, 'the disease assumed a higher profile than in reality it deserved' (Marcombe 136). There were clearly more complex reasons for the widespread foundation of leper houses in Western Europe than the scale of the leprosy problem itself.

Many of the medical characteristics of leprosy were little understood in the Middle Ages. It has been argued that the disease was perceived to be very contagious, and to be sexually transmitted. It was believed that women, particularly prostitutes, who had intercourse with lepers might become immune to the disease, but remain capable of passing it on to other male partners (Jacquart and Thomasset 185, 188–90). Thus, there was fear of not only the disease itself, but also of its sufferers and those close to them. The shocking physical appearance of lepers increased the aversion of the healthy to them (Marcombe 136).

The fact that lepers were isolated in institutions specifically dedicated to their care, situated outside urban settlements, points to the intentional marginalization and exclusion of this group. However, leper houses were also religious institutions, providing not only medical but also spiritual care for their leprous residents (Rawcliffe, *Leprosy* 337–43). According to Touati (*Maladie* 188–201), in the course of the twelfth century, leprosy increasingly came to be seen not as a divine punishment, but as an invitation by God to convert to a religious life, and thereby attain salvation. God particularly pitied those whom he afflicted with leprosy: this encouraged healthy Christians to pity them likewise. The widespread charitable patronage for leper houses in the twelfth and thirteenth centuries, therefore, may reflect not a wish to exclude lepers, but rather a concern to support them in the pursuit of their religious vocation. Indeed, the attachment of leper communities to prominent monasteries such as Fontevraud and Le Grand-Beaulieu at Chartres reflects a concerted drive to integrate lepers into the religious life (Touati, 'Saint-Lazare' 225, 236).

The Lepers of Twelfth- and Thirteenth-Century Rouen

The leper house of Mont-aux-Malades, an Augustinian priory dedicated to St James, was established around 1130 on a hill northwest of Rouen. Around 1174, Mont-aux-Malades was refounded by Henry II, king of England (1154–89) and duke of Normandy (1150–89), in dedication to St Thomas Becket (Langlois 83–4, 86–7). By the mid-thirteenth century, as revealed in the visitation records of Eudes Rigaud, archbishop of Rouen

(1248–75), the community consisted of five different groups. These included the prior and canons, male lepers, female lepers, lay brothers, and lay sisters (*Regestrum* 513; *Register* 585). Mont-aux-Malades thus catered to lepers of both sexes, and also accommodated healthy religious and lay personnel. Although there were several other leper houses in the area surrounding Rouen (Deschamps 31–2), Mont-aux-Malades was by far the largest and most significant institution of its kind in the Rouen area.

In Mont-aux-Malades' rich archive (Rouen, Archives départementales de la Seine-Maritime, deposit 25HP) there is very little direct information concerning the lepers of Rouen themselves and their identities, medical condition, and treatment. Nonetheless, the documentary and material evidence for this institution and the leper house of Salle-aux-Puelles, established by Henry II for high-status leprous women around 1185–8, tells us a great deal about the perception of lepers, and the response to leprosy, in twelfth- and thirteenth-century Rouen. Salle-aux-Puelles was located at Petit-Quevilly, opposite Rouen on the other side of the river Seine. The situation of Mont-aux-Malades and Salle-aux-Puelles outside the city walls, like that of so many other leper houses, implies that Rouen's healthy citizens endeavoured to keep lepers away from their midst. Significantly, however, through the charity of these citizens, lepers at Mont-aux-Malades and Salle-aux-Puelles received bodily and spiritual care.

It is notable that not only lepers but also healthy members of the laity entered Mont-aux-Malades. On 1 April 1264, for instance, there were twelve male lepers, seventeen female lepers, five lay brothers, and sixteen lay sisters at the leper house (*Regestrum* 513; *Register* 585). Many of these men and women may have been single and/or elderly persons who joined the community in order to find sustenance and accommodation in a supportive environment. In April 1233, for example, Lawrence Bouguenel granted in perpetuity to Mont-aux-Malades the annual rent of nine sous that his mother, Laurentia Bouguenel, had donated when she entered the leper house (Lawrence Bouguenel). Presumably, Laurentia's son was an adult; he may have reconfirmed his mother's grant upon her death. This would suggest that Laurentia had retired to Mont-aux-Malades as an elderly woman, probably a widow, in order to spend her last years there. Similarly, in 1296, Matilda Piguet, widow, donated three pieces of land and twenty-two sous annual rent to the leper house, 'in order to find her living there sufficiently for as long as she should live' ['pour trouver ly son Vivre suffisalment tant comme elle Vivra' (Matilda Piguet)].

Although the laymen and women who entered Mont-aux-Malades were to some degree motivated by self-interest, their decision to join a community of lepers as opposed to a healthy monastic community suggests that they were not afraid to live in close proximity to lepers, and were sympathetic towards the plight of these individuals. The high number of lay sisters at Mont-aux-Malades might indicate that those laywomen who were still sufficiently active undertook nursing duties. Given the symptoms of leprosy described above, these nurses would have dedicated much of their time to dressing the lepers' sores and the wounds on their hands and feet. In addition, those lepers in whom the disease had reached an advanced stage must have required particular care. These lepers were significantly disabled: nerve damage to the hands and feet rendered them immobile, facial degeneration made it difficult for them to breathe, speak, eat, or drink, and some of them may also have become blind. It is therefore possible that those who were very ill were each attended by a personal nurse.

A set of statutes issued by Archbishop Eudes Rigaud for Salle-aux-Puelles in August 1249 (*Regestrum* 101–2; *Register* 115–17) points towards the practical aspects of the care of lepers, and to the fact that some sufferers were very sick indeed. The archbishop's language distinguishes 'the more sick' ['infirmioribus'] and 'the more gravely ill' ['gravioribus'] (*Regestrum* 101, 102; *Register* 116, 117). Interestingly, this suggests that he appreciated the different phases of leprosy. Eudes instructed that 'For those who are more sick, and those bled outside the community, the prior should make provision according to their needs, as God wills it, as seems appropriate' (*Regestrum* 101; *Register* 116). This tenet reveals that bloodletting, a fundamental aspect of medical practice and the regular religious life, could take place outside Salle-aux-Puelles itself. Bloodletting was 'a routine prophylactic and therapeutic measure' by which what were believed to be excess quantities of blood were removed from the veins (Rawcliffe, *Leprosy* 232). It was used to treat lepers as a result of 'the theory that the retention and corruption of blood were the worst causes of leprosy' (Demaitre 261). By the sixteenth century, it also formed part of the process by which leprosy was diagnosed, since blood drawn from the right arm was then examined (Demaitre 196, 206). However, it was believed that, while in the early stages of leprosy the evacuation of blood was beneficial, in advanced cases bleeding would not cure but rather would weaken the sufferer. Nonetheless, venesection was deployed in certain instances: to alleviate the breathing problems of very sick lepers, and on 'female lepers who had failed to menstruate' (Rawcliffe, *Leprosy* 233–4).

Bloodletting was also an important part of the religious calendar, taking place between three and nine times per year. It was followed by a three-day period of recovery, thus marking an opportunity for religious to abstain from the rigours of the regular life. Eudes Rigaud ordered that, at Salle-aux-Puelles, 'The sisters should be bled at the proper times, if they wish, and they should have a competent female bloodletter' (*Regestrum* 102; *Register* 117). Thus, bloodletting was a voluntary procedure at the leper house. The archbishop made responsible provision for the welfare of the women at Salle-aux-Puelles, specifying that a proficient bloodletter was to be used there. Furthermore, the women were to have a female bloodletter, indicating that it was deemed inappropriate for this procedure to be performed on leprous women by a member of the opposite sex.[1] Bleeding was presumably also practised at Mont-aux-Malades, on both the sick and the healthy residents.

Most significantly, Eudes Rigaud instructed: 'they should have linen clothes, that is, two blouses and two linen sheets, at least once a year, and if more ought to be made for the more gravely sick on account of their needs, they should be made according to the judgement of the prioress. Indeed, the prioress should be discreet, so that she recognizes and shows pity towards the infirmities of the sisters, according to the available resources of the house' (*Regestrum* 102; *Register* 116–17). Théodose Bonnin notes that the archbishop was often opposed to religious communities using linen sheets and clothing (presumably due to the expense involved), indicating that, here, he made a special exception 'out of pity for the sick' (*Regestrum* 102n2). The provision of linen fabric facilitated the care of lepers, enabling them to have a soft, cool material next to their raw skin. However, although Archbishop Rigaud provided for the lepers at Salle-aux-Puelles to have linen, he instructed the prioress to judge their needs with discretion, and not to spend money on this commodity beyond the leper house's means.

Eudes Rigaud's specifications concerning linen point to his awareness of the medical reality of leprosy: as a result of the wounds and sores that afflicted the lepers' bodies, their sheets and clothing must have quickly became bloodstained. This provision suggests that the archbishop expected a high standard of care to be maintained at Salle-aux-Puelles: as far as resources permitted, lepers were to have clean linen in the same way that this is a basic essential in modern-day hospitals. It appears that clean linen was also important at other medieval hospitals: for example, the statutes of the Hôtel-Dieu-le-Comte at Troyes, issued on 10 June 1263, provided for the sheets of the sick to be washed at least once a week, and once a day if necessary (*Statuts* 116). The statutes of the leper house of Grand-Beaulieu at Chartres (January 1264) instructed that the clothes of the healthy were not to be washed with those of the sick (*Stat-*

uts 217). This suggests that sheets and clothing were associated with the transmission of leprosy, indicating an additional reason why the lepers of Salle-aux-Puelles were to have new blouses and sheets at least once a year.

Like the women at Salle-aux-Puelles, at least some of the lepers of Mont-aux-Malades were of high social status. In May 1237, Peter de Collemezzo, archbishop of Rouen (1236–44), forbade Mont-aux-Malades' canons from accepting entrance gifts on behalf of lepers (Peter de Collemezzo, fol. 1r–1v). This implies that the lepers previously had to sponsor their own admission; this practice may well have continued after 1237 in spite of the archbishop's prohibition. Thus, the lepers admitted to Mont-aux-Malades either had their own financial resources or received personal backing from elsewhere. Furthermore, lepers from Rouen's other religious houses entered Mont-aux-Malades. In October 1261, Henry, prior of La Madeleine hospital, an Augustinian priory adjacent to Rouen cathedral, acknowledged the 'special grace' ['gratiam specialem'] by which the leper house had admitted a leprous canon, Roger, and a leprous sister, Haisia, from La Madeleine (Henry, prior of La Madeleine). Canon Roger was to have the same entitlement to food and drink as a brother of Mont-aux-Malades, while Sister Haisia was entitled to the same victuals as a sister. Since Haisia is not described as a canoness in Prior Henry's charter, she was presumably a lay sister who had undertaken nursing duties at La Madeleine. Although the male and female lepers at Mont-aux-Malades were technically brothers and sisters of the community, the specification concerning food indicates that Roger and Haisia were to have a superior diet to the other lepers, sharing that of the canons/lay brothers and lay sisters. Significantly, this charter suggests that at Rouen the care of lepers was firmly separated from that of other groups of the sick and needy. La Madeleine itself catered to the acutely sick, pilgrims, and the elderly, but sent its own leprous staff to Mont-aux-Malades (Hicks 157–8; Boulanger 18–19).

On 18 February 1297, Prior Richard of Mont-aux-Malades confirmed the privileges to be extended to leprous monks from the Benedictine abbey of St-Ouen, Rouen, when resident at the leper house (Richard, prior of Mont-aux-Malades). Monks from St-Ouen enjoyed the same special entitlements to food and drink as the canons of Mont-aux-Malades, had their own manservants, and could return to the abbey whenever they needed to. Clearly, these monks were high-status men, singled out from the other lepers at Mont-aux-Malades. The fact that they were free to return to the abbey perhaps indicates a lack of concern regarding the contagiousness of leprosy. However, it is significant that, as at La Madeleine,

St-Ouen itself, which had its own infirmary, was not considered to be an appropriate place for the care of lepers (*Regestrum* 326–7; *Register* 373–4).

Evidently, leprous religious from Rouen's other monastic houses were accorded special status at Mont-aux-Malades, distinguishing them from the majority of the lepers. Thus, the other lepers were not so privileged in terms of diet, service, and freedom of movement. In 1297 the prior of Mont-aux-Malades explicitly associated St-Ouen's leprous monks with his own canons, indicating that the two groups ate and perhaps even worshipped together. These monks had servants, underlining their high social standing. Yet these religious were still lepers, and their association with the healthy canons and lay personnel may also have encouraged overall interaction between the different resident groups.

Although the experiences of the lepers at Mont-aux-Malades varied according to their religious/social status, they and the leprous women at Salle-aux-Puelles clearly lived in better circumstances than the other lepers at Rouen. The will of John Hardi, of the parish of St-Martin-du-Pont, Rouen, dated 1304, reveals that there were many other, less fortunate, leper communities in the local area. John's will is an extremely long document, bequeathing money and possessions to numerous persons, institutions, and religious and secular communities (John Hardi). John appears to have been a wealthy burgess landholder: the tenure of land by a John Hardi at Quincampoix, northeast of Rouen, was listed in the *Livre des Jurés* (a register of rural possessions) of the abbey of St-Ouen between 1299 and 1302 (*Censier* vii–viii, 369). It is very likely that this John Hardi and the John Hardi of the will were the same person.

John remembered Mont-aux-Malades and Salle-aux-Puelles, but also left money in his will to the lepers of Répainville and Darnétal, and 'to the lepers of the four gates of Rouen' ['leprosis quatuor portus Rothom']. Significantly, he distinguished Mont-aux-Malades and Salle-aux-Puelles, as 'priories,' from the lepers of Répainville, Darnétal, and 'the four gates,' as groups of 'lepers.' Mont-aux-Malades was to receive twenty sous, Salle-aux-Puelles ten sous, 'the lepers of the four gates' twenty sous, and the lepers of Répainville and Darnétal five sous each. This suggests that John was discriminating in terms of both the size of these communities and the status of the resident lepers. Eudes Rigaud's *Register* reveals that there were approximately thirty lepers and thirty healthy residents at Mont-aux-Malades in the third quarter of the thirteenth century (*Regestrum* 203–4, 325, 513; *Register* 221–2, 371, 585). Salle-aux-Puelles, housing ten leprous women, a prior, a prioress, and a small number of staff, was a much smaller community, hence enjoying a bequest of ten sous rather than twenty sous (*Regestrum* 101, 102, 325; *Register* 115, 117, 371). In turn, the leper houses at Répainville (immediately northeast of Rouen) and Darnétal (further eastwards), to which John granted only five sous, each presumably accommodated fewer than ten lepers and a few healthy individuals. These leper houses do not appear to have been Augustinian priories; thus, their inferior status as institutions in relation to Mont-aux-Malades and Salle-aux-Puelles may also explain the smaller bequests they received.

John's gift of twenty sous 'to the lepers of the four gates' suggests that there were also small groups of lepers resident outside each of Rouen's four main gates, the Portes Cauchoise, Beauvoisine, de Robec, and du Pont (Musset 54). These too were to receive five sous each. Leper hostels may have been maintained at these gates to house lepers who had recently had to leave the city, and to deter wandering, begging lepers from entering. In the late twelfth and early thirteenth centuries, leper houses were established outside four of the city gates of Toulouse, suggesting that it was not uncommon for lepers to be accommodated at these sites (Mundy 185–6). Finally, John included a third category of lepers, the 'poor lepers,' among the beneficiaries of his will. He donated twenty sous of Tours 'to the poor lepers who flock together at Rouen on Good Friday' ['pauperis leprosis qui confluent apud rothom' in die beneris crucis adorante']. The same sum was granted 'to the poor lepers who flock together at Rouen on the Monday, Tuesday, Wednesday, and Thursday of the Ascension' ['pauperibus leprosis qui confluent rothom' diebus lune martis mercurii et ascensione domini quolibet die'].

Although the term 'poor' may signify the status of all lepers as the poor of Christ, rather than their financial situation, this data could indicate that there were numerous 'poor lepers' in Rouen and the surrounding area who lacked the necessary resources to become members of leper house communities. These lepers appear to have received alms on important holy days, perhaps at the city gates or even within Rouen.[2] They may also have targeted nearby religious houses, such as Mont-aux-Malades itself. John Hardi bequeathed money to other groups of the poor in his will, awarding twenty sous to the 'poor pilgrims' on the day after Easter Day, and a total of forty sous to the 'poor prisoners' in the castle, the court of the official of Rouen, and the mayor's prison. Thus, John was categorizing the poor lepers with other poor groups who had no fixed abode and depended on the charity of others. This suggests that, like pilgrims, poor lepers wandered alone or in groups, and were viewed as a subcategory of 'the poor.'

The stark distinction in John Hardi's will between the different categories of lepers at Rouen indicates the superior status and living conditions of the lepers at Mont-aux-Malades and Salle-aux-Puelles. John's reference to both these leper houses as 'priories' reinforces the fact that the resident lepers were members of religious communities, which provided them with shelter, food, and religious facilities. In his statutes for Salle-aux-Puelles drawn up in August 1249, Eudes Rigaud ordered the prior to ensure that remnants of food were kept 'for poor lepers outside' ['pauperibus leprosis extraneis' (*Regestrum* 101; *Register* 116)]. This instruction might suggest that poor, begging lepers were sometimes present outside the leper house, and that they could not be admitted but came to solicit alms. However, Eudes may have envisaged charity to lepers outside Salle-aux-Puelles more broadly, since on 11 February 1265/6 he reported that the community was conserving the remaining fragments of food for a female leper at Moulineaux, southwest of Salle-aux-Puelles (*Regestrum* 538; *Register* 614–15). There was clearly a marked difference in the circumstances of the relatively privileged lepers within the two leper houses and those of the poor, hungry lepers outside. The pre-existing social and religious status of individual lepers, therefore, which had little to do with the disease afflicting their bodies, played a crucial role in determining their fate.

Bodies and Souls: The Metaphysical Associations of the Leprous Body

(a) Lepers as a Focus of Piety

Although Mont-aux-Malades was situated outside Rouen, the leper house community remained in contact with the city. Furthermore, the healthy citizens themselves visited the leper house on specific occasions, implying that they were not afraid of the possibility of encountering the lepers. Between 1151 and 1154, Henry II established an annual eight-day fair at Mont-aux-Malades, to be held from 1 to 8 September (Langlois 7). The fair quickly became an important commercial event, and attracted many people to the leper house. Significantly, regulations laid down by Hugh of Amiens, archbishop of Rouen (1130–65), and renewed by his successor Rotrou de Beaumont-le-Roger (1165–84) around 1165, characterized a visit to the fair as a form of pilgrimage. Those travelling to and from Mont-aux-Malades at this time did so under the protection of the Church of Rouen, and received remission of one third of their penance for that year. Any person who troubled them on their journey would be excommunicated until they had made amends. Local deans and clerics were instructed to receive the visitors' clerics kindly in their churches (Rotrou de Beaumont-le-Roger).

There is no evidence that patrons of the fair came into direct contact with the lepers: indeed, the lepers may have been kept away from the area (presumably a field within Mont-aux-Malades' grounds) where the fair took place. Nonetheless, visitors may have risked touching agricultural produce and other items that the lepers had handled, and those lepers who were not too sick may plausibly have assisted at the event. It is possible that the 'pilgrims' who patronized the fair, from Rouen and further afield, were actually attracted by the possibility of encountering the lepers and offering them charity. They may have hoped thereby to enjoy the benefits of the lepers' prayers, believing that this particularly holy group would intercede with Christ on their behalf. The medieval topos of the kissing of lepers and the washing of their feet, as exemplified by the actions of Hugh of Lincoln and Matilda of Scotland, wife of Henry I, king of England (1100–35), indicates that bodily contact with lepers, although repellent, was deemed to be spiritually beneficial (Rawcliffe, *Leprosy* 144–5; Peyroux 173, 183; Kealey 90). The popularity of Mont-aux-Malades' annual fair may indicate the importance of lepers as a focus of piety.

Other evidence from the twelfth and thirteenth centuries suggests that the prayers of the community at Mont-aux-Malades were particularly sought after. Probably in 1145–50, a fraternity of prayers was concluded between the leper house community and the palmers of Rouen, a confraternity of pilgrims to Jerusalem (Nicholas, prior of Mont-aux-Malades). According to this arrangement, the palmers would make an annual procession to Mont-aux-Malades on the day of the Finding of the Holy Cross (3 May), with an alms contribution from their profits through pilgrimage and work, and seven pints of wine. The prior and community of Mont-aux-Malades pledged that, when one of the palmers died, they would celebrate a full service for the individual just as they did for their own deceased.

The fact that the palmers chose to associate with Mont-aux-Malades suggests that the latter was perceived as a reputable, pious community. Simultaneously, the definition of the alliance as a fraternity of prayers implies that the leper house's prior and canons deemed this link with pilgrims who had visited the Holy Land to be spiritually beneficial, although they must also have been attracted by the palmers' alms. Indeed, this was a reciprocal arrangement: the pilgrim fraternity ensured that funeral services for its members would be performed in the leper house church, while Mont-aux-Malades received the annual alms gift of money and wine. The palmers' procession to the leper house was a public religious ritual, symbolizing the association between the two communities.

It is significant that the palmers made an annual visit to Mont-aux-Malades, since they, like patrons of the annual fair, thereby completed a journey akin to a pilgrimage. The palmers appear to have been concerned to benefit from services in the church at Mont-aux-Malades, implying that they sought the enhanced spiritual value of the prayers of lepers. They wished to visit the leper community in person, and to facilitate the fulfilment of divine worship in a church in which lepers prayed. This suggests that the healthy perceived a direct link between lepers, piety, and their own salvation.

In July 1219, Nicholas Pigache, mayor of Rouen in 1208–9 and 1219–20, established a family priest at Mont-aux-Malades, donating an annual revenue of ten livres of Tours to maintain him. Nicholas instructed that the priest was to celebrate Mass daily on behalf of himself, his wife, his parents, and other ancestors, at the altar of St Mary Magdalene in the leper house church, in the presence of female lepers (Nicholas Pigache). In 1285, on the Saturday before the feast of St Mary Magdalene, Nicholas's son, John Pigache, mayor of Rouen in 1255–6, 1262–3, and 1271–3, increased the chaplain's stipend by thirty sous (Langlois 100). The visitation records of Archbishop Eudes Rigaud, recording his visit to Mont-aux-Malades on 1 April 1264, refer to the secular priest celebrating Mass 'in the Pigache chapel' ['in capella Pyage' (*Regestrum* 513; *Register* 585)]. This reveals that the priest fulfilled his duties in a private chantry chapel in the church at Mont-aux-Malades. The leper house was, therefore, an important focus for the piety of the Pigaches, a leading merchant family of thirteenth-century Rouen (Sadourny 84). The Pigache family's pious activities were particularly linked to the prayers of female lepers and the cult of St Mary Magdalene.

Female lepers appear to have been viewed as a special, holy group, as indicated by the existence of Salle-aux-Puelles, a priory specifically for leprous women. Thus, Nicholas Pigache may have believed that the prayers of the female lepers at Mont-aux-Malades were particularly efficacious. He was clearly concerned regarding the spiritual welfare of this group; perhaps he was related to, or acquainted with, one of the female lepers at Mont-aux-Malades. Mary Magdalene, whose cult flourished in this period, was an exemplar saint for laywomen and, as a sinner who was redeemed through her penitence, represented a poignant model for these leprous women (Garth 19–21; Farmer 357–8). Furthermore, Mary Magdalene was often conflated with Mary of Egypt, a penitent former prostitute (Farmer 358). This was a significant attribute in light of the medieval belief that prostitutes played a role in the transmission of leprosy, and the association of leprosy with sexual excess (Rawcliffe, *Leprosy* 122; Jacquart and Thomasset 190). Like Mary Magdalene, the female lepers might obtain 'complete forgiveness' through their repentance (Rawcliffe, *Leprosy* 122).

(b) The Care of Lepers' Souls

In the medieval conception of medical care, the care of the body was inextricably linked to that of the soul. Indeed, 'in all hospitals, the first line of treatment for bodily illness was reconciliation with God, and spiritual healing and preparation for death by confession and enjoined penance preceded bed-rest and medical treatment' (Bird 103). Chapels, often situated within or near sick wards, were an essential feature of medieval hospitals, ensuring that Masses and prayers could be performed regularly within the sight or hearing of the sick (Bird 103). In the preacher Jacques de Vitry's idealized picture of life in hospitals (*Historia occidentalis*, chapter 29, composed in 1219–21), he envisaged that the chaplains 'continually celebrate the divine offices in a common chapel so that all the infirm can hear them from their beds' (Jacques de Vitry 110).

In many respects, the notion of spiritual care resulted from the close association of Christ with the suffering and needy. John Henderson (114–15) underlines 'the ubiquity of the image of Christ in the medieval and Renaissance hospital,' and argues that such images drew particular attention to Christ's suffering. Simultaneously, however, Christ was attributed with an active role in the cure of souls. St Augustine presented the idea of Christ as a divine physician, healing the soul in the same manner that mortal physicians treated human bodies. Moreover, Christ was more effective than human physicians in curing both the souls and the bodies of the sick, since, according to St Augustine, 'God, however, made your body, God made your soul. He knows how to restore what He has made' (Henderson 113–14). The concept of Christ as a holy physician helps to explain why, in medieval eyes, spiritual care was just as essential as physical care: the former was guaranteed to bring comfort to both body and soul.

At Mont-aux-Malades, the Augustinian canons were no doubt familiar with the ideas presented by St Augustine. From the foundation of the Augustinian priory at the leper house, the sick were cared for as members of a religious community, a situation confirmed by the decree issued at the Third Lateran Council (1179) that communities of lepers should have their own church, cemetery, and priest (*Decrees* 1:222). Thus, Mont-aux-Malades' lepers benefited spiritually from the religious services performed in the leper house church, and from prayers on their behalf offered by the canons, lay personnel, and even their fellow lepers. Furthermore, they were ensured proper funerary services and a place of burial.

In the context of both the importance ascribed to spiritual care, and the reality that lepers would not recover and thus needed to be prepared for death, providing for the health of the lepers' souls was presumably a high priority for Mont-aux-Malades' prior, canons, and lay personnel. Although there is little evidence for the structure of daily life at Mont-aux-Malades, it was undoubtedly based around the performance of religious worship. Even apparently non-religious activities, such as eating and sleeping, took on a religious dimension within monastic communities: Biblical readings were recited in the refectory, and men and women ate and slept separately to ensure that they remained chaste (Jacques de Vitry 109–10).

Confession and the performance of Mass were among the most important aspects of religious provision for lepers. The former enabled the leper to embark upon the route to spiritual recovery, while the latter, 'regular exposure to the body and blood of Christ,' was understood to be particularly beneficial to the soul, especially when received immediately prior to death (Rawcliffe, *Leprosy* 338, 339–40, 342). At the English leper house at Sherburn, County Durham, the foundation charter (1184–9) of Hugh Le Puiset, bishop of Durham (1153–95), provided for both a church and a separate infirmary chapel. The leper house's new statutes drawn up in the first quarter of the fourteenth century by Bishop Richard Kellaw (1311–16) established another chapel for the sick, perhaps so that the male and female lepers could remain segregated during worship. Thus, the sick convened in their own separate chapels. Bishop Kellaw stipulated the performance of a daily Mass in the new chapel, indicating that Mass was performed once a day throughout the leper house. At the much smaller leper house of St Thomas's, Bolton, Mass took place only three times a week, suggesting that only the more distinguished institutions, which had sufficient religious personnel – by the first part of the fourteenth century, four priests and four clerks were serving Sherburn's leper house – provided daily religious services (Rawcliffe, *Leprosy* 258, 338, 339).

Although Mont-aux-Malades was smaller than Sherburn, which accommodated sixty-five lepers of both sexes, Nicholas Pigache's provision for a daily Mass before female lepers in the church at Mont-aux-Malades (discussed above) reveals that here too Mass was performed once a day for at least some of the resident lepers (Rawcliffe, *Leprosy* 296, 319). At religious houses like Mont-aux-Malades and Sherburn, lepers expected to benefit from spiritual care and, in particular, 'the provision made for death, burial and commemoration' (Rawcliffe, *Leprosy* 342). It was also crucially important for the lepers regularly to engage in prayer, since this was 'one of the few forms of penance available to them in their weakened state' (Bird 103). Penance was essential 'for the divine healing of body and soul' (Bird 103), and Touati ('Les léproseries' 9) argues that the very act of being a member of a monastic community was penitential, since it required an individual to renounce the world and live in obedience to a rule.

The religious status of the lepers of Mont-aux-Malades, therefore, was essential to ensuring that they received spiritual care. From the end of the twelfth century, lepers were widely understood to possess a *status* in medieval society 'comparable in many respects to the religious condition' (Touati, 'Les léproseries' 5). The assignment of this status to lepers reflects a more general concern to impose uniformity over the many different forms of religious life, as revealed by the decrees of the Fourth Lateran Council of 1215 (Touati, 'Les léproseries' 5). However, it does not indicate how lepers who remained outside monastic communities, such as the 'poor lepers' cited in the will of John Hardi, were perceived.

The strongest evidence for the spiritual care received by Mont-aux-Malades' lepers simply consists of acknowledgment of their religious status. Charters that refer to 'the community, both healthy and sick,' such as acts of the Rouen burgess Silvester du Marché (issued in 1195 or 1198–1200), Prior Robert of Mont-aux-Malades (1193–4 or 1201–3), and Prior William (May 1233), testify to the general understanding that the lepers were full members of the monastic community at the leper house (Silvester du Marché; Robert, prior of Mont-aux-Malades; William, prior of Mont-aux-Malades). The phraseology of Prior Nicholas's act establishing the fraternity with Rouen's palmers is particularly vivid: he issued the charter with 'the whole community ... of canons and poor lepers regularly ... living in their chapter' ['omnis conuentus ... canonicorum et pauperum leprosorum regulariter ... uiuentium in capitulo suo' (Nicholas, prior of Mont-aux-Malades fol. 1v)]. The charter was drawn up 'in the chapter of the sick, in the presence of the prior, the canons and the sick' ['in capitulo infirmorum coram priore et canonicis et infirmis' (fol. 2r)]. Thus, the lepers fully participated in the establishment of the pious association with the palmers, whose prayers were no doubt intended to benefit the lepers' souls. Furthermore, the lepers followed the same regular rule as the Augustinian canons of Mont-aux-Malades, and apparently formed their own chapter. It is significant that the priors in particular self-consciously described their community as one formed of both healthy and leprous members, since this indicates that they encouraged the lepers to assume a religious identity.

Preaching and the reading of the gospels, especially on important religious festivals, were central to the spiritual care of lepers. Richard Kellaw's statutes for Sherburn provided for one of the four priests to 'read the gospel on feast days and festivals in the *domibus leprosorum* to those who were too ill to go to church' (Rawcliffe, *Leprosy* 338, 339). Thus, when necessary, the gospel was read inside the lepers' lodgings at Sherburn. By the mid-thirteenth century, the archdeacon of every French diocese was responsible for preaching regularly to lepers, in person or via a deputy (Touati, 'Les léproseries' 22–3). Thirteenth-century collections of sermons *ad status* provide examples of the sermons delivered to lepers. These texts are among the richest sources of attitudes to the leprous since, from the sermons of Jacques de Vitry (edited 1229–40) onwards, they address lepers and other sick people as a distinct social and religious group or *status* (Touati, 'Les léproseries' 24; Bériou 37–8). According to de Vitry, the Church consisted of thirty different *status*, which he placed in order according to their various states of perfection. The religious preceded the laity in this hierarchy: clerics were placed first, followed by monks and all those who lived in fraternities, including hospital communities. Among the laity, lepers and other sick persons were placed in the highest category, which also included the poor, the grieving, pilgrims, and those who had taken the cross. Since members of this group were being tested by God, they were spiritually superior to the rest of the laity. The two other categories of laypeople were active professionals, and, in the lowest spiritual state, married people, servants, women, and children (Bériou 39–40).

Lepers and the sick, therefore, immediately followed the healthy religious personnel of hospitals in Jacques de Vitry's classification, suggesting that, within leper house and hospital communities, the religious status of the healthy and the sick was relatively equal. Nicole Bériou (40–1) argues that the manner in which de Vitry addressed 'lepers and the other sick' in his sermons also indicates that he deemed lepers to be representative of the sick in general. Thus, the spiritual characteristics of leprosy reflected the manner in which sickness in every form marked God's intervention.

The first of Jacques de Vitry's two sermons to lepers and the sick, Sermon 41 of his *Sermones vulgares*, is based on an extract from the New Testament (James 5:11): 'You have heard about the patience of Job, and you have seen the death of the Lord' (Bériou 41, 101). The sermon equates Job's suffering with that of the sick, suggesting that the latter are afflicted physically in order that their souls may be healed. The spiritual benefits of sickness are listed, encouraging the sick to accept their suffering gladly. Leprosy in particular is described as a divinely inflicted penitential test. It is also emphasized that, since Christ consented to his own suffering, his death confirms that the sick will be resurrected (Bériou 41–2).

The sermon's subject matter confirms that leprosy and other diseases were seen as being inflicted by God, so that individuals might suffer in this life in order to be redeemed in the next. It implies that the sick were viewed sympathetically, as a suffering group among the faithful, linked to Christ himself. When delivered, the sermon catered to the religious needs of the sick by encouraging them to have faith in God and the world to come. Equally, however, it played a more immediate pastoral role, urging the sick to come to terms with their condition by accepting it as God's will. Thus, it provided for the welfare of their souls while they were still alive, encouraging them to make sense of their suffering and to find solace in the fact that it would ultimately bring spiritual rewards.

The preface to the sermon explicitly states that it is intended to soothe the physical pain of the sick: 'For the moisture of the word of God cools the heat and difficulty of sickness, and the word of the Lord cuts through the flame of fire, so that while the spirit is restored, the pains of the body are soothed ... Indeed, no corporeal alms can soothe pain as effectively as the word of comfort, which is like a sweet ointment' (Bériou 102). These lines imply that preaching was understood to result in not only spiritual but also physical benefits, confirming the medieval belief that the care of the body and that of the soul were closely connected. Thus, the word of God brought both emotional and physical relief to the sick. The belief in the physical benefits produced by preaching is particularly significant in light of the fact that medieval physicians could offer little medical treatment for leprosy and many other diseases. Jacques de Vitry also suggests here that preaching is more effective than material alms in meeting the needs of the sick, underlining the perceived importance of spiritual care.

Conclusion

The evidence for the perception of lepers in twelfth- and thirteenth-century Rouen points to the great variation in the experiences of lepers, and the complexity of social attitudes, in the Middle Ages. There was clearly more than one category of lepers at Rouen, since while some became members of the monastic communities of Mont-aux-Malades and Salle-aux-Puelles, others were housed in less wealthy hostels, or did not benefit from institutional charity at all. This indicates that additional factors, namely, the social and religious status of lepers before they became sick, shaped their fate. The bodily characteristics of leprosy undoubtedly played an important role in determining responses to the leprous, particularly since the disfigurement caused by the disease was deeply shocking, and it entailed disabilities such as blindness and immobility. Yet the multiple statuses occupied by lepers suggest, above all, that a person's bodily appearance had only a limited significance in shaping the process by which others responded to them. Instead, the social identity of each individual was ultimately responsible for the place he or she occupied in medieval society.

NOTES

This chapter is adapted from sections of my PhD thesis, 'Charity in Rouen in the twelfth and thirteenth centuries (with special reference to Mont-aux-Malades)' (Emmanuel College, University of Cambridge, 2007). I gratefully acknowledge the financial assistance of Emmanuel College, Cambridge, the Lightfoot Fund, Faculty of History, Cambridge, and the Wellcome Trust, London. I also thank Professor Elisabeth van Houts for her excellent supervision. Translations from Latin and French are my own unless otherwise indicated. Quotations from manuscript sources do not include transcription marks.

1 I am grateful to Professor Monica Green for drawing my attention to the fact that 'minutricem' in the original Latin signifies a female bloodletter.
2 It is also plausible, however, that the lepers who received alms at Rouen on holy days were actually those of Mont-aux-Malades and Salle-aux-Puelles, as suggested to me by Dr Richard E. Barton at the International Medieval Congress, University of Leeds, in July 2007.

WORKS CITED

Bériou, Nicole. 'Les lépreux sous le regard des prédicateurs d'après les collections de sermons *ad status* du XIIIème siècle.' In *Voluntate dei leprosus: Les lépreux entre conversion et exclusion aux XIIème et XIIIème siècles*. Ed. Nicole Bériou and François-Olivier Touati. Testi, Studi, Strumenti, 4. Spoleto, Italy: Centro italiano di studi sull'alto Medioevo, 1991. 33–163.

Bird, Jessalynn. 'Medicine for Body and Soul: Jacques de Vitry's Sermons to Hospitallers and Their Charges.' In *Religion and Medicine in the Middle Ages*. Ed. Peter Biller and Joseph Ziegler. York Studies in Medieval Theology 3. Woodbridge, UK: York Medieval Press, 2001. 91–108.

Boulanger, Marc. *Les hôpitaux de Rouen: Une longue et attachante histoire. Des origines à nos jours*. Luneray, France: Bertout, 1988.

Brody, Saul N. *The Disease of the Soul: Leprosy in Medieval Literature*. Ithaca, NY: Cornell University Press, 1974.

Un censier normand du XIIIe siècle. Le Livre des Jurés de l'abbaye Saint-Ouen de Rouen. Ed. Denise Angers, Catherine Bébéar, and Henri Dubois. Documents, Études et Répertoires publiés par l'Institut de Recherche et d'Histoire des Textes, vol. 62. Paris: CNRS Éditions, 2001.

Demaitre, Luke. *Leprosy in Premodern Medicine: A Malady of the Whole Body*. Baltimore: Johns Hopkins University Press, 2007.

Deschamps, Philippe. 'Léproseries et maladreries rouennaises. Le prieuré du Mont-aux-Malades et ses rapports avec Thomas Becket.' *Revue des Sociétés Savantes de Haute-Normandie* 48 (1967): 31–46.

Eudes Rigaud. *Regestrum visitationum archiepiscopi Rothomagensis. Journal des visites pastorales d'Eude Rigaud, archevêque de Rouen. MCCXLVIII–MCCLXIX*. Ed. Théodose Bonnin. Rouen: Auguste Le Brument, 1852.

– *The Register of Eudes of Rouen*. Ed. Jeremiah F. O'Sullivan. Trans. Sydney M. Brown. Records of Civilization, Sources and Studies, no. 72. New York: Columbia University Press, 1964.

Farmer, David H. *The Oxford Dictionary of Saints*. 5th edition. Oxford: Oxford University Press, 2003.

Garth, Helen M. *Saint Mary Magdalene in Mediaeval Literature*. The Johns Hopkins University Studies in Historical and Political Science, series 67, no. 3. Baltimore: Johns Hopkins University Press, 1950.

Henderson, John. *The Renaissance Hospital: Healing the Body and Healing the Soul*. New Haven, CT: Yale University Press, 2006.

Henry, prior of La Madeleine hospital, Rouen. Charter regarding the admission of two members of the community at La Madeleine to Mont-aux-Malades, Monday after the feast of St Rémy, October 1261. Paris, Archives Nationales S4889B, dossier 13, nos. 17 (seventeenth-century copy) and 18 (original).

Hicks, Leonie V. 'Women and the Use of Space in Normandy, c. 1050–1300.' Unpublished PhD thesis, University of Cambridge, 2002.

Jacquart, Danielle, and Claude Thomasset. *Sexuality and Medicine in the Middle Ages*. Trans. Matthew Adamson. Cambridge, UK: Polity Press, 1988.

Jacques de Vitry. 'Texts on Hospitals: Translation of Jacques de Vitry, *Historia occidentalis* 29, and edition of Jacques de Vitry's sermons to hospitallers.' Ed. and trans. Jessalynn Bird. In *Religion and Medicine in the Middle Ages*. Ed. Peter Biller and Joseph Ziegler. York Studies in Medieval Theology, 3. Woodbridge, UK: York Medieval Press, 2001. 109–34.

John Hardi. Will, dated the Monday after the circumcision of the Lord, 1304 (in an original *vidimus* of the official of Rouen, 1353). Rouen, Archives départementales de la Seine-Maritime G1236.

Kealey, Edward J. *Medieval Medicus: A Social History of Anglo-Norman Medicine*. Baltimore: Johns Hopkins University Press, 1981.

Langlois, Pierre. *Histoire du prieuré du Mont-aux-Malades-lès-Rouen, et correspondance du prieur de ce monastère avec saint Thomas de Cantorbéry, 1120–1820*. Rouen: Fleury, 1851.

Lawrence Bouguenel. Charter granting to Mont-aux-Malades the annual rent donated by his mother, Laurentia Bouguenel, April 1233. Rouen, Archives départementales de la Seine-Maritime 25HP1, folder 17, doc. (viii).

Marcombe, David. *Leper Knights. The Order of St Lazarus of Jerusalem in England, 1150–1544*. Woodbridge, UK: Boydell Press, 2003.

Matilda Piguet. Charter donating three pieces of land and twenty-two sous annual rent to Mont-aux-Malades, Thursday after Easter, 1296. Rouen, Archives départementales de la Seine-Maritime 25HP1, folder 24, doc. (vii).

Mundy, John H. 'Hospitals and Leprosaries in Twelfth- and Early Thirteenth-Century Toulouse.' *Essays in Medieval Life and Thought: Presented in Honor of Austin Patterson Evans*. Ed. John H. Mundy, Richard W. Emery, and Benjamin N. Nelson. New York: Biblo and Tannen, 1955. 181–205.

Musset, Lucien. 'Rouen au temps des Francs et sous les ducs (Ve siècle – 1204).' *Histoire de Rouen*. Ed. Michel Mollat. Univers de la France et des pays francophones, vol. 43. Toulouse: Privat, 1979. 31–74.

Nicholas Pigache. Charter establishing a family priest at Mont-aux-Malades, July 1219 (in a *vidimus* of the official of Rouen, 1249). Rouen, Archives départementales de la Seine-Maritime 25HP10, doc. (viii).

Nicholas, prior of Mont-aux-Malades. Charter establishing a fraternity of prayers between the community at Mont-aux-Malades and the palmers of Rouen, undated (c. 1135–73, probably ca 1145–50). Rouen, Archives départementales de la Seine-Maritime 25HP54^2, fol. 1v –2r (late seventeenth-century copy).

Peter de Collemezzo. Reforms for Mont-aux-Malades, May 1237. Paris, Archives Nationales S4889B, dossier 13, doc. (xxi) (seventeenth-century copy), fol. 1r–2r.

Peyroux, Catherine. 'The Leper's Kiss.' *Monks and Nuns, Saints and Outcasts: Religion in Medieval Society. Essays in Honor of Lester K. Little*. Ed. Sharon Farmer and Barbara H. Rosenwein. Ithaca, NY: Cornell University Press, 2000. 172–88.

Rawcliffe, Carole. 'Learning to Love the Leper: Aspects of Institutional Charity in Anglo-Norman England.' *Anglo-Norman Studies* 23 (2000): 231–50.

– *Leprosy in Medieval England*. Woodbridge, UK: Boydell Press, 2006.

Richard, prior of Mont-aux-Malades. Charter confirming the privileges enjoyed by leprous monks from the abbey of Saint-Ouen, Rouen, at Mont-aux-Malades, 18 February 1297. Rouen, Archives départementales de la Seine-Maritime 14H660, doc. (i).

Richards, Peter. *The Medieval Leper and His Northern Heirs*. Cambridge: D.S. Brewer, 1977.

Robert, prior of Mont-aux-Malades. Charter granting a tenement to Ralph de Cailli, undated (1193–4 or 1201–3). Rouen, Archives départementales de la Seine-Maritime 25HP1, folder 10, doc. (xiii).

Rotrou de Beaumont-le-Roger. Charter confirming the rules for the annual fair at Mont-aux-Malades, undated (1165–84, probably ca 1165). Rouen, Archives départementales de la Seine-Maritime 25HP1, folder 10, doc. (xi).

Sadourny, Alain. 'L'époque communale (1204 – début du XIVe siècle).' *Histoire de Rouen*. Ed. Michel Mollat. Univers de la France et des pays francophones, vol. 43. Toulouse: Privat, 1979. 75–98.

Satchell, Max. 'The Emergence of Leper-houses in Medieval England, 1100–1250.' Unpublished D.Phil thesis, University of Oxford, 1998.

Silvester du Marché. Charter selling an annual revenue of twelve sous to Mont-aux-Malades, undated (1195 or 1198–1200). Paris, Archives Nationales S4889B, dossier 13, nos. 9 (seventeenth-century copy) and 11 (original).

Statuts d'Hôtels-Dieu et de léproseries. Recueil de textes du XIIe au XIVe siècle. Ed. Léon Le Grand. Paris: Picard, 1901.

Tanner, Norman P., ed. *Decrees of the Ecumenical Councils*. 2 vols. London: Sheed & Ward and Washington, DC: Georgetown University Press, 1990.

Touati, François-Olivier. 'Les léproseries aux XIIème et XIIIème siècles, lieux de conversion?' In *Voluntate dei leprosus: les lépreux entre conversion et exclusion aux XIIème et XIIIème siècles*. Ed. Nicole Bériou and François-Olivier Touati. Testi, Studi, Strumenti, 4. Spoleto, Italy: Centro italiano di studi sull'alto Medioevo, 1991. 1–32.

– *Maladie et société au Moyen Âge. La lèpre, les lépreux et les léproseries dans la province ecclésiastique de Sens jusqu'au milieu du XIVe siècle*. Bibliothèque du Moyen Âge, 11. Brussels: De Boeck Université, 1998.

– 'Saint-Lazare, Fontevraud, Jérusalem.' In *Robert d'Arbrissel et la vie religieuse dans l'ouest de la France. Actes du colloque de Fontevraud 13–16 décembre 2001*. Ed. Jacques Dalarun. Disciplina Monastica, 1. Turnhout, Belgium: Brepols, 2004. 199–237.

William, prior of Mont-aux-Malades. Charter granting a tenement to William Peteum and his wife Matilda, May 1233. Rouen, Archives départementales de la Seine-Maritime 25HP1, folder 10, doc. (ii).

11 The Feminine Flesh in the *Disputacione betwyx the Body and Wormes*

WENDY A. MATLOCK

In the late fifteenth-century morality play *Mankind*, the title character laments that his body has reversed the natural order of things by gaining dominance over his soul, just as a wife might gain dominance over her husband:

> My name ys Mankynde, I have my composycyon
> Of a body and of a soull, of condycyon contrarye.
> Betwyx þem tweyn ys a grett dyvisyon;
> He þat xulde be subjecte, now he hath þe victory.
> Thys ys to me a lamentable story;
> To se my flesch of my soull to have governance.
> Wher þe goodewyff is master, þe goodeman may be sory! (ll. 194–200)

On stage, an actor literally embodies Mankind – his body and his movements animate the character. Mankind's speech, however, asserts that a human being has a dichotomous composition and characterizes the relationships between both bodies and souls and wives and husbands as contentious binaries situated in hierarchical arrangements. The explanation that Mankind has a body and a soul divides him into two parts, but, as the actor embodies the character, the soul remains invisible. If the doctrine is accepted, the performance on stage unifies these two entities in one individual, the actor. The marriage metaphor works similarly. Upon marriage, two individuals, a husband and a wife, unite in one conjugal unit.[1] Contested dichotomies such as these pervade medieval discussions of the relationship between the body and the soul. In particular, medieval debate poems featuring recently deceased bodies that dispute with their souls depend upon the division of the disputants in order to teach how both together determine an individual's fate. These poems demand our attention because body and soul debates formed one of the most popular genres of medieval poetry.[2]

Among the extant examples of debate poetry concerning the body, one – *A Disputacione betwyx the Body and Wormes* – stands out because it features, uniquely among Middle English and perhaps all debate poems, a female corpse.[3] Like the morality play *Mankind*, *A Disputacione betwyx the Body and Wormes* equates femininity and corporeality. Unlike the play, however, in the poem, the body emerges as a specifically female character. Klaus Jankofsky, for example, finds the body in the *Disputacione* to be 'a very specific corpse, that of a woman, a highranking noble lady, possibly a duchess or queen; the body is also seen as an image and an expression of a uniquely unified personality and not as the traditional dualistic separation of the body and soul' (140). The poem, thus, provides important insight into the perceived relationship between femininity and carnality so frequently asserted in medieval texts.

The poem incorporates the first-person speeches of the disputants within a first-person narrative frame and is a model of late medieval accretive textuality. Although there are no records of how the poem was read, and it was probably never performed, it, like *Mankind*, relies on first-person speeches to characterize the three personages who participate in the poem – the narrator, the body, and the worms (who speak as one even though they are described as numerous). The single extant manuscript version of the poem clearly differentiates the body's lines from worms' by indicating changes in speakers with rubricated notes like 'Wormes speke to þe body' and 'Þe body spekes to þe wormes' (see fig. 11.1). The poem looks dramatic on the page and relies on that performative aspect to construct a distinctly feminine corpse. Yet even as it relies on the equation of femininity and corporeality to characterize the body, the poem challenges the dichotomies and hierarchies that it, like *Mankind*, might superficially seem to reinforce. The poem inscribes a first-person account of a vision that begins with the narrator seeing a newly forged tomb, an image which invites readers to identify with the corpse in order to prepare for their own deaths. The *Disputacione* relies on layers of first-person narrative and dialogue to produce this lesson. The poem's multiplicity of images and voices conforms to the late medieval textual practice identified as accretive by James Simpson. Simpson explains that 'writers in such a textual culture often represent themselves as readers, whose rereading of old texts produces a rewriting. This rewriting reveals a complex layering of textuality, where texts from different sources are juxtaposed to form a composite

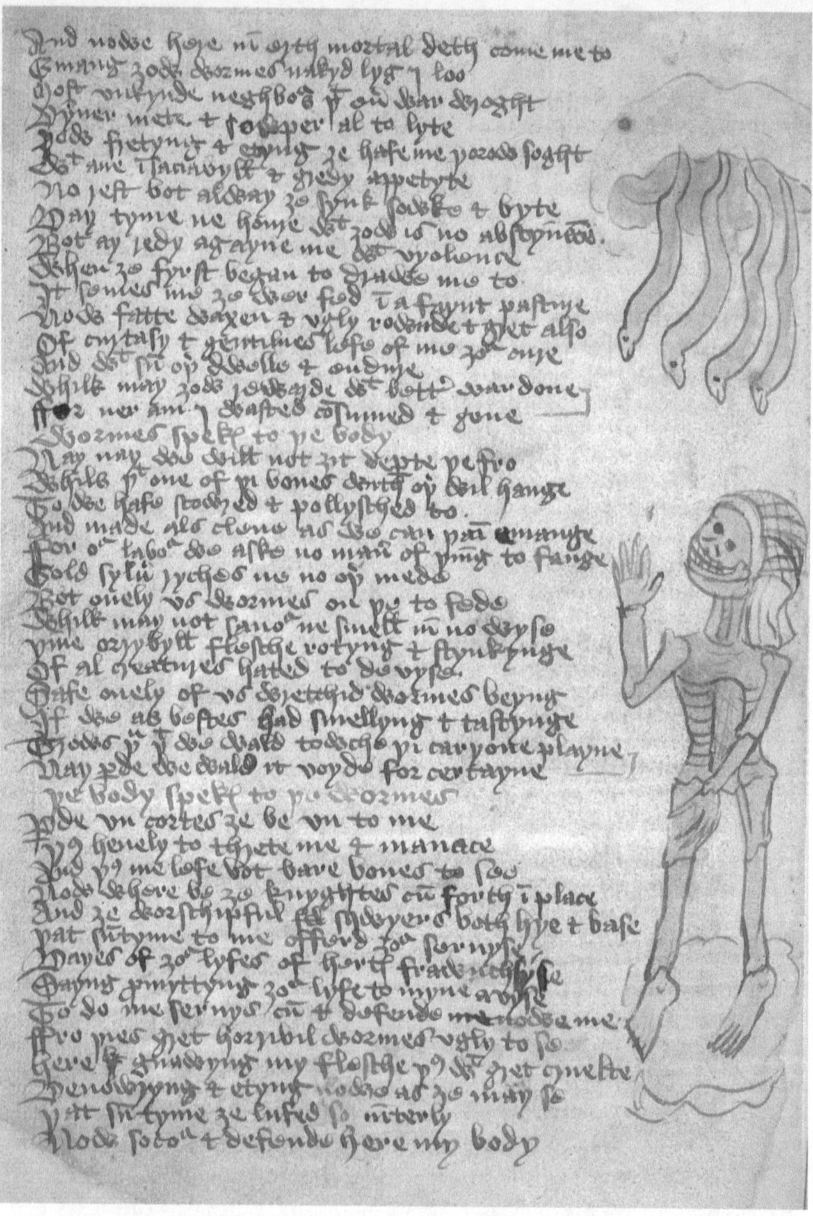

Fig. 11.1 The disputants in *The Disputacione betwyx the Body and Wormes*. London, BL Additional MS 37049, fol. 33v.

yet heterogeneous whole' (64). In *A Disputacione betwyx the Body and Wormes*, the initial text that inspires the poem is a sculpture, a tomb, rather than an old book, but the effect is similar. The poem weaves a composite whole from the original artefact and three different first-person speakers. Furthermore, in the manuscript, several images of death and devotion accompany the poem and create additional layers of imagery that connect the body performed in the text to the bodies illustrated on the page and to the bodies of readers. The poem, thus, links male and female, living and dead, and text and image though juxtapositions of these distinct parts.

The *Disputacione betwyx the Body and Wormes*, like *Mankind*, is usually dated ca 1460–70 and is preserved in the late fifteenth-century manuscript British Library, MS Additional 37049.[4] Scholars have connected the manuscript with the culture of English Carthusian charterhouses but have been unable to associate it with any specific charterhouse (Doyle 128; Gray 100). Because the origins and use of the manuscript remain uncertain – Marlene Villalobos Hennessy cautiously refers to the 'Carthusian community of readers who produced, compiled, and read' the manuscript (311), while Douglas Gray maintains that it may have been intended for the education of lay brothers (100) – a precise audience cannot be identified. The manuscript's most distinctive feature is the coloured pen drawings that accompany and directly relate to the texts. As several scholars have demonstrated, the manuscript carefully matches specific illustrations to each of the vernacular texts in its extensive collection.[5] Gray maintains that the pairings are 'designed to operate in an interactive way, sometimes as mnemonic guides to doctrine, sometimes as aids for the pious reader in his devotion, sometimes to intensify the emotional impact of the text, sometimes to create proto-emblematic poems' (100). As Hennessy asserts, the manuscript's 'conflation of reading and seeing, and the direct textual reference to an attendant illustration ... is one of its most distinctive and intriguing features' (314).

In addition, the *Disputacione betwyx the Body and Wormes* is the only debate poem featuring a recently deceased corpse in which the body is not engaged in a dispute with its soul. The substitution of worms for the soul focuses the debate on the body and its inescapable death and decay. W.A. Davenport in 'Patterns in Middle English Dialogues' has identified dialogues as dividing into two main groups, 'the "equal" contest and the "unequal" teacher/pupil dialogue' (127–8), but observes that Middle English writers artfully varied such patterns (129). The worms in the *Disputacione* serve as teachers to the body – they remind her of Church doctrine and present an untroubled understanding of their place in God's order in contrast to the body's confusion about her fate; however, they don't articulate complex theological arguments about the need for repentance before death or about the idea of the soul as the principle of life and site of reason and will.[6] Such understanding underlies the characterization of the body as female but is never explicitly articulated. Indeed, the worms understand that they were created to aid in and oversee the natural decomposition of the body, yet they prove to be successful instructors only in reconciling the body to the decay that is the fate of all bodies without authoritatively judging her worthiness of salvation. Their knowledge does not extend beyond this world into the afterlife. Indeed, while the characterization of the body as a fundamentally flawed woman might suggest that the body will not attain heaven, the poem ends inconclusively without an account of the body's fate after the resurrection. The characterization of the worms artfully combines the learned teacher role with the limited understanding of vermin.

The femininity of the body in the *Disputacione* first becomes evident in the image that precedes it in the manuscript (see the cover image to this volume). Like a *transi* tomb, the striking illustration that faces the opening page of the debate portrays a deceased lady as a pristine corpse or a resting woman in all her colourful finery on top and as a decayed and vermin-ridden corpse below.[7] The upper level of the illustration fills about half of the page and emphasizes her former beauty, rank, and fashionable garments,[8] while the lower level occupies about a quarter of the page and depicts her current repulsive state. In the upper part, a long red-orange skirt cascades over her feet, and her bodice appears to be of ermine with brown specks on a white background. She wears a horned headdress, which highlights her taste for fashion, and a crown, which asserts her high status, as do the heraldic shields that decorate her tomb. Her head rests on a tasselled pillow and her hands meet on her chest in prayer, prompting Marjorie M. Malvern to observe that she 'seems to rest in peace amidst her worldly glory' (420). In the lower level of the illustration, however, the body, wrapped in a shroud with its grinning skull tilted towards the viewer, lies surrounded by worms and toads and is less peaceful. Her right hand grips the shroud against her belly as if she is trying to protect herself from the ravenous vermin, and her left hand seems to be trying to brush them away from her left leg. Although the lower level occupies less of the illustration, the gaze of the skull engages the viewer and draws attention from the larger, more colourful image above.

The illustration confronts viewers with the contrast between idealized femininity above and its decay below. Given this contrast, the accompanying verse is surprisingly gender neutral. Beneath the illustration, the corpse speaks:

> Take hede vnto my fygure here abowne
> And se how sumtyme I was fressche & gay
> Now turned to wormes mete & corrupcone
> Bot fowle erth & stynkyng slyme & clay
> Attend þerfore to þis disputacione written here
> And writte it wisely in þi hert fre
> Þat þer-at sum wisdom þou may lere
> To se wat þou art & here aftyr sal be
> When þou leste wenes. venit mors te superare
> When þi grafe grenes. bonum en mortis meditari.[9]

The injunction to meditate on the fate of the body, 'Bot fowle erth & stynkyng slyme & clay,' eliminates distinctions between male and female bodies. The verse makes no mention of the corpse's gender and commands readers to think about death regularly because it vanquishes *all* mortal creatures, an injunction repeated frequently throughout the manuscript.[10] The verse suggests that, despite the feminine gender of the body in the illustration (and the poem), *everyone* should write the disputation that follows in their hearts.[11]

The manuscript includes a second *transi* illustration (fol. 87r) that demonstrates the immediacy of the corpse's address to readers in the first. The second illustration features a male corpse – in this case an emperor – which also serves as a reminder that death will come for everyone. Both *transi* illustrations rely on the understanding that images connect the living and the dead through remembrance. In the case of the second illustration, however, the inclusion of the emperor's son, who engages in a dialogue with his father, serves as an inscribed audience and diffuses the immediacy of the image by mediating between the depicted corpse and the reader's body. The verse accompanying the illustration describes the emperor as proud and his son as 'more wykkyd of lyfynge þan euer was his fader before hym' (Matsuda 243). At the end of the dialogue, the narrator explains that when the son

> had sene þis sight & hard þis noyse, he went home & gart bryng hym a paynter. And in hys bed chawmer he gart paynt þe lyknes of his fader as he lay in his graue. And when he was styrred to any syn, he beheld þe ymage of his fader knawyng wele þat he come fro þe erthe and suld turne to þe erthe. And

> on þis wyse he ouercome his synne. So þou þat wyll ouercum syn take heede at þis insawmpyll.

The image and narrative exemplify James Simpson's assertion that 'the social function of images is everywhere apparent and implicit in late medieval society' (431). By commissioning and viewing a painting of a decaying corpse like the one depicted in the bottom half of the manuscript's illustration of the emperor's tomb, the son commemorates his father and recalls his own future fate; he also serves as an intermediary between image and audience. Hennessy observes that the narrative distances readers from the image but simultaneously offers the son's response to the image of his father's corpse as a model for devout readers of the manuscript: 'While the painting in the story is made for the moral and spiritual benefit of the emperor's son, the illustration on fol. 87r is made for the reader-viewer's. Thus the figure of the son finds its embodiment in the person of the reader, who makes the text and image the basis of her or his own *memento mori* exercise' (315). This distance highlights the directness of the first *transi* illustration: in the 'Dialogue of the emperor and his dead father,' the reader embodies the son, while in the verses accompanying the illustration preceding the *Disputacione betwyx the Body and Wormes*, the reader embodies the female corpse.

The presence of the son in the 'Dialogue' mediates between the reader/viewer and the corpse and models the reader's desired response in an even more literal way than the male dreamer who narrates the *Disputacione* does. That poem begins when a pilgrim, depicted as a man in the accompanying illustration and travelling 'in þe ceson of huge mortalitie' (l. 1), discovers a newly erected tomb in an abandoned church. This tomb, like the upper portion of the first *transi*-tomb illustration, depicts 'a fresche fygure fyne of a woman' with many coats of arms painted on it (l. 21). As the narrator offers prayers, he falls asleep and hears a debate between the body and the worms devouring it. At the debate's conclusion, the narrator relates the dream to a 'holy man,' who advises him to write it down 'to styr & to mefe / Man & woman to be acceptabyll / Vnto our Lord' (ll. 207, 213–15). Men and women alike benefit from the contemplation of the final disgusting fate of this woman's body. Rosemary Woolf has argued that the impersonal posture of medieval authorship, in which a deliberately unidentified 'I' allows anyone to occupy the position, expresses not personal feeling but rather serves as an exercise for readers to use (5–8). In the *Disputacione*, the layers of first-person speakers complicate this exercise. Whereas the lines of verse that give voice to the dead woman depicted in the *transi* illustration ask viewers to identify with her, in the poem proper, the narrator asks everyone reading the account of his vision to identify with him *and* with the female corpse. In the poem, the initial image of the woman's figure unites the anonymous narrator with the unknown woman in the prefatory manuscript image, and the poem itself connects the dreamer with his readers, who then come to occupy his place through the undifferentiated narrative 'I.'

The intended audience for the *Disputacione* cannot be identified with any precision, but the illustrations that introduce the poem and its dream framework offer models for how it should be read. The first image that accompanies the debate poem proper suggests that men could be the intended audience. The illustration (see fig. 11.2) shows what James Hogg has identified as a Carthusian lay brother with 'surprisingly long' hair kneeling before Christ crucified on the cross and with wounds covering his body (*Illustrated Yorkshire* 44). This identification is problematic – Malvern, for example, associates him with the poet-persona (422), Hennessy calls him a 'praying hermit' (319), and Jankofsy tentatively refers to him as 'author, narrator, rubricator' (147) – but, despite the figure's long hair, critics have agreed that he is a man, perhaps because of his beard. The narrator, whose opening devotions may be represented in the illustration, undergoes a transformation when he is confronted by a tomb of a woman much like that depicted in the illustration on fol. 32v: he is able to overhear the debate between the woman's body and the worms and, in a sense, embodies the disputants by giving voice to both the female corpse and the devouring worms when he inscribes their dialogue. The narrator's performance of the dead body in writing down the vision collapses the distinction between the woman whose tomb provides the inspiration for his dream and himself. The poem invites readers to transform themselves similarly by experiencing the body's debate with the worms and its decay, which will eventually be theirs, much as the opening *transi* illustration instructs viewers inspired by that woman's fate to think on their own deaths. This relationship between images and texts creates a fluid connection between entities often dichotomized as discrete units in the Middle Ages. The text itself connects the bodies of corpse, narrator, and readers, whether men or women, by offering unmediated identification with the decaying body. In this way, the poem corresponds to the dominant late medieval vernacular devotional aesthetic, which collapses boundaries, especially temporal ones to, in Shannon Gayk's words, 'enable affective, participatory memory' (177). The only textual mediation of the experience comes from the authority who instructs the narrator to write down

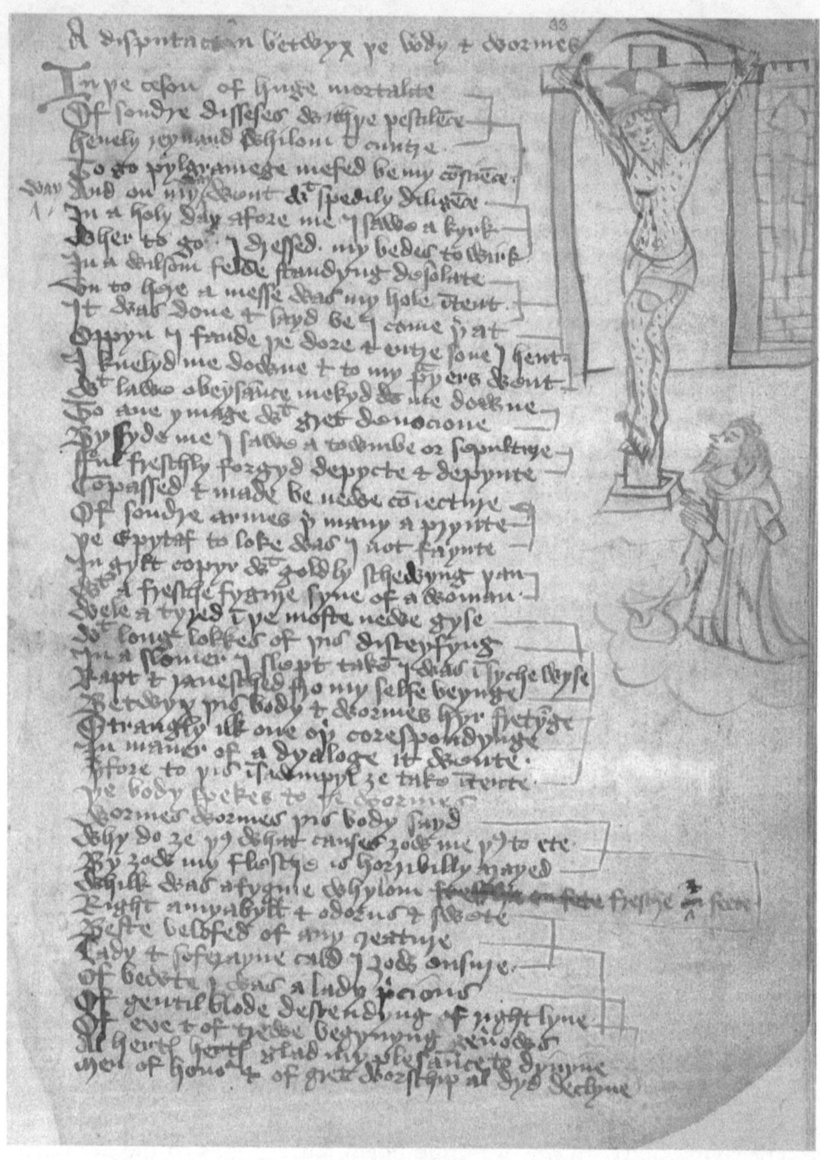

Fig. 11.2 A man praying, possibly the narrator of *The Disputacione betwyx the Body and Wormes*. London, BL Additional MS 37049, fol. 33r.

his dream in order 'to styr & to mefe' readers ('Disputacione' ll. 213). The poem emphasizes embodiment even as it dissolves differences between bodies to make the image of the decaying body and devouring worms 'experientially present' (Gayk 182).

While the narrative frame dissolves temporal and gender differences, the debate itself relies on the body's femininity to characterize the body and its potential for corruption. Both the opening image of the body in life and death and the debate the body engages in with the worms depend upon stark contrasts, especially regarding her gender, for their effectiveness. The deceased body in the poem still identifies herself as the beautiful noblewoman she was in life. She boasts:

> Of bewte I was a lady precious,
> Of gentil blode desendyng, of right lyne
> Of Eve, and of trewe begynyng generows;
> Al hertes glad my plesaunce to dyuyne,
> Men of honour & of gret worschip al dyd declyne. (ll. 37–41)

The corpse unambiguously and without shame or irony aligns herself with feminine lineage, concerns, and conduct. She frequently reveals both her obsession with courtly culture and her complete ignorance regarding spiritual concerns. At one point in the dispute she complains about her discourteous neighbours, the worms, and commands her male admirers to save her from them:

> Now where be ȝe knyghtes, cum forth in place,
> And ȝe worschiþful sqwyers, both hye & base,
> Þat sumtyme to me offred ȝour seruyse,
> Dayes of ȝour lyfes, of hertes frawnchsyse,
> Saying permyttyng ȝour lyfe to myne avyse?
> To do me seurys, cum & defende nowe me
> Fro þies gret horribil wormes vgly to se,
> Here gnawyng my flesche þus with gret cruelte. (ll. 75–82)

Here, the body alludes to courtly conventions that urge men to serve and protect women. She expects men will react to her plight with pity and solicitude, and indeed they have: the narrator describes the tomb beside which he kneels as newly made, finely painted with many coats of arms, and topped with an elaborate sculpture. This woman *has* been looked after by the living, but she misses the import of that service: it is not designed to preserve her earthly beauty, but to ensure her salvation, something she shows little or no interest in.

The body's emphasis on her physical beauty contrasts with her current state of carnal decomposition and demonstrates that even the most desirable flesh is nothing but food for worms, a common late medieval motif.[12] Woolf maintains that the use of a female body amplifies the lesson that all flesh decays: 'The rotting of feminine beauty gave a turn of the screw to the theme of putrefaction' (318). The worms themselves remind readers that this woman's body represents the fate of all fair women in their final speech:

Rememor ȝe sal with will of ȝour hert fre
In holy scripture, & ȝe wole behalde
Þat þe fayrnes of women talde
Is bot vayne þinge & transitory. (ll. 172–5)

The debate's emphasis on the corpse's former beauty depicts her as special and extraordinary; in particular, she herself reminds the worms of her elevated social status, thus providing an example of pride.[13] Just as the emperor and his dead father in the dialogue accompanying the other *transi* illustration are characterized by their pride and elevated by their class, the dead woman is elevated by her former beauty to serve as a negative example of pride, yet her characterization in the debate depends upon her femininity – the body brags that she descends from Eve's line while the worms remind her that only 'women dredyng God sal be praysed holy' (l. 176).

The other illustrations that accompany the debate also highlight the levelling effects of death and decay. Although they depict the corpse in its elaborate headgear interacting with three worms, the corpse's skeletal and decaying state renders it an object of disgust for moral and physical reasons (see fig. 11.1). Samantha Mullaney points to the 'popular horned and veiled head-dress of a noble lady' worn by this corpse as the singular identifying mark of the figure's femininity (80). The headdress corresponds to the debate's characterization of the body as prideful, for late medieval moralists frequently harangue women who wear stylish clothes. For example, John Lydgate's 'Horns Away' explains that 'Off God and kynde procedith al bewte; / Crafft may shewe a foreyn apparence, / But nature ay must haue the souereynte' (ll. 1–3). Lydgate singles out the fashion of horned headdresses as a particularly egregious example of counterfeiting craft by ending each stanza of the poem proper with the line 'Beute wol shewe, thogh hornes wer away' (ll. 8, 16, 24). (The last two stanzas before 'Lenvoye' vary the formula, and the poem proper ends, 'Lyst nat of pryde, ther hornes cast away' [l. 40].) 'Lenvoye' itself explicitly addresses 'noble pryncessis, of meek benyvolence' and commands them to follow the example of the Virgin Mary and their 'hornes cast away' (ll. 71–2). Thus, according to Lydgate, modest women should not wear elaborate headgear, which would mark them as prideful. Even in an advanced state of decay, the body depicted in the illustrations maintains her proud horns. The headgear marks her as feminine and sinful, even as the skeletal body represents the shared fate of all mortal bodies.

The skeletal figure also inspires sensory dread. The worms themselves regard their meal as 'orrybyll flesche, rotyng & stynkynge' and note that it is 'Of al creatures hated to devyse / Safe onely of vs wretchid wormes beyng,' because they were created for their work without the senses of taste and scent (ll. 67–8). Despite the body's description of the worms horribly attacking her flesh (l. 32), the illustrations of the body debating the worms separate the disputants on individual plots of grass. The light brown colouring of the skeleton, however, matches the colouring of the worms, indicating the close connection between the disputing entities.[14] The body reviles this connection, revealing her ignorance of Church teachings about the fate of the body. She is both a repulsive figure and one whose need for instruction potentially mirrors the reader's. While the representation of the wealthy, fashionable woman on top of the tomb and the body's reminiscence of her mortal beauty elevate the body to the highest levels of the earthly hierarchy, the opening injunction and her posthumous corruption implore readers to identify with her in order to avoid her fate.

Her lack of spiritual understanding throughout the debate further allies her with readers needing moral instruction. The body consistently falls short of good moral conduct and her contributions to the debate are riddled with ignorance of spiritual concerns. The dead lady repeatedly draws attention to the violence the worms do to her, which she believes causes her decay. The verbs she uses in describing the worms' treatment of her deal with eating and digestion and, in an effort to stop their gluttony, she warns that their meal is nearly done, 'For ner am I wasted, consumed, & gone' (l. 57). The body castigates the worms for their poor manners, exclaiming, 'Of curtasy & gentilnes lefe of me ȝour cure,' and, 'Parde, vncortes ȝe be vnto me, / Þus heuely to threte me & manace / And þus me lefe bot bare bones to see' (ll. 54, 72–4). Her experience is not one of gradually coming to understand the ephemeral nature of the body but merely one of discomfort and dismay. The body associates a monstrous appetite with the devouring worms and does not recognize that her own appetites – for fashion, male company, and other earthly pleasures – are the appetites that must be controlled if the body is to overcome death. In the debate, the body fails to realize that she would decay even without the worms' attentions, because the body's destruction is an inevitable event that began, as the worms attempt to explain to her, before their arrival. Nor does she comprehend that they were created specifically to help the process. After death the body remains unaware of the sins she committed in life and, in fact, continues to evince the same moral shortcomings she demonstrated in life, especially pride. Alive, she spent no time preparing for death, and dead, she fails to recognize the need to repent. Injunctions to prepare for death, like those that frame the debate, caution that one cannot wait until after death to relinquish worldly desires, implying that after death such a truth cannot be avoided, especially after the soul has departed from the body. The body in the *Disputacione* cannot reach this understanding; she does not fully comprehend her errors even when the worms have nearly cleaned the flesh from her bones.[15] Through the dialogue, the worms teach her and readers identifying with her to understand that the body's fate is inevitable and divinely ordained.

In the body's initial incomprehension, the *Disputacione betwyx the Body and Wormes* develops a particular view of the female body as a disruption of the proper balance between spirit and flesh and between appetites and devotion. Caroline Walker Bynum explains that medieval writers frequently associated femininity with flesh for both medical and theological reasons (98–101). For example, Aristotelian physiological theories, which some medieval scientists followed, most clearly associate woman with flesh by maintaining that the mother provides matter and the father form to the fetus. The competing Galenic tradition asserts that seeds from both parents were needed but that the mother's body provides the necessary material for the fetus's growth (100). The theory of complexions, however, relies on the idea that the four qualities – hot, cold, moist, and dry – are in both sexes, but finds female bodies to be colder and moister than male ones (Cadden 170–88). This last theory was used to explain women's irrationality and susceptibility to uncontrolled passions. The female body in the *Disputacione* speaks and is animated despite the absence of a soul, and her rhetoric is characterized by passionate if irrational commands that her former suitors save her from the worms and that the worms obey her commands. In death, the body prioritizes her fleshly desires and forsakes all devotional practices, just as she did in life. Her failure is gendered female, but it is a lesson applicable to all Christians about the relationship between body and soul.

The theological traditions Bynum mentions are even more important in explaining the danger the body represents to order and good conduct in the *Disputacione*. As Karma Lochrie argues, medieval theological writers frequently represent the 'principle of influx' that alienates and disorders the body and soul as a woman (21). In such figures, woman becomes the means by which the proper hierarchies of body and soul are overturned. In the 'Exposition of Psalm 140,' Augustine elucidates the relationship between an individual and the chastised body, answering the question 'If someone chastises his body, does that mean that he hates his body?' by listing a series of hierarchical relationships – master/slave, parent/child – before examining 'an even more intimate relationship' – husband and wife – and explaining that 'your flesh is like a wife to you' (20.316). He expands the simile, saying, 'Your flesh lusts against you like a wife opposing your wishes, so you must both love it and discipline it until undivided concord reigns, through the reformation of your whole self.' The body ought to be subordinate, but carnal sensibilities tempt, mislead, and, indeed, cause disorder, as Eve did in paradise.[16]

The image of Eve, whom the body cites as an esteemed ancestor in the *Disputacione*, is a powerful image of corruption in medieval theology. For example, Bernard of Clairvaux maintains that the body is not evil, but merely subject to the desires of the will in conjunction with the senses. He explains, 'The will is your Eve' (*Selected Works* 76). In associating the will with Eve, Bernard equates the body's permeability with woman, a permeability that began with the Fall. In a sermon describing 'How reason and will engage in a dispute on behalf of the body,' he personifies the body as a lazy servant while will is a domineering, wild, and unkempt old woman, whose already decaying body is covered with ulcers: 'Little old will gnashes her teeth. Her mind is maddened; she grows voluble, contentious, and loud. She stalks out with her chest uncovered, her hair a tangle, and covered with horrible running sores' (*The Parables and the Sentences* 200). She is initially described as lying in a 'harmful languor,' but once the debate with reason begins she becomes an 'angry viper' (199, 200). In this sermon, reason convinces will to accede to his rule by describing the pleasures she will find in paradise: '"Reason prudently entices will to enter the garden and gradually begin to taste its fruits until, full of delight, she will shout: 'Nourish me with flowers, restore me with apples, for I languish with love"' (201).The will in Bernard's personification, like the body in the *Disputacione*, insists on sensory experience even *after* she is convinced to follow reason. *Before* consenting to reason, the will's emphasis on hunger and sex, sound and taste, lead to the corruption represented by the ulcers, and pleasures that she 'longed for so ardently that never could the eye see or the ear hear them enough' become 'a cause of revulsion to her' after her conversion (201). For Bernard, the body is torn between reason and will, and without reason's dominance, it remains in a 'dungheap' (200). In this understanding, the feminine body in *A Disputacione betwyx the Body and Wormes* is equated with the will and the disjunction between body and soul. Rather than being controlled by reason, the body and her sensory experiences dominate the dead lady's thoughts even after death.

The soul never appears in the *Disputacione betwyx the Body and Wormes*; in fact, no mention is made of it at all. Therefore, readers' understanding of its fate depends on what happens to the body over the course of the poem, suggesting an unbreakable relationship between the body and the soul. The debate never raises the question of whether the body or the soul is responsible for the sins the lady committed during her life (a topic frequently addressed in most body and soul debate poetry), so while the will may separate body and soul in theory, the two are indistinguishable in the poem. Thus, the body represents Augustine's 'whole self' (20.316). Despite the fact that God sent messengers to remind her to meditate on death, the lady lived a sinful life and died unprepared and unshriven. In their role as teachers, the worms explain that they sent their representatives, lice and nits and fleas, to prepare her for death and to 'warne ȝow of vs, to make ȝow redy,' but she ignored them (l. 134). They remind her that priests also forewarn her of mortality on each Ash Wednesday, when 'with asses blisses to hafe rememoraunce, / What þu art & wher to þou sal turne agayne' (ll. 149–50). The lady's responses betray her failure to apprehend and obey these warnings; she was too busy pursuing her sinful ways to contemplate death, making her ability to comprehend her body's decay and the coming judgment more difficult if not impossible. Neither the soul's absence, nor its responsibility, figure into her musings, perhaps contributing to the difficulty she has in understanding the worms' work, but also implying the unity of body and soul: *both* are responsible for the lady's actions.

The manuscript containing the *Disputacione* does not rely entirely on the text's silence for an understanding of how a body and a soul constitute an individual, however, since it also contains the prose *Dysputacion betwyx þe Saule & þe Body*. The prose debate is filled with mutual antagonism and vituperation, as the soul begins by calling the body, 'Þou wretchyd body, so horribill and fowle stynkyng, wormes mete & noreschyng of corrupcion' (Hogg, 'Selected Texts' 85); the body replies by immediately blaming the soul for any horrible filth it may see. Despite the vehemence of the argument, this prose debate is the only Middle English dispute between body and soul that explicitly posits the salvation of the protagonist. It is a translation of part of Guillaume de Guilleville's *Pèlerinage de l'âme* and concludes with an angel's sermon that announces that body and soul will be saved.[17] It might seem that the antagonism between body and soul in the prose *Dysputacion betwyx þe Saule & þe Body* reflects their sinfulness and damnation, but the text proffers the idea that even a saved person's body and soul can become embroiled in an altercation, just as the *Disputacione betwyx the Body and Wormes* demonstrates that an apparently unified body and soul can be sinful. The angel ends the prose debate, saying:

> Pes & stynt of ȝour pleyng, for it is not ȝour avaylyng betwyx ȝow twoo to stryfe on swylk maner of wyse be swylk wordes & to be mefed. For ȝe are predestinate to saluacion & hereafter sal be ioyned again togeder. Betwene þaim swilk stryfe of wordes suld be mefyd whilk þat ar perpetually dampned & ordand to þe payne of helle. (88)

At first, the angel suggests that the souls and bodies of saved people should not experience such discord, but this speech asserts that even such an antagonistic body and soul as the one engaged in this disputation can be united and saved. The prose *Dysputacion* ends when the angel reminds all creatures to consider the fate of the body after death and announces that everyone should 'discretly hald vnder his flesche with helful discyplyne, þat it may be obedient to þe wil & þe reson of þe saule, & þe saule obedient vnto God in kepyng his commandments right, & þan sal þai bothe be gloryfyed togeder in euerlastyng ioy' (89). The angel establishes a hierarchy in which the body should be obedient to the will and reason of the soul and the soul should be obedient to God. The prose *Dysputacion* thus asserts a hierarchical connection between body and soul and maintains that the individual human should not be divided into warring components. The angel's speech concludes the prose debate, as it presents an exemplum to further explain the interdependence of the body and soul, and the body and soul in this debate learn the lesson. They stop arguing because the angel tells them that they are among those predestined for salvation, providing authoritative and positive closure – body and soul must work together to govern the flesh, the ungoverned version of which is so vividly portrayed by the body in *A Disputacione betwyx þe Body and Wormes*.

The debate between the body and the worms concludes with the body's celebration of concord with the worms and a glorious vision of her fate after the Last Judgment:

With þe body glorified to be,
And of þat nowmbyr þat I may be one,
To cum to þat blis of heuen in fee,
Þorow þe mene & þe mediacione
Of our blissed Lord, our verry patrone,
Þar in abilite to be for his hye plesaunce.
Amen. Amen. (ll. 198–204)

Whether we accept the body's jubilant celebration or the worms' more cautious final statement that only women dreading God will be called holy, she reflects an interest in the importance of the flesh and uneasiness with the simplified equation of carnality with corruption and femininity. The poem never asserts simply that the sinful flesh unprepared for death merits damnation. Rather, it reveals larger cultural anxieties about death and doubts about the judgment that will be visited upon sinful individuals who die unrepentant. *A Disputacione betwyx the Body and Wormes* both relies upon traditional equations of woman with corruption and the body, and dissolves those simplistic binaries. It can be helpful to divide complex ideas into discrete categories – male and female, body and soul – but ultimately the text demonstrates that these divisions are more fluid and less concrete than they initially appear.

As an allegorical representation of all humanity, Mankind's discussion of the body in the morality play suggests that our bodies and bodily experiences provide common ground for all humans, but they also jeopardize our salvation. From his first line, 'Of þe erth and of þe cley we have owr propagacyon,' Mankind characterizes humanity as embodied and mortal, but also as immortal, deriving from 'þe prouydens of Gode' (ll. 186–7). While he hopes that 'onto Hys blysse ye be all predestynatt,' such an end requires the renunciation of bodily desires (ll. 189):

Every man for hys degree I trust xall be partycypatt,
Yf we wyll mortyfye owr carnall condycyon
Ande owr voluntarye dysyres, þat ever be pervercyonatt,
To renounce þem and yelde ws wnder Godys provycyon. (ll. 190–3)

The female corpse in *A Disputacione betwyx the Body and Wormes* relies upon many of the prevalent misogynistic attitudes towards women – their irrationality and emotionality, their ability to disrupt order and hierarchy – but the poem is more nuanced in its characterization of the body. As in *Mankind*, the main character represents all embodied humanity as being propagated from 'þe erth' and 'þe cley' and serves as a reminder that fleshly desires are 'pervercyonatt' and must be renounced, but it is less certain that failure to do so will result in damnation.

The *Disputacione betwyx the Body and Wormes* rehearses a performance of the feminine flesh to convince men and women to embrace their own deaths by preparing themselves for its inevitability. Such preparation allows individuals to become almost heroic, as opposed to the body in the *Disputacione* who remains ignorant about death even after her own, since foreknowledge is the mark of a hero's death. As Philippe Ariès asserts, the death of a heroic knight in medieval literature does 'not come as a surprise, even when it is the accidental result of a wound or the effect of too great an emotion, as was sometimes the case. Its essential characteristic is that it gives advance warning of its arrival' (6). While the warnings Ariès discusses tend to be within days of the hero's death, lessons about the need to foreknow death and suppress fleshly desires are embodied by the female corpse in *A Disputacione betwyx the Body and Wormes*. If followed, these lessons demonstrate how to prepare for death and die heroically. Despite its macabre characters, the poem is more concerned with how the living govern themselves than with eschatological questions about the fate of the body after death. The dead body of the corpse is embodied by the narrator's act of composition and becomes the living body of the attentive reader. The poem asserts and then dissolves divisions between male and female, text and image, dead and living in a complex layering of performance and textuality.

NOTES

1 Accounts of marriage often cite scriptural texts such as 'Wherefore a man shall leave father and mother, and shall cleave to his wife: and they shall be two in one flesh' (Genesis 2:24) to endorse this view.

2 Body and soul debate poems exist in Latin and in most late medieval European vernaculars. Wright lists nineteen debates between the body and soul in languages as diverse as Greek and Netherlandish in the appendix to his collection of Latin poems. Walther lists 132 extant manuscripts of the enormously popular Latin debate, the *Dialogus inter corpus et animam*. Additionally, Brock and Drijvers edit four medieval Syriac disputes, and Gragnolati explores the versions of the theme associated with three thirteenth-century Italian poets (Uguccione da Lodi, Giacomino da Verona, and Bonvesin de la Riva).

3 Conlee discusses the tradition in *Middle English Debate Poetry: A Critical Anthology* (xxiv–xxvii). See also Utley.

4 Bevington dates *Mankind* as ca 1465–70 (901), and Scherb describes it as 'probably dating from the 1460s' (24). Doyle and Gray place British Library, MS Additional 37049 in the middle or third quarter of the fifteenth century (128 and 99, respectively). Scott is more specific, dating it to after 1460–70 (2.193).

5 See, for example, Brantley, Gray, Hennessy, Malvern, and Mullaney.

6 For a discussion of how the poem incorporates popular rather than learned theology, see Ackerman.

7 For descriptions of actual *transi* tombs, see Boase 97–103. For example, Boase includes the fifteenth-century tomb of Chaucer's granddaughter, the Duchess of Suffolk, at Ewelme: 'The Duchess lies in prayer, her finely-drawn, aging features almost certainly a portrait; above is a choir of angels while on the sarcophagus other angels hold armorial shields; but below, through a tracery panel, can be seen a decomposing corpse, carved with infinite detail despite the obscurity of its position, stretched on its shroud, the long hair still falling from the skull' (97).

8 For a discussion of the fashions depicted in the manuscript, see Mullaney.

9 Conlee 53 nn. to l. 19. All quotations of the poem come from this edition.

10 See, for example, the *Danse Macabre* verses in fols. 31v and 32r as well as fol. 69r, 'Memento Mori' (Hogg, 'Selected Texts' 266–7) and 'The Harper' in fol. 84v (Ross, 281).

11 Similar commands appear in other artistic and poetic contexts, especially in depictions of the *Danse Macabre* and *The Three Dead and the Three Living*.

12 Johan Huizinga's discussion of works developing the theme of 'the decomposition of all that had once constituted earthly beauty' focuses particularly on the aging and decay of *female* bodies (157).

13 The *dance macabre* in particular emphasizes that every stratum of human society is susceptible to death with its depiction of different professions and estates. For an English version of the poem, see Lydgate's *Danse Macabre*. A version featuring women was available in French. See Harrison.

14 Malvern also notices the similarity of colouring: 'The Body, like the Worms, is colored light brown' (428).

15 For an examination of the worms' pastoral authority and the debate's irresolution concerning the body's salvation, see my 'Vernacular Theology in *The Disputacione betwyx the Body and the Wormes*.'

16 In the second exposition of Psalm 29, Augustine explains how Job's wife, 'like Eve, made herself the devil's accomplice, instead of her husbands support,' also representing the site of disruption as an unmastered woman (15.306).

17 BL Additional 37049 contains twelve excerpts from the *Pèlegrinage de l'âme*, primarily from books 2 and 5, between fols. 69v and 84. Each extract generally begins with a calligraphic initial, has its own format, and works as a complete text independent of the whole. For a description of the relevant sections, see McGerr xcii–xciv. The work in its entirety tells of a dreamer's soul taken on a journey by its attendant angel to see the universe. At one point, the soul sees its own body and engages it in a debate over their respective responsibility for past sins. Although the debate is not between a recently deceased body and its soul, but between the body and soul of a visionary dreamer, the issues debated are similar to those in the more traditional body and soul debates. Furthermore, the excerpt of body and soul debate included in BL Additional 37049, fols. 82–4, contains no frame to establish the state of the body at the time of the debate. Readers unfamiliar with the longer poem must rely on the ambiguous title, 'A disputacion betwyx þe saule & þe body when it is past oute of þe body,' that begins the debate.

WORKS CITED

Ackerman, Robert W. 'The Debate of the Body and the Soul and Parochial Christianity.' *Speculum* 37 (1962): 541–65.

Ariès, Philippe. *The Hour of Our Death*. Trans. Helen Weaver. New York: Alfred A. Knopf, 1981.

Augustine. *Expositions of the Psalms 1–32*. The Works of Saint Augustine. Part 3. Vol. 15. Trans. Maria Boulding. Hyde Park: New City Press, 1990.

– *Expositions of the Psalms 121–150*. The Works of Saint Augustine. Part 3. Vol. 20. Trans. Maria Boulding. Hyde Park, NY: New City Press, 1990.

Bernard of Clairvaux. *Bernard of Clairvaux: Selected Works*. Trans. G.R. Evans. New York: Paulist Press, 1987.

– *Bernard of Clairvaux: The Parables and the Sentences*. Trans. Michael Casey and Francis R. Swietek. Kalamazoo, MI: Cistercian Publications, 2000.

Bevington, David, ed. *Medieval Drama*. Boston: Houghton Mifflin, 1975.

Boase, T.S.R. *Death in the Middle Ages*. New York: McGraw-Hill, 1972.

Brantley, Jessica Caroline. 'Reading in the Wilderness: A Contextual Study of a Carthusian Miscellany (British Library MS Additional 37049).' Diss., University of California, Los Angeles, 2000.

Brock, Sebastian. 'Syriac Dispute Poems: The Various Types.' In *Dispute Poems and Dialogues in the Ancient and Mediaeval Near East: Forms and Types of Literary Debates in Semitic and Related Literatures*. Ed. G.J. Reinink and

H.L.J. Vanstiphout. Orientalia Lovaniensia Analecta 42. Leuven: Departement Oriëntalistiek, 1991. 109–19.

Bynum, Caroline Walker. *Fragmentation and Redemption: Essays on Gender and the Human Body in Medieval Religion*. New York: Zone Books, 1991.

Cadden, Joan. *Meanings of Sex Difference in the Middle Ages: Medicine, Science, and Culture.* Cambridge: Cambridge University Press, 1993.

Conlee, John W., ed. *Middle English Debate Poetry: A Critical Anthology*. East Lansing, MI: Colleagues Press, 1991.

Davenport, W.A. 'Patterns in Middle English Dialogues.' In *Medieval English Studies Presented to George Kane*. Ed. Edward Donald Kennedy, Ronald Waldron, and Joseph S. Wittig. Woodbridge, UK: Boydell and Brewer, 1988. 127–45.

'A Disputation between the Body and the Worms.' *Middle English Debate Poetry: A Critical Anthology*. Ed. John W. Conlee. East Lansing, MI: Colleagues Press, 1991. 50–62.

Doyle, A.I. 'English Carthusian Books Not Yet Linked with a Charterhouse.' In *'A Miracle of Learning': Studies in Manuscripts and Irish Learning. Essays in Honour of William O'Sullivan*. Ed. Toby Barnard, Dáibhí Ó Cróinín, and Katharine Simms. Aldershot, UK: Ashgate, 1998. 122–36.

Drijvers, Han J.W. 'Body and Soul: A Perennial Problem.' In *Dispute Poems and Dialogues in the Ancient and Mediaeval Near East: Forms and Types of Literary Debates in Semitic and Related Literatures*. Ed. G.J. Reinink and H.L.J. Vanstiphout Reinink. Orientalia Lovaniensia Analecta 42. Leuven: Departement Oriëntalistiek, 1991. 121–34.

Gayk, Shannon. 'Images of Pity: The Regulatory Aesthetics of John Lydgate's Religious Lyrics.' *Studies in the Age of Chaucer* 28 (2006): 175–203.

Gragnolati, Manuel. *Experiencing the Afterlife: Soul and Body in Dante and Medieval Culture*. Notre Dame, IN: University of Notre Dame Press, 2005.

Gray, Douglas. 'London, British Library, Additional MS 37049 – A Spiritual Encyclopedia.' In *Text and Controversy from Wyclif to Bale: Essays in Honour of Anne Hudson*. Ed. Helen Barr and Ann M. Hutchison. Turnhout, Belgium: Brepols, 2005. 109–18.

Harrison, Ann Tukey. *The Danse Macabre of Women: MS. Fr. 995 of the Bibliothèque Nationale.* Kent, OH: Kent State University Press, 1994.

Hennessy, Marlene Villalobos. 'The Remains of the Royal Dead in an English Carthusian Manuscript, London, British Library, MS Additional 37049.' *Viator* 33 (2002): 310–54.

Hogg, James, ed. *An Illustrated Yorkshire Carthuian Religious Miscellany British Library London Additional MS. 37049*. Analecta Carthusiana 95. Salzburg, 1981.

– 'Selected Texts on Heaven and Hell from the Carthusian Miscellany, British Library Additional MS. 37049.' *Zeit, Tod, und Ewigkeit in der Renaissance Literatur*. Analecta Cartusiana 117. Salzburg: Institut für Anglistik und Amerikanistik, Universität Salzburg, 1987. 63–89.

Huizinga, Johan. *The Autumn of the Middle Ages*. Trans. Rodney J. Payton and Ulrich Mammitzsch. Chicago: University of Chicago Press, 1996.

Jankofsky, Klaus. 'A View into the Grave: "A Disputacion betwyx þe Body and Wormes" in British Museum MS Add. 37049.' *Taius* 1 (1974): 137–59.

Lochrie, Karma. *Margery Kempe and Translations of the Flesh*. Philadelphia: University of Pennsylvania Press, 1991.

Lydgate, John. *The Dance of Death: Edited from MSS. Ellesmere 26/A.13 and B.M. Lansdowne 699*. Ed. Florence Warren. EETS, O.S. 181. London: Oxford University Press, 1931.

– 'Hornes Away.' *The Minor Poems of John Lydgate: Part II*. Ed. Henry Noble MacCracken. EETS, O.S. 192. London: Oxford University Press, 1934. 662–5.

Malvern, Marjorie M. 'An Earnest "Monyscyon" and "Þinge Delectabyll" Realized Verbally and Visually in "A Disputacion Betwyx Þe Body and Wormes," a Middle English Poem Inspired by Tomb Art and Northern Spirituality.' *Viator* 13 (1982): 415–50.

'Mankind.' *Medieval Drama: An Anthology*. Ed. Greg Walker. Oxford: Blackwell, 2000. 258–79.

Matlock, Wendy A. 'Vernacular Theology in *The Disputacione betwyx the Body and the Wormes*.' *Feast, Famine, and Fasting: Food and Material Consumption in Medieval and Renaissance Culture*. Ed. Laura Hollengreen. Arizona Studies in the Middle Ages and Renaissance 13. Turnhout, Belgium: Brepols, 2008. 113–27.

Matsuda, Takami. *Death and Purgatory in Middle English Didactic Poetry*. Cambridge: D.S. Brewer, 1997.

McGerr, Rosemarie Potz, ed. *The Pilgrimage of the Soul: A Critical Edition of the Middle English Dream Vision*. Vol. 1. New York: Garland, 1990.

Mullaney, Samantha. 'Fashion and Morality in BL MS Add. 37049.' *Texts and Their Contexts: Papers from the Early Book Society*. Ed. John Scattergood and Julia Boffey. Dublin: Four Courts Press, 1997. 71–86.

Ross, Thomas W. 'Five Fifteenth-Century "Emblem" Verses from Brit. Mus. Addit. MS. 37049.' *Speculum* 31 (1957): 274–82.

Scherb, Victor I. *Staging Faith: East Anglian Drama in the Later Middle Ages*. Madison, NJ: Fairleigh Dickinson University Press, 2001.

Scott, Kathleen L. *Later Gothic Manuscripts, 1390–1490*. Vol. 2. London: H. Miller, 1996.

Simpson, James. *Reform and Cultural Revolution*. The Oxford English Literary History. Vol. 2: 1350–1547. Oxford: Oxford University Press, 2002.

Utley, Francis Lee. 'Dialogues, Debates, and Catechisms.' In *A Manual of the Writings in Middle English, 1050–1500*. Ed. John Edwin Wells, Jonathan Burke Severs, and Albert E. Hartung. Vol. 3. New Haven: Connecticut Academy of Arts and Sciences, 1967. 669–745, 829–902.

Walther, H. *Das Streitgedicht in der lateinischen Literatur des Mittelalters*. Quellen und Untersuchungen zur lateinischen Philologie des Mittelalters. Munich: Oskar Beck, 1920.

Woolf, Rosemary. *The English Religious Lyric in the Middle Ages*. Oxford: Clarendon, 1968.

Wright, Thomas, ed. *The Latin Poems Commonly Attributed to Walter Mapes*. Camden Society Publications 16. New York: AMS Press, 1841. 321–4.

12 Death as Metamorphosis in the Devotional and Political Allegory of Christine de Pizan

SUZANNE CONKLIN AKBARI

The essays in this volume have highlighted the interplay between the individual body and the communal body: that is, the way in which the community is figured as a body that contains mutually interdependent members, and excludes that which lies outside its boundaries. This closing essay focuses on how the body's apparent stability is undercut by its necessarily changeable nature: just as the individual human body appears different over time, just as it matures, eventually weakens, and finally dies and decays, so too the communal body is subject to alteration. Change is in its nature. In the Christian vision of community, however, the collective body of the Church could be understood as immutable because its template is the eternal and unchanging form of Christ. In this view, the perfect flesh of the Incarnation, remaining eternally whole as resurrected body, models the wholeness of the community of the Church that is at once a mirror of Christ and his bride.

Secular notions of community were somewhat different. Even though notions of the body politic were modelled upon conceptions of the Christian community, the immutability that could be assumed by the Church was not so readily available to the nation. On the contrary, mutability was written into the very fabric of the nation, not only in the lived realities of political conflict and continually redrawn national boundaries, but also in the elaborate (and, often, imaginary) genealogical relationships that underlay medieval European constructions of the nation. Change, in other words, had to be reckoned with in the effort to describe the contours of the late medieval body politic. This effort is the focus of the present essay, which explores the tension between the individual and the communal body in two works by Christine de Pizan, both of which portray the necessary phenomenon of change: the *Livre du corps de policie*, written in 1406–7, and the *Livre des fais et bonnes meurs du sage roy Charles V*, written in 1404. In each of these works, *vertu* is presented as the mediating property that both guarantees flux and ensures continuity. In the *Corps de policie*, *vertu* appears as a liquid, flowing substance that vivifies the body politic; in the biography of Charles V, it appears as a property of the king himself. In both cases, however, *vertu* is central to Christine's figurative representation of the formation and maintenance of the community, whether expressed in terms of political allegory (as in the *Corps de policie*) or devotional allegory (as in the biography of Charles V). The life of the body politic is maintained through the circulation of *vertu* throughout the community, while its leadership is perpetuated through the expression of *vertu* in the person of the nation's ruler. While the death of the king might threaten to interrupt the continuity of the body politic, Christine presents a vision of kingship in which death is, paradoxically, both a beginning and an ending, a time of change that is also a moment of supreme stability. Through the devotional allegory of her biography of Charles V and the political allegory of her *Corps de policie*, Christine constructs a figurative model of the body politic that reaffirms the fundamental stability of the French nation, defying the political and social turmoil of the period.

By the early fifteenth century, writers had come to think differently about the relationship of language to knowledge, and about the role of affective devotion in the act of knowing. No longer an intellectual process that could be described simply through tropes of vision, allegorical knowing came to be articulated in terms of bodily process, in which the flow of tears, blood, and humoral fluids were the signs through which knowledge was mediated. In this setting, metamorphosis – that is, bodily change – came to be used as an extended metaphor for other kinds of transformation: historical, ecclesiastical, social, and spiritual. Christine de Pizan's work manifests this perspective on the relationship of language to knowledge with particular clarity: she describes death in terms of metamorphosis, and uses it as a figure for transformation in general, expressed through the literary modes that she refers to as 'poesie' and 'methafore.'

While this essay will argue that Christine's biography of Charles V can be read as an expression of 'devotional allegory,' it is important to note that it is nothing new to point out devotional elements in the writing of Christine de Pizan. Her commentary on the seven penitential psalms, her *Epistre de la prison de vie humaine*, and, most famously, the legends of saints found in the third book of her *Cité des dames* clearly identify Christine as a writer deeply concerned with the literary expression of religious piety. It is somewhat more unusual, however, to point out the integration of these devotional elements within Christine's allegory. In part, this is the result of Christine's own practice of signalling continuities between her writings and earlier works in the allegorical tradition, such as the *Roman de la rose* or Dante's *Commedia*; in part, this is the result of a modern tendency to separate what one might call 'secular' allegory from other uses of figurative language in a devotional setting. I myself have been guilty of contributing to this tendency, having argued that the writings of Christine de Pizan are particularly representative of standard late medieval secular allegory (Akbari, *Seeing* 236–43).

While there are good reasons to read Christine's work as part of a lineage of allegorical literature, I have come to think that it is misleading to use the harsh dichotomy of 'secular allegory' and 'devotional writing' to characterize her writings. Following the argument of Barbara Newman that a number of medieval allegories can be seen as representative of a mode of writing we might call 'imaginative theology' (Newman 292–304), I would suggest that Christine can productively be read as a writer of 'devotional allegory.' Like the subgenre of 'devotional romance' that several readers (including myself) have proposed in recent years,[1] the subgenre of 'devotional allegory' may allow us to perceive the cross-fertilization of genres and figurative modes so characteristic of the early fifteenth century, an age of transition in many respects. Similarly, Christine's use of political allegory can be fruitfully studied in the context of the 'decision allegories' found in the work of Nicole Oresme, as well as in the broader framework of the late medieval proliferation of allegories focused on civic, national, and ecclesiastical division.[2] For Christine, as for other late medieval allegorists, the purposes of the enigmatic mode had moved far away from the abstruse philosophical allegories of the twelfth century; instead, allegory had come to be a figurative mode that could be used to describe the changes taking place in the surrounding world, and to account for the place of the individual within the swirl of time.

The Body Politic

The *Livre du corps de policie* is a political treatise concerning the welfare and conduct of the body politic: linking together its political counsel, however, is what we might call the 'political allegory' of the body. While this political allegory is threaded throughout the work as a whole, it is most succinctly articulated in a passage that appears in the third book of the *Corps de policie*, which focuses on the 'menu peuple,' that is, the 'little people' or 'commoners.'[3] Christine addresses to them a parable or 'fable' concerning the parts of the body:

> [H]ere is a moral tale composed in the guise of a fable.
>
> Once upon a time there was a great murmuring between the belly of the human body and its limbs ... Therefore the limbs stopped working, and the belly was no longer nourished, and so it began to grow thin, and the limbs to fail and become feeble. And thus, due to spite of the one toward the other, all perished together. Similarly, when the prince demands more of the people than they can provide, and when the people murmur against the prince, and rebel out of disobedience – in such discord, all perish together.
>
> And for this reason, the union of accord is the conservation of all the said body politic.[4]

> [C]hiet une telle moralité fourmee en guise de fable a propos.
>
> Une fois sourdit moult grant murmuracion entre le ventre de corps humain et les membres ... Si cesserent les membres de oeuvre, et le ventre plus ne fu nourri, si commença a amagrir et les membres a deffaillir et a affoibloier. Et ainsi en despit l'un de l'autre tout peri ensemble. Semblablement avient quant prince demande plus a peuple qu'il ne peut fournir, et que peuple murmure contre prince et se rebelle par desobeissance: tel descort perist tout ensemble.
>
> Et pour ce conclus que union d'accord est la conservacion de tout le dit corps de la policie. (3.1; Kennedy 92.6–25)

Versions of this 'fable' date back to the twelfth century, appearing in John of Salisbury's *Polycraticus* and, in a more developed version, in the *Fables* of Marie de France.[5] The need for all members of the body politic to work together for the good of the whole is stated in the starkest of terms: without the cooperation of all of the parts, the body becomes 'thin' and 'feeble,' and finally 'all perish together.' Here, death truly is the end, both of the individual and of the community as a whole.

One might expect to find this concise allegorical summary of the body politic placed at the opening of the work; instead, however, Christine opens the *Corps de policie* with a more oblique evocation of the body politic, one that focuses on her own role within the community. This is in keeping with Christine's approach throughout her allegorical works, in which the position of the autobiographical narrator is used as a kind of staging ground for the broader aims of the work as a whole. For example, her *Livre de la mutacion de Fortune* prefaces the account of the great movements of nations in its universal history with an allegorical autobiography of Christine herself, recounting how she too was changed by Fortune, while her *Livre de la cité des dames* opens with Christine alone in her study, unhappily contemplating a vast heritage of misogynistic literature before moving into a wide-ranging account of the great women of history and myth. Similarly, the *Livre du corps de policie* opens with Christine's identification of her own role within the body politic, one which, significantly, is defined by the obligation of the individual member of the community to express her *vertu*.

Consistently throughout her writings, Christine de Pizan expresses a passionate concern for the welfare of her community, whether that community be defined in terms of nation, in terms of gender, or in terms of a common allegiance to certain intellectual and philosophical principles. Nowhere, however, is Christine's concern for the welfare of the community expressed more passionately than in the opening lines of the *Corps de policie*:

> If it is possible for virtue to be born of vice, it pleases me very well, in this respect, to be impassioned as a woman. Thus, since many men assume that the female sex does not know how to keep quiet or to silence the abundance of their hearts, now come boldly, then, and be shown, through many clear streams, the source and inexhaustible fountain of my heart, which cannot be restrained from pouring forth the desires of virtue. Oh, Virtue, thing noble and divine, how can I dare to put myself forward by speaking of you, when I know that my understanding does not know you well and cannot express you?

> Se il est possible que de vice puist naistre vertu, bien me plaist en ceste partie estre passionnee comme femme. Ainsi que plusieurs hommes au sexe femenin imposent non savoir taire ne tenir soubz sillence l'abondance de leur courage, or viengne donc hors hardiement et se demonstre par plusieurs clers ruisseaux la source et fontaine interissable de mon couraige que ne peut estancher de getter hors les desirs de vertu. O vertu, chose digne et deifiee, comment m'ose-je vanter de parler de toy, quant je congnois que mon entendement ne te sauroit bien au vif comprendre ne exprimer? (1.1; Kennedy 1.6–14)

In this powerful passage, the passionate outpouring of *vertu* from the pen of the writer is representative of the same *vertu* that should infuse every member of the body politic, ensuring that the community is knit together in a state of social health, linked by the 'love' (1.1; Kennedy 2.4) expressed by each member towards all of the other members of the body.

As a number of scholars, including Kate Forhan and Cary Nederman, have pointed out, Christine's *Livre du corps de policie* draws upon John of Salisbury's extended metaphor of the body politic in order to outline the remedies available to the late medieval French state.[6] Christine alters John's anatomical metaphor, however, in order to elaborate on what one might call the 'physiological' aspects, illustrating how the social health of the body politic must be actively maintained. Nederman has shown that Christine's physiological amplification of John's fundamentally anatomical metaphor has parallels in the work of her contemporary Nicole Oresme: in his *De moneta*, Oresme emphasizes the role of economic exchange in dynamically maintaining the fiscal – and social – health of the nation.[7] Other studies of Christine's development of the metaphor of the body politic have focused on the crucial role of gender in Christine's imagining of the nation. Tsae Lan Lee Dow has gone so far as to suggest that Christine's reworking of John's metaphor actually 'feminizes' the body politic, constructing an idea of the nation that is not founded on the normative 'virile' body of the male (227–43). In a complementary study, Karen Green has argued that the personification of 'Felicité Vertueuse' [or 'virtuous happiness'] in the opening chapters of the *Corps de policie* is part of Christine's programmatic reworking of masculine normative forms in order to lay the groundwork not only for a specifically feminine poetics, but also for the exercise of political power by women.[8] In a series of articles focused on Christine de Pizan's writing about the French nation, Lori Walters has proposed that the opening of the *Corps de policie* features a 'female voice' that initially presents itself through 'female bodily metaphors,' but ultimately constructs a 'semimystical body combining male and female characteristics.'[9]

I propose to draw back from readings focused primarily on gender difference (which tends to be foregrounded in studies of Christine's work) in order to more fully explore the function of *vertu* in the *Livre du corps de policie*, showing how Christine expresses it in terms of two distinct discourses: that is, the devotional and the humoral. In each of these discourses, *vertu* functions as a liquid, mediating property that acts as a catalyst to enable motion and change. Within the terms of devotional discourse, *vertu* functions like blood or milk, calling forth an empathetic, affective response in the reader. Within the terms of Galenic discourse, *vertu* functions like one of the four humours whose balance is essential to the health of the body.[10] Within devotional discourse, *vertu* serves as a metonym for the nourishing, spiritually revivifying liquid of the divine presence; within the humoral discourse, *vertu* serves as a metaphor for the fluids that animate the body. Through *vertu*, the philosophical figure of the body politic and the affective figure of the suffering Christ are drawn together into a single quality that the narrator both offers as a remedy to her readers and adduces as the source of her own poetic inspiration.

In medieval Latin, as in vernacular languages of the late Middle Ages, the term *vertu* has several different meanings. On the level of created nature, *vertu* is life sustaining and regenerative, conveyed through the natural moisture that infuses all living things. Such uses of the term are ubiquitous in medieval culture: for example, in the thirteenth-century encyclopedia of Bartholomaeus Anglicus, *vertu* refers to the power of animation, the power of fecundity, of thought, of precious stones, of seeds, of eggs, of music, and so on.[11] Nowhere, however, are the multiple meanings of natural virtue more fully on display than in medieval medical writings, where every aspect of the physiology of the living body is articulated through the expression of virtue – from the digestive powers located in the stomach and liver, to the generative powers of reproduction, to the expulsive powers driving fluids out of the body, to the humours that actively maintain and propagate the smooth workings of all of the body's parts. The faculties of the mind as it thinks and the faculties of the senses as they mediate between the outside world and the interior, sensitive soul are all characterized in terms of *vertu*.

The extraordinary accomplishment of the *Livre du corps de policie* is that, in it, Christine draws together the various applications of natural *vertu* and integrates them with ethical virtue: in other words, the expression of moral virtues such as prudence or temperance is characterized in terms of natural processes that (in medical writing) are also expressed in terms of *vertu*. Such integration is not unprecedented in medieval culture: late medieval philosophers and theologians worked hard to amalgamate Aristotelian and Augustinian notions of virtue,[12] and a popular, vernacular audience was addressed on this topic by Brunetto Latini in the late thirteenth century. In book one of his *Tresor*, Brunetto describes the 'vertu' of the soul, including sense perception (1.15, pp. 12–13), and the 'vertus' of the body, including the 'apetitive, retentive, digiestive et espulsive' (1.102, pp. 66–7). Book two, titled 'on vices and virtues' ('des vices et de vertus'), devotes its first fifty chapters to a vernacular translation of Aristotle's *Ethics* before turning to a compendium of authorities ranging from Cicero and Seneca to Augustine and Bernard, all centring on the nature of 'vertu' (2.52; pp. 203–6). Brunetto thus integrates Aristotelian philosophy with Christian theology in a synthetic redefinition of *vertu*, and implies – but does not state explicitly – that this *vertu* is to be identified, at least figuratively, with the virtues that animate the body.

It is precisely this synthesis that Christine de Pizan effects in her *Livre du corps de policie*. Christine coordinates natural *vertu* with the ethical expression of *vertu*, indicating that this quality must be expressed not only by the ruler (as head of the body politic), but also by the knightly class (as its arms and hands), and by the 'common people' (as its belly and lower limbs):

> which three kinds of estate ought to be in one single polity just like a real living body, according to the teachings of Plutarch who, in a letter that he sent to Trajan the emperor, compares the republic ['chose publique'; cf. *res publica*] to a living body, in which the prince or the princes hold the place of the head ... The knights and the nobles hold the place of the hands and the arms ... The other types of people are like the belly and the feet and the legs, for just as the belly receives everything into itself that is provided by the head and the limbs, just so the workings of the prince and the nobles must be directed to the good, and for the love of the public, as will be explained more fully later on. And just as the legs and the feet sustain the deeds of the human body, similarly the laborers sustain all the other estates.
>
> lesquelz trois genres d'estat doivent estre en une seule policie ainsi comme un droit corps vif, selon la sentence de pultarque qui en une epistre qu'il envoya a Trajen l'empereur compare la chose publique a un corps aiant vie, auquel le prince ou les princes tiennent le lieu du chief ... Les chevaliers et les nobles tiennent le lieu des mains et des bras ... Les autres gens de peuple sont comme le ventre et les piez et les jambes, car si comme le ventre reçoit tout en soy ce que prepare le chief et les membres, ainsi le fait de l'exercite du prince et des nobles doit revertir ou bien et en l'amour publique, si comme cy aprés sera plus declairiée. Et ainsi comme les jambes et piez soustiennent le fais du corps humain, semblement les laboureurs soustiennent tous les autres estas. (1.1; Kennedy 1.27–33, 2.1–7)

Each of the three parts of the *Livre du corps de policie* corresponds to each of the three 'estas'; each estate is, in turn, instructed in the expression of moral virtue. Such expression of moral virtue will lead to the health and growth of the body politic, a process which is articulated in physiological terms based on the workings of natural virtue in the living body.

Christine's use of *vertu* in the *Corps de policie* is, as I have begun to suggest, polysemous, and this polysemy is further enriched by the description of personified virtue in the opening sections of the work. In a passage that has attracted attention from a number of scholars, Christine describes an 'image' of 'Felicité Vertueuse' 'in the form of a very beautiful and very delightful queen seated on a royal throne' ['en guise d'une tres belle et tres delictative royne qui en une chaiere royal seoit' (1.2; 2.29–30)], surrounded by the personified virtues of Prudence, Justice, Force, and Temperance ('Atrempance'). As Karen Green points out, Christine's modification of her source, Augustine's *City of God*, is based not in an erroneous reading of Augustine but rather a deliberate reworking of the image: Green argues that the effect is to emphasize the role of the feminine – and, perhaps, the role of actual women rulers – in the exercise of political power (Green 134). Here, however, I would like instead to draw attention to the way in which the personification of Felicité Vertueuse forms the basis of Christine's physiological, dynamic model of the body politic, where *vertu* functions as the nutritive fluid of the state. Each of the personified virtues maintains the health of the body politic: Prudence ensures that Felicité Vertueuse 'is able to reign for a long time, and remain healthy, and in a secure state' ['peust longuement regner et estre saigne et en estat seur' (1.2; 2.33–5)], while Force makes sure that, 'if any sorrow come to her body, that she moderate it by resistant and virtuous thought' ['se aucune douleur venoit a son corps qu'elle l'amoderast par resistant et vertueuse pensee' (1.2; 2.36–7)]. Temperance ensures the health of the body politic by ensuring that she only moderately consume 'wines and meats and other delightful things' ['vins et viandes et autres choses delictables' (1.2; 2.37–3.1)]. That is to say, the personification of Felicité Vertueuse is significant not simply in terms of gender, but also in terms of embodiment: the virtuous quality of this felicity lies in its active maintenance of the flow of life forces within the body politic.

This dynamic flow of life forces through the medium of *vertu* recalls the opening passage of the *Livre du corps de policie*, discussed above, in which Christine's narrator explicitly couches the call to health that she directs to the people of France in terms of the upwelling of *vertu*. Here, *vertu* is explicitly characterized as that which is 'born' from vice, and which manifests itself as a 'pouring forth,' a liquid stream that offers revivifying nourishment to the body politic in the form of exhortation towards moral and ethical virtues. This liquid quality of *vertu* appears once again in the passage that immediately follows the long description of the personified Felicité Vertueuse:

> Now we have to discuss virtue, to the profit of the order of living for all three different estates; by this said virtue, human life must be regulated in all works and, without it, no man may attain honor; and so that it be the right degree of honor, Valerius says that the most plenteous nourishment of virtue is honor.

Ainsi doncques nous avons a traictier de vertu au proufit d'order de vivre en trois differences d'estas par laquelle dicte vertu vie humaine doit estre ruillee en toutes oeuvres et sans qui ne peut homme a honneur ataindre, et que elle soit le droit degré de honneur dit Valere que les tres plantureux nourissement de vertu est honneur. (1.2; Kennedy 2.9–13)

In this passage, *vertu* nourishes each part of the body politic, thereby leading to the nourishment of the whole. Such proper flowing of liquid virtue is what conduces towards not just the nourishment but also the health of the body politic:

And thus by this present description, one may understand that being virtuous is nothing other than having within oneself all the things that draw towards good, and which draw outward and away all that is bad and full of vice. Therefore, it is necessary that, in order to govern the public body politic, the head be healthy, that is, virtuous. For if it should be sick, all [parts] will feel it as well. Therefore let us begin to speak of the medicine for the head, that is, for the king or the princes.

Et ainsi par ceste presente descripcion puet-on entendre que estre vertueux n'est autre chose fors avoir en soy toutes les choses qui tirent a bien et qui retraient et tirent en sus de mal et de vice. Doncques est-il neccessaire pour bien gouverner le corps de la policie publique que le chief soit sain, c'est a savoir vertueux. Car s'il estoit malade, tout s'en sentiroit. Sy commencerons a dire de la medicine du chief, c'est a savoir du roy ou des princes. (1.2; Kennedy 3.3–9)

The first of the book's three sections will exhort the 'head' of the body politic towards virtue, which is to say, towards 'health': 'if the head [of the body] is healthy,' Christine writes – 'that is, virtuous' – the parts of the body will follow. *Vertu* itself is defined as precisely the 'having within oneself all the things that draw toward good, and which draw outward and away all that is bad and full of vice.' Here, *vertu* functions like the natural *vertu* described in humoral theory, having the property to attract or repulse, to draw things inward or to drive them outward.

The proper working of *vertu* thus leads toward nourishment and health of the body politic, and also leads away from the incipient dangers of dismemberment and disease:

For just as the human body is not at all whole, but rather defective and deformed when one of its members is lacking, similarly the body politic cannot be perfect, whole, or healthy unless all the estates under discussion be in a good conjunction and union all together, so that they can succour and aid one another, each one exercising the office it must serve; which various offices ought to serve only for the conservation of all together, just as the members of the human body aid in the movement and nourishing of the whole body. And just as soon as one of them fails to serve, it follows that the whole body feels it and it and suffers famine by it.

Car tout ainsi comme le corps humain n'est mie entier, mais deffectueulx et diffourmé quant il lui fault aucun de ses membres, semblablement ne peut le corps de policie estre parfait, entier ne sain se tous les estas dont nous traictons ne sont en bonne conjonction et union ensemble, si qu'ilz puissent secourir et aidier l'un a l'autre, chascun excercitant l'office de quoy il doit servir, lesquelz divers offices ne sont a tout considerer establis et ne doivent servir ne mes pour la conservacion de tout ensemble, tout ainsi comme les membres de corps humain aident a gouverner et nourrir tout le corps. Et si tost comme l'un d'eulx deffault, couvient que tout le corps s'en sente et en ait disete. (3.1; Kennedy 91.16–26)

For perfect health of the body politic to exist, unity is necessary: all the various 'estates' must be 'in a good conjunction and union all together,' so that each aids the other. If one part fails, the body is dismembered; if the body loses the good of one member, the whole falls into starvation and corruption.

This unity of the various parts of the body politic through the medium of *vertu* is enabled through a related, complementary medium, one which is expressed not through affections of the body but through affections of the soul. This medium is love, as Christine makes clear in the opening of the third book of the *Corps de policie*, where she exhorts the common people to virtue:

just as we spoke before about the love and care that the good prince ought to have toward his subjects and his people, and similarly of the office of the nobles, who are established for the care and the defense of the said people, now we must speak of the love, reverence, and obedience that the good people ought to have toward the prince. So let us speak universally to all, to the extent that it relates to this matter, how all estates owe to the prince the selfsame love, reverence, and obedience.

comme nous avons devant dit de l'amour et cure que le bon prince doit avoir vers ses subgiez et peuple, et aussi de l'office des nobles, lesquelz sont establis

> pour la garde et deffence du dit peuple, dire nous couvient de l'amour, reverence et obeissance que bon peuple doit avoir envers prince. Si dirons universelement a tous en tant que touche ceste matiere, comme tous estas doient au prince une meisme amour, reverence et obeissance. (3.1; Kennedy 91.30–6)

Christine describes a reciprocal arrangement that involves all three estates that make up the body politic, but which seems to exist with a greater specificity between the first and the remaining parts of the state, that is, between the ruler and all of his people, both nobles and commons. Just as the prince must express 'amour' towards his subjects, so too the people owe to their 'prince une meisme amour,' the self-same love that he expresses towards them. This common love is exactly the same 'amour publique' that circulates among and thus unites all parts of the 'chose publique' or republic of France (1.1; 1.27–2.7).

This love is also evident in the passionate exhortation expressed by the narrator in the opening lines of the *Corps de policie*: she is motivated by love of the French people and their king to express moral teachings that will lead to the renewed *vertu* – and, therefore, health – of the state. This 'amour' that unifies the king and his people can, moreover, be more fully contextualized with reference to the theological template for the body politic, that is, the loving relationship of Christ to the Church, which is simultaneously both bride and body of Christ. The sacramental language of *vertu*, used to describe the quality that unites Christ with his Church, provides a template for the conceptualization of a specifically Christian model of kingship that Christine expresses most fully in her biography of Charles V. Like the language of *vertu* used in the *Corps de policie* to describe the health and security of the body politic, the sacramental language of *vertu* is frequently expressed in liquid terms. For example, the holy water used for baptism is commonly said to be imbued with 'virtue,' while the transubstantiation of water into wine, bread into flesh, is said to take place 'through the virtue of the Mass.'[13] In order to understand this allegorical function of *vertu* more fully, it is necessary to turn to Christine's devotional allegory in her biography of Charles V.

The King's Body

It is strange but true that Christine de Pizan's most explicit articulation of her preferred genre of allegory appears not in her specifically allegorical works, but rather in her biography of the late ruler of France, Charles V. Before turning to her statement of allegory in the *Livre des fais et bonnes meurs du sage roy Charles V*, however, it is useful to look more closely at Christine's position within the literary tradition of late medieval allegory, and at the unusual way in which she defines the genre. Because Christine self-consciously presents herself as a writer following in the tradition of earlier allegorists, especially Boethius, Alan of Lille, Jean de Meun, and Dante, it is tempting to read her allegories as part of a continuous literary genealogy linking a series of writers with shared assumptions regarding the function of figurative language. Christine's assumptions differ significantly, however, from her predecessors. Instead of describing figurative language in terms of 'alegorie' (a term she reserves to describe allegoresis, or allegorical exposition), she uses the terms 'poesie' and 'methafore.' Both of these terms are central to my argument here, with 'poesie' being closely connected to a form of allegorical exegesis in Christine's biography of Charles V, and 'methafore' being closely connected to Christine's depiction of moments of stark corporeal change. In both cases, whether expressed in terms of 'poesie' or 'methafore,' the transformative property of death – whether in the last days of the king or in the mythical figure of Atropos – appears as the fundamental mediator of all change, whether ontological or epistemological.

Christine's two most explicit definitions of 'poesie' appear in a preface to her last allegorical work, the *Advision Cristine*, and in her biography of Charles V.[14] In the third and last part of her biography of the late king, Christine includes what appears at first to be a digression 'concerning understanding and ways of knowing' ['de l'entendement et des sciences']. The apparent digression begins with an account of the senses and ends with a description of 'poesie,' which, Christine says, uses figurative language to convey meanings that 'cannot be expressed clearly' ['clerement ne se pevent enseigner' (3.68)]. Although Christine refers to this kind of language as 'poesie,' her description of it closely resembles typical medieval definitions of allegory. Christine writes that 'poesie' is generally taken to be any 'narration or introduction openly signifying one sense, and covertly signifying another or many others' ['narracion ou introduction apparaument signifiant un senz, et occultement en segnefie un aultre ou plusieurs']. More properly, Christine continues, 'poesie' is a mode 'whose end is truth, and the process of which is teaching, clothed [*revestue*] in words of delightful ornament and in the appropriate colors of rhetoric; with those clothes [*revestemens*] being of unusual styles in keeping with the purpose that one desires, and the colors of rhetoric according to appropriate figures' ['dont la fin est verité, et le proces doctrine revestue en paroles d'ornemens delictables et par propres couleurs, lesquelz revestemens soient d'estranges guises au propos dont on veult' (3.68)]. In this definition, Christine uses several terms that are conventional to descriptions of allegory: the text signifies one thing openly, another covertly; it may have several levels of meaning; its purpose is to convey truth; and it clothes meaning with pleasant words, an allusion to the *integument* (a technical term, particularly common in the twelfth century), which is literally a veil or covering. Finally, among writers of 'poesie' Christine goes on to list several allegorists, including Boethius, Martianus Capella, and Alan of Lille.

After offering this description of 'poesie,' however, Christine abruptly draws back from this mode of writing, she states, 'because, to the many who have not learned it, this language may seem strange, and consequently bore them, let us return to our first objective' ['pour cause que a maint pourroit le lengage sembler estrange, qui apris ne l'ont, et par consequent tourner a anui, retournerons a nostre premier objett' (3.69)] – that is, to the thread of the biography's narrative line, currently at the account of Charles's death. Overtly, then, Christine indicates that a political biography is not the place for language that veils its meaning in order to restrict interpretation to a few. Covertly, however, she signals that, for those few who do understand such 'strange language,' it may be possible to find a veiled significance in the biography of the former king. To put it another way, the historical narrative of Charles's life is the ground for figurative explication, in the same way that sacred histories of the Bible are subject to exegesis, or the historical narratives evoked in Dante's *Commedia* are unfolded within the hermeneutics of the 'allegory of theologians.' The fact that Christine identifies this form of figurative language as 'poesie' suggests, moreover, that 'poesie' can refer to veiled language that does not necessarily have a fiction as its literal level. On the contrary, we can read historical narrative – such as the life of Charles V – as 'poesie' just as we can more conventionally read the *narratio fabulosa*, or 'fabulous narrative,' of the integument. In this striking move, biography is assimilated to the genre of allegory, with the exemplary figure being not a personification, but a person – that is, Charles, king of France.[15]

Critics who discuss Christine's treatment of 'poesie' in the biography of Charles V generally overlook one of the most interesting and revealing features of that treatment, namely, the placement of those chapters. Significantly, Christine's definition of 'poesie' appears in conjunction with her account of the king's death, recounting the paradoxical disruption and continuity of that moment in the life of the nation. The substance that maintains this continuity is, as in the *Livre du corps de policie*, *vertu*. In the biography of Charles V, the virtues of the king – that is, his deeds and good morals – are at the centre of a narrative that treats the life of the ruler and the life of the state as a single entity. The death of the king's natural body does not entail the death of the state, however, because the *vertu* of kingship is perpetual, passed on in an endlessly renewed chain of descent. In this context, the final chapters of the biography – which constitute an extended meditation on 'ends' or 'fins' – are of special importance, for they chronicle the paradoxical moment when the end of the king's natural body is subsumed into the continued perpetual health of the body politic. The concept of the 'fin' or 'end' in the biography of Charles V is polysemous, with 'ends' denoting not just the chronological terminus of a process but also its *telos*, that is, the culmination or fruition of a process. In this multivalent sense, the 'end' of the biography of Charles V includes 1) the chronological end or completion of the book itself; 2) the conceptual end or goal of the book; 3) the end – that is, the death – of the subject of the biography, the monarch Charles V; and 4) the end – that is, the enduring legacy, that which remains – of Charles's reign. The meditation on the 'end' of Charles – that is, the ending of his mortal life, and the purpose of his existence – is central to the articulation of what we might call 'devotional allegory' in Christine's work.

Leading up to the culminating dozen or so chapters of the biography, Christine begins to signal that the meditation on 'ends' is at hand:

> And it is now time that I draw toward the end of my work, in ending the process of the particular praising of the deeds and good mores of this wise king, whom I have described; but ... my last conclusion will be of wisdom alone.

> Si est dès or temps que je tire vers la fin de mon oeuvre, en terminant le procès des particulieres louenges des fais et bonnes meurs de cestui sage roy, dont j'ay traittié; mais ... ma desreniere conclusion sera de sapience aucunement. (ch. 62; 158)

As Christine draws towards the 'end' of the work, she approaches the 'end' of 'this wise king'; her 'conclusion,' however, will be purely of wisdom, as 'deeds and good mores' drop away and are eclipsed by the simple light of wisdom. How are these multiple 'ends' integrated together? On a narrative level, simply enough, the discourse of the biography draws to a close as the life of the biographical subject draws to a close.[16] On a more complex level, however, the 'end' denotes not just termination, but *telos*: that is, destination, trajectory, fulfilment. In this sense, the 'end' is the harvest or fruition of all that has come before. 'Sapience,' or wisdom, for Christine is part of this harvest. It is therefore unsurprising that the various chapters nested within the introduction to the 'end' of the work, and the final three chapters of the work, which recount the death of the king, concern topics such as understanding and knowledge, sense perception, prudence, the sciences and metaphysics, and, finally, 'poesie' ('de l'entendement et des sciences' [63–4], 'des sens du corps' [65], 'prudence' [66], 'des sciences, et de ceulz qui les trouverent' [67], 'poesie' [68]). All of these things are the 'end' of the work, that is, they are both situated *at* the end of the work, in narrative terms, and *are* themselves the end, that is, the goal or *telos*.

The language of 'ends' is repeatedly threaded throughout these chapters. To cite just one example, in the chapter on prudence, Christine alludes to how this virtue has been 'interwoven throughout the abundance of other matters leading to the end' ['Pour ce que cy devant fu entamée la matiere de traittier de la vertu de prudence, entrelaissié par l'abondence des autres matieres traire à ffin' [66; 167]). Here again, the end is both the end of the narrative and the goal of the endeavour. The penultimate chapter, which immediately precedes the account of Charles's death, accordingly focuses on 'what goods come from the things spoken of below' ['quel bien vient des choses susdittes' (69)], that is, the harvest that grows out of the narrative of the life of Charles, and the harvest that grows out of his life itself. These latter goods are spiritual benefits that accrue both to the individual soul of the king and to the community he leaves behind him. The former goods (those that grow out of the biography) are also spiritual benefits, which permit future generations to partake in the same abundant goods as did those who were fortunate enough to live during Charles's reign.

Following this exposition of the good that flows out of the 'end' of Charles, Christine turns sharply to the account of the death itself: she states, 'let us return to our first object,' 'it is time to come to an end' ['retournerons à nostre premier objett' (178); '[il] est temps de terminer' (179)]. The rubrics of the three final chapters sufficiently indicate their focus: one on 'the approach of the end of King Charles,' one on 'the passing away and beautiful end of the wise King Charles,' and one on 'the end and conclusion of this book' (70: 'l'aprochement de la fin du roy Charles'; 71: 'le trespassement et belle fin du sage roy Charles'; 72: 'la fin et conclusion de ce livre'). The termination of the king, and of the book, are mirrored and fulfilled in the ends – that is, the bountiful rewards – they provide:

> Just as it is clearly known and understood that all created things have an end, for all things are drawn this way, in getting near to the end of our work, let us

speak of the last period of this wise one, concerning whom we took up this matter and contents of this book; and just so says the common proverb, 'In the end one may know the perfection of the thing,' we may truly, in the last end of our said wise king, know the perfection of his very highly elevated virtues and wisdom.

Ainsi comme clerement est sceu et cogneu toutes choses creées avoir fin, car ad ce se trayent toutes ycelles, en aprestant la fin de nostre oeuvre, dirons du desrenier terme d'ycellui sage, ouquel avons prise la matiere et contenu de ce livre; et tout ainsi que dit le commun proverbe: 'En la fin peut on cognoistre la perfection de la chose,' povons vrayement, à la perfin de nostre dit sage roy cognoistre la perfection de ses tres preesleues vertus et sapience. (*Charles V* 3.70; Solente 180)

The duality of the polysemous 'end,' appearing in the simultaneity of the 'fin' of the king and of the narrative, and in the 'fin' – that is, the 'goods' – arising from his reign and from the biography of him, is amplified dramatically in the detailed account of Charles's death. His death is recounted in terms of a whole series of binary oppositions. While he suffers from a terminal 'enfermeté,' he continues to display 'sain entendement' and 'saine discrecion' ['healthy understanding' and 'healthy discretion' (182)]. While his body displays the 'signes mortelz' of approaching death, the king continues to utter prayers and make 'signs of great faith in Our Lord' ['signes de grant foy à Nostre Seigneur' (185)]. This duality is finally emblematized in the episode of the two crowns:

He requested that the crown of thorns of Our Lord be brought to him by the bishop of Paris, and also that the abbé of Saint-Denis bring him the crown for the coronation of the kings. That of thorns he received with great devotion, tears, and reverence, and had it raised up high before his face; that of the coronation he had placed at his feet. Then he began to utter prayers to the holy crown: 'Oh, precious crown ...' And he said long prayers there and very devout. After that, he turned his words toward the crown of France, and said, 'Oh, crown! How precious you are, and how extremely vile!'

[Il] requist que la couronne d'espines de Nostre-Seigneur par l'evesque de Paris lui fust aportée, et aussi par l'abbé de Saint-Denis la couronne du sacre des roys. Celle d'espines receupt à grant devocion, larmes et reverence, et haultement la fist mettre devant sa face; celle du sacre fist mettre à ses piez. Adonc commença telle oroison à la sainte couronne: 'O couronne precieuse ...' Et longue oroison y dist moult devote. Après, tourna ses paroles à la couronne de France, et dist: 'O couronne! Quan tu es precieuse, et precieusement tres vile!' (3.71; 187)

This duality, emblematized in the two crowns, is more than a reaffirmation of the birth of the soul into eternal life even as the body descends into death. It is an integral part of Christine's devotional allegory, in which typology affirms destiny.

In the chapter on 'poesie' that precedes the concluding account of the death of Charles, Christine recalls that 'figures' (that is, figurative language) are amply attested both in the literature of the ancients and in the sacred page of the Bible. She writes, 'the Old Testament was entirely made up of figures, and similarly Jesus Christ spoke in figures' ['l'ancien Testament fu tout fait par figures, meismement aussi Jhesu-Crist si parla par figures' (67; 177)]. It is not remarkable to cite Jesus's parables as a precedent for the use of figurative language; to describe the entire Old Testament as made up of 'figures,' however, sets up a typological relationship of type and antitype, anticipation and fulfilment, that will be a crucial substrate of Christine's account of the 'end' of Charles V. As he suffers, moving ever closer to his 'end,' Charles mirrors the suffering Christ, and he offers spiritual gifts to those who sorrowfully attend his last days. Charles's reflection of Christ's passion, and his people's reflection of Charles's own passion, becomes increasingly apparent as the text goes on. His words, 'full of such great faith, devotion, and knowledge of God,' move 'all hearing them ... to great repentance and tears.' Passages similar to this one, in which those who observe Charles's suffering come to participate in it, appear frequently in this part of the biography.[17]

This mirroring of the Passion culminates, finally, in a passage that highlights the typological relationship fundamental to Christine's devotional allegory:

A little later, approaching the period of the end ['le terme de la fin'; literally, 'the end of the end'], in the manner of the ancient patriarchs of the Old Testament, he had brought before him his elder son, the dauphin; then, in blessing him, he began to speak this way: 'Just as Abraham [with] his son Isaac ...' This mystery completed ... he blessed all those present, saying this, 'May the blessings of God the Father, the Son, and the Holy Spirit, descend upon you and remain forever'; the which benediction everyone received upon their knees, with great devotion and tears.

Un peu après, en approchant le terme de la fin, en la maniere des anciens Peres patriarches du viel Testament, fist amener devant lui son filz ainsné, le daufin;

> alors, en le beneissant, commença ainsi à dire: 'Ainsi comme Abraham son filz Ysaac ...' Ce mistere fait ... beney tous les presens, disant ainsi: 'Benedicio Dei, Patris et Filii et Spiritus sancti, descendat super vos et maneat semper'; laquelle beneïçon receurent tous à genoulz, à grant devocion et larmes. (3.71; 190–1)

As in a series of preceding passages, the affective response of the assembled community reflects their participation in the spectacle of the death of the king. His suffering knits together the community into the imagined community of the nation, just as the suffering of Christ unites the body of the Church. Here, however, Charles is both Abraham and Christ, both the father who bestows the blessing on his offspring and the Son who accepts the will of the Father. In Charles, then, the blessings of the Trinity appear in microcosm, and serve as a nexus that binds together the Christian nation of France – even if only temporarily.

It is this very temporariness, however, that Christine refutes in her polysemous notion of the 'end' in the devotional allegory of Charles's life. In chronological terms, the life of Charles – and his biography – has reached its 'end.' In eternal terms, however, the life of Charles has its 'end' (that is, its fulfilment) in the eternal present, in which the bounty of his life, and Christine's recounting of his life, continue perpetually to bear spiritual fruit. The protracted process of Charles's death, which extends over the last eleven chapters of the biography, beginning with Christine's promise to 'draw toward the end of [her] work,' continues to be drawn out as a series of successive signs of suffering, and signs of affective response, mark the slow progress towards the moment of death – towards the 'end.' This is heightened still more in Christine's account of Charles's last moments: 'He listened to the whole story of the Passion, and almost to the end of the gospel of John, and began to labor toward his last end' ['(Il) oy toute l'ystoire de la Passion, et aucques près de la fin de l'Euvangile saint Jehan, commença a labourer à sa desreniere fin' (71; 191–2)]. The narrative Charles hears, 'almost to the end,' brings him closer – but not quite – to 'his last end' ['sa desreniere fin']. This stretched-out process of time enables the reader to approach – but not quite touch – the moment of change, when body is left behind and the soul departs, when the king's reign ends and only the 'biens' or 'goods' remain, when the biographical narrative concludes and the memory lingers.

The Ends of Virtue

In Christine's biography of Charles V, virtue appears in the ethical and moral rectitude of this exemplary ruler and has its supreme expression in the hours and days leading up to his death. The moment of death witnesses the perfect convergence of the king's two bodies: as the body natural fades away, the body politic is renewed, mediated through the virtue of Christian kingship. The virtue of the king, and his surpassing wisdom, lie in the transcendence of his ethical, political virtue by spiritual, devout virtue. To put it another way, Charles expresses moral and ethical virtues in an exemplary manner; his own *vertu*, however, his transformative power to renew and regenerate the body politic, is mediated not through his virtuous life but, more specifically, through his way of dying. The death of the king is paradoxically a moment of both change and stability. This same paradox is also the focus of Christine de Pizan's narratives of Ovidian metamorphosis, in which (as in the *Ovide moralisé*) transformation entails a paradoxical reaffirmation of essential identity.[18] For Christine, 'methafore' – an unusual term in medieval allegory – is intimately intertwined with metamorphosis, and it finds its most profound expression, unsurprisingly, in the greatest transformation of them all: that is, death.

Christine's best-known use of the term 'methafore' appears in the famous autobiographical scene that concludes book one of the *Livre de la mutacion de Fortune*, where she recounts how she was miraculously transformed by the goddess from a woman into a man, a change that enabled her to become the financial and social supporter of her family. The same term reappears later in the same work, in the course of her description of Atropos, one of the Fates, who together with three personifications guards the four entrances to Fortune's castle. The curious inclusion of Atropos within a group of personifications is explained by Christine as a use of 'methafore,' a usage reinforced in the account of Atropos given in Christine's first allegorical work, the *Epistre Othea*. In the *Mutacion*, as in the *Epistre Othea*, Atropos represents the liminal point that marks not the end of life, but the transition from one state of being (life on earth) to another (eternal life of the soul). She therefore makes an appropriate emblem of transformation, whether realized in the form of Ovidian metamorphosis or in the form of figurative change – that is, metaphor.

The notion of metamorphosis in late medieval translations of and commentaries on Ovid was conceived in terms that explicitly framed death as an agent of the final metamorphosis. Like a butterfly emerging from its shell, the experience of death was understood as a gateway from the confines of the material world to the liberation of the eternal life of the soul. The extent to which Ovidian descriptions of metamorphosis served as the template for medieval images of death can be seen in a brief quotation from a manual on how to die well written by Jean Gerson, chancellor of the University of Paris and close associate of Christine de Pizan:

> My hands grow cold, my face grows pale, my eyes turn backward and are sunken in my head ... My strength grows faint, my mouth is blackened, my tongue fails and my breath also. I cannot see at all.
>
> Les mains me [f]roidissent, la face me paslist, mes yeulx me tournent et parfondissent en la teste ... Mon pouoir commence a defaillir, la bouche me noircist, la langue me fault et mon alaine aussi. Je ne voy plus goutte. (Gerson 119)

Reading this passage, it is difficult not to recall the 'fearful changes' experienced by figures in the *Metamorphoses*, as the bark closes over the face of Myrrha, or Daphne reaches upward as her arms are clothed with leaves. Death was understood as a kind of metamorphosis, and metamorphosis was expressed most fully at the moment of death, when flesh would fall away and the new, true form of the soul would emerge.[19]

As a writer of allegory, in which the trope of language clothes meaning within a beautiful and obscuring veil, Christine sought to integrate such conceptions of metamorphosis with her usage of figurative language. Her treatment of metamorphosis as a paradoxical revelation of essential identity, therefore, was aligned in her writing with a conception of language as a covering which paradoxically exposes the truth that lies behind. In the *Mutacion de Fortune*, Christine asserts that 'it is not a lie to speak according to metaphor, which does not put the truth in front' ['qui ne met la verité fore']. In this definition of allegorical language as metaphor, figurative language appears as that which places truth *behind* – that is, conceals it behind a veil or covering. In the biography of Charles V, by contrast, Christine defines allegorical language as 'poesie,' language 'whose end is truth' ['dont la fin est verité']. Figurative language, then, places truth either behind (as in 'methafore') or ahead (as in 'poesie'). In each case, knowledge of truth is displaced spatially: wherever it is, it is not where we are.

Within the terms of the devotional allegory of the biography of Charles V, the deferral of full, unmediated knowledge of truth is in keeping with the Christian expectation that the soul's full knowledge of God will come only with the experience of the Beatific Vision, when the individual can hope to see the divine 'face to face.' Within the terms of the political allegory of the *Corps de policie*, however, the deferral of full knowledge is more problematic and, arguably, unsatisfactory. The *Corps de policie* acts as a kind of handbook of conduct, like Christine's *Livre des trois vertus*; it does not, however, address the deeper questions of how and why the body politic comes into being. One might say that it is directed towards practical rather than theoretical knowledge.

As early as the twelfth century, with John of Salisbury, the metaphor of the body politic was explicitly formulated on the model of Christian community, in which the Church is itself the body of Christ. Just as Christ has a natural body and a spiritual body, made up of the community of the Church, so too the king has a natural body and a 'body politic.' While John of Salisbury explicitly grounds his conception of the body politic in classical antiquity, citing Plutarch's address to Trajan as his source (though no such source appears to exist), explicitly Christian antecedents lie behind John's formulation: these include not only the foundational Pauline analogy of the body of Christ (1 Cor. 12:12–28), but also twelfth-century elaborations of the parallelism between the power of the Church and of the State expressed by figures such as Robert Pullen.[20]

The late fourteenth and early fifteenth centuries witnessed a renewal and an elaboration of the devotional underpinnings of the metaphor of the body politic, as Lori Walters has shown in her work on Christine's use of Augustine's *City of God* and its role in the emergence of medieval forms of French national identity.[21] A particularly pointed example of the convergence of sacramental language and the expression of national identity can be found in the early fifteenth-century English Parliament rolls, in which an extended analogy is drawn between the Parliament and the Mass, with the king in the place of the priest:

> The said Commons put forth to the king that it seemed to them that the Parliament could be likened to a Mass ... And in the middle of the Mass, when the sacrifice is offered to God on behalf of all the Christians, the King, to accomplish this goal, has at the Parliament many times declared plainly to all his liegemen that his will is that the faith of Holy Church should be sustained and governed just as it was in the time of his noble progenitors ... And, moreover, at the end of the Mass it is necessary to say, 'Ite missa est, et Deo gratias'; similarly, it is performed by the Commons.

> Les dites Communes monstrerent au Roy, Coment leur sembloit, que le fait de Parlement purroit estre bien resemblez a une Messe ... Et a la mesne de la Messe, qe feust la sacrifice d'estre offertz a Dieux pur toutz Cristiens, la Roi mesmes a cest Parlement pur acomplir celle mesne, pleuseurs foitz avoit declarez pleinement as toutz ses lieges, Coment sa volunte feust, que la Foie de Seinte Esglise serroit sustenuz et governez en manere come il ad este en temps

de ses nobles progenitours ... Et auxint au fyne de chescun Messe y covient de dire, Ite missa est, et Deo gratias. Semblement y feust monstrez par mesmes les Communes. (*Rotuli parliamentorum* 3:466 [15 March 1400/1])[22]

In its patterning of the body politic on the body of Christ – that is, the community of the Church – this record from the English Parliament is relatively conventional. What is striking is the way in which the 'Commons' are drawn into the performance of the body politic, affirming their participation in a political ritual that is presented as a secular reflection of the ecclesiastical ritual of the Mass. Further, it is striking that this reaffirmation of the unity of the body politic was uttered in the Parliament of Henry IV just months after the deposition and execution of his cousin, the former Richard II. In the face of disruption and discontinuity of rule, the incorporate nature of the body politic had to be reaffirmed in the strongest terms, namely, in terms of the eucharistic body of Christ.

While France did not suffer the removal and execution of its king, the political unrest of the first years of the fifteenth century was certainly comparable to the state of affairs across the Channel. Christine's biography of Charles V, written in 1404, was both a celebration of the virtuous rule of the former king and a prayer, one might say, that a similar time of peace and benign rule might be at hand. Her *Corps de policie*, written just a few years later, expresses even more plainly the extent to which the restoration of national harmony depended on more than just leadership from the head of the body politic: it required active participation by all members of the body, including the 'menu peuple' or commons. Like their king and the chivalric ranks, they too were expected to express *vertu*. This was a new development, for fourteenth-century descriptions of *vertu* in sacramental terms were restricted to the role of the king. This can be seen, for example, in the early fourteenth-century *Ovide moralisé*, one of the literary sources that Christine drew upon most frequently. In this passage, which describes the shield of Perseus, sacramental language is used to express chivalric virtue:

The shield has a round form
In order to make it known
That God is without beginning
And without end, eternal:
He is the triangular alpha
And the omega, simple and singular,
Who begins all, and ends all,

And encompasses all, by divine virtue.
...
The fourth heraldic stripe represents the sacrifice
That the priest celebrates and consecrates,
When by the virtue of the holy sacrament
The bread and wine upon the altar
Become divine flesh and blood,
Just as God consecrated them
Who blessed his flesh and his blood
When he wanted to give his peace
To his apostles at Cana.
It is the body of God, who was hung
Upon the cross, and the blood poured forth
When for our redemption
The Son of God endured his passion.
It is the food, it is the life,
That gives the soul peace and vivifies it,
Of which God said that there was never one who lived
Who did not worthily eat and drink
His flesh and his blood.

Si puet reonde forme avoir
Li escus pour fere assavoir
Que Diex est sans commencement
Et sans fin pardurablement:
Il est a 'Alpha' trianguliers
Et 'O' simples et singuliers,
Qui tout commence et tout affine
Et comprent par vertu divine.
...
Li quars [labiaux] note le sacrefice
Que li pretres celebre et sacre,
Quant par la vertu dou saint sacre
Sor l'autier li pains et li vins
Devienent char et sans devins,
Ensi com Dieux le consacra,
Qui sa char et son sanc sacra,
Quant il vault de son sanc demaine
Ses apostres paistre en la Chaine;
C'est li cors Dieu, qui fu pendus

En crois, et li sans espandus,
Quant pour nostre redempcion
Souffri la filz Deu passion;
C'est la viande, c'est la vie
Qui l'ame paist et vivifie,
Dont Diex dist que ja ne vivroit
Qui ne mengeroit et buvroit
Sa char et son sanc dignement. (*Ovide moralisé* 5.1195–1213)

The shield of Perseus, himself an exemplary figure of knightly virtue (as in Christine's *Epistre Othea*), is here figured in terms of the all-embracing power of divine *vertu*. The shield's heraldic marking represents the sacrifice of the Mass, actualized by the transformative power – or *vertu* – that makes flesh out of bread, and blood out of wine. The death of Charles V, as recounted in Christine's biography, reflects and even participates in this sacramental quality, as the death of the king entails the renewal of the body politic in the same way that the crucifixion, commemorated in the sacrifice of the Mass, entails the renewal of the body of Christ in the Church.

It is necessary to recall this devotional and Christological template for the construction of national identity in order to fully appreciate the integrated role that humoral and devotional discourses play in Christine's *Livre du corps de policie*. These discourses share a common vocabulary concerning the process of change, with *vertu* consistently serving as the transformative element. The role of devotional discourse is particularly worth pointing out in the *Corps de policie* if only because scholarship on this work has tended to emphasize precisely Christine's *lack* of engagement with the role of the Church and, especially, the clergy in her prescription for the health of the body politic. As Nederman puts it, Christine goes beyond even Oresme in her 'anticlerical' perspective: 'Christine's use of the organic metaphor extends medieval precedent by imputing to it a noticeably anticlerical orientation ... Her organic model disposes her to count the priestly function as essentially a civil office.'[23] Nederman is surely right in emphasizing Christine's omission of significant attention to the role of the clergy; a closer examination of Christine's perspective on the Schism and its impact on French society might help to explain this omission. Neglect of the role of the clergy, however, did not preclude Christine from emphasizing the sacramental role of kingship and construing that role in explicitly devotional and even Christological terms: this approach is particularly evident in her biography of Charles V, and also more subtly imbues her description of the body politic in the *Corps de policie*, where *vertu* is the nourishing, revitalizing fluid that unites the metaphorical body just as surely as the blood of Christ unites his flock.

It is beyond the scope of this essay to describe Christine's use of *vertu* as a polysemous term elsewhere in her writings; here, I will just sketch out the rough outlines of the larger picture. In the *Advision Cristine*, *vertu* is both a property resident in natural objects and a quality that, in the viewer, enables the recognition of the *vertu* resident in the thing and, consequently, the formation of a philosophical and poetic community.[24] In the *Cité des dames*, the *vertu* of the sibylline stones is recalled in the overflowing *vertu* of the virgin martyrs of the third book, whose bodies run with milk and blood in a corporeal representation of the sacramental *vertu* they bear. And, as we have seen, in the biography of Charles V, the king's *vertu* appears not only in his moral, ethical qualities, but in the Christological role he plays relative to the body politic, in imitation of the relationship of Christ to his own mystical body, the Church. Finally, in the *Livre du corps de policie*, ethical *vertu* is articulated in terms of a discourse of natural *vertu* that is expressed in the relatively technical terms of Galenic medicine: in this discourse, the health, wholeness, and nourishment of the body are achieved through the smooth flow of *vertu* throughout the parts and, therefore, throughout the whole of the body politic. *Vertu* is the catalyst that enables the perpetuation of life, both natural and political: it marks an ongoing, dynamic process that is – paradoxically – the very basis of stability.[25]

NOTES

1 For an overview of 'devotional romance,' see Akbari, 'Incorporation' 22–4.

2 On Oresme's 'decision allegories,' see Sherman 35–174; on Christine's use of Oresme, see Akbari, 'Movement' 143–4. On late medieval allegories of civic, national, and ecclesiastic division, including the work of Honoré Bouvet, John Gower, and John Lydgate, see Akbari, *Seeing* 234–43.

3 On the 'little people' in Christine's works, see Dudash 788–831.

4 All translations from Middle French are my own unless otherwise noted.

5 On the body politic fable in Marie de France, see Akbari, 'Between Diaspora' 26–8.

6 The relevant passages in the *Polycraticus* are 5.2, 4.3 (Nederman 67, 32). On the dissemination of this analogy, see the foundational work of Kantorowicz, *The King's Two Bodies*, esp. 208–11. See also Forhan; Nederman.

7 Nederman argues that both Oresme and Christine use 'the corporeal analogy ... to express equilibrium and equity.' Yet while, in the *De moneta*, 'Oresme constantly sketches a circulatory image of the body politic, stressing the need to "normalize" the flow of fluids between the bodily parts so as to prevent unhealthy "enlargements,"' Christine 'stress[es] the need for the limbs and organs to cooperate in their active coordination and interconnection of functions' (Nederman 32).

8 'The image asserts that there is nothing inappropriate about a woman on the throne ... One cannot help wondering whether Christine does not choose this passage also to promote a literal queen' (Green 128–35; quotation from 134).

9 Walters, 'Christine de Pizan as Translator' 36; see also Walters, 'Magnifying' 243–7.

10 For a useful overview of the system of humoral physiology, see Paster 77–134 (chapter 2, 'Love Will Have Heat'). For a specifically fourteenth-century French context, focusing on the *Chirurgia magna* (1363) of Guy de Chauliac, see Ogden 272–91. On medieval Galenism and humoral theory as known in medieval Paris, see Jacquart, *Milieu* and *Médecine médiévale*; on medieval Galenism more broadly, see Temkin, *Galenism* 95–116.

11 On the virtues (intellective and sensitive powers) of the soul, see Bartholomaeus Anglicus, *De proprietatibus rerum* book 3; ed. Long 149–88. On the virtues (vital spirits) of the body, see book 5, especially the overview of the spirits, including the retentive and expulsive virtues, in chapter 1, pp. 114–19 of the incunable edition, Frankfurt 1601 [no modern edition for book 5 has yet been published]; on the virtue of generation, see book 5, chapters 48–50, pp. 204–9; on the virtues of precious stones, see book 16, pp. 715–71.

12 For an overview of scholastic integration of Aristotelian and Augustinian concepts of virtue, see Michel, 'Vertu,' especially cols. 2748–53.

13 On the 'vertue' given to the water in baptism, see Higden 4:257; on the 'vertu' of the transubstantiated host in the Mass, see *The Lay Folks' Mass Book* 54–5. Both examples are from the fourteenth century.

14 For a fuller account of 'poesie' in Christine's work, see Akbari, 'Movement' 139–44.

15 '[N]ous couvient recuillir em briefves paroles les motifs de ceste oeuvre pris en un seul suppost, qui est le sage roy Charles devant dit' (179). Here, Charles is the focus of the allegorical narrative, similar to – but different from – a personification.

16 In her perceptive reading of Christine's biography of Charles V, Delogu points out the extent to which Christine highlights the simultaneous conclu-

sion of the biography and the death of the monarch (181). Delogu argues that this is part of a broader strategy to align the author with her subject, so that she is 'uniquely and intimately associated with him, at once his double, partner, and successor' (160).

17 In one passage, Charles identifies himself with the suffering Christ as he approaches death: 'Quant la crois lui fu presentée, la baisa, et, en l'embraçant, commença a dire, regardant la figure de Nostre-Seigneur: '"Mon tres doulz Sauveur et Redempteur, qui en ce monde daignas venir, affin que moy et tout l'umain lignage, par la mort, laquelle, voulontairement et sanz contrainte, vouls souffrir"' (70; 189). In another, Charles listens to the gospel account of Christ's death as he 'works towards' his own death: ['[Il] oy toute l'ysstoire de la Passion, et aucques près de la fin de l'Euvangile saint Jehan, commença a labourer à la desreniere fin' (71; 191–2). In a third passage, Charles's suffering causes those around him to empathetically identify with his experience, in an imitation of pious devotion to the suffering Christ: 'Celle oroison finée, se fist tourner la face vers les gens et peuple, qui là estoit, et dist ... [asks their pardon]. Et adonc se fist haulcer les braz, et leur joingny les mains; si povez savoir se grant pitié et larmes y ot gittées de ses loyaulz amis et serviteurs' (70; 190).

18 On metamorphosis in the *Ovide moralisé* and Christine's *Mutacion de Fortune*, in which the 'outer form comes to reflect the inner form' (88), see Akbari, 'Metaphor and Metamorphosis' 86–9.

19 For a more detailed account of death as metamorphosis in Christine's work, see Akbari, 'Metaphor and Metamorphosis' 82–5.

20 On Pullen as a source for John of Salisbury, see Forhan 45–75.

21 On Christine's use of Augustine, see Lori Walters's monograph in progress, early fruits of which can be found in her numerous articles, especially her 'Réécriture de saint Augustin par Christine de Pizan' and 'Christine de Pizan, Primat, and the '"noble nation françoise."'

22 *Rotuli parliamentorum* 3:466 (15 March 1400/1). Translations are my own. For a fuller analysis of this and related passages in the Parliament rolls in connection with late medieval expressions of English national identity, see Akbari, 'Hunger' 214–16.

23 Nederman 28.

24 For a fuller account of the polysemous nature of *vertu* in the *Advision Cristine*, see Akbari, 'Movement' 146–8.

25 Earlier versions of this material were presented at the Medieval Academy (Toronto, 12–14 April 2007) and the International Congress on Medieval Studies (Kalamazoo, MI, 8–11 May 2008). Thanks very much to Ben Semple and Lori Walters for their constructive comments.

WORKS CITED

Akbari, Suzanne Conklin. 'Between Diaspora and Conquest: Norman Assimilation in Petrus Alfonsi's *Disciplina Clericalis* and Marie de France's *Fables*.' In *Cultural Diversity in the British Middle Ages: Archipelago, Island, England*. Ed. Jeffrey Jerome Cohen. New Middle Ages. New York: Palgrave Macmillan, 2008. 17–37.

– 'The Hunger for National Identity in *Richard Coer de Lion*.' In *Reading Medieval Culture: Essays in Honor of Robert W. Hanning*. Ed. Robert M. Stein and Sandra Pierson Prior. Notre Dame, IN: University of Notre Dame Press, 2005. 198–227.

– 'Incorporation in the *Siege of Melayne*.' In *Pulp Fictions of Medieval England: Essays in Popular Romance*. Ed. Nicola McDonald. Manchester: Manchester University Press, 2004. 22–44.

– 'Metaphor and Metamorphosis in the *Ovide moralisé* and Christine de Pizan's *Mutacion de Fortune*.' In *Metamorphosis: The Changing Face of Ovid in Medieval and Early Modern Europe*. Ed. Alison Keith and Stephen Rupp. Toronto: Centre for Reformation and Renaissance Studies, 2007. 77–90.

– 'The Movement from Verse to Prose in the Allegories of Christine de Pizan.' In *Poetry, Knowledge and Community in Late Medieval France*. Ed. Rebecca Dixon and Finn E. Sinclair. Woodbridge, UK: Boydell and Brewer, 2008. 136–48.

– *Seeing Through the Veil: Optical Theory and Medieval Allegory*. Toronto: University of Toronto Press, 2004.

Bartholomaeus Anglicus. *De proprietatibus rerum*. Frankfurt, 1601. Rpt. Frankfurt: Minerva, 1964.

– *De proprietatibus rerum, Books 1–4*. Book 3. Ed. R. James Long. General editor Baudouin Van den Abeele. Vol 1. Turnhout, Belgium: Brepols, 2007.

– *De proprietatibus rerum, Book 16*. Ed. Iolanda Ventura. General editor Baudouin Van den Abeele. Vol. 6. Turnhout, Belgium: Brepols, 2007.

Brunetto Latini. *Li Livres dou Tresor*. Ed. Spurgeon Baldwin and Paul Barrette. Tempe: Arizona Center for Medieval and Renaissance Studies, 2003.

Christine de Pizan. *Le Livre des fais et bonnes meurs du sage roy Charles V*. Ed. Suzanne Solente. 2 vols. Paris: Champion, 1936, 1940.

– *Le Livre du corps de policie*. Ed. Angus J. Kennedy. Paris: Champion, 1998.

Delogu, Daisy. *Theorizing the Ideal Sovereign: The Rise of the French Vernacular Royal Biography*. Toronto: University of Toronto Press, 2008.

Dow, Tsae Lan Lee. 'Christine de Pizan and the Body Politic.' In *Healing the Body Politic: The Political Thought of Christine de Pizan*. Ed. Karen Green and Constant J. Mews. Disputatio 7. Turnhout, Belgium: Brepols, 2005. 227–43.

Dudash, Susan J. 'Christine de Pizan and the "menu peuple."' *Speculum* 78 (2003): 788–831.

Forhan, Kate Langdon. *The Political Theory of Christine de Pizan*. Aldershot, UK: Ashgate, 2002.

Gerson, Jean. *Gerson Bilingue: Les deux rédactions, latine et française, de qualques oeuvres du chancelier parisien*. Ed. Gilbert H. Ouy. Paris: Champion, 1988.

Green, Karen. 'Philosophy and Metaphor: The Significance of Christine's "Blunders."' *Parergon* 22 (2005): 119–36.

Higden, Ranulph. *Polychronicon Ranulphi Higden monachi Cestrensis*. Vol. 4. Ed. Joseph Rawson Lumby. London: Longman, 1872.

Jacquart, Danielle. *La médecine médiévale dans le cadre parisien, XIVe–XVe siècles*. Paris: Fayard, 1998.

– *Le milieu médical en France du XIIe au XVe siècle*. Geneva: Droz, 1981.

Kantorowicz, Ernst H. *The King's Two Bodies: A Study of Mediaeval Political Theology*. Princeton, NJ: Princeton University Press, 1957.

Lay Folks' Mass Book, The. Ed. T.F. Simmons. E.E.T.S. 71. 1879. Rpt. Oxford: Oxford University Press, 1968.

Michel, A. 'Vertu.' *Dictionnaire de théologie catholique*. Vol. 15, part 2. Paris, 1950. Cols. 2739–99.

Newman, Barbara. *God and the Goddesses: Vision, Poetry and Belief in the Middle Ages*. Philadelphia: University of Pennsylvania Press, 2003.

Nederman, Cary. 'The Living Body Politic: The Diversification of Organic Metaphors in Nicole Oresme and Christine de Pizan.' *Healing the Body Politic: The Political Thought of Christine de Pizan*. Ed. Karen Green and Constant J. Mews. Disputatio 7. Turnhout, Belgium: Brepols, 2005. 19–33.

Ogden, Margaret S. 'Guy de Chauliac's Theory of the Humors.' *Journal of the History of Medicine* 24 (1969): 272–91.

Paster, Gail Kern. *Humoring the Body: Emotions and the Shakespearean Stage*. Chicago: University of Chicago Press, 2004.

Sherman, Claire Richter. *Imaging Aristotle: Verbal and Visual Representation in Fourteenth-Century France*. Berkeley: University of California Press, 1995.

Temkin, Owsei. *Galenism: Rise and Decline of a Medical Philosophy*. Ithaca, NY: Cornell University Press, 1973.

Walters, Lori J. 'Christine de Pizan as Translator and Voice of the Body Politic.' *Christine de Pizan: A Casebook*. Ed. Barbara K. Altmann and Deborah McGrady. New York: Routledge, 2003. 25–41.

– 'Christine de Pizan, Primat, and the "noble nation françoise."' *Cahiers de Recherches Médiévales* 9 (2002): 237–46.

– 'Christine's Symbolic Self as the Personification of France.' *Christine de Pizan:*

Une femme de science, une femme de lettres. Ed. Juliette Dor and Marie-Elisabeth Henneau, with Bernard Ribémont. Paris: Champion, 2008. 191–215.

– 'Constructing Reputations: *Fama* and Memory in Christine de Pizan's *Charles V* and *L'Advision Cristine*.' *Fama: The Politics of Talk and Reputation in Medieval Europe*. Ed. Thelma Fenster and Daniel Lord Smail. Ithaca, NY: Cornell University Press, 2003. 118–42.

– 'La réécriture de saint Augustin par Christine de Pizan: De *La cité de Dieu* à la *Cité des dames*.' In *Au champ des escriptures. IIIe Colloque international sur Christine de Pizan, Lausanne, 18–22 juillet 1998*. Ed. Eric Hicks, Diego Gondalez, and Philippe Sion. Études christiniennes 6. Paris: Champion, 2000. 197–215.

– '"Magnifying the Lord": Prophetic Voice in *La Cité des Dames*.' *Cahiers de Recherches Médiévales* 13 (2006): 239–53.

– 'The Royal Vernacular: Poet and Patron in Christine de Pizan's *Charles V* and the *Sept psaumes allégorisés*.' In *The Vernacular Spirit: Essays on Medieval Religious Literature*. Ed. Renate Blumenfeld-Kosinski, Duncan Robertson, and Nancy Warren. New York: Palgrave, 2002. 145–82.

Contributors

Suzanne Conklin Akbari is Professor of English and Medieval Studies, and was educated at Johns Hopkins and Columbia. Her research focuses on the intersection of English and comparative literature with intellectual history and philosophy, ranging from Neoplatonism and science in the twelfth century to national identity and religious conflict in the fourteenth century. Akbari's books are on optics and allegory (*Seeing Through the Veil* [2004]), European views of Islam and the Orient (*Idols in the East* [2009]), and travel literature (*Marco Polo* [2008]); she is currently at work on *Small Change: Metaphor and Metamorphosis in Chaucer and Christine de Pizan*. She is the volume editor for the *Norton Anthology of World Literature, Volume B: 100–1500* and co-editor of the *Norton Anthology of Western Literature*, and is at work on *The Oxford Handbook to Chaucer*.

Amy Appleford received her doctorate from the University of Western Ontario and is presently Assistant Professor of English at Boston University. Her publications include 'The Dance of Death in London: John Carpenter, John Lydgate, and the *Daunce of Poulys*,' *Journal of Medieval and Early Modern Studies* 38:2 (2008): 285–314; 'The "Comene Course of Prayers": Julian of Norwich and Late Medieval Death Culture,' *Journal of English and Germanic Philology* 107, no. 2 (2008): 190–214; and 'Shakespeare's Katherine of Aragon: Last Medieval Queen, First Recusant Martyr,' *Journal of Medieval and Early Modern Studies* 40, no. 1 (2010): 149–72. Appleford's current book project, *Learning to Die in London, 1350–1530*, is a study of death in English literary, religious, and civic culture in the late medieval and early Reformation period, and has been supported by a fellowship at Stanford University's Humanities Center.

Elma Brenner is a doctoral graduate in History and is currently Specialist, Medieval and Early Modern Medicine, at the Wellcome Library, London. Her research focuses on the history of leprosy, hospitals, and charity in medieval Western Europe, and is currently supported by a Wellcome Trust-funded project titled 'Leprosy and Society in Rouen, c. 1100–c. 1500.' Brenner is working on a book provisionally titled *Leprosy and Charity in Medieval Rouen*, as well as co-editing two essay collections: *Memory, Commemoration and Medieval Europe* and *Society and Culture in a Medieval City: Rouen 989–1300*. Her most recent publications include 'The leper house of Mont-aux-Malades, Rouen' in *Étude des lépreux* (2007) and 'Recent Perspectives on Leprosy in Medieval Western Europe,' *History Compass* 8, no. 5 (2010): 388–406.

Linda G. Jones completed her doctoral degree in Religious Studies at the University of California at Santa Barbara and a Masters in Arabic and Islamic Studies at Berkeley. She studies the religious cultures of Muslim Iberia and the Maghreb, medieval Islamic preaching, and religion, gender, and embodiment in medieval Muslim and Christian Iberia. Jones is co-author of the *Handbook to Life in the Medieval World* (2008). Her forthcoming monograph, titled *'The Good Eloquent Speaker': The Power of Oratory in the Medieval Islamic World*, is now under contract, and she is currently editing a monograph on Jewish, Christian, and Muslim preaching in the Middle Ages (2012). Among her many articles are 'Islamic Masculinities,' in *Debating Masculinity* (2009). She is currently a Professor in the Master's program in the History of Religions at the University of Barcelona and an affiliated research professor in the Institución Milà i Fontanals' Department of Medieval Studies in Barcelona, Spain.

Christine Kralik is currently completing her doctorate in the History of Art at the University of Toronto, with a study titled 'A Matter of Life and Death: The Three Living and the Three Dead in Late Medieval Manuscripts.' Her publications include 'The "Macabre" Image as Devotional Aid: The Illumination of the Three Living and the Three Dead in the Berlin Hours of Mary of Burgundy and Maximilian I,' in *Constructions of Death* (2006), as well as forthcoming articles titled 'Dialogue and Violence in Late Medieval Illuminations of the Three Living and the Three Dead' (in *Mixed Metaphors: The Danse Macabre*).

Wendy A. Matlock, a doctoral graduate of Ohio State University, is currently Assistant Professor of English at Kansas State University. Among her publications are '"And long to sue it is a wery thing": Legal Commentary in *The Assembly of Ladies*,' *Studies in Philology* 101, no. 1 (2004): 20–37 and 'Secrets, Gossip and Gender in William Dunbar's *The Tretis of the Tua Mariit Wemen and the Wedo*,' *Philological Quarterly* 83 (2004): 209–35. Matlock's current research considers the cultural significance of Middle English debate poems from the thirteenth through fifteenth centuries.

Sylvia Parsons completed her doctorate in Medieval Studies at the University of Toronto, and subsequently served as Assistant Professor of Classics at St John's University and Louisiana State University. She is currently pursuing advanced studies in Information Studies and Book History while completing a book titled *The Representation of the Body in Twelfth-Century Latin Epic*, which focuses particularly on the *Alexandreis* of Walter of Châtillon and the *Ylias* of Joseph of Exeter. Parsons' research centres on the ways that medieval Latin poets incorporate references to concrete writing and reading practices into their images of authorship.

Catherine Rider received her doctorate from the University of London, has been a research fellow at Christ's College, Cambridge, and is currently Lecturer in the Department of History at the University of Exeter. Her research focuses particularly on the history of magic and the Church's attitude to magic, including the fields of religious history, history of medicine, and somatic history. Rider is the author of *Magic and Impotence in the Middle Ages* (2006), an investigation of the surprisingly diverse opinions held by medieval people concerning what magic was, how it worked, and whether it was ever legitimate to use it. Rider is currently examining the priests' manuals written by church reformers in thirteenth- to fifteenth-century England, probing their attitude to magic and finding what light they might shed on late medieval religion more generally.

Jill Ross is a graduate of the University of Toronto and currently Associate Professor at Toronto's Centre for Comparative Literature and Centre for Medieval Studies. Her research on the Castilian, Latin, Catalan, and Hebrew literatures written in medieval Iberia focuses on constructions of the feminine and on medieval poetic theory, expressed cogently in *Figuring the Feminine: The Rhetoric of Female Embodiment in Medieval Hispanic Texts* (2008), as well as in her publications on rhetorical theory and practice, including articles on the Latin poet Prudentius. Ross is currently working on a study of medieval theories of metaphor in both Romance and Hebrew literatures, ranging from its conceptual importance in the areas of Eucharistic transformation and religious conversion to the development of an idea of ethical literary character.

Sarah Sheehan earned her doctorate in Medieval Studies at the University of Toronto and has just completed a postdoctoral fellowship from the Social Sciences and Humanities Research Council of Canada. She is the co-editor, with Ann Dooley, of a collection of essays titled *Constructing Gender in Medieval Ireland*, and is currently at work on two book projects: *Gender and Sexuality in Early Irish Saga* and *Women and Gender in Medieval Irish Classical Adaptations*. She has already published several articles, including two on Welsh literature: 'Matrilineal Subjects: Ambiguity, Bodies, and Metamorphosis in the Fourth Branch of the *Mabinogi*,' *Signs* 34, no. 2 (2009): 319–42, which was one of three finalists for the Catharine Stimpson Prize for Outstanding Feminist Scholarship, and 'Giants, Boar-Hunts, and Barbering: Masculinity in *Culhwch ac Olwen*,' *Arthuriana* 15, no. 3 (2005): 3–25.

Anna Taylor received her doctorate from the University of Texas at Austin, taught at the University of Notre Dame, and is currently Assistant Professor of History at the University of Massachusetts at Amherst. She studies the monastic history of the early and central Middle Ages and the classical tradition, and also has an interest in monster theory. She is currently finishing her first book, *Epic Lives*, which explores saints' lives written in epic Latin verse. Her next project is entitled *A Cultural History of the Imaginary Book*.

Danielle M. Westerhof received her doctorate from the University of York, UK, and is a freelance writer and a rare-book cataloguer working for the National Trust. She is an Honorary Visiting Fellow at the School of Historical Studies, University of Leicester, and a Research Associate at the Centre for Medieval Studies, University of York. She has published a monograph titled *Death and the Noble Body in Medieval England* (2008), which explores the ways in which during the Middle Ages the body was used to demonstrate widely held social assumptions concerning virtue and nobility, not only through the idealized 'art' of dying but also through the elaborate executions of aristocratic traitors. Westerhof has edited a collection of essays titled *The Alchemy of Medicine and Print: The Edward Worth Library* (2010). Her current research interests focus on concepts of health in the medieval and early modern period, in particular in terms of ownership and readership of manuscripts and incunabula covering the subject of health and the prevention of illness.

Index